RICHARD GROSS

BEING HUMAN

Psychological and Philosophical Perspectives

HODDER
EDUCATION
AN HACHETTE UK COMPANY

First published in Great Britain in 2012 by
Hodder Education, An Hachette UK Company,
338 Euston Road, London NW1 3BH

www.hoddereducation.com

Hachette UK's policy is to use papers that are natural, renewable and
recyclable products and made from wood grown in sustainable forests.
The logging and manufacturing processes are expected to conform to the
environmental regulations of the country of origin.

The advice and information in this book are believed to be true and
accurate at the date of going to press, but neither the authors nor the publisher
can accept any legal responsibility or liability for any errors or omissions.

British Library Cataloguing in Publication Data
A catalogue record for this book is available from the British Library

Library of Congress Cataloging-in-Publication Data
A catalog record for this book is available from the Library of Congress

ISBN: 978 1 444 128 864
1 2 3 4 5 6 7 8 9 10

Typeset in Minion Pro 11/13pt by DC Graphic Design Limited, Swanley Village, Kent.
Printed and bound in Dubai

Cover image: © Barking Dog

What do you think about this book? Or any other Hodder Education title?
Please send your comments to educationenquiries@hodder.com

CONTENTS

Preface

For me, the beauty of Psychology as an academic discipline is that it allows and enables (and sometimes requires) you to explore and draw on other disciplines (such as anthropology, archaeology, biology, chemistry, genetics, history, literature, mathematics, music, philosophy and physics).

You may have noticed two things about the foregoing list: first, the disciplines appear in alphabetical order; second, the named disciplines represent some of the major influences on the evolution of Psychology as a discipline in its own right in the latter half of the 19th century.

Regarding the second point, it's perhaps not too surprising that Psychology still has links with those 'parent' disciplines; regarding the first, I generated it simply by going through the alphabet, in my head, picking out those disciplines that began with the next letter, then moving on. Underpinning that apparently simple procedure lies an enormous amount and range of cognitive processing, most of it unconscious, including attention, language, memory, imagery, abstract concepts and semantics. (Each of these could itself be 'unpacked' to reveal many layers and levels of knowledge, understanding and information processing.)

None of this, of course, would be possible without a certain kind of brain, which, in turn, relies for its development on genetic processes. This is biology informing and complementing our understanding of cognitive (i.e. psychological) processes. At the same time, none of what takes place in the brain (*with* or *via* the brain) does so in a vacuum: there must be cultural knowledge and content for the brain to process in the first place, just as cultural knowledge/content wouldn't have accumulated without the human brain. In an even broader context, both the brain and culture are products of evolution, which is studied by a whole host of academic disciplines including those listed above.

So, we've sort of come full circle, just as I have in my own academic journey. I chose to study Psychology because I wanted to understand people and believed that Psychology offered the most effective route. In the course of my teaching – and, more especially my writing – career, I've come to see how the full richness and complexity of being human can really only be reflected in the combination of mirrors that different disciplines hold up to *Homo sapiens.*

Just a few things to point out before you start:

- The 'Key Questions' at the beginning of each chapter are intended to give you a flavour of what's to follow and to get you thinking about the key issues that are discussed.

- The 'Time for Reflection' breaks that recur within each chapter are aimed at getting you to think in a more specific, focused, way about particular theories, concepts, ideas and experiences. Often, the questions posed here are answered in the text that follows – but not always; where they're not, you're either being asked to consider something very personal or the question is deliberately very general/wide-ranging (which might lend itself to a seminar paper or even a class debate).

- The Glossary provides definitions of (selected) key terms, many of which are used in more than one chapter. Usually (but not in every case), the Glossary terms appear **in bold** the first time they appear in the text.

I hope you learn as much from reading this book as I did from writing it.

Richard Gross

August, 2011

Acknowledgements

I'd first like to thank Jasmin Naim for commissioning the book and having faith in an author she hadn't worked with before. Thanks, too, Ruben Hale, for (probably) supporting my proposal 'behind the scenes'. Thanks also to Naomi Wilkinson, for taking over from Jasmin during her absence (congratulations, Jasmin), Rebecca Norman, for her conscientious copy-editing, and Sarah Stubbs for her efficient and supportive desk-editorship. Last but not least, thanks to Julie Joubineaux for a brilliant cover design.

Dedication

In memory of the unique Audrey Bernhard, whose charm, sense of humour, *joie de vivre*, and all-round larger-than-life persona are greatly missed.

Picture Credits

The author and publisher would like to thank the following for permission to reproduce material in the book:

Figure 5.1 © 2010 davidevison – Fotolia; figure 5.2 © Ghost – Fotolia; Figure 5.3 © NHPA/SuperStock; Figure 5.4 © Bettmann/Corbis; Figure 7.4 © John B. Carnett/Bonnier Coorporation via Getty Images; Figure 8.1 © Joseph Siroker; Figure 8.2 © Hulton Archive/Getty Images; Figure 8.4 © 1996 M.Freeman/Photodisc/Getty Images; Figure 8.5 © Signal Corps US Army/Library of Congress Prints and Photographs Division Washington

Every effort has been made to obtain necessary permission with reference to copyright material. The publishers apologise if inadvertently any sources remain unacknowledged and will be glad to make the necessary arrangements at the earliest opportunity.

Chapter 1: Introduction: Quantitative or qualitative difference?

Key questions

- What is meant by the terms 'quantitative difference' and 'qualitative difference' and how does this affect the debate regarding the differences between humans and non-humans?

- What characteristics, abilities and behaviours have been claimed for human uniqueness (i.e. what makes us an exceptional species)?

- What connotations does the term 'human exceptionalism' evoke when comparing humans with other species?

- What criticisms have been made of the human exceptionalism argument?

- Is the human exceptionalism argument consistent with Darwin's theory of evolution?

- What is meant by 'human nature' and how does this concept relate to the human exceptionalism and continuity arguments?

- When and how did human beings (*Homo sapiens*) evolve as a distinct species?

- How can we account for the increase in the size of the brain during human evolution?

- What is it about the human ability to speak (as distinct from the capacity for language *per se*) that was so important in the evolution of *Homo sapiens*?

- Is the size of the human brain continuing to increase – or does technology make this increasingly unnecessary?

Introduction

Trying to understand what 'Being human' involves (or what it *means* to be human) can be approached from many different directions and viewpoints emanating from a wide range of scientific, philosophical and religious perspectives. While it may be possible to draw up a list of characteristics, attributes and abilities, etc., that describe (or even define) what a human being is like, what we really want to know is what it is that makes human beings unique as a species, what makes us different from non-humans and what makes us special?

According to those who believe in **human exceptionalism**, human beings are unique as a species, implying a *qualitative* difference (a difference in kind, a different 'order' of being) and not (merely) a *quantitative* difference (one of degree, a relative difference). But no sooner has the concept of human exceptionalism been introduced than it runs into trouble, partly because of the notion of uniqueness, and partly because of the near impossibility of describing human beings without *comparing* humans with other species (i.e. exceptional compared with what?). In turn, most scientists and others (with the exception of creationists) agree that we can only understand ourselves by taking an *evolutionary* approach: if we have evolved from other species, then we must have abilities and behaviours in common with these species (especially those to whom we are most closely related), which implies *continuity* (rather than exceptionalism). Before we consider these problems in more detail, let's look at some of the claims that have been made for human exceptionalism.

> ### Time for reflection
> ● Whether or not you consider yourself to be an exceptionalist, what abilities and behaviours do you think might have been identified as making us unique?

The case for human uniqueness: What makes us exceptional?

Descartes' deep-chasm argument

One of the most frequently cited arguments for human exceptionalism was made by the seventeenth-century French philosopher, René Descartes. According to his theory of philosophical dualism (1637), the world is composed of two kinds of substance: (a) the kind that has length, breadth, weight and other material properties (*res extensa*) and (b) the mind (*res cogitans*), which has none of these properties. In relation to human exceptionalism, the crucial point is that only human beings have a mind. While the body – including the brain – can be studied scientifically (as with other aspects of the physical world), the mind can only be examined through introspection; only humans have this capacity. Almost every action of an animal could be simulated by an inanimate machine or automaton. Indeed, '... there is nothing which leads weak minds further astray than to imagine that the souls of animals are of the same nature as ours.' (Descartes, 1637). Only creatures with a mind have free will (the ability to choose how to act), so, by definition, animals lack free will.

> ### Time for reflection
> ● What do you understand by 'free will'?
> ● Do you agree with Descartes that only human beings possess free will? (See Gross, 2009.)

Descartes cites language as distinguishing between 'men and beasts'. While 'magpies and parrots can utter words as we do', they cannot speak: these sounds are not the expression of thought but a natural mechanism which works according to the 'disposition of their organs' as a clock works according to its construction. He concludes not that animals have less reason than we do, but that they have *none at all*; while human and animal bodies share a place in the natural realm, our souls or minds (or 'consciousness') are 'independent of it'. Clearly then, we are a different *kind* of being altogether.

Descartes' view is an example of what Forsey (1999/2000) calls a 'deep chasm' argument. While there is plenty of evidence for animal cognition (including heated debate regarding the non-human capacity for language), it's still possible to find modern deep-chasm arguments. For example, Davidson (1984, 1985) argues that thought is impossible without language and thought appears to be an all-or-none affair – you either have it or you don't (Forsey, 1999/2000). Of even more importance (and relevance to the 'language debate') is Chomsky's (e.g. 1957, 1979) claim that children are born with a **language acquisition device** (**LAD**), which enables them to identify the features shared by all languages (*linguistic universals*) and which represents a distinct mental module or 'organ'. (Language is further discussed in Chapter 6.)

Hauser's 'humaniqueness'

Arguably, the best example of a very recent deep-chasm argument is Hauser's (2009), neatly summed up in his concept of '**humaniqueness**'. After pointing out that Charles Darwin argued in *The Descent of Man* (1871) that the difference between human and non-human minds is 'one of degree and not of kind', Hauser claims that mounting evidence indicates that:

> *...in contrast to Darwin's theory of continuity of mind between human and other species, a profound gap separates our intellect from the animal kind. This is not to say that our mental faculties sprang fully formed out of nowhere. Researchers have found some of the building blocks of human cognition in other species. But these building blocks make up only the cement footprint of the skyscraper that is the human mind ...*(Hauser, 2009)

So, while acknowledging that human cognition has *evolved*, Hauser maintains that it has evolved so far beyond other species' abilities that it has become qualitatively different. According to Hauser's (2009) concept of humaniqueness, there are four key ingredients that distinguish the human mind from those of non-humans:

1. **Generative computation** enables humans to create a virtually limitless variety of words and things, and central to this is 'recursion', the repeated use of a rule to create new expressions. Interestingly, critics of the linguistic universals argument (such as Evans & Levinson (2009) and Everett (2009a and 2009b) (see below)) have focused on recursion, claiming that not all languages display this feature.

2. **Promiscuous combination of ideas** allows the mingling of different domains of knowledge, such as art, sex, space, causality and friendship.

3. **Mental symbols** encode sensory experiences, both real and imagined; these symbols can be kept to oneself or communicated to others as words or pictures.

4. **Abstract thought** allows us to consider things beyond our actual – or even possible – sensory experience (such as unicorns, nouns, infinity and God).

Hauser's humaniqueness is further discussed in Chapter 5.

Symbols, meaning and imagination

Other candidates for human exceptionalism include Carroll's (2006) claim that: '...the need to produce and consume aesthetic imaginative artefacts is as real and vital a need as the need to eat, to have sex, to tend offspring, and to develop and sustain relations within a social network.' Here, Carroll is referring to literature specifically, but this is only one of the ways in which human beings construct systems of meaning; other examples include narratives, art, music, myths, religions, ideologies, philosophies and science. Carroll disagrees with Pinker's (e.g. 2006) claim that these are merely non-adaptive by-products of other cognitive processes.

Consistent with Carroll's argument, Tattersall (2007) maintains that: '... without any doubt, the differences [between humans and the great apes] that most *significantly* differentiate us from them are the cognitive ones...' (Italics in original.)

We are *symbolic* creatures, while the great apes (i.e. other **primates**) are not, and language is the ultimate symbolic activity. Through language:

> *...we can and do constantly remake the world in our heads; and it is in this mentally reconstructed world that we human beings live, rather than in the world as presented directly by Nature – which is the one on which, to the best of our knowledge, all other living creatures live.* (Tattersall, 2007)

Similarly, according to Dunbar (2007): '... [it] is in humans' capacity for culture, to live in a world constructed by ideas, that we really differ from the other apes ...' What we can do, which they cannot, is step back from the real world and ask: could it have been otherwise than we experience it? According to Dunbar (2007): '... in that simple question lies the basis for everything that we would think of as uniquely human ...'

Once again, literature and science feature prominently in this imagined world (albeit using very different methods and often asking very different questions). One aspect of this imaginative ability is contemplation of alternative universes, which has led to the development of religion. Once again, language plays a fundamental role (see Chapter 6). (Religion is discussed in Chapter 8 in relation to our fear of death (also see below)).

Baron-Cohen (2006) also regards the ability to imagine (second-order representation) as a central feature of human cognition. More specifically, second-order- and other meta-representations are essential for **mind-reading**: the ability to put yourself in someone else's shoes, to imagine the other person's thoughts and feelings (Baron-Cohen, 1995). Mind-reading, or **theory of mind** (**ToM**), is essential for both face-to-face social interaction and, more broadly, the development and maintenance of culture.

Tools, culture and memes

The making and use of tools were once taken to be uniquely human behaviours, but since Goodall's pioneering observational study of wild chimpanzees during the 1960s and 1970s (e.g. Goodall, 1988), these no longer constitute the 'deep chasm' argument they used to. Tool-making and use are now more likely to be discussed in the context of culture, which itself has assumed deep chasm proportions. Based on the definition of culture as 'knowledge and habits [that] are acquired from others', which may explain why 'two groups of the same species may behave differently' (de Waal, 2001), many species of animals can be viewed as 'cultured'. Chimpanzees, for example, possess 39 cultural habits, each of which is peculiar to the group and is acquired by individual members through imitating others within the group (Whiten *et al.*, 1999). But according to Malik (2006), humans are entirely different kinds of cultural beings (an exceptionalism argument):

> *Humans ... do not simply acquire habits from others. We also constantly innovate, transforming ourselves, individually and collectively, as we do so. There is a fundamental difference between a process by which certain chimpanzees have learnt to use two stones to crack open a palm-nut and a process through which humans have engineered the industrial revolution, unravelled the secrets of their own **genome** and developed the concept of universal rights.* (Malik, 2006)

His deep chasm argument is summarised by claiming that 'All animals have an evolutionary past. Only humans make history'. However, this argument has been challenged by another, equally deep chasm but much more controversial argument, the **meme machine** argument. Based on Dawkins' (1976) concept of the **meme**, defined as a unit of culture (itself based on his selfish **gene** theory), Blackmore claims that memes inhabit, or rather parisitise, our brains: '... Instead of thinking of our ideas as our own creations, and working for us, we have to think of them as autonomous selfish memes, working only to get themselves copied ...' (Blackmore, 1999).

Blackmore argues that there are no such things as beliefs or selves, 'only a person arguing, a brain processing the information, memes being copied or not.' Only humans are meme machines and '... memetics provides the best explanation of what makes us human.' (Blackmore, 2007)

Based on Herskovits (1948), culture is usually defined as the 'man-made part of the environment' (Segall *et al.*, 1999). Segall *et al.* maintain that:

> *Human behaviour can best be understood as the product of learning, particularly learning that results from experiences with other people or with ideas, institutions, or other products of the behaviour of other people. In short, we are largely what we are because of culturally based learning ... No other animal has this capacity [to benefit from the lessons of experience...] to the same extent ... No other animal learns as much. As a result, we display many forms of behaviour that are uniquely human, many of which are part of what we call culture ...*
> (emphasis in original.) (Segall *et al.*, 1999)

This sounds a little like a blend of deep chasm and **continuity arguments** (qualitative and quantitative differences). It is undeniable that culture is the context in which all human activity takes place (including cognitive activity 'within the head'), and even the most social of species (such as ants and wasps) don't display anything remotely resembling cultural learning. However, as we've seen, evidence exists which suggests that chimpanzees (and other primates) might display cultural learning, depending partly on how culture is defined (e.g. Kendal, 2008; Workman & Reader, 2008). This debate (as well as meme theory) is discussed further in Chapter 9.

Memory and the perception of time

According to Corballis and Suddendorf (2007), what makes humans unique is *mental time travel* (MTT) – the ability to transcend time. While other species react to what is happening here and now (what is in their immediate environment), humans are able to remember the past (what has already happened) and think about the future (what has not yet taken place). MTT may lie at the heart language and Corballis and Suddendorf believe that language and MTT probably co-evolved. In turn, these are both related to *memory*.

According to some, 'memory' describes a uniquely human – even a uniquely personal – activity, so that it doesn't really make sense to use the word in relation to non-human animals (Rose, 2003). But this begs the question if we consider *learning* and memory (i.e. the *retention* of learning) to be two sides of a coin, then animals must be able to remember. However, if the learning that humans are capable of far outstrips that of non-humans (partly because of brain differences and, related to this, our possession of language – see Chapters 3 and 6), then it follows that the kind of memory we possess will differ too. A distinction that may help to highlight this difference is that between remembering *how* and remembering *that*: not only can humans (like non-humans) acquire skills that are demonstrated in behavioural change (**non-declarative**

memory), but they acquire knowledge which often is not expressed through behaviour at all (**declarative memory**). This knowledge can be of a very general, public kind, for example 'Paris is the capital of France', or very personal, for example, 'I visited Paris in summer 2007'). These personal (**episodic** or autobiographical) **memories** represent a fundamental feature of our sense of who we are – in other words, our identity and what we mean by 'I'.

Corballis and Suddendorf describe features that declarative language, memory and MTT have in common; these include (a) *combinatorial structure*; and (b) *generativity*, which is related to **recursion** (one aspect of Hauser's humaniqueness – see above). They believe that recursion is as much a property of episodic memory as it is of language. As we also saw above, recursion is one of the linguistic universals identified by Chomsky. A third feature shared by language, memory and MTT is the role of time.

Memory plays a crucial role in our ability to estimate time. For example, amnesic patients (who have suffered damage to those regions of the brain involved in learning and recalling new facts) develop major disturbances in their ability to place past events in the correct epoch and sequence. They also lose the ability to estimate the passage of time accurately at the level of hours, months, years and decades (Damasio, 2006). This is an example of '**mind time**' or 'brain time', as distinct from '**biological time**'. The brain possesses a 'stopwatch' (the so-called **interval timer** (**IT**)), which can track seconds, minutes and hours; it operates in conjunction with memory, perception and conscious thought. A major biological clock, the circadian clock, affects the daily rhythms of many basic physiological processes (such as body temperature, blood pressure and hormone secretion), as well as tuning our bodies to the cycles of sunlight and darkness (Wright, 2006). While all species display various biological clocks, mind time seems to be uniquely human. It can be manifested in various ways, such as the experience of time speeding up as we get older (Draaisma, 2004), the greater accuracy of time estimations the smaller the intervals we are trying to estimate (e.g. Weardon in Fox, 2009), and the speed at which time seems to pass in different situations (such as the slow-motion experience reported by people undergoing extremely stressful or traumatic situations (e.g. Eagleman, in Fox, 2009).

Consciousness and the 'givens of existence'

Memory and the experience of time are major aspects of consciousness. According to Libet (1985), when someone deliberately flexes his or her finger or wrist, it is an unconscious brain process that starts the action off, rather than the conscious decision to act. In other words, there is a delay (that we are unaware of) between the brain's response (which comes first) and our conscious intention. This has serious implications for our belief in free will, another characteristic that is usually taken to be uniquely human. Memory and the perception of time are discussed further in Chapter 7.

Another fundamental feature of human consciousness is what Yalom (e.g. 2008) calls the '**givens of existence**', namely:

● awareness of our mortality and fear of death
● freedom – are we really in control?
● existential isolation – the need to be connected to others
● meaninglessness – the need to believe that our lives have meaning.

Language, MTT, declarative memory and imagination all converge to make these issues distinctively and uniquely human. While they have traditionally been addressed by existentialist philosophers (such as Jean-Paul Sartre) and novelists (such as Albert Camus), in recent years they have increasingly been investigated by experimental psychologists (Jones, 2008; Pyszczynski *et al.*, 2004). This has led to the emergence of **experimental existential psychology** (known as XXP), focusing on Yalom's four 'givens' (see above), plus identity – 'who am I and what's my place in the world?' Of these, fear of death has received the greatest attention. (Yalom's givens of existence are discussed further in Chapter 8.)

Table 1.1 Summary of the major exceptionalism arguments
Summary of abilities/behaviours claimed as being uniquely human

● Possessing a mind, the ability to reason, free will.	Descartes (1637)
● Language (Language Acquisition Device/LAD)	Chomsky (1957, 1979)
● Language and thought	Davidson (1984, 1985)
● (i) Generative computation (ii) Promiscuous combination of ideas (iii) Meutal symbols (iv) Abstract thought } Humaniqueness	Hauser (2009)
● Use of symbols, meaning-making, imagination	Baron-Cohen (2006) Carroll (2006) Dunbar (2007) Tattersall (2007)
● Culture	Malik (2006)
● Imitation/meme machines	Dawkins (1976) Blackmore (1999, 2006)
● Mental time travel (MTT)	Corballis & Suddendorf (2007)
● Declarative (vs. non-declaritive/ procedural memory) } Consciousness	Cohen & Squire (1980) Tulving (1985)
● (i) Awareness of mortality/ fear of death (ii) Freedom (iii) Existential isolation (iv) Meaninglessness + (v) Identity } 'Givens of existence' } [Existential concerns/ 'the human condition' (Pyszczynski *et al.*) 2004]	Yalom (1980)

The case against uniqueness: The continuity argument

> ## Time for reflection
> ● Can you think of any arguments against the notion of human uniqueness?

As we noted above, the concept of uniqueness is problematical. By definition, *all* species are unique (Rose, 2005). As Ridley (2003) puts it: '... in the animal kingdom, there is nothing exceptional in being unique. Every species is unique.'

More seriously, perhaps, belief in the uniqueness of human beings implies belief in our superiority, that is, humans are the pinnacle of evolutionary achievement and enjoy some sort of privileged position over the rest of the natural world (Forsey, 1999/2000). The alternative view is that every species has survived because it has *adapted* successfully to the particular environmental circumstances it has had to face during its evolutionary history, and this applies equally to ants, fish, crocodiles and humans. So, instead of asking what makes us unique or special (i.e. superior), we could ask what attributes and behaviours are likely to distinguish humans from other species (especially chimpanzees); that is, are there any human *species-specific* characteristics? This avoids the pitfalls of the exceptionalism argument, while at the same time acknowledging that (a) humans, like other species, have evolved through the process of natural selection; and (b) we clearly are different. In order to appreciate how – and to what extent – we are different, the most logical place to start would be to *compare and contrast* ourselves with other species. While (some of) the differences between humans and, say, fish, are too obvious to be very helpful, those between ourselves and our closest genetic and evolutionary relatives, chimpanzees (*Pan troglodytes*) are less obvious or extreme. For this reason, attempts to define 'human nature' are usually made by comparison with chimpanzees rather than with species lower down the evolutionary (**phylogenetic**) **scale**.

> ## Time for reflection
> ● Given what has been said above regarding the implication of human superiority, how might we justify the continued use of the concept of 'lower' and 'higher' species?

However, comparison with many other 'lower' species is also very informative, especially when considering our *biological* make-up (e.g. our genetic make-up and the kind of brain we possess). In these cases, there is likely to be a *continuity* between closely related species; in other words, the differences between species are likely to be merely quantitative. For example, the basic process of genetic transmission (whereby characteristics are passed from parents to offspring) is the same in all species. In addition, humans and chimpanzees share almost 99 per cent of their genetic make-up (**genome**). Efforts to identify those regions of the human genome that have changed the most since chimps and humans diverged from a common ancestor have helped pinpoint the DNA sequences (i.e. genes) that make us human. These findings provide insights into how chimps and humans can differ so profoundly, despite having almost identical genetic blueprints (Pollard, 2009). This is discussed further in Chapter 2.

Again, all brains are made of the same basic 'stuff' (nerve-cells or **neurons**, connections between these cells) and function according to the same basic processes (electrochemical transmission involving neurotransmitters). What distinguishes the human brain might be its size relative to body size, or its overall structure, including the amount of brain space not obviously devoted to specific behavioural or cognitive functions. Or might there be brain cells that are only found only in higher primates (including humans)? These issues are discussed in Chapter 3.

As we have seen, language is (probably) the most commonly cited example of human exceptionalism. One way of investigating the claim that language is unique to humans is to try to teach language to non-humans, in particular chimpanzees. A leading researcher in this field is Sue Savage-Rumbaugh (e.g. 1994), who believes that there's only a quantitative difference between the language abilities of chimps and humans. Her work is discussed in Chapter 6.

According to Goodall (1988), there are 'striking similarities' between the whole range of human and chimpanzee postural and gestural communication. This suggests that:

> ... man and chimp either have evolved gestures and postures along a most remarkable parallel or that we share with the chimpanzees an ancestor in the dim and very distant past; an ancestor, moreover, who communicated with his kind by means of kissing and embracing, touching and patting and holding hands. (Goodall, 1988)

However, Goodall goes on to acknowledge that one of the major differences between ourselves and chimpanzees is that they have not developed the power of speech, which she describes as a 'truly gigantic stride forward in man's evolution'. This gigantic stride is also discussed in Chapter 6.

Is there an alternative to the exceptionalism and continuity arguments?

A third approach is adopted by the philosopher, Charles Taylor (1985), whose argument is outlined in Box 1.1.

Box 1.1 Humans as self-interpreting animals (Taylor, 1985)

According to Taylor, humans can only be understood as 'beings who exist in, or are partly constituted by language'. We are 'self-interpreting animals: interpretation represents what it means to be human. Things matter deeply to us; we make sense of ourselves and our lives by evaluating and choosing between our various goals and desires. In these ways, we define and redefine what it means to be human. Language is necessary in two ways:

1. 'Human life is both fact and meaningful expression.' Feelings that are ill-defined or confused become determinate and unambiguous only through their expression in a certain vocabulary (i.e. put into appropriate words). To say that 'language articulates our feelings' is to say that language defines them, gives them a form they wouldn't have if they had remained unexpressed.

2. Language is not a set of tools that can be used to convey ideas that are already somehow fully formed in our minds. Rather, language is a 'web' or 'pattern of activity' which defines a community of users and forms a 'horizon' in which they live. What is characteristically human is that we understand and define ourselves through participation in dialogue with others in a linguistic community. We are born into a world of language, which carries the meanings of the evaluative terms we use. Through language, we operate within a culture that helps create understandings of ourselves, each other, and the world around us.

Time for reflection
- This second function of language is reminiscent of a major account of cognitive development, which emphasises the socio-cultural nature of individual development. Thinking back to what you have read so far, whose theory comes to mind?
- In what ways is Taylor's account relevant to the debate regarding the relationship between language and thought? (See Gross, 2010.)

Taylor's approach is not deep chasm: he does not stress what differentiates us from the natural realm, but rather the central role of language in defining human nature. Language is the vehicle through which we define ourselves and realise our humanity (Forsey, 1999/2000).

When discussing consciousness in relation to exceptionalism (see above, page 9), what we really meant was self-consciousness('knowing that we know' or explicit awareness), rather than the capacity for experiencing pain, hunger, fear, sexual arousal, etc., (or sentience) which is shared by all species with a **limbic system** or 'old mammalian brain' (see Chapter 3). If this truly separates humans from all non-humans, it's likely to have at least something to do with the kind of brains we possess (again, see Chapter 3) and our possession of language, which itself is related to the human brain (see Chapter 6). However, there's plenty of evidence for self-consciousness in chimpanzees (in the form of mirror self-recognition), which suggests that the difference between humans and non-humans may be merely quantitative. This is discussed in Chapter 4.

Human beings as a distinct species: When and how did this happen?

Throughout the preceding discussion, one fundamental – and pivotal – assumption has been made, namely that *Homo sapiens* ('wise man') constitutes a distinct species. While this in itself is not controversial, the question as to just when – and how – modern humans became 'us', and how exactly we differ from our **hominid** ancestors (and how, they, in turn, evolved from the great apes), is a matter of on-going (and often heated) debate between anthropologists and other academics concerned with human origins. To pose the question 'when did human beings evolve?' in a way begs the very question that this book is trying to answer: at what point, and by virtue of what attributes, both physical/biological (such as walking upright and having a particular kind of brain), psychological (such as consciousness, language, memory, time perception), and cultural, do we judge human beings to have become a distinct species?

Box 1.2 provides a brief account of how human beings evolved into a distinct species.

Box 1.2 A brief history of human evolution: two legs and bigger brains

Like all evolving species, human beings had ancestors and cousins who shared some of our abilities but became extinct. Our physical and behavioural adaptations, most strikingly brain size and language, were focused on surviving the struggle with our greatest enemy – the worsening climate (Oppenheimer, 2007).

The human family of species is commonly referred to as hominid, with *Homo* (human) being reserved for people like us (i.e. those that display our own level of intelligence, moral sense, and depth of introspective consciousness (see text above) (Leakey, 1994). Leakey regards the evolution of upright locomotion (**bipedalism**) as fundamental for distinguishing ancient hominids from other apes of the time and for influencing the subsequent course of human history. For this reason, he believes that we should call *all* hominid species 'human'. At its most basic, the designation 'human' simply refers to bipedal apes.

Habitual bipedalism marks a split between our ancestors and those of chimps, but predates humans (i.e. *Homo sapiens*) by several million years. The first clear evidence of bipedalism is seen in skeletons of **Australopithecus anamensis**, a walking ape dating from 4 million years ago (found on the shores of Lake Turkana, in north Kenya); such claims have also been made for *Ardipithecus ramidus* (4–5 million years ago) and *Orrorin tugenensis* (6 million years ago) (Oppenheimer, 2007; Wong, 2009).

These early walking apes, including 'Lucy' (**Australopithecus afarensis**) (found in Hadar, Ethiopia), were shorter than us, and still closer to chimps above the neck with brain volumes of 375–500 cm^3. A different two-legged version (**Australopithecus africanus**) lived 2–3 million years ago, and although the same size, had a slightly larger than average brain size than chimps (420–500 cm^3). However, over the few million years during which the **Australopithecines** ('southern apes') and their immediate ancestors walked the African grasslands, there was only a moderate, not dramatic, increase in brain size (Oppenheimer, 2007).

Soon after the start of the *Pleistocene* period (just under two million years ago), *Australopithecines* were replaced in the African savannah by two diverging lines of walking apes, both with larger brains:

1. the first line of the meat-eating *Homo* genus characterised by their stone tools

2. the vegetarian *Paranthropus*.

One of the earliest human tool-makers, *Homo habilis* (found in Olduvai Gorge, Tanzania), had an average brain volume of 650cm^3.

Well before 2 million years ago, there must have already been some aspect of our behaviour, perhaps to do with how we responded to extremes of climate change, that gave large, energy-expensive brains survival value. By one million years ago, brain volumes of various human species living both within and outside Africa had increased from 400 to 1,000cm^3 and even into the modern size range. In other words, human brains had grown to three-quarters of their modern size long before *Homo sapiens* appeared (Oppenheimer, 2007). Between the earliest *Homo habilis* and the first *Homo rhodesiense* fossils of 1.1–1.3 million years ago (about 700,000 years) brain volume increased two-and-half times. During the following 1.2 million years, there were modest increases in Asian **Homo erectus** and European **Homo neanderthalensis** (first found in Engis, Belgium), but their brains were now 94 per cent of the size of today's human brains. In fact, there has been an overall *decrease* in brain volume in modern humans over the past 150,000 years (Oppenheimer, 2007).

> **Box 1.2** *Continued*
>
> **Homo ergaster** (first found in Lake Turkana, Kenya) was the first hominid to leave Africa (1.95 million years ago) to become the Asian *Homo erectus*. They were smaller than us and spread rapidly to the Middle East, Russia, India, the Far East and Southeast Asia. **Homo habilis**, which probably also migrated at the same time, was a possible precursor to *Homo floresiensis* (first found in Flores, Indonesia), the latest-surviving extinct hominid (as recently as 18,000 years ago) and nicknamed the 'Hobbits' because of their miniature stature (Connor, 2010).
>
> *Homo sapiens* was born around 200,000 years ago. When modern humans finally spread out of Africa to the rest of the world around 70,000–80,000 years ago, Eurasia was still inhabited by several other human species. The European Neanderthals, and possibly the Southeast Asian *Homo erectus*, persisted until less than 30,000 years ago, but no specific genetic traces remain in living humans (Oppenheimer, 2007). A finger bone found in Denisova Cave in southern Siberia in 2008 is thought to have belonged to a hominid species that was neither Neanderthal nor human; 'X woman' dates from 30–48,000 years ago (Connor, 2010).

What made our brains grow?

Oppenheimer (2007) sums up by saying that the greatest acceleration in relative brain size occurred before 1.5 million years ago (rather early in hominid history), then gradually slowed down. This contrasts with our relatively very recent explosion in knowledge and technology, in particular the species-specific use of symbols.

> *... the extraordinary invention and sophisticated flowering of writing happened 5000 years ago, and the invention of musical notation much more recently. These two coded non-oral systems of communication unleashed, arguably, the highest peaks of human achievement, yet we do not invoke a new species with special genes and a new brain to account for each of them.* (Oppenheimer, 2007)

What Oppenheimer is describing is *cultural evolution*. While most researchers agree that culture is a very recent human evolutionary development, there is considerable disagreement regarding (a) the relationship between cultural evolution and brain growth; and (b) the role of spoken language in evolved culture.

The place of the 'deep social mind': What makes humans human

According to Whiten (1999, 2007), humans are more social – more deeply social – than any other species on earth (including chimpanzees). By 'deep', Whiten means a special degree of cognitive or mental penetration between individuals; this goes beyond the sociality of species such as ants, which often involves self-sacrifice and innate infertility. The **deep social mind** comprises four main elements, some of which have already been discussed above in relation to human uniqueness. These four elements are described in Box 1.3.

Box 1.3 The four elements of the Deep Social Mind (Whiten, 1999, 2007)

1. *Mind-reading*: Adult humans are mentalists (rather than behaviourists), predicting and explaining others' actions in relation to a complex system of 'everyday psychology', key constructs in which are states of mind such as thinking, wanting and believing (Wellman, 1990; Whiten & Perner, 1991: see Gross, 2009). This view is similar to Humphrey's (1986) claim that we are 'natural psychologists' (**Homo psychologicus**). As important as the evolution of human *practical* intelligence may have been (bipedalism, tool-making, hunting and fire-lighting), the real mark of a human-like ape would have been the ability to 'manipulate and relate himself – in human ways – to the other apes around him' (i.e. *social* intelligence). Humphrey argues that consciousness (i.e. self-awareness) evolved *in order* to help us understand how *others* think and feel and therefore behave. (Mind-reading in humans and non-humans is discussed in Chapter 4.)

2. *Culture*: Evidence from both cultural anthropology and the study of language acquisition shows that the contents of mature human minds are 'massively shaped by cultural acquisitions'. Human minds are 'unprecedently deeply social': vast amounts of both 'knowing how' and 'knowing that' (see page 8) are acquired socially, i.e. from other minds. Mind-reading, of course, plays a crucial role in this process of cultural transmission.

3. *Language and communication*: Compared with forms of communication used by non-human species, language enables us to transmit to other minds 'what one has in mind' (e.g. intentions, ideas and knowledge). Some of these transmissions will form the basis for cultural transmission. So, while language is often cited an example of human exceptionalism (see page 5–6), it could equally well be seen as a *tool* through which mind-reading and cultural transmission operate particularly powerfully.

4. *Cooperation*: This can take two forms: (a) a group as a whole acts like a well-coordinated organism. While pack-hunting mammals may show elementary forms of such coordination, ant colonies have often been compared to a giant organism, with individuals playing the parts of organs, each with their distinct, yet coordinated, roles directed at the well-being of the colony as a whole (e.g. Wilson, 1975); (b) capacities which emerge in certain contexts to act in egalitarian ways, such as distributing resources and power relations equitably. Again, this reflects a 'submerging' of individual social minds in relation to group-level processes, achieved in a unique, human mental way.

Whiten's deep social mind account is not a deep chasm approach: regarding mind-reading, culture and cooperation, at least, there is clearly evidence of continuity with other species. His major argument is that it is the *combination* of these characteristics which is distinctively human. This combination represents what biologists call an *adaptive complex*: the functional significance of each is amplified by the others, with natural selection favouring their combined effect. The evidence he cites in support of his deep social brain hypothesis is derived mainly from present-day hunter-gatherers around the world.

Consistent with Whiten's deep social brain hypothesis is Dunbar's (e.g. 1996) claim that the ability to recognise and groom a large number of conspecifics (members of the same species) may be associated with a large brain. Language may have been an energetically cheap means of social grooming in this context (Aiello & Dunbar, 1993). Dunbar's hypothesis is described in Box 1.4.

> **Box 1.4** Grooming, gossip and the evolution of language (Dunbar, 1986)
>
> Apes probably use their highly developed manual dexterity as much when searching for ticks in each other's fur as they do when picking fruit. In primates that live in large social groups, grooming becomes extremely time-consuming. Humans started living in such large groups that it became necessary to invent a form of social grooming that could be carried out on several others at the same time.
>
> Dunbar notes that people do not use language just to communicate useful information; they use it mainly for social gossip: 'Why on earth is so much time devoted by so many to the discussion of so little?' The answer is that social gossip, like grooming in other primates, helps the formation of social bonds between members of a community.
>
> This 'grooming hypothesis' is part of a more general claim that intelligence evolved in order to maintain large group sizes: the more individuals you live with, the more demands that are put on you to keep track of each individual and of the relationships between them. To meet these cognitive demands, there needs to be an increase in brain size. In support of this general claim, Dunbar (1993) plotted the ratio of neocortex (the most recently evolved part of the brain used for higher cognitive abilities, including language) to total brain volume, against the average size of their group for a range of non-human primates. In support of the social brain hypothesis, Dunbar found a strong positive correlation between group size and neocortex ratio.
>
> If the value for human neocortex size is plotted on the same graph, the predicted average group size for humans comes to around 150 individuals. Consistent with this prediction, many hunter-gatherers live in bands of 100–200 (with an average of 150). Dunbar also suggests that people in the Western world are able to call on an average of 150 others for help (such as to borrow money).
>
> It has been estimated that if humans were to maintain group sizes of 150 individuals by using one-to-one grooming, then we would need to spend about 50 per cent of our time grooming, and this would prevent us from attending to our other duties. Consequently, our ancestors developed language as an alternative form of grooming (the *language-as-social-grooming hypothesis*).

Time for reflection

- To support Dunbar's language-as-social-grooming hypothesis, we would need to establish that everyday language is used most often for gossiping and other social chitchat rather than for giving instructions or imparting information. In your experience, is this true?
- Does people's use of texting and social networking sites on the internet support Dunbar's hypothesis?
- Can you think of arguments against Dunbar's claim that language evolved to enable humans to 'groom' more than one other at a time?

Oppenheimer (2007) doubts that such a networking effect could have fuelled each jump in human brain size over the past 2.5 million years. The human brain consumes a huge relative amount of bodily energy and is a major cause of maternal and foetal death due to obstructed labour. In addition, it's hard to believe that complex spoken language – our own unique skill – evolved more as a tool for reciprocal grooming and gossip than as a means to extend our cooperation productively and to teach our offspring by transmitting practical information and planning food acquisition. He also disagrees with Blackmore's claim (1999, 2007) (see page 8)

that human-evolved culture (their 'meme complex') drove brain growth. Oppenheimer asks how could this have occurred usefully before complex language itself had developed?

> ...it is much more likely that we were already communicating usefully and deliberately 2.5 million years ago, and that this drove our brain growth, than that our brain grew until some threshold size was reached and we miraculously discovered we could talk. (Oppenheimer, 2007)

The special nature of speech

According to Oppenheimer (2007):

> ...of all the mental and practical skills that philosophers, biologists and theologians have put forward as qualitative differences between modern humans and chimps, the only one that remains is human speech ... For the past 2 million years humans have been improving on the walking-ape model by using their brains, but they may have been aided in this by speech-driven coevolution in brain size.

Similarly, Gentilucci & Corballis (2007) argue that it's not language *per se* that distinguishes *Homo sapiens* from other hominids (as described earlier, one of the most common claims made for human exceptionalism), but rather the conversion from a primarily visual form of language to one that is conveyed largely through the medium of *sound*. As Gentilucci and Corballis claim, 'What distinguished our species was the power of speech.'

The consequences of speech

The advantages of using sound, whereby the message can be conveyed without actually seeing the speaker, may explain the so-called 'human revolution' (Mellars & Stringer, 1989). This is manifested in the dramatic appearance of more sophisticated tools, bodily ornamentation, art and, perhaps, music, dating from about 40,000 years ago in Europe, and probably earlier in Africa (McBrearty & Brooks, 2000; Oppenheimer, 2003). With the hands free from their role in gesture, they could be put to other uses. The estimated date of the mutation of the **FOXP2** gene is 40,000 years ago, which may have been the final step in the evolution of autonomous speech (see Chapter 6).

The claim made by some that the human revolution was a result of the emergence of symbolic language itself implies that language must have evolved very late – and quite suddenly – in hominid evolution (such as 170,000 years ago with the arrival of *Homo sapiens*, (Bickerton, 1995)). However, given the complexity of syntax, it is unlikely that such 'big bang' theories of language evolution can be correct (Gentilucci & Corballis, 2007). Gentilucci and Corballis say that language is much more likely to have evolved *incrementally* (e.g. Pinker & Bloom, 1990), perhaps beginning with the emergence of the genus *Homo* around 2 million years ago.

Chomsky (e.g. 1975) has long been the champion of the view that the capacity for language (in spoken or any other form) is unique to humans (a deep chasm theory). But he and his colleagues (Hauser *et al.*, 2002) have recently highlighted a *continuity* between primate and human communication; again, this suggests a gradual evolution of human language.

> ## Time for reflection
> - Is this continuity view inconsistent with Hauser's humaniqueness argument? (See page 6, the discussion below and Chapter 5.)

Hauser *et al.* fail to consider the possibility that speech evolved from manual and facial gestures, nor do they speculate as to precisely when the 'faculty of language in the narrow sense' (i.e. the uniquely human component) emerged in hominid evolution. As Gentilucci & Corballis (2007) point out, if syntactic language evolved gradually over the past 2 million years, then it seems reasonable to suppose that it was already well developed by the time *Homo sapiens* appeared.

According to Gentilucci & Corballis (2007):

> *...what has really distinguished us from all other hominids was the honing of language into a cost-efficient mode that freed the hands and arms for other activities, and allowed humans to communicate in a wider range of environmental contexts than is possible in a purely visual medium. That mode was speech.*

Language is part of human nature, with speech the 'default option'; that is, children with normal brains and raised under normal circumstances, *acquire* speech. The vast majority of children begin to talk at about 12 months, and their speech becomes increasingly adult-like through the course of the next few years, without anyone having to teach them or having to *learn*. By contrast, reading and writing are skills have to be taught and learned and so are part of human *culture* (see Chapter 9). The hand could once again be used to communicate, but now it was freed from the need to be seen by the person we were communicating with: written language transcends space and time. But also, ironically, modern technology has made it possible for speech to be carried across continents: it's now possible to communicate with someone thousands of miles away, in real time, using just the default option of speech (and the technology, of course).

> ## Time for reflection
> In his book, *The Artificial Ape* (2010), Taylor argues that technology has played a pivotal role in shaping the human species. The genus *Homo* is a product of the realm of technology: it underpinned our evolution and turned us into a highly intelligent creature.
> - What do you make of this hypothesis?
> - Is there a chicken-and-egg problem? In other words, was it not the case that highly developed intelligence was necessary for tools (the first technology) to be produced in the first place?
> - List some of the socio-psychological advantages and disadvantages of being so technology-dependent.

Box 1.5 The artificial ape (Taylor, 2010)

According to Taylor, once our *Homo* ancestors discovered how to make stone tools for making spears, they could kill wild animals, remove their skins with knives and make a sling for carrying their babies. Without the slings, women would have expended more biological energy carrying their children in their arms than they would have used on providing them with milk (lactation).

The implications of this development were enormous. Meat from wild animals provided the protein-rich diet necessary for the evolution of bigger brains. Babies could continue to develop outside the womb and their brains would continue to grow: they were not constrained by the size of their mothers' pelvis. The proportion of the human lifespan spent as immature and dependent on adults for survival is huge compared with other species (including chimpanzees). Its purpose is to allow brain growth in particular to continue for several years post-natally.

However, just as technology aided this evolution, so over time it came to reduce the need for ever-larger brains; the use of symbols, for example, could replace the need for sheer memory-power. Indeed, we are now 'outsourcing' our intelligence at an ever greater speed, with the development of powerful personal computers, for example. Taylor predicts that in the long run, humans will continue to become less biologically intelligent. He gives the example of eyesight. On average, the eyesight of *Homo sapiens* is probably deteriorating: if we had to survive now by being able to spot a deer and then shoot it down with a bow and arrow, then many of us would not be here. But we can see not only deer, but microbes and distant galaxies with the aid of powerful microscopes and telescopes. In these ways, our eyesight is better than our early human ancestors – but only in the sense that we have become biotechnological creatures.

Conclusions: Quantitative and qualitative differences revisited

Because most of us probably share belief in the basic principles of evolutionary theory, most of us would also accept that human attributes and abilities did not suddenly and dramatically appear where they had not previously existed. By definition, they emerged gradually, so we should not be surprised to find many examples of typically human behaviour displayed by chimpanzees in at least some rudimentary form. Perhaps the key question is, just when does a quantitative change (a difference of degree) become a qualitative one (a difference of kind)? Put another way, are the human exceptionalism and continuity arguments necessarily mutually exclusive? Can there be evidence of some ability (e.g. language in chimpanzees) that is so much more advanced in humans that we want to regard it as a feature of human nature or a human species-specific behaviour? To find it in chimps in some rudimentary form is exactly what we would expect from the continuity perspective; at the same time it forms part of our definition of *Homo sapiens* and is what makes us different. As Hauser (2009) would put it, a quantitative difference can be sufficiently great that it becomes a qualitative difference. Whether you agree with him or not, is,ultimately, as much a matter of opinion and definition as it is a matter of biology, psychology or evolutionary theory.

Chapter summary

- According to a human exceptionalism viewpoint, human beings are a qualitatively different species from all other species. This contrasts with the comparative and evolutionary approaches, which imply continuity (quantitative differences only).

- Descartes' 'deep chasm' argument claimed that only humans possess a mind (*res cogitans*) and language. Consistent with this is Chomsky's concept of an innate language acquisition device (LAD).

- Hauser's concept of humaniqueness is a deep chasm argument that identifies generative computation, promiscuous combination of ideas, mental symbols and abstract thought as uniquely human.

- Other candidates for human uniqueness include literature, narratives, art, music, myths, religions, philosophies and science; these are all examples of systems of meaning.

- Tattersall argues that humans are symbolic creatures, with language the ultimate symbolic activity. According to Dunbar, both literature and science enable us to step back from the real world and imagine how it may have been different from how it is.

- Imagination is a form of second-order representation; this, and other meta-representations, are essential for mind-reading or theory of mind (ToM).

- Until quite recently it was believed that only humans used and made tools, but Goodall's study of wild chimpanzees showed this to be false.

- The use and making of tools are commonly discussed in relation to culture; according to certain definitions, chimpanzees possess this along with humans. While this implies continuity, Malik's deep chasm argument claims that humans and chimpanzees are qualitatively different kinds of cultural beings.

- Based on Dawkins' concept of the meme, Blackmore regards human beings uniquely as meme machines.

- According to Corballis and Suddendorf, what makes humans unique is mental time travel (MTT); this probably co-evolved with language, and both are related to memory.

- While humans and non-humans share the capacity for non-declarative memory, declarative memory (including episodic or autobiographical memory) is unique to humans.

- Memory is crucial for the estimation of time, as demonstrated by its disruption in amnesic patients.

- While all species display various biological clocks (such as the circadian clock/rhythm), 'mind (or 'brain') time' (as demonstrated by the brain's interval timer) seems to be uniquely human.

- Memory and the experience of time are major aspects of human self-consciousness or explicit awareness; this is contrasted with sentience which is shared by all species with a limbic system.

- Another core feature of self-consciousness is what Yalom calls the 'givens of existence'. While these have traditionally been addressed by existentialist philosophers and novelists, they are now the focus of experimental existential psychology (XXP), with fear of death receiving the greatest attention.

- While belief in human uniqueness implies human superiority, the continuity argument stresses successful adaptation to environmental conditions; this applies equally to all species.

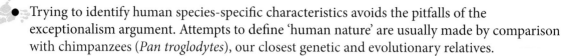

- Trying to identify human species-specific characteristics avoids the pitfalls of the exceptionalism argument. Attempts to define 'human nature' are usually made by comparison with chimpanzees (*Pan troglodytes*), our closest genetic and evolutionary relatives.

- Just as the basic process of genetic transmission is the same in all species, so all animal brains are composed of the same 'stuff' and function according to the same basic processes.

- While some attempts to teach language to chimpanzees suggests that there may only be a quantitative difference between their language ability and that of humans, the evolution of speech represents an enormous difference. Speech, rather than language *per se*, may be what distinguishes *Homo sapiens* from other hominids.

- An alternative to both the exceptionalism and continuity arguments is represented by Taylor's view of humans as self-interpreting animals.

- The human family of species is commonly referred to as hominid, with *Homo* denoting people like us (modern humans). Basically, 'human' simply refers to bipedal apes.

- While habitual bipedalism predates humans by several million years, *Homo sapiens* emerged around 200,000 years ago.

- While most researchers agree that culture is a very recent human evolutionary development, they disagree regarding (a) the relationship between cultural evolution and brain growth; and (b) the role of speech in evolved culture.

- According to Whiten's deep social mind theory, it is the combination of mind-reading, culture, language and communication, and cooperation that is distinctively human. This is consistent with Dunbar's language-as-social-grooming hypothesis.

Suggested further reading

Pasternak, C. (ed.) (2007) *What Makes Us Human?* Oxford: Oneworld. An excellent collection of original chapters by some of the world's leading thinkers and researchers, who give their views regarding what distinguishes humans from non-humans, including Susan Blackmore, Ian Tattersall, Stephen Oppenheim, Andrew Whiten and Lewis Wolpert.

Wells, R.H. & McFadden, J. (eds) (2006) *Human Nature: Fact and Fiction*. London: Continuum. Another collection of original chapters by distinguished scientists and academics, including Steven Pinker (The biology of fiction), Ian McEwan (Literature, science and human nature), Joseph Carroll (Literature and evolution), Simon Baron-Cohen (The biology of the imagination), and Philip Pullman (Do we need a theory of human nature in order to act?).

Workman, L. & Reader, W. (2008) *Evolutionary Psychology: An Introduction* (2nd edn). Cambridge: Cambridge University Press. One of the classic textbooks of evolutionary psychology, which discusses many of the topics and issues that recur throughout *Being Human*, including genetics, evolution, language and culture.

Selected websites

Howard Hughes Medical Institute 'Holiday Lectures' (2005): *Evolution: Constant Change and Common Threads. www.hhmi.org/biointeractive/evolution/lectures.html*

Text-based account of the evolution of *Homo sapiens. http://www.bbc.co.uk/sn/prehistoric_life/human/human_evolution/*

Video discussion of 'Does Evolution Explain Human Nature?' at Yale University. Includes links to other related videos. *http://www.youtube.com/watch?v=9Cz8ZwaJe24*

University of California Museum of Palaeontology (UCMP) Exhibition Halls: Evolution. *www.ucmp.berkeley.edu/history/evolution.html*

The Evolution of the Human. Includes links to the TalkOrigins Archive. *http://www.onelife.com/evolve/manev.html*

The Leakey Foundation: What Makes Us Human? Includes lots of useful links. *http://www.youtube.com/watch?v=9JvNwEMXLD8&NR=1*

Chapter 2: The genetics of being human

Key questions

- What is a gene?

- What are the basic principles of genetics?

- How do the human and chimpanzee genomes compare with each other – and with that of gorillas?

- How are we to make sense of the very close genetics relationship we have with chimpanzees?

- Are there specifically human genes or (merely) human forms of the same basic gene shared by all mammals?

- How can relatively small genetic differences between species account for such large physical, cognitive and behavioural differences between them?

- Are there specific genes that have mutated very recently in evolutionary terms that can explain distinctive human abilities (such as speech)?

- Is there any evidence that *Homo sapiens* interbred with other *Homo* species (such as Neanderthals) before the latter became extinct?

- How and when did *Homo sapiens* become the 'naked ape' and what physical and social consequences might this have had?

- Is it possible that it is the loss of certain genetic material that accounts for our uniquely human characteristics?

Introduction

According to Bodmer (2007), a biologist and a geneticist interested in evolution, the obvious explanation for what makes us human must lie within the genetic differences that distinguish *Homo sapiens* from other species, especially chimpanzees.

> *Every species has, more or less by definition, a unique DNA sequence signature that distinguishes it from every other species. Our challenge, however, is to discern those human features which make* Homo sapiens *qualitatively distinct from all other species, especially with respect to its cognitive and related abilities.* (Bodmer, 2007)

Time for reflection

- What kind of argument is Bodmer putting forward?

- Can you see any irony in Bodmer's claim that humans can (at least, in principle) be distinguished from other species in terms of their genetic make-up? What kind of difference is he asking us to identify? (See Chapter 1.)

The irony of this deep chasm argument is that, unlike other claims for **human exceptionalism, genes** are physical entities that can be seen under a microscope and can be counted, objectively identified and so on – in other words, they can be quantified.

Bodmer cites research by Pollard *et al.* (2006) on the analysis of human, chimpanzee and other mammalian DNA sequences that has shown how it may be possible to identify those sequences that may be most relevant to human uniqueness. The research of Pollard and her colleagues is discussed below.

Pasternak (2007), a biochemist, adopts a continuity approach. He considers two interpretations of the finding that humans and chimpanzees have 95 per cent of their **genes** in common. (Other researchers give the figure as almost 99 per cent; see below).

1. The five per cent dissimilarity might indicate that some five per cent of genes are specifically 'human' or 'chimpanzee-like'. Since there are thought to be about 25,000 genes (stretches of DNA) in chimpanzees and humans, 125 of these might be specific for one or other species.

2. The total set of genes (the **genome**) is, on average, five per cent dissimilar: some more, some less. The dissimilarity reflects not different genes, but merely different **mutations** within genes that are common to ape and man.

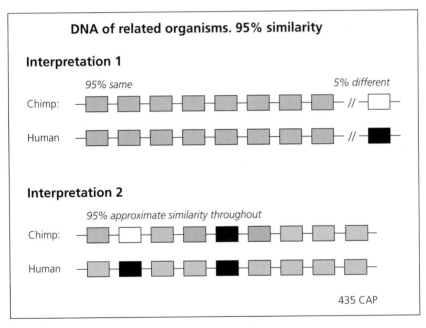

▲ **Figure 2.1** Interpretations of 95 per cent similarity between DNA of chimpanzees and humans. (Reproduced from Pasternak (2003a) by permission of the publisher.)

Pasternak favours the second argument, concluding that specifically 'human genes' do not exist. The exact nature of genes – what they do and how they do it – are all discussed below.

An outline of genetics

Ridley (1999) asks us to imagine that the human genome is a book.

- The book comprises 23 chapters (the number of human *chromosomes*, each person inheriting one member of each pair from each parent).

- Each chapter contains several thousand stories (*genes*). (In fact, the number now appears to be about 23,500 (Le Page, 2010)).

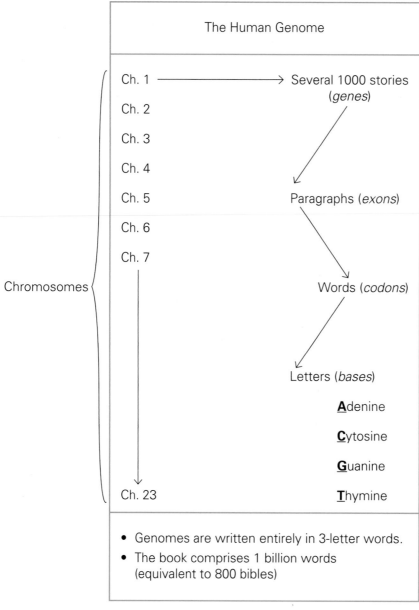

▲ Figure 2.2 The human genome represented as a book

● Each story is composed of paragraphs (*exons*), which are interrupted by advertisements (*introns*).
● Each paragraph is made up of words (*codons*).
● Each word is written in letters (*bases*); there are an estimated 3 billion bases. (Pollard, 2009.)
● There are one billion words in the book (as long as 800 Bibles).

According to Ridley, the idea of the genome as a book is literally true. A book is a piece of digital information (every letter is of equal importance), written in linear, one-dimensional and one-directional form and defined by a code that produces a large collection of meanings from a small alphabet of signs; so is a genome. But whereas English books are written in words of variable length using 26 letters, genomes are written entirely in three-letter words, using only four letters: A (which stands for *adenine*), C (*cytosine*), G (*guanine*) and T (*thymine*). In addition, instead of being written on flat pages, these words are written on long chains of sugar and phosphate called DNA molecules; the bases are attached as side rungs. Each chromosome is one pair of very long DNA molecules. Ridley describes the genome as a 'very clever book': in the right conditions, it can both photocopy itself (**replication**) and read itself (**translation**).

Box 2.1 Replication and translation

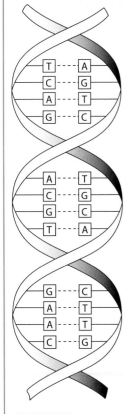

Replication works because of an ingenious property of the four bases: A pairs only with T, and G pairs only with C. So, a single strand of DNA can copy itself by assembling a complementary strand with Ts opposite all the As, As opposite all the Ts, Cs opposite all the Gs, and Gs opposite all the Cs. In fact, the usual state of DNA is the famous double helix of the original strand and its complementary pair intertwined.

So, to make a copy of the complementary strand brings back the original text: the sequence ACGT becomes TGCA in the copy, which transcribes back to ACGT in the copy of the copy. In this way, DNA can replicate indefinitely, while still containing the same information.

Translation begins with the text of a gene being transcribed (translated) into a copy by the same base-pairing process described above. But this time, the copy is made of RNA – a very slightly different chemical. RNA can also carry a linear code and uses the same letters as DNA, except that it uses U (*uracil*) instead of T. This RNA copy (called *messenger RNA*) is then edited by removing all introns and the splicing together of all exons (see above). *Ribosomes* (made partly from RNA) then move along the messenger, translating each three-letter codon (word) in turn into one letter of a different alphabet; this consists of 20 different amino acids, each brought by a different version of a molecule called *transfer RNA*. Each amino acid is attached to the last to form a chain in the same order as the codons. When the whole message has been translated, the

| thymine | is bound to | adenine |
| cytosine | is bound to | guanine |

▲ Figure 2.3

Box 2.1 *Continued*

chain of amino acids folds itself up into a distinctive shape that depends on its sequence. It is now referred to as a protein. Every protein is a translated gene.

> *Almost everything in the body, from hair to hormones, is either made of proteins or made by them ...* (Ridley, 1999)

In particular, the body's chemical reactions (including replication and translation) are catalysed by proteins known as enzymes. Proteins are also responsible for switching genes on and off, by physically attaching themselves to promoter and enhancer sequences near the start of the gene's text. Different genes are switched on in different parts of the body.

Mutations: When replication goes wrong

Mistakes can and do occur when genes are replicated. A letter (base) is occasionally missed out or the wrong letter inserted. Whole sentences or paragraphs are sometimes duplicated, omitted or reversed. These errors are called mutations. As Ridley (1999) points out, many mutations are neither harmful nor beneficial. Human beings accumulate about 100 mutations per generation and while this may not seem much, given that there are over a million codons in the human genome, in the wrong place even a single one can be fatal.

Box 2.2 Mitochondria and 'junk DNA': exceptions to the rule (Based on Ridley, 1999)

- Not all human genes are found on the chromosomes; a few live inside little blobs called **mitochondria**.
- Not all genes are made of DNA; some viruses use RNA instead.
- Not all genes are recipes for proteins; some are transcribed into RNA but not translated into protein, with the RNA going directly to work either as part of a ribosome or as a transfer RNA.
- Not all DNA spells out genes. In fact, most of it is a jumble of repetitive or random sequences that is rarely or never transcribed ('**junk DNA**'). According to Le Page (2010), 85–95 per cent of our DNA is useless, without any demonstrable function.

Comparing the human and chimpanzee genome

How similar are we?

As we saw above, Pasternak (2007) adopts a continuity approach when trying to account for genetic differences between humans and chimpanzees. This is consistent with his view of behavioural and cognitive continuity: chimpanzees display the use of tools, the ability to reason and language ability (claimed to be unique to humans, according to exceptionalism). Also, they can stand upright for short periods of time (though not to walk any distance), grasp objects with precision grip (though more clumsily, and with much less force, than a human), and utter a variety of sounds (enough, when combined with gestures, for meaningful communication between themselves).

The anatomical differences between humans and chimpanzees are also relatively minor, including the skeleton and the voice box. The chimpanzee voice box at birth resembles that of a human baby quite closely (each can swallow and breathe at the same time), but the human larynx develops quite differently after that (and at the age of two a child can no longer swallow and breathe simultaneously) (Pasternak, 2007).

According to Dunbar (2007), by the end of the 1980s our whole understanding of ape evolutionary history had been turned on its head. Far from being a separate evolutionary lineage with deep roots (as human exceptionalists would have claimed):

> *... we humans were in fact embedded within the great ape family. Indeed ... we were kith and kin to the chimpanzees – genetically more closely related to the two chimpanzee species (the common chimpanzee and the bonobo) than any of the three of us was related to the gorilla ...* (Dunbar, 2007).

Indeed, it's since been shown that we're more closely related to each other than the two gorilla species (the physically barely distinguishable eastern and western gorillas) are related to each other! According to Dunbar, the universally accepted position is that now the big split in the great ape family isn't between humans and the other great apes, but between the Asian orang-utan and the four (or should it be five?) species of African great apes (one of which is *Homo sapiens*). 'Humans are now, strictly speaking, firmly ensconced within the chimpanzee family' (Dunbar, 2007). As Jones (1994) puts it: ' ... Any idea that humans are on a lofty genetic pinnacle is simply wrong. A taxonomist from Mars armed with a DNA hybridisation machine would classify humans, gorillas and chimpanzees as members of the same closely related biological family.'

Time for reflection

- What is your initial response to Dunbar's final statement and the quote from Jones?
- In what ways are they relevant to the human exceptionalism and **continuity arguments** discussed in Chapter 1?
- Even in terms of the continuity approach, we are still very different from our ape cousins (e.g. Dunbar, 2007). Is there a contradiction between these two positions, namely (a) the claim that we are very different from chimpanzees; and (b) the claim that we are more closely related (biologically) to chimpanzees than the two species of gorilla are to each other?

(Consider the discussion of genetics above, including Pasternak's (2007) preference between the two human-chimp difference arguments.)

What are the key differences between humans and chimpanzees?

As we've seen, humans have 23 pairs of chromosomes. However, chimpanzees, gorillas and orang utans have 24 pairs! As Ridley (1999) says, this is rather surprising: we are the exception to the rule among the great apes. What has happened is that chromosome 2, the second largest of the human chromosomes, has formed from fusion of two medium-sized ape chromosomes.

According to Pollard (2009), the DNA blueprints of humans and chimpanzees are almost 99 per cent identical; that is, of the three billion letters that make up the human genome, only 15 million of them – less than one per cent – have changed in the six million or so years since the human and chimp lineages diverged. While evolutionary theory maintains that the vast majority of these changes had little or no effect on our biology, somewhere among those roughly 15 million bases lay the differences that made us human.

The rate at which genes randomly accumulate spelling changes gives a firm indication of relationships between different species (Ridley, 1999). Pollard (2009) wrote a computer program that would scan the human genome for the pieces of DNA that have changed the most since humans and chimps split from a common ancestor. Because most random genetic mutations neither benefit nor harm an organism, they accumulate at a steady rate that reflects the amount of time that has elapsed since two living species had a common ancestor (the 'ticking of the molecular clock'). An accelerated rate of change in some part of the genome is a hallmark of positive selection, in which mutations that help an organism survive and reproduce are more likely to be passed on to future generations. In other words: ' … those parts of the code that have undergone the most modification since the chimp-human split are sequences that most likely shaped humankind.' (Pollard, 2009)

At the top of a list of rapidly evolving sequences is **human accelerated region 1** (*HAR1*), a stretch of 118 bases. *HAR1* is found in the genomes of mice, rats, chickens, 12 other vertebrate species, as well as chimps and humans, so, in this sense, there are no specifically human genes (see above). However, until humans came along, *HAR1* evolved extremely slowly. In chickens and chimps (whose lineages diverged about 300 million years ago), only two of the 118 bases differ, compared with 18 differences between humans and chimps (who 'split' much more recently). According to Pollard (2009): ' … The fact that *HAR1* was essentially frozen in time through hundreds of millions of years indicates that it does something very important; that it then underwent abrupt revision in humans suggests that this function was significantly modified in our lineage.' So, what might this important function of *HAR1* be?

Earlier research had detected *HAR1* activity in two samples of human brain cells (neurons). While the human brain is well known to differ considerably from the chimpanzee brain in terms of size, organisation and complexity, as well as other traits (see Chapter 3), the developmental and evolutionary mechanisms underlying these differences are poorly understood. According to Pollard (2009), *HAR1* had the potential to 'illuminate this most mysterious aspect of human biology'.

In 2005, Pollard collaborated with Vanderhaeghen, who designed a fluorescent molecular tag that would light up when *HAR1* was activated in the living cells, that is, when it was translated from DNA into RNA. The labelling revealed that *HAR1* is active in a type of neuron that plays a key role in the pattern and layout of the developing cerebral cortex. When something goes wrong in this process, it may result in a severe, often fatal, congenital disorder known as **lissencephaly** ('smooth brain'): the cortex lacks its characteristic folds (**convolution**) and there's a much reduced surface area. Malfunctions in these same neurons are also linked to the onset of schizophrenia in adults. So, *HAR1* is active at the right time and place to be instrumental in the formation of a normal human cortex. However, exactly how this piece of the genetic code affects cortex development is still unclear (Pollard, 2009).

Part of what makes *HAR1* distinctive is that it's part of just 1.5 per cent of our total DNA which encodes RNA (Bodmer, 2007; Pollard *et al.*, 2006) (see Box 2.2 above). It's also the first documented example of an RNA-encoding sequence that appears to have undergone positive selection (Pollard, 2009).

As Pasternak (2007) observes, we might suppose that genes that play a role in the development of upright gait, mobile thumb, vocal cords and cortical neurons are the ones that show the greatest difference between chimpanzee and human. But we'd be mistaken. This is illustrated by the case of the **FOXP2** gene, which contains another of the fast-changing sequences (like *HAR1*) and is known to be involved in speech (see Box 2.3).

Box 2.3 The KE family and the speech gene: *FOXP2*

Half of the members of an extended English family (the KE family) are affected by a speech and language disorder, which is evident from an affected child's first attempts to speak and persists into adulthood (Vargha-Khadem *et al.*, 1995). The disorder is now known to be due to a point mutation on the *FOXP2* gene on chromosome 7 (Fisher *et al.*, 1998; Lai *et al.*, 2001). To acquire normal speech, two functional copies of *FOXP2* seem to be necessary.

It has been claimed that *FOXP2* is involved in the development of **morphosyntax** (Gopnik, 1990), that is, understanding of the internal structure of words (morphology) and how words are put together to form phrases and sentences (syntax, a part of 'grammar'). Pinker (1994) went as far as identifying it as the 'grammar gene' – although he has more recently acknowledged that other genes probably also played a role in the evolution of grammar (Gentilucci & Corballis, 2007). However, subsequent research suggests that the core deficit in affected members of the KE family is one of articulation (i.e. speech), with grammatical impairment a secondary outcome (Watkins *et al.*, 2002a). Lai *et al.* (2001) reported that the disorder involves the inability to make certain subtle, high-speed facial movements needed for normal human speech, despite possessing the cognitive ability needed for processing language.

This view of the disorder was supported by the use of brain-scanning (Liegeois *et al.*, 2003). Using **fMRI (functional magnetic resonance imaging)**, the researchers recorded brain activity in both affected and unaffected members of the KE family while they covertly (silently) generated verbs in response to nouns. Whereas unaffected individuals showed the expected activity concentrated in **Broca's area** in the left hemisphere (an area specialised for speech production: see Chapter 3), affected individuals showed relative *under*-activation in *both* Broca's area and its right-hemisphere *homologue* (the corresponding area) as well as in other cortical language areas. They also showed *over*-activation in both hemispheres (*bilaterality*) in regions not associated with language. However, there was bilateral activation in the posterior superior temporal gyrus; the left side of this region overlaps with *Wernicke's area*, associated with language comprehension. This suggests that affected individuals may have generated words in terms of their sounds, rather than in terms of articulatory patterns. Their deficits weren't attributable to any difficulty with verb generation itself: affected and unaffected individuals showed similar ability to generate verbs overtly (out loud), and the patterns of brain activity were similar to those recorded during covert verb generation.

According to Pasternak (2007), the human-chimpanzee genome difference that has arisen over the 6 million years since they split from their common ancestor reflects mainly 'silent' mutations (irrelevant mutations that have no effect on function). It's a much smaller number of relevant mutations, some of which don't alter the *structure* of a protein at all, but merely the *amount* that's synthesised (Donaldson & Gottgens, 2006), which appear to have been critical in human evolution. *FOXP2* differs by less than 0.1 per cent between chimpanzee and human, while genes that specify proteins of identical function (such as insulin or haemoglobin) differ by more (Pasternak, 2007).

It's not only chimpanzees that have *FOXP2*; in fact, the gene is unusually similar in all mammals, from monkeys to mice. Clearly, then, merely possessing the gene doesn't make speech possible, but perhaps having the peculiar human form of the gene is a prerequisite of speech (Ridley, 2003). Ridley points out that, since the split with chimpanzees ('a mere yesterday'), there have already been another two very recent changes that alter the protein. These changes occurred through a 'selective sweep', that is, 'elbowing all other versions of the gene aside in short order'.

> *... Sometime after 200,000 years ago, a mutant form of FOXP2 appeared in the human race ... and that mutant form was so successful in helping its owner to reproduce that his or her descendants now dominate the species to the utter exclusion of all previous forms of the gene.*
> (Ridley, 2003)

According to Pollard (2009) whole-genome comparisons in other species have provided another crucial insight into why humans and chimps can be so different despite being so much alike in their genomes. *Where* DNA substitutions occur in the genome can make a big difference – rather than *how many* changes overall there are; in other words:

> *You do not need to change very much of the genome to make a new species. The way to evolve a human from a chimp-human ancestor is not to speed the ticking of the molecular clock as a whole. Rather the secret is to have rapid change occur in sites where those changes make an important difference in an organism's functioning.* (Pollard, 2009)

Both *HAR1* and *FOXP2* are two such sites. *FOXP2* is highly conserved in mammals, and in humans differs in only three places from that in the mouse. Two of these three changes occurred on the human lineage *after* the split from the common chimp/bonobo-human ancestor (Gentilucci & Corballis, 2007). According to Enard *et al.* (2002), the more recent of these mutations occurred 'since the onset of human population growth, some 10,000 to 100,000 years ago'. If this is so, fully articulate vocal language may not have emerged until *after* the appearance of *Homo sapiens,* some 170,000 years ago in Africa. *FOXP2* was probably just the final step in a series of progressive changes (Gentilucci & Corballis, 2007).

Pollard (2009) cites research (in 2007) which involved sequencing *FOXP2* extracted from a Neanderthal fossil and found that these extinct humans possessed the modern human version of the gene – perhaps enabling them to enunciate as we do. Current estimates for when the Neanderthal and modern human lineages split suggest that the new form of *FOXP2* must have emerged at least 500,000 years ago. Box 2.4 discusses comparison of the human and Neanderthal genomes as a whole.

It was also found that Neanderthals shared more genetic variants with present-day humans in Eurasia than with present-day humans in sub-Saharan Africa. This suggests that gene flow from Neanderthals into the ancestors of non-Africans occurred *before* the divergence of Eurasian groups from each other (Green *et al.,* 2010). This has been confirmed by another genetic study. Long (in Callaway, 2010) presented results from nearly 100 modern human populations, showing that Eurasians acquired genetic diversity from breeding with other *Homo* species *after* they left Africa. In addition, there was a spike in genetic diversity in Indo-Pacific peoples, dating to around 40,000 years ago. Since Neanderthals never travelled that far south, the diversity may have arisen from interbreeding with *Homo erectus* and species related to *Homo floresiensis* (again, see Chapter 1, pages 14–15).

Box 2.4 Modern humans' Neanderthal origins

A long-awaited rough draft of the Neanderthal genome (Green *et al.,* 2010) has revealed that our own DNA contains clear evidence that early humans interbred with Neanderthals; nor were Neanderthals the only other *Homo* species that early *Homo sapiens* mated with. These findings cast doubt on the familiar story that modern humans left Africa around 100,000 years ago and swept aside all other *Homo* species as they made their way around the globe. A more likely scenario is that as *Homo sapiens* migrated, they met and interbred with other *Homo* species that have all since died out (Callaway, 2010) (see Chapter 1, pages 14–15).

Green *et al.* (2010) presented a draft sequence of the Neanderthal genome comprising more than 4 billion nucleotides from three individuals; this was compared with the genomes of five present-day humans from different parts of the world. This comparison resulted in identification of several genomic regions that may have been affected by positive selection in ancestral modern humans, including genes involved in metabolism and in cognitive and skeletal development. The genome of humans today is 1–4 per cent Neanderthal.

Genes, language, and the brain

As important as *FOXP2* may be for understanding human language (especially speech), most of what distinguishes human language from vocal communication in other species reflects differences in cognitive ability, and these, in turn, are correlated with brain size. **Primates** generally have a larger brain that would be expected from their body size (but see Chapter 3, pages 45–47). However, human brain volume has more than tripled since chimps and humans shared a common ancestor (Pollard, 2009).

One of the best-studied examples of a gene linked to brain size in humans and other species is *ASPM*. Genetic studies of people with **microcephaly**, in which the brain is reduced by up to 70 per cent, have revealed the role of *ASPM*, as well as three other genes – *MCPH1*, *CDK5RAP2* and *CENPJ* – in controlling brain size. *ASPM* has been shown to have undergone several bursts of change over the course of primate evolution, suggesting positive selection. At least one of these bursts occurred in the human lineage since it diverged from that of chimps and so was potentially instrumental in the evolution of our large brain (Pollard, 2009).

Other parts of the genome may have influenced the evolution of the human brain less directly. The computer scan that identified *HAR1* also found 201 other HARs (human accelerated regions), most of which don't encode proteins or even RNA. Instead, they appear to be *regulatory sequences*, telling nearby genes when to turn on and off. More than half the genes located near HARs are involved in brain development and function, and as with *FOXP2*, the products of many of these genes go on to regulate other genes. According to Pollard (2009): '... even though HARs make up a minute portion of the genome, changes in these regions could have profoundly altered the human brain by influencing the activity of whole networks of genes.'

Genes beyond the brain

HAR2 (a gene regulatory region and the second most accelerated site on Pollard's list) drives gene activity in the wrist and thumb during pre-natal development; the ancestral version in non-human primates cannot. As Pollard (2009) says: '... This finding is particularly provocative

because it could underpin morphological changes in the human hand that permitted the dexterity needed to manufacture and use complex tools.' (See Chapter 9.)

In addition to undergoing changes in bodily form, our ancestors also underwent behavioural and physiological shifts that helped them adapt to changed circumstances and migrate to new environments. For example, the conquest of fire more than a million years ago and the agricultural revolution about 10,000 years ago made foods high in starch more accessible. But to exploit these calorie-rich foods, cultural shifts had to be matched by genetic adaptations. Changes in the **AMY1** gene, which encodes salivary amylase, an enzyme involved in digesting starch, represent one such adaptation. The mammalian genome contains multiple copies of this gene, with the number of copies varying between species (and even between individual humans). But overall, compared with other primates, humans have an especially large number of copies (Pollard, 2009).

Another famous example of dietary adaptation cited by Pollard involves the gene for lactase (**LCT**), an enzyme that allows mammals to digest the carbohydrate lactose (or milk sugar). In most species, only nursing infants can process lactose. But around 9,000 years ago – very recently, in evolutionary terms – changes in the human genome produced versions of *LCT* that allowed adults to also digest it. Modified *LCT* evolved independently in European and African populations, enabling carriers of the gene to digest milk from domesticated animals. Today, adult descendants of these ancient herdsmen are much more likely to tolerate lactose in their diets compared with adults from other parts of the world; many Asian and Latin American adults are lactose-intolerant, having the ancestral primate version of the gene.

A different kind of example of genetic change that can help explain the evolution of *Homo sapiens* as a distinct species relates to the loss of fur and the acquisition of dark skin. This is discussed in Box 2.5.

Box 2.5 The human *MC1R* gene and the 'naked ape'

Humans are the only primate species that has mostly naked (i.e. fur-less) skin. Loss of fur was an adaptation to changing environmental conditions that forced our ancestors to travel longer distances in search of food and water (Jablonski, 2010).

Rogers *et al.* (2004) examined sequences of the human **MC1R** gene, which is one of the genes responsible for producing skin pigmentation (i.e. skin colour). They found that a specific gene variant always found in Africans with dark pigmentation originated as many as 1.2 million years ago. Early human ancestors are thought to have had pinkish skin covered with black fur, much like chimpanzees, so the evolution of permanently dark skin was presumably a requisite evolutionary follow-up to the loss of our sun-shielding body hair. Rogers's estimate, therefore, provides a *minimum* age for the dawn of nakedness (Jablonski, 2010).

Less certain than why and when we became naked is how hominids evolved bare flesh. The genetic evidence for the evolution of nakedness has been difficult to locate because several genes contribute to the appearance and function of our skin. However, comparison of the human and chimp genomes reveals that one of the most significant differences lies in the genes that code for proteins that control properties of the skin. The human versions of some of those genes encode proteins that help to make our skin particularly waterproof and scuff-resistant – critical properties in the absence of protective fur. This finding implies that the appearance of those gene variants contributed to the origin of nakedness by helping to reduce its (potentially harmful) consequences (Jablonski, 2010).

Box 2.5 *Continued*

The outstanding barrier capabilities of our skin stem from the structure and makeup of its outermost layer, the stratum corneum (SC) of the epidermis. Most of the genes that direct the development of the SC are ancient, and their sequences are highly conserved among vertebrates. The distinctiveness of the human SC genes suggests very strongly that their appearance was important to survival (Jablonski, 2010).

Going furless had profound consequences for subsequent phases of human evolution. According to Jablonski (2010), the loss of most of our body hair and the gain of the ability to get rid of excess body heat through eccrine sweating (the epidermis comprises mainly eccrine glands, which permit improved cooling compared with furry animals) helped to make possible the dramatic enlargement of our brain – our most temperature-sensitive organ. As Jablonski puts it, '... shedding our body hair was surely a critical step in becoming brainy'.

Time for reflection

- Jablonski (2010) claims that our furlessness also had *social* consequences. What do you think the functions of fur might be, bearing in mind that it is unique to mammals (indeed, it is a defining characteristic)?

- Based on your answer to the above question, how might the loss of fur have affected communication between humans? (Another way of asking the question is to ask 'How do humans communicate *non-verbally* in ways that might be the equivalent of hairy mammals' use of their fur'?).

Less is more: Is the loss of DNA the key to human uniqueness?

A recent, ground-breaking study by McLean *et al.* (2011) has demonstrated experimentally for the first time how specific differences between human DNA and that of chimpanzees can account for traits that make us uniquely human. Crucially, it provides insight into how genetic changes helped us evolve our most prized asset – 'a large brain that enables us to reason, imagine, think forwards and backwards in time and unravel our own genetic and cosmological origins.' (Coghlan, 2011).

The key changes don't involve bits of DNA that humans acquired as we evolved (as we saw above, there are *no* specifically human genes); rather, it's the loss of several hundred 'snippets' of DNA that McLean *et al.* believe are crucial in explaining human distinctiveness. The snippets or chunks in question aren't genes at all, but DNA sequences that lie between genes and act as switches, regulating the turning on and off (and where and when in the body this occurs) of specific genes throughout the course of an animal's development. The loss of these regulatory regions caused our ancestors to lose certain features, such as facial whiskers, and added new ones, including brain cells in crucial locations.

McLean *et al.* (2011) compared the genomes of humans, chimps, macaques, chickens and mice. They specifically looked for regulatory regions that are uniquely *absent* in humans but apparently vital to the other species. They identified 510 instances where the loss of DNA removed a sequence that is highly conserved in other animals, suggesting that the deletions were likely to have had functional consequences for humans. They then focused on two of these instances, both *enhancers* (they boost the production of a protein): the first is located next to *AR*, a gene that makes receptors for male hormones; the second switches on *GADD45G*, a gene that inhibits the growth of brain tissue.

Through the use of genetic engineering, McLean *et al.* (2011) found that the *AR* gene causes the growth of sensory whiskers on the faces of foetal mice and spines on the surface of the mouse penis. Loss of this control sequence explains why we have lost both features. Penile spines are common in species where several males compete to fertilise the same female. The loss of such spines may have allowed humans to prolong sex (which, in turn, may have made it more intimate) and helped establish the emotional bonds between partners (monogamous relationships) needed for the prolonged task of raising children.

The *GADD45G* gene was found to be active in layers of the brain where cells that ultimately form the cortex are born. Specifically, in mice and chimps it *suppresses* the development of brain regions which in humans are involved in higher cognitive functions (such as conscious thought and language). The loss of this regulator gene may have been a pivotal moment in human evolution, as it allowed parts of the human brain to expand into the most complex known entity in the universe (see Chapter 3).

While it would be premature – and a little rash – to claim that the loss of this regulatory DNA was the only genetic change that made us human, the study does demonstrate the profound impact that such change can have. McLean *et al.*'s findings have been hailed by other researchers (Coghlan, 2011).

Interestingly, a comparison with the Neanderthal genome revealed that, like *Homo sapiens*, Neanderthals too had lost features possessed by a common ancestor, including penile spines and facial whiskers. This means that the crucial loss of DNA took place more than 800,000 years ago, when our human ancestor split from the Neanderthal lineage (see Chapter 1).

Conclusions

Echoing what we said in Chapter 1, and contrary to 'deep chasm' arguments, Ridley (1999) claims that the human species is by no means the pinnacle of evolution. Evolution has no pinnacle and there is no such thing as evolutionary progress (these are just value-judgements made by human beings): 'Natural selection is simply the process by which life-forms change to suit the myriad opportunities afforded by the physical environment and by other life-forms ...' (Ridley, 1999)

However, human beings are an ecological success. They are probably the most abundant large animal on the entire planet and have shown a remarkable capacity for colonising different habitats: cold or hot, dry or wet, high or low, marine or desert. In addition (and perhaps of fundamental importance): 'They [human beings] have, perched between their ears, the most complicated biological machine on the planet ...' (Ridley, 1999.) The brain is the subject of the next chapter.

Chapter summary

- Bodmer's deep chasm argument claims that what makes humans unique is their genetic differences from other species, especially chimpanzees.

- By contrast, Pasternak believes that the human genome/chimpanzee genome dissimilarity doesn't reflect different genes, but merely different *mutations* (replication errors) within genes that are common to the two species. This is consistent with the claim that there are no specifically 'human genes'.

- Ridley compares the genome with a book, comprising 23 chapters (chromosomes), each consisting of several thousand stories (genes), and each story made up of paragraphs (exons) and interrupted by advertisements (introns). Each paragraph comprises words (codons), with each word written in letters (bases).

- Genomes are written entirely in three-letter words, using only four letters: **A**denine, **C**ytosine, **G**uanine, and **T**hymine.

- The words are written on long chains of sugar and phosphate called DNA molecules; each chromosome is one pair of very long DNA molecules.

- Two fundamental processes carried out by genes are *replication* (making copies of themselves) and *translation* (reading themselves). In translation, the DNA is converted into RNA, which uses the same letters as DNA except for **U**racil instead of **T**. This RNA copy is called messenger RNA.

- Ribosomes move along the messenger, translating each codon in turn into one letter of a different alphabet comprising 20 amino acids; these are brought by transfer RNA. The end-product of the translation process is a protein, which forms the basis of almost everything in the body.

- The body's chemical reactions (including replication and translation) are catalysed by proteins called enzymes. Proteins are also responsible for switching genes on and off.

- Most DNA is rarely or never translated/transcribed and is called 'junk DNA'.

- It's now widely accepted that humans are genetically more closely related to the common chimpanzee and bonobos than any of these three species is to the gorilla.

- While humans have 23 pairs of chromosomes, chimpanzees, gorillas and orang-utans all have 24 pairs. However, less than one per cent of the human genome has changed in the six million years or so since the human and chimpanzee lineages diverged.

- Research by Pollard has helped identify the sections of DNA that have changed the most rapidly since chimpanzees and humans split from a common ancestor. One noteworthy example is *human accelerated region 1 (HAR1)*.

- While only two of the 118 bases comprising *HAR1* differ between chickens and chimpanzees, there are 18 differences between humans and chimpanzees. This implies a very important function for the gene in humans.

- *HAR1* is active in a type of neuron that plays a key role in the pattern and layout of the developing cerebral cortex; a disruption to this process can result in lissecephaly ('smooth brain').

- *HAR1* is part of the mere 1.5 per cent of our total DNA which encodes RNA. It's also the first case of an RNA-encoding sequence that appears to have been positively selected.

- *FOXP2* is another of the fast-changing sequences and is known to be involved in speech, as demonstrated by study of the KE family. While the gene is very similar in all mammals (from monkeys to mice), the peculiar (mutant) human form of the gene may be a prerequisite for speech. Neanderthals possessed the modern human version of *FOXP2*, and the total genome of modern human is 1–4 per cent Neanderthal.

- Genetic studies of people with microcephaly have revealed the role of *ASPM*, as well as three other genes – *MCPH1*, *CDK5RAP2* and *CENPJ* – in controlling brain size. *ASPM* has been shown to have undergone several bursts of change over the course of primate evolution, suggesting positive selection.

- Other genetic adaptations correlate with behavioural and physiological adaptations to changing environmental conditions. For example, the *AMY1* gene aids the digestion of starch (made more accessible by the conquest of fire and the agricultural revolution) and *LCT* aids the digestion of lactose (milk sugar) from domesticated animals.

- Recent evidence suggests that what's distinctive about the genetic make-up of *Homo sapiens* is the loss of certain enhancer DNA (one located next to *AR*, a second that switches on the *GADD45G* gene). These make receptors for male hormones and inhibit the growth of brain tissue, respectively.

Suggested further reading

Jones, S. (1993) *The Language of the Genes: Biology, History and the Evolutionary Future.* London: Flamingo. A very readable and informative account of a highly technical subject. However, as the sub-title suggests, this is much broader in its scope than just an explanation of the fundamentals of genetics.

Plomin, R. (1994) *Genetics and Experience: The Interplay Between Nature and Nurture.* Thousand Oaks, CA: Sage. A detailed discussion of the major principles of genetics by a leading behaviour geneticist.

Ridley, M. (1999) *Genome: The Autobiography of a Species in 23 Chapters.* London: Fourth Estate. Published before publication of the entire human genome in 2000, Ridley selects one newly discovered gene from each of the 23 pairs of human chromosomes and tells its story in the context of the evolution of *Homo sapiens.*

Selected websites

http://genome.ucsc.edu

University of California, Santa Cruz, Genome Bioinformatics website. It includes a page on the Encyclopaedia of DNA elements (ENCODE), the Neanderthal genome and the chimpanzee (*Pan troglodytes*) genome. Not an easy ride, but well worth the effort.

www.sanger.ac.uk

Wellcome Trust: Sanger Institute. (The Human Genome Project.)

www.kumc.edu/gec

Genetics Education Centre: University of Kansas Medical Centre.

Chapter 3: The human brain: What makes it so special?

Chapter 3: The human brain: What makes it so special?

Key questions

- What are the major structures and sub-divisions of the human brain?
- How did the human brain evolve from our fish, amphibian, reptilian and early mammalian ancestors?
- How does the human brain differ from those of other (present-day) mammals?
- What is the relationship between intelligence and brain size?
- How does the human brain compare with those of chimpanzees?
- How does knowledge of post-natal brain development help us understand what distinguishes the human brain from those of other mammals (including other apes)?
- What is meant by the human brain's 'plasticity' and is this what makes it special?
- How are the long period of human immaturity and brain development related?
- Are handedness and functional lateralisation (or hemispheric asymmetry) uniquely human characteristics?

A brief outline of the human brain: Major structures

During the first five weeks of foetal life, the neural tube changes its shape to produce five bulbous enlargements. These are generally accepted as the basic divisions of the brain, namely:

- the **myelencephalon** (comprising the medulla oblongata)
- the **metencephalon** (pons and cerebellum)
- the **mesencephalon** (tectum and tegmentum)
- the **diencephalon** (thalamus and hypothalamus)
- the **telencephalon** (cerebral hemispheres or cerebrum, basal ganglia and limbic system).

'Encephalon' means 'within the head'.

During foetal development the outside of the brain gradually becomes more folded/wrinkled (convolution) (see Figure 3.1). This is necessary if its 2,500 cm² surface area is to fit inside the relatively small skull.

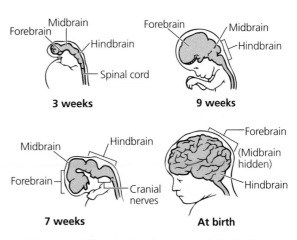

▲ **Figure 3.1** Foetal development of the brain

An overlapping, but broader, division into hindbrain (**rhombencephalon**), midbrain (mesencephalon) and forebrain (**prosencephalon**) is shown in Figure 3.2, while Figure 3.3 shows a lateral (side-on) view of the left cerebral hemisphere.

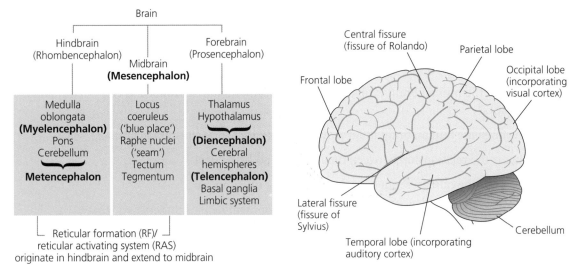

▲ **Figure 3.2** Division into hindbrain, midbrain and forebrain

▲ **Figure 3.3** Lateral view of the left cerebral hemisphere

Mammalian brains

According to Rose (2005), the evolutionary development from the amphibians through the reptiles to mammals (including humans) resulted in the dominance of the furthest forward part of the brain (the telencephalon). In mammals this developed from the olfactory lobes (responsible for the sense of smell) swelling outwards, enlarging and folding over all other brain regions to form the cerebral hemispheres (see Figures 3.1 and 3.3. above). With mammals, the cerebrum took over the task of coordination and control from the thalamus; some areas of the latter became mere staging posts or relay stations en route to the cortex.

However, the hypothalamus (with the thalamus, forming the diencephalon) and the pituitary gland (located near the hypothalamus, but actually the master endocrine/hormonal gland and not part of the brain at all) remain crucially important for controlling mood, emotion and complex behavioural patterns. The hypothalamus contains groups of neurons concerned with the regulation of appetite, sexual drive, sleep and pleasure; the pituitary (in conjunction with the hypothalamus) regulates the production of many key hormones and forms the major link between the nervous and endocrine hormonal systems.

Rose (2005) describes as 'popularising behavioural determinists' those who stress continuity with other species, pointing out as they do how critical these drives and behavioural states are for human beings, how they dominate the totality of human behaviour, and what a large proportion of human life is devoted to activities associated with or driven by them. One very influential example of a serious scientific account, which is often depicted in cartoon form showing a straight line of fish emerging onto land to become reptiles, mammals, **primates**, then humans, is MacLean's (1973) **triune brain model** (TBM) (see Box 3.1). This specifies 'primitive' complexes in the human brain inherited from animal ancestors, reflecting traditional ideas about sequential evolution (Patton, 2008/2009). Originally proposed in the 1960s, MacLean's TBM has been widely popularised and claims that human brains are the culmination of *linear* evolution progressing from simpler species.

Time for reflection

- What do you think is meant by 'linear evolution'?

Box 3.1 MacLean's triune model of the brain

Drawing on the work of pioneering comparative neuroanatomist, Ludwig Edinger, MacLean (a neuroscientist and psychiatrist) conceived of the brain not as a unity but as *three brains in one*, each with a different phylogenetic history, each with 'its own special intelligence, its own special memory, its own sense of time and space, and its own motor functions' (MacLean, 1973). In fact, he proposed four sequential steps:

1. A *'neural chassis'* corresponding to the brains of fish and amphibians.

2. A *reptilian complex*, comprising the basal ganglia (dominant in the brains of reptiles and birds). This evolved about 300 million years ago and is shared by all terrestrial vertebrates; it has remained remarkably unchanged during that time period. The basal ganglia include the olfactostriatum (the olfactory tubercle and nucleus acumbens) and part of the corpus striatum (the caudate nucleus, putamen, globus pallidus and satellite collections of grey matter). Emotions had not yet evolved, and behavioural responses were largely controlled by instinct (Stevens and Price, 2000). According to Bailey (1987, quoted in Stevens and Price): ' ... The reptilian carry-overs provide the automatic, compulsive urgency to much of human behaviour, where free will steps aside and persons act as they have to act, often despising themselves in the process for their hatreds, prejudices, compulsions, conformity, deceptiveness and guile.'

3. A *paleomammalian component*, consisting of the limbic system (which, supposedly emerged with the appearance of mammals and which was responsible for emotional behaviour). The limbic system includes the **hippocampus**, hypothalamus and thalamus, and the pituitary gland (see above). It is a homeostatic mechanism, maintaining not only control of hormone levels but also balances hunger against satiation, sexual desire against gratification, thirst against fluid retention, and sleep against wakefulness. It also plays an indispensable role in memory (Stevens and Price, 2000).

   By this evolutionary stage, fear and anger have emerged, as well as love and attachment, together with their associated behavioural response patterns, bonding and mating. MacLean (1985) draws particular attention to three forms of behaviour that most clearly distinguish the evolutionary transition from reptiles to mammals: (i) nursing and maternal care; (ii) audiovocal communication for maintaining mother–offspring contact; (iii) play. The separation call is the most primitive and basic mammalian vocalisation, which originally served to maintain mother–offspring proximity; later, it helped to maintain contact between group members. Likewise, MacLean claims that play evolved to promote group harmony. These behaviours depend on the thalamocingulate division of the limbic system, which has no counterpart in the reptilian brain. The amygdalar and septal divisions are involved in self-preservation behaviour and reproduction, respectively.

Box 3.1 *Continued*

Conscious awareness is more evident at this evolutionary stage and behaviour is less rigidly determined by instincts (although they're still very apparent). The limbic system also includes the paleocortex – the most primitive part of the evolving cerebral cortex.

4. A neomammalian component, consisting of the neocortex, which is the site of higher cognitive functions, as opposed to emotional (limbic) and instinctive (basal ganglia) behaviour. According to Stevens and Price (2000).

... Behaviour arising in the neocortex is usually described as 'conscious', 'voluntary', and 'rational', reflecting the fact that there is a sense of personal control over such behaviour. At this level there is a high degree of awareness, unlike the partial awareness and limited sense of control that characterises emotional behaviour, and the relative lack of control, and often only retrospective awareness, that is typical of instinctive behaviour.

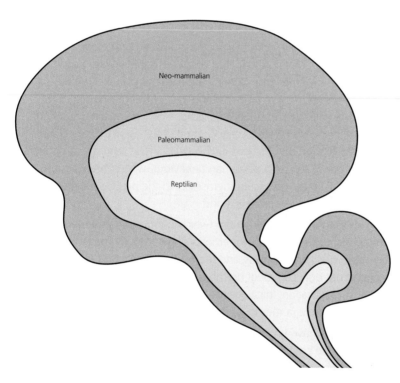

▲ **Figure 3.4** MacLean's three brains

Time for reflection
- How is awareness/consciousness different from self-awareness/self-consciousness?
- How does this difference correlate with differences between different species?
(See Chapters 1 and 4.)

An evaluation of MacLean's TBM

Stevens and Price (2000) cite research which indicated that human emotional responses depend on neuronal pathways linking the limbic system with parietal and frontal areas of the right cerebral cortex. Furthermore, this system appears to be under the control of the *left* frontal cortex, suggesting that the 'cold' dominant left hemisphere represses or inhibits the emotionally toned 'hot' paleo-mammalian brain. Does this evidence support the claims of Rose's popularising behavioural determinists?

Rose (2005) agrees that in the brain's evolution, few structures have ever totally disappeared. Rather, as new ones have developed, the old ones have become less important and relatively smaller, but many of the connections and pathways remain. It's also true that the hypothalamus is of considerable importance in controlling mood and behaviour in mammals – including humans. However, '... to extrapolate from these facts towards the claim that because similar brain structures exist in people and frogs, people's behaviour is inevitably froglike, is nonsense. It is like arguing that we think by smelling because the cerebral hemispheres evolved from the olfactory lobes...' (Rose, 2005.)

Brain regions may survive, but their functions are transformed or partially superseded by others. Fish, amphibians, reptiles and birds survive today because they're fully 'fit' for the environmental conditions they find themselves in; they're all at least as fit and 'evolved' as humans are. As Rose (2005) puts it, '... adaptation is about survival; our brains evolved as a strategy for survival, not to solve abstract cognitive puzzles, do crosswords or play chess.'

Time for reflection

- How do Rose's comments regarding adaptation relate to the **human exceptionalism/ uniqueness arguments** discussed in Chapter 1?

- Is there a case for claiming that human abilities and behaviours are *inherently* superior (or 'more evolved') or are they subject to the same qualifications as other species-specific behaviours (i.e. they can only be judged in terms of how they have helped the animal survive in its particular habitat)?

A further criticism of the TBM is that the brains of present-day reptiles have undergone independent evolution during the past 250 million years and can hardly be assumed to be identical with the brain of the common ancestor we share with the reptiles (Butler and Hodos, 1996). However, Stevens and Price (2000) argue that the TBM's basic principles remain valid. The increase in size and complexity of the human brain since the reptilian stage has equipped us with three *central processing assemblies* or decision-making units, each of which responds in its characteristic way to environmental changes. While there is some coordination between the activity of these three assemblies, each retains a degree of autonomy.

Stevens and Price also claim that the TBM provides a home for what might be called the 'triune mind'. Many thinkers, including Plato, St Augustine, La Rochefoucauld, Freud and Jung, have observed that the mind seems to possess separate functional components which compete with one another for overall control of behaviour.

...Variously attributed to such organs as the 'head', the 'heart', and the 'bowels', reason, emotion, and instinct may display differing intentions when it comes to choosing a mate during courtship or displaying valour on the field of battle ... MacLean's anatomical studies give useful support to this long-standing concept of three minds in one (the neurological 'holy trinity'). (Stevens and Price, 2000)

Time for reflection

- Can you think of expressions commonly used in everyday language which reflect this 'triune mind'? (An example would be 'My heart tells me to ... but my head ...')
- Are these just figures of speech that reflect out-dated – and invalid – beliefs about human functioning (for example, that the heart is the seat of emotion), or do you agree with Stevens and Price's argument that the TBM provides a 'home' for the 'triune mind'?

Not all mammalian brains are the same

The cerebral hemispheres have undergone considerable change even within the genus of mammals itself. Marsupials (such as the Australian duck-billed platypus or the North American opossum) have well-developed forebrains by comparison with the reptiles, whose cerebral hemispheres have a cortex just a single layer of cells thick. By contrast, even the early mammals have a cortex with many layers of cells, although this was almost entirely olfactory in function. However, the integration of information from different sensory modalities increasingly depended on cerebral dominance over thalamic control. The greatest expansion occurs with the formation of the neocortex. As this increases in area, so the older cortical regions are forced deeper into the brain structure, becoming curved in the process to form the hippocampus. This plays a central role in memory (especially spatial memory: see Chapter 7) and has been called 'a cognitive map' (O'Keefe and Nadel, 1978). An index of this development is the fact that while in mammals like the hedgehog the ratio of the volume of the neocortex to hippocampus is 3:2, in monkeys it has increased to 30:1 (Rose, 2005).

All the cerebral regions, except the neocortex, have some sort of rudimentary equivalent in reptiles: it's the layered cortex which is unique to mammals. How it's taken over thalamic functions can be shown by mapping the connections between neocortex and thalamus, which all arrive within specific layers of the cortical neurons: each thalamic region matches an appropriate neocortical area. In the earliest mammals (as in today's marsupials), most of the neocortex is devoted to the motor area and the cortical targets of thalamic neurons. The major development in the later-evolving mammals is the expansion of the area of neocortex between the sensory and motor regions; these contain **association areas**, which don't have direct connections outside the cortex. Instead, they 'talk' only to each other and to other cortical neurons: they relate to the outside world only after several stages of neuronal mediation. In humans, these association areas include the massive *prefrontal lobe* and regions of the *occipital*, *temporal* and *parietal* lobes (Rose, 2005). This relative ballooning of the cortex in humans endows it with far more neural tissues than is needed for the mundane tasks of keeping the rest of the body running (Oppenheimer, 2007). In other words, in humans (and to a lesser extent in modern apes), there's a huge volume of apparently redundant cortex without a civil service role (Deacon, 1997).

Intelligence and the brain: does size matter?

Time for reflection
- Is it the size of the human brain that gives us our superior intelligence?
- Is it possible to have small brains and still display intelligent behaviour?
- Might there be brain characteristics other than size which determine species differences?

According to Patton (2008/2009), in recent decades scientists have rejected a linear, sequential view of brain evolution in which the human brain incorporates components resembling those of modern fish, amphibians, reptiles and birds. This is partly because of the observation of abilities, in non-human species, previously taken to be limited to humans, or, at least, to primates. Among birds, for example, parrots and **corvids** (a group that includes crows, jays, ravens and jackdaws) have been shown to be capable of some amazing cognitive feats (see Chapters 5 and 6). How do we square these findings with the popular 'put down', whereby someone displaying limited intelligence is called 'birdbrain'?

Absolute versus relative size

The traditional view of birds as rather unintelligent creatures is reflected in the fact that, objectively and relatively, their brains are small. Conversely, the view of humans as the most highly intelligent species (whether this is from an exceptionalism or continuity perspective – see Chapter 1) is consistent with our possession of the largest brain of all species. But is it?

According to Rose (2005), a number of questions have been posed by those concerned with brain evolution. Is there a correlation between brain size and cognitive or affective abilities? Are big brains better? Is there some scale on which humans are top of the brain tree? What scale would be appropriate? Is there a distinction between actual size and effective size?

Clearly, the brain of *Homo sapiens* isn't the biggest brain on the planet in *absolute* terms: whales and elephants outdo us by up to six times, and the dolphin brain is also larger than ours (Motluk, 2010; Rose, 2005). However, it's equally clear that larger bodies require bigger brains: the larger organs and muscles of larger animals need more brain to control them, or at least a minimum share of the attention the brain pays to the larger body bulk (Oppenheimer, 2007; Rose, 2005). So, perhaps brain weight *relative* to body weight might be a better measure. In general, brain weight and body weight increase in step and the brain weight/body weight ratio is fairly predictable in most mammals. One early study concluded that, taking body size into account, the human brain is exceptionally large, as much as seven times larger than those of other mammals (Jerison, 1955). But it's not a simple ratio: if it were, then adult mice, for example, would have much smaller brains than they actually possess. Both mice and chicks have brains representing 4 per cent of body weight – twice the human brain weight/body weight ratio of 2 per cent (with brain weight averaging between 1,300–1,500 g) (Rose, 2005). The relationship becomes even less straightforward in the higher mammals: the brain weight/body weight ratio has been distorted in several fundamental ways. For example, primates have proportionately larger adult brains than other mammals, because they have bodies that, from early life, grow more slowly for the same absolute rate of brain growth (Oppenheimer, 2007).

Again, although, in general, bigger-brained animals tend to be more versatile and creative, the correlation doesn't seem to hold up *across* taxonomic orders (Motluk, 2010). For example, the brains of hoofed animals (the ungulates), such as cows and horses, are 4–5 times larger than monkey brains, but monkeys have abilities that are clearly more complex. Similarly, the capybara, a giant Amazonian rodent, cannot do with its 75 g brain what a capuchin monkey can do with its more modest 52 g. In the past, such differences were explained away in terms of an extension of the 'bigger bodies need bigger brains' argument discussed above:

- The bigger the animal, the larger the individual neurons; this means that fewer of them can be packed into any given brain volume.
- The bigger the brain, the more space was taken up with the hardware for transmission in the form of longer, thicker and better insulated neural pathways.

As a result, a 65 kg capybara might still have far less mental processing power than a 4 kg capuchin monkey (Motluk, 2010). Herculano-Houzel *et al.* (2006) found evidence to support this traditional explanation, but using a method that hadn't been used before. This is described in Box 3.2.

Box 3.2 Counting brain cells in rodents and humans (Azevedo *et al.*, 2009; Herculano-Houzel *et al.*, 2006)

Herculano-Houzel and her colleagues suspected that the brains of animals in different orders (e.g. rodents) might be constructed along different lines. Specifically, they wanted to know exactly how many neurons there are in any given brain and whether human brains are exceptional within their order (i.e. primates).

Most textbooks state that the human brain contains 100 billion neurons – but no one seems to have actually counted them! The same appears to be true for **glial cells** (or glia), which are mostly smaller than neurons and 9–10 times more numerous. Once thought to merely play a maintenance role, they're now regarded as playing a vital role in processes such as the formation and modification of synapses (the connections between neurons) (Fields, 2004).

Counting brain cells is a time-consuming process, typically using the *stereological method*: taking thin slices of brain and counting the cells, hoping that the slices contain a representative number of cells, then extrapolating to the whole brain. Herculano-Houzel used a different method, the 'isotropic fractionators', which involves 'turning fixed brains into soup' (Motluk, 2010). This is faster and more accurate.

Herculano-Houzel *et al.* (2006) first used this method with a mouse brain, then with a range of other rodents: hamsters, guinea pigs, rats, agoutis and capybaras. They found that as size increased, so there were more neurons and more glial cells, and also that individual neurons got bigger. So, among rodents at least, the long-held assumptions about brain size (see earlier discussion) were supported: (a) bigger brains tend to have more raw processing power; and (b) bigger animals tend to have bigger neurons and, therefore, require bigger brains.

Box 3.2 *Continued*

But would these assumptions hold up in the case of primates (including humans)? Azevedo *et al.* (2009) used the isotropic fractionators with six different primates (including marmosets, owl monkeys, squirrel monkeys and macaques). As expected, primate brains were different: larger brains didn't have larger neurons, and there were many more neurons per volume of brain than found in rodents. So, even if a rodent brain and a primate brain were the same size, the primate brain would have more neurons. Put another way, if a rodent had the same number of neurons as a primate, its brain would be about six times the size.

What about humans? Based on what they knew from studying the other primates, the researchers estimated that a primate with the average human body mass of 70 kg should have a brain of about 1,300 g, containing about 90 billion neurons – quite close to the commonly cited 100 billion. Using the brains of a 70-year-old and three 50-year-old males, they found an average weight of 1,500 g and an average neuron count of 86 billion. Azevedo *et al.* concluded that the human brain is nothing more than 'a linearly scaled-up primate brain'.

Are human brains not so special after all?

According to Montgomery *et al.* (2010), it's often assumed that increasing brain size was a general evolutionary trend in primates. However, as we saw in Chapter 1, recent fossil discoveries have documented brain size *decreases* in some lineages; this raises the question of how general a trend there was for brains to increase in mass over evolutionary time.

Montgomery *et al.* carried out the first study to reconstruct brain evolution (in terms of absolute brain mass, absolute body mass and relative brain mass) across all primates: 37 existing and 23 extinct species. They found that both absolute and relative brain mass did generally increase over evolutionary time, but body mass didn't. Nevertheless, there were instances where brain size has declined within several lineages, including mouse lemurs, marmosets, mangabeys and possibly also humans (as suggested by the 2003 discovery of *Homo floresiensis*, or the 'hobbit', whose brain was about one-third the size of *Homo sapiens*: see Chapter 1, page x).

These findings suggest that we should be cautious when taking the brain weight/body weight ratio as evidence of our cerebral superiority (see above). When Montgomery *et al.* (2010) evaluated how body size evolved in primates, they found no overall trend. In some cases, such as gibbons and colobus monkeys, as their brains got bigger, their bodies got smaller. In others, like the gorillas, brain mass grew but body mass grew a lot more. They concluded that primate brains and bodies evolved in response to different selection pressures, so that their sizes aren't necessarily correlated.

Herculano-Houzel (in Motluk, 2010) agrees with these conclusions. Using the neuron-counting technique used in previous studies (see Box 3.2) with orang-utan and gorilla brains, she found that they conform to the same neuronal scaling rules found in other primates, with a high density of neurons per volume and no increase in neuron size with body size. Where the great apes *do* differ from other primates is that their bodies are bigger than would be expected from their brain size, '... so although a gorilla weighing about the same as a human has a brain just one-third of the size, it is actually the body size of the gorilla rather than the brain size of the human which is the outlier ...' (Motluk, 2010).

Looking elsewhere for what makes human brains special

According to the 'developmental constraint hypothesis' of comparative mammalian neuroanatomy, brain structures increase in size predictably as the entire brain grows – both **ontogenetically** (as part of individual development) and **phylogenetically** (as part of the evolution of species) (Rilling and Insel, 1998). Rilling and Insel used magnetic resonance imaging (MRI) to scan the whole brain and cerebellum volumes of 44 primates from 11 **haplorhine species** (which include New and Old World monkeys, including apes and humans). After controlling for overall brain volume, they found that the cerebellum in both **pongid** (chimpanzees, orang-utans and gorillas) and **hylobatid** (such as gibbons) apes is, on average, 45 per cent larger than in monkeys.

Rilling and Insel (1998) concluded that not all primate brains are organised in the same way and that developmental constraints don't prevent selection for increased cerebellar volume independent of selection on overall brain size.

Time for reflection
● What do you understand by Rilling and Insel's conclusion?

Another way of looking at their conclusion is that during the evolution of different primate species, having a larger cerebellum conferred advantages on those particular species over-and-above their possessing an overall bigger brain.

In a second study, also using MRI scans, Rilling and Insel (1999) found (as predicted) that the human neocortex is significantly larger than expected from a primate of our brain size. They also found that the human brain is significantly more convoluted than expected for our brain size. These findings provide additional insights into human brain evolution beyond the important observation that brain volume approximately trebled in the hominid lineage: they demonstrate that the neocortex (independently of overall brain size) was uniquely modified throughout hominid evolution. These modifications may constitute part of the neurobiological substrate that supports some of *Homo sapiens'* most distinctive cognitive abilities (Rilling and Insel, 1999) (see Chapters 4–7).

Development of the human brain: Is this what makes it unique?

We noted above the distinction between ontogenesis and phylogenesis, which refer to development of the individual, and evolution of the species, respectively. Could the way the human brain develops (before and after birth) point us towards what its distinctive characteristics are?

According to Oppenheimer (2007), compared with other apes, humans have a slower clock for brain maturation. In all mammals, brain growth switches off before body growth in a way that matches the functional needs of the adult body size. But in the case of humans, our internal clock keeps our brains growing for longer than would be expected for our final body size as primates. (This mirrors the finding cited above that the great apes differ from other primates in that their bodies are bigger than would be expected from their brain size.) The result of this prolongation of foetal and infant development is a brain size more appropriate for a 1,000 kg ape such as the extinct *Gigantopithecus* (Deacon, 1997).

Developmental cognitive neuroscience (DCN) and brain plasticity

Developmental cognitive neuroscience (**DCN**) is a new subfield in which researchers are specifically interested in relating developmental changes in perception, cognition and behaviour in the developing child to the underlying growth of the brain (Johnson, 2005). One of the factors contributing to the emergence of DCN has been increasing evidence for the **plasticity** of the brain; in turn, this is critically related to the slower clock for brain maturation described above. Far from being the unfolding of a rigid genetic plan, postnatal human brain development involves a two-way interaction between brain structure and emerging functions (Johnson, 2005). In other words:

> ... the postnatal structural and functional development of the brain is influenced by the environment in which it is raised. This is particularly so for humans since our postnatal brain development is considerably slowed down even relative to our most closely related primate cousins ... (Johnson, 2009)

Time for reflection
- What do you understand by the term 'environment' in this context?
- How is Johnson's description of human brain development relevant to the nature–nurture debate? (See Gross, 2009.)

According to Johnson (2009), the environment that helps shape our brains involves not only the physical world of objects, surfaces, gravity, etc., but also the social world of other human beings. For Gerhardt (2004), it's the baby's responsiveness to human interaction that is the distinguishing characteristic of human beings compared with other newborn mammals.

Humans share with other mammals a core brain which ensures survival (echoing MacLean's TBM – see above). A newborn baby has a basic version of these systems in place: a functioning nervous system that enables him or her to breathe, a visual system that allows the tracking of movements and seeing faces close up, a core consciousness (based in the brainstem) that reacts to sensory experiences and assesses them in terms of survival. What makes the human infant special is its *sociability*: '... Human beings are the most social of animals and are already distinctive in this way at birth, imitating a parent's facial movements and orienting themselves to faces very early on.' (Gerhardt, 2004)

Box 3.3 Development of the social brain

According to Turner (2000), as the emotional (i.e. mammalian) brain evolved in humans, we became more emotionally complex and sophisticated: more alternatives and choices arose in our social interactions. This required a capacity for thinking about and reflecting on our emotions, which led to the development of the cortex, in particular, the **prefrontal cortex** (PFC). The PFC has a unique role, linking the sensory areas of the cortex with the emotional and survival-oriented subcortex and is found only in humans (Gopnik, 2010). A key region within the PFC, and the first to mature, is the **orbitofrontal cortex (OFC)** (lying behind the eyes, next to the amygdala and anterior cingulate gyrus).

Box 3.3 *Continued*

Time for reflection
- The OFC, together with other parts of the PFC and the anterior cingulate gyrus, is probably the area of the brain most responsible for what Goleman (1996) calls 'emotional intelligence' (Gerhardt, 2004).
- What do you understand by the term 'emotional intelligence'?
- How might this be relevant to the human exceptionalism/**continuity arguments** (see Chapter 1)?

Without an intact and properly functioning OFC, it becomes impossible to empathise with other people (to mentally put yourself in their shoes). Gerhardt (2004) describes it as 'so much about being human'. Not only is it larger in the right hemisphere, but Schore (2003) believes that the OFC is the controller for the whole right hemisphere, which is dominant throughout infancy. It develops almost entirely postnatally, not maturing until toddlerhood. However, while the functions supported by the PFC clearly become more advanced during childhood, this region is active from at least the first few months after birth (Johnson, 2005).

Crucially, there's nothing automatic about the maturation of the OFC. As Gerhardt (2004) puts it, '... the kind of brain that each baby develops is the brain that comes out of his or her particular experiences with people. It is very 'experience dependent ...'

This building up of the brain through experience makes good evolutionary sense: it means that each individual child can be moulded to his or her environmental niche. '... Precisely because we are so dependent as babies, and our brains at this stage are so 'plastic' (that is, easily changed), we can learn to fit in with whatever culture and circumstances we find ourselves in ...' (Gerhardt, 2004).

Similarly, Johnson (2009) observes that the influence of the environment on the brain includes not only aspects of the social and physical world that are specific to individuals (such as being exposed to spoken English), but also aspects that are common to almost all human beings (such as being exposed to language of some kind or other). This suggests that some of the common aspects of human brain structure and function could arise not only because we have **genes** in common, but also because we share a common environment (Johnson, 2009).

Time for reflection
- How does Chomsky (e.g. 1957) explain the connection between the 'specifics' and 'universals' of language? (See Chapters 1 and 6 for a discussion of Chomsky's theory of language acquisition.)

The self-organising brain

What Gerhardt claims for the OFC in particular, a majority of researchers involved in DCN claim for the brain as a whole. There is considerable evidence that human functional brain development is a *constructive process*, in which the state of the brain at one (earlier) stage helps it to select the appropriate experience needed for advancing to the next (later) stage (Johnson, 2009). In other words, human post-natal brain development is a *self-organising process* (Mareschal *et al.*, 2007).

According to Eliot (1999), neurons are remarkably plastic:

> *... The brain itself is literally moulded by experience: every sight, sound, and thought leaves an imprint on specific neural circuits, modifying the way future sights, sounds, and thoughts will be registered. Brain hardware is not fixed, but living, dynamic tissue that is constantly updating itself to meet the sensory, motor, emotional, and intellectual demands at hand.*

Interestingly, more intelligent children have been found to possess a particularly plastic cortex (Shaw *et al.*, 2006).

The relatively primitive nature of babies' brains has been explained in terms of our evolutionary history (see Chapter 1). Our upright posture and bipedal lifestyle sets limits on pelvic size, so women can only squeeze out a baby with a relatively small head; this means that its brain is only partially developed. But, as Eliot (1999) points out, other mammalian species are born just as helpless as humans (such as rats and cats, who don't even open their eyes for several days postnatally).

However, humans take relatively longer to complete their development because they have more functions (especially cognitive ones) to add – we have further to go. This observation suggests an alternative explanation for why babies' brains are poorly developed: it is to allow them to learn to add these additional functions. Echoing Mareschal *et al.*'s concept of brain development as a self-organising process, Eliot (1999) states that: '... Babies' brains are learning machines. They build themselves, or adapt, to the environment at hand. Although the brain is often appropriately compared to a computer, this is one way in which they differ: The brain actually programs itself ...'

Time for reflection
● What other differences between brains and computers can you think of? (See Gross, 2009.)

Eliot goes on to say, 'Such adaptability is a property of the brain from its very first emergence. While genes program the *sequence* of neural development, at every turn the *quality* of that development is shaped by environmental factors ...' Box 3.4 discusses the complementary nature of plasticity and **specificity**.

Box 3.4 Specificity and plasticity

Rose (2005) describes the two intertwined, complementary processes of specificity and plasticity as a 'developmental double helix'.

Without specificity, the brain wouldn't be able to become accurately wired; for example, nerves wouldn't be able to make the right connections between the retina and the visual cortex to enable binocular vision, or between the motor cortex and muscles (via the spinal cord).

Without plasticity, the developing nervous system would be unable to repair itself following damage, or to mould its responses to changing aspects of the outside world in order to create an internal model or representation of that world (a plan of how to act on the world). This is the function of (human) brains to provide such models. '... It is specificity and plasticity rather than nature and nurture that provide the dialectic within which development occurs, and both are utterly dependent on both genes and environment.' (Rose, 2005) '"Plasticity"' is also used to refer to the in-built "redundancy" characteristic of all developing systems: there are multiple possible pathways to a successful outcome ...' (Rose, 2005).

Perhaps the clearest example of babies seeking out those aspects of the environment necessary for their own later brain development is the attention and effort they devote to interacting with other humans, especially their primary caregivers (Johnson, 2009). This brings us neatly back to the social brain.

Dependent infants and the maturing PFC

Gopnik (2010) asks, from an evolutionary perspective, why humans have such an unusually long period of immaturity: why make babies so helpless for so long, thus requiring adults to put so much work and care into keeping their babies alive?

Across the animal kingdom, the intelligence and flexibility of adults are correlated with babies' immaturity. **Precocial** species (such as chickens) rely on highly specific innate capacities, adapted to one particular environmental niche, and so they mature more quickly. By contrast, **altricial** *species* (including humans) rely much more on learning. For example, crows can take a new object (such as a piece of wire) and work out how to turn it into a tool (see Chapter 9). But young crows depend on their parents for much longer than chicks do.

To solve the 'problem' of dependent offspring, evolution has created a division of labour between babies and adults. Babies get an extended period for learning about their environment without having to actually do anything; when they become adults, they can use their learning to help them survive and reproduce, taking care, in turn, of the next generation. Agreeing with Eliot, Gopnik (2010) states that 'Fundamentally, babies are designed to learn'. The PFC plays a key role in human learning, underpinning the adult capacities for focusing and planning ahead. Wiring within the PFC may not be complete until the mid-20s.

As we saw above, the PFC inhibits inappropriate emotion and allows us to empathise with others; it also inhibits irrelevant thoughts and actions. While such inhibition may be essential in adults, in babies and young children lack of inhibition may help them to explore freely.

According to Gopnik (2010):

> ... Far from being mere unfinished adults, babies and young children are exquisitely designed by evolution to change and create, to learn and explore. Those capacities, so intrinsic to what it means to be human, appear in the purest forms in the earliest years of our lives. Our most valuable human accomplishments are possible because we were once helpless dependent children and not in spite of it. Childhood, and caregiving, is fundamental to our humanity.

Handedness and functional lateralisation: Are these uniquely human?

Handedness is a form of asymmetry in which one side is proficient and the other less so (i.e. right- or left-handed) (Coren, 1992). While about 54 per cent of cats, rats and mice have a dominant paw (much as humans are right- or left-handed), their pawedness seems to be equally split between right and left (i.e. around 50 per cent are right-pawed and around 50 per cent are left-pawed). By contrast, approximately 90 per cent of all humans are right-handed. Indeed, this observation has been verified so many times in so many cultures and countries, that we can take right-handedness as a human predisposition (Coren, 1992).

As interesting as these species differences might be, what's really important is what handedness tells us about the brain. Because the right hand is controlled by the left hemisphere (and vice versa), the predominant human preference for the right hand implies dominance of the left hemisphere. Regardless of handedness, two major specialised parts of the brain responsible for language (**Broca's area** and **Wernicke's area**) are found *only* in the left hemisphere (see Chapter 6). This is an example of **functional lateralisation** (or hemispheric asymmetry). A crucial question we need to ask is: is hemispheric asymmetry unique to human beings?

According to MacNeilage *et al.* (2009), 40 years ago it was widely believed that, in addition to language, right-handedness and the specialisation of the right hemisphere (among other things) for providing our sense of how objects are spatially interrelated, were uniquely human. Other animals were believed to have no hemispheric specialisation of any kind.

These beliefs fit well with the human exceptionalism view of our evolutionary status.

Biologists and behavioural scientists generally agreed that right-handedness evolved in our hominid ancestors as they learned to make and use tools, about 2.5 million years ago (see Chapters 1 and 9). Right-handedness was also thought to underlie speech (see Chapters 1, 2 and 6). However, more recent studies of several other species, including birds and mammals, have shown that their two hemispheres also have distinctive roles.

Based on a review of this evidence, MacNeilage *et al.* (2009) hypothesise that the specialisation of each hemisphere in the human brain was already present in its basic form when vertebrates emerged about 500 million years ago. They proposed that the more recent specialisations of the brain hemispheres, including those of humans, evolved from the original ones via the Darwinian process of **descent with modification**. (In this, capabilities relevant to ancient traits are changed or co-opted in the service of other developing traits.) MacNeilage *et al.*'s hypothesis holds that:

> ... the left hemisphere of the vertebrate brain was originally specialised for the control of well-established patterns of behaviour under ordinary and familiar circumstances. In contrast, the right hemisphere, the primary seat of emotional arousal, was at first specialised for detecting and responding to unexpected stimuli in the environment.

In early vertebrates, such a division of labour probably got started when one or other hemisphere developed a tendency to take control in particular circumstances. From that simple beginning, the right hemisphere took primary control in potentially dangerous circumstances that required a quick response (such as detecting a nearby predator); it became the seat of environmentally motivated behaviour ('bottom-up control'). Under 'safer' conditions, control passed to the left hemisphere, which became the seat of self-motivated behaviour ('top-down control'). For example, one routine behaviour with a right side (and, hence, left brain) bias is feeding (Schultz, 2010). Fish, reptiles, toads and humpback whales have all been shown to retain what was probably an ancestral bias towards the right. The processing that directs more specialised behaviours (such as language, tool-making and face recognition) evolved from those two basic forms of control (MacNeilage *et al.*, 2009).

MacNeilage *et al.* also state that more than 12 recent studies have now shown that primates also display this bias, including monkeys (baboons, *Cebus* monkeys, and rhesus macaques) and apes (especially chimpanzees). In addition, they propose that feeding behaviour may also have given rise to the left hemisphere specialisation for language (see Chapter 6).

Conclusions

So what, if anything, is special about the human brain? As Rose (2005) points out, our biochemistry is virtually identical to that of no-brain species. Even under the most powerful microscope our neurons look the same as those of any other vertebrate species and they communicate with one another using exactly the same electrical and chemical signals. Our sensory and motor skills are better in some ways, worse in others. Our brains aren't the biggest, either in absolute terms or in terms of brain weight/body weight ratio. But they do have some unique features, such as the relative enlargement of the frontal lobe and, specifically, the PFC.

We have seen that we're not unique in displaying handedness or the related hemispheric specialisation. However, the *nature* of that specialisation may still distinguish us from all other species (including chimpanzees), as in our possession of left hemisphere areas (Broca's and Wernicke's) devoted to language (see Chapter 6). We've also noted that the long period of infancy and childhood has evolved in order to allow the 'learning machine' (that is, the human brain) to develop and mature. That learning machine is also special in the way that it constructs itself, adapting to the particular environmental conditions it confronts. For humans, these conditions can be summarised as 'culture', which both creates and is created by human brains (see Chapter 9).

Rose (2005) believes that part of what makes us unique is our *versatility*:

> *... we are the only species that can ... run a kilometre, swim a river and then climb a tree. And for sure we are the only species that can then go on to tell others of our kind of our achievements, or write a poem about them. We have above all a deeper range of emotions, enabling us to feel empathy, solidarity, pity, love, so far as we can tell, well beyond the range of any other species ... We have language, consciousness, foresight. We have society, culture, technology ...*

Empathy is discussed in Chapter 4 in relation to consciousness, language in Chapter 6, and culture in Chapter 9.

Chapter summary

- The five basic divisions of the brain are the myelencephalon (the medulla oblongata), metencephalon (pons and cerebellum), mesencephalon (tectum and tegmentum), diencephalon (thalamus and hypothalamus), and telecenphalon (cerebral hemispheres/cerebrum, basal ganglia, and limbic system).

- A broader, overlapping division is that between hindbrain (rhombencephalon), midbrain (mesencephalon) and forebrain (prosencephalon).

- In mammals, the telencephalon developed from the olfactory lobes, swelling outwards and enfolding the other brain regions to form the cerebral hemispheres.

- The cerebrum took over the task of coordination and control from the thalamus, but the hypothalamus and the pituitary gland remain crucially important for controlling mood, emotion, appetite, sexual drive, sleep and pleasure.

- MacLeans's triune brain model (TBM) identifies 'primitive' complexes in the human brain inherited from animal ancestors, reflecting traditional ideas regarding sequential/linear evolution.

- According to the TBM, the brain really comprises three brains in one, involving four sequential steps: a 'neural chassis' (corresponding to the fish and amphibian brains), a reptilian complex (the basal ganglia), a paleomammalian component (the limbic system, comprising the hippocampus, hypothalamus, thalamus, and pituitary gland), and a neomammalian component (the neocortex).

- According to MacLean, nursing and maternal care, audiovocal communication for maintaining mother–offspring contact, and play, all depend on the thalamocingulate division of the limbic system, which has no counterpart in the reptilian brain. The amygdalar and septal divisions are involved in self-preservation behaviour and reproduction, respectively.

- Behaviour arising in the neocortex is usually described as 'conscious', 'voluntary' and 'rational', in contrast with the partial awareness and limited sense of control associated with emotional behaviour.

- While few structures have ever totally disappeared during the brain's evolution, older ones have become less important, relatively smaller, and their functions transformed. But many of the connections and pathways remain.

- All species are equally well adapted to their environmental conditions and all brains evolved as a strategy for survival.

- The TBM is consistent with the 'triune mind' theory, the long-standing concept of three minds in one (the neurological 'holy trinity').

- The cerebral hemispheres have undergone considerable change even within the genus of mammals, with the greatest expansion occurring in the formation of the layered neocortex; this is unique to mammals.

- A feature of the neocortex of later-evolving mammals are association areas, which relate to the outside world only after several stages of neuronal mediation. In humans, these include the massive prefrontal lobe and regions of the occipital, temporal, and parietal lobes.

- While whales, elephants, and dolphins all have larger brains than humans, larger bodies require bigger brains. This suggests that brain weight relative to body weight is a more useful measure than absolute weight/size, although the former is not a simple ratio.

- According to Azevedo *et al.* (2009) the human brain is no more than a linearly scaled-up primate brain. Montgomery *et al.* (2010) concluded that primate brains and bodies evolved in response to different selection pressures, so that their sizes aren't necessarily correlated. Compared with other primates, great apes' bodies are larger than would be expected from their brain size.

- The 'developmental constraint hypothesis' claims that the brain structures of mammals increase in size predictably as the overall brain size increases. For example, during the evolution of different primate species, a larger cerebellum conferred advantages on those particular species over-and-above their possession of an overall larger brain.

- Similarly, the human neocortex is significantly larger than expected from a primate of our size, and the human brain is significantly more convoluted than expected for its overall size. The neocortex was uniquely modified throughout hominid evolution.

- Factors contributing to the emergence of developmental cognitive neuroscience (DCN) include the increasing evidence for the brain's plasticity and the slower internal clock for brain maturation.

- Especially in humans, postnatal structural and functional brain development is influenced by the environment; this involves not only the physical world but the social world of other human beings. What makes the human infant special is its sociability.

- The prefrontal cortex (PFC) is unique to humans, and a key region within it (and the first to mature) is the orbitofrontal cortex (OFC). An intact and properly functioning OFC is necessary for empathising with others. The OFC doesn't mature automatically, but depends on the particular social and cultural environment the child is exposed to.

- The brain as a whole is also very 'experience-dependent': human functional brain development is a constructive or self-organising process. The brain is literally moulded by experience and is poorly developed at birth, allowing for the learning of additional – especially cognitive – functions.

- The plasticity of the brain is complemented by its specificity, without which it couldn't become accurately wired.

- Evolution has solved the 'problem' of humans' long period of immaturity by creating a division of labour between babies and adults; childhood and caregiving are fundamental to our humanity.

- Regardless of handedness, Broca's and Wernicke's language areas are found only in the left hemisphere; this illustrates functional lateralisation (or hemispheric asymmetry).

- Contrary to the traditional view that hemispheric specialisation is uniquely human, evidence now exists that the hemispheres have distinctive roles in several other species, including birds and mammals. The Darwinian process involved is descent with modification.

Suggested further reading

Ramachandran, V.S. & Blakeslee, S. (1998) *Phantoms in the Brain*. London: Fourth Estate. A highly readable, extremely informative account of some of the relationships between mind and brain. Full of fascinating case histories.

Rose, S. (2003) *The 21ST Century Brain: Explaining, Mending and Manipulating the Mind*. London: Vintage Books. Almost a one-stop book – everything you need to know about the human brain: its evolution, its development in the individual human being, the relationship between mind and brain. Rose (Professor of Biology at the Open University) also discusses what the brain can do and how it makes us different from non-humans, as in language, consciousness, and culture.

Toates, F. (2001) *Biological Psychology: An Integrative Approach*. Harlow: Pearson Education Ltd. A very detailed but accessible text, which assumes no prior knowledge of biology. The diagrams are excellent.

Selected websites

http://www.cbcd.bbk.ac.uk

Centre for Brain and Cognitive Development, Birkbeck College, London. Links to Department of Psychological Studies, giving details of internationally renowned research.

http://www.alisongopnik.com/

Alison Gopnik's website.

http://www.stevenroseonline.net/SPRR/Welcome.html

Steven Rose's website.

www.cf.ac.uk/plasticity/index.html

Medical Research Council (MRC) Co-Operative on Neuronal Plasticity, Learning and Memory.

Chapter 4: Consciousness and self-consciousness

Key questions

- What do we mean by the term 'consciousness'?
- What is the difference between consciousness and self-consciousness?
- How do we know that other people are conscious?
- Is it possible for people in a vegetative state to be conscious?
- Do we need to have a body in order to be conscious?
- How do we determine whether any non-human animals are conscious?
- Do non-human primates possess a theory of mind (ToM)?
- Can non-humans understand intention?
- Are non-humans capable of lying and deception?
- How and why did consciousness evolve?
- What is (self-) consciousness for?

The nature of consciousness

According to Chalmers (2007), 'consciousness' is an ambiguous term, referring to many different phenomena, some of which are easier to explain than others. The 'easy' problems of consciousness are those that seem directly accessible to the standard methods of cognitive science and include the:

1. ability to discriminate, categorise and react to environmental stimuli
2. integration of information by a cognitive system
3. reportability of mental states
4. ability of a system to access its own internal states
5. focus of attention
6. deliberate control of behaviour
7. difference between wakefulness and sleep.

All of these phenomena are associated with the notion of consciousness, and there is no real argument about whether they can be explained scientifically (in terms of computational or neural mechanisms). This is what makes them 'easy', implying *not* that we have a complete explanation for them, only that we know how to go about finding one. For Chalmers, the 'hard' problem of consciousness is *the problem of experience*:

> *...When we think and perceive, there is a whir of information-processing, but there is also a subjective aspect. As Nagel (1974) has put it, there is something it's like to be a conscious*

organism. The subjective aspect is experience. When we see, for example, we experience visual sensations: the felt quality of redness, the experience of dark and light, the quality of depth in a visual field. Other experiences go along with perception on different modalities: the sound of a clarinet, the smell of mothballs. Then there are bodily sensations, from pains to orgasms; mental images that are conjured up internally; the felt quality of emotion, and the experience of a stream of conscious thought. What unites all these states is that there is something it's like to be them ... (Chalmers, 2007)

Time for reflection

● If you have not already done so, try to focus on something red, close your eyes and experience the darkness, open them and experience the light, focus on depth in the room you are reading this in, and so on. What are those experiences like?

While this might seem relatively straightforward, even natural, for Chalmers the 'hard problem of consciousness' is trying to explain the *relationship* between (a) an individual's subjective experience and (b) his or her brain activity or information-processing. Philosophers have been discussing this for centuries in the form of the **mind–brain** (or **mind–body**) **problem** (see Gross, 2009).

Consciousness and qualia

These subjective experiences that Chalmers describes are known as **qualia** – the collection of personal, subjective experiences, feelings and sensations that accompany awareness. According to Edelman (1992), qualia are phenomenal states, 'how things seem to us as human beings'. Consciousness manifests itself in the form of qualia.

For Edelman, what Chalmers calls the 'hard problem' amounts to an apparent discrepancy between subjective and objective: 'The dilemma is that phenomenal experience is a first-person matter, and this seems at first glance, to prevent the formulation of a completely objective or causal account.' (Edelman, 1992)

Since science is a **third-person account**, how can we produce a scientific account of consciousness that (must) include qualia?

Time for reflection

● As 'real' as subjective experience is, discussion of qualia seems to raise a number of fundamental issues:

   (a) The age-old philosophical problem of other minds. It's all very well having access to our own consciousness (if not to our 'mind'), but how do we know that *anybody else* is conscious? (This is discussed in Box 4.1 below.)

   (b) Are non-humans conscious in the same way as humans are? This is partly answered by Edelman's distinction between **primary consciousness** and **higher-order consciousness** (see text below), partly by studies of self-recognition in children and other species (also discussed below), and partly by studies of what is called animal cognition (again, see below).

   (c) Could a machine have consciousness? (See Gross, 2009.)

Edelman's (1992) proposed solution to the 'first-person/third-person dilemma' is to accept that other people and oneself do experience qualia, to collect first-person accounts, and to correlate them in order to establish what they all have in common – bearing in mind that these reports are inevitably 'partial, imprecise and relative to ... personal context'.

Box 4.1 What is it like to be a bat?

A potential danger involved in trying to solve the first-person/third-person dilemma (although not in Edelman's case) is **reductionism**: a powerful third- person account, such as neuroscience, is likely to take precedence over the subjective, first-person qualia account, with the consequence that qualia are 'explained away' (reduced to brain processes).

A well-known attempt to protect first-person experience (qualia) from reduction to third-person talk (as in neuroscience) is Nagel's (1974) 'What is it like to be a bat?' (See the quote from Chalmers (2007) above.) The essence of Nagel's argument is that no amount of descriptive knowledge could possibly add up to the experience of how it feels to be a bat, or what it's like to perceive by sonar. Conscious experience is 'what it's like' to be an organism to that organism. Attempts to reduce that subjective experience must be considered unsuccessful as long as the reducing theory (for example, pain is the firing of neurons in some brain centre) is logically possible without consciousness (the 'zombie problem'). A theory of consciousness should be able to distinguish us from zombies (Bem and Looren de Jong, 1997).

Although we may never know animals' or other people's minds, or have an adequate language to describe subjective experience, this doesn't mean it isn't real, complex, rich or highly specific in nature (Nagel, 1974).

Nagel's reference to the reality of subjective experience coincides with one of Searle's (2007) seven criteria for defining conscious states. These are described in Box 4.2.

Box 4.2 Major criteria for defining conscious states (Searle, 2007)

1. Conscious states are *qualitative*: there is a qualitative feel to being in any particular conscious state. This is Searle's (2007) way of describing qualia and mirrors Nagel's 'batness' argument, albeit at the level of different conscious states (e.g. tasting beer and listening to a Beethoven Symphony) as opposed to whole organisms (e.g. bats).

2. Such states are also *ontologically subjective:* they only exist as experienced by a human being or non-human animal. While physical objects, as well as natural features such as mountains, have an objective (or third-party) ontology/existence, conscious states (such as pains and itches) exist only when experienced by a person or animal (they have a subjective or first-person ontology).

3. At any moment in your conscious life, all your conscious states are experienced as part of a *single, unified conscious field*. The unity of consciousness is the starting point for Edelman and Tononi's (2000) information integration theory of consciousness (see text below and Figure 4.1).

4. Most, but not all, conscious states are **intentional**, in the philosophical sense that they are about, or refer to, something (objects or states of affairs). For example, my states of thirst, hunger and visual perception are all directed at something, in contrast with undirected, generalised feelings of well-being or anxiety. Edelman (1992) makes the same observation.

Box 4.2 *Continued*

5. Conscious states are real parts of the real world and cannot be reduced to something else (they are irreducible) (see Box 4.1). According to Searle:

> *If it consciously seems to me that I am conscious, then I am conscious. We can make lots of mistakes about our own consciousness, but where the very existence of consciousness is in question we cannot make the appearance-reality distinction, because the appearance of the existence of consciousness is the reality of its existence.*

Wise (1999) extends this argument to consciousness in non-human animals (see text below).

6. We cannot reduce consciousness to more fundamental neurobiological processes (again, see Box 4.1). We cannot show that the subjective, first-person ontology of consciousness is 'nothing but' brain processes (with their third-person, objective ontology). However, this is different from the claim that conscious states are *caused by* brain processes, which Searle believes isn't in dispute (although exactly how this happens is still unknown).

7. Conscious states have *causal efficacy*. (This is discussed at the end of this chapter in relation to how – and why – consciousness evolved.)

Consciousness and self-consciousness

Time for reflection

- What do you understand by the term 'self-consciousness' and how does it differ from 'consciousness'?

Edelman (1992) makes what he believes is a fundamental distinction between primary and higher-order consciousness.

- *Primary consciousness* refers to the state of being mentally aware of things in the world, of having mental images in the present. An animal with primary consciousness alone is strongly tied to the succession of events in *real time*. It's not accompanied by any sense of being a person with a past and a future. In other words, to be conscious doesn't necessarily imply any kind of 'I' who is aware and having mental images. (It can be described as *sentience*: the ability to have bodily sensations, including hunger, thirst, pain, and more emotional states, such as fear and anger.) This is why at least some non-human species are likely to be conscious, despite not possessing language (see Chapter 6). Edelman believes that chimpanzees are almost certainly conscious, and, in all likelihood, so are most mammals and some birds; probably those animals without a cortex (or its equivalent) are not (see Chapter 3).

- *Higher-order consciousness* involves the recognition by a thinking subject of his or her own acts or affections, embodying a model of the personal, and of the past and future as well as the present. It involves *direct awareness* – '... the noninferential or immediate awareness of mental episodes without the involvement of sense organs or receptors. It is what we as humans have in addition to primary consciousness. We are conscious of being conscious.' These abilities cannot develop without a symbolic memory. In order to become conscious of our consciousness, systems of memory must be related to a conceptual representation of a true self (or social self) acting on an environment, and vice versa.

Edelman (1992) believes that human beings are in a 'privileged position' (see Chapter 1):

... While we may not be the only conscious animals, we are, with the possible exception of the chimpanzee, the only self-conscious animals. We are the only animals capable of language, able to model the world free of the present, able to report on, study, and correlate our phenomenal states with the findings of physics and biology'.

... Accordingly, beings with primary consciousness alone cannot construct theories of consciousness – even wrong ones!'

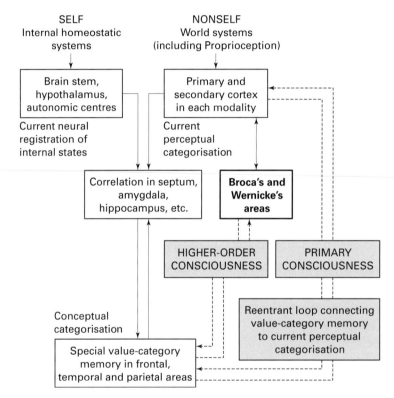

▲ **Figure 4.1** A re-entrant loop

The primary/higher-order consciousness distinction is a central feature of Edelman and Tononi's (2000) information integration theory (IIT) of consciousness. As we noted in Box 4.2, the unity of consciousness is the starting point for IIT, according to which consciousness corresponds to the capacity of a system to integrate information (Tononi, 2007). This is summarised in Figure 4.1. The figure shows a re-entrant loop, which appeared during the evolution of hominids and the emergence of language. The acquisition of a new kind of memory via semantic capabilities, and ultimately language, produced a conceptual explosion. As a result, concepts of the self, the past and future could be connected to primary consciousness. Consciousness of consciousness now became possible (Blackmore, 2010).

Primary and higher-order consciousness correspond to consciousness and self-consciousness respectively. As Wise (1999) points out, the *International Dictionary of Psychology* (1989) warns against confusing consciousness with self-consciousness: to be conscious it is only necessary to be aware of the external world.

This distinction between primary and higher-order consciousness is sometimes presented as that between **phenomenal consciousness** and **self-consciousness** (Allen and Bekoff (2007):

- *Phenomenal consciousness* refers to the qualitative, subjective, experiential or phenomenological aspects of conscious experience, sometimes identified with qualia (i.e. sentience). While not everyone would agree with Nagel's (1974) argument that it's not possible to know, imagine or describe scientifically what it is like to be a bat, and his assumption that there is something it's like (see Box 4.1), there's broad, commonsense agreement that phenomenal consciousness is more likely in mammals and birds than it is in invertebrates (such as insects, crustaceans or molluscs, with the possible exception of some cephalopods, notably octopi). Reptiles, amphibians and fish constitute an enormous grey area.

- *Self-consciousness* usually refers to an organism's capacity for second-order representations of its own mental states ('thought about thought'); this is closely related to questions about **theory of mind** (ToM) in non-humans, i.e. the ability to attribute mental states to others (see below, page 80).

Allen and Bekoff (2007) make the further distinction between two non-controversial senses of consciousness and **access consciousness**:

- Two ordinary senses of consciousness that aren't in dispute when applied to non-humans are (a) being awake rather than asleep or in a coma; and (b) the basic ability of organisms to perceive and thereby respond to selected features of their environment, thus making them conscious or aware of those features. Consciousness in both these senses can be identified in non-humans belonging to a wide variety of taxonomic groups.

- A more technical sense of consciousness, *access consciousness* (Block, 1995) captures the sense in which mental representations may be poised for use in rational control of action or speech. While Block believes that many animals possess access consciousness (he doesn't make speech a requirement: see Chapter 6), Descartes, who as we saw in Chapter 1, denied speech and language to animals, would also deny them access consciousness.

According to Allen and Bekoff (2007), some modern philosophers, while rejecting Cartesian dualism (see Chapter 1), support Descarte's views regarding the necessary involvement of linguistic processing in human consciousness: '... Such insistence on the importance of language for consciousness underwrites the tendency of philosophers such as Dennett (1969, 1997) to deny that animals are conscious in anything like the same sense that humans are ...' (Allen and Bekoff, 2007). The special role of language is discussed in Chapter 6. (Also see the discussion in Chapter 1.)

How do we know that anyone else (or any non-human animal) is conscious?

> ## Time for reflection
> - Do we just *assume* that everyone else is conscious, like us?
> - Or is there some kind of *evidence* that we base our assumption on?
> - What *social* processes depend on us making this assumption?

According to Wise (1999), the strongest available argument that you (as well as chimpanzees and baboons) are conscious is 'by analogy':

1. I know I am conscious.

2. We are all biologically very similar.

3. We all act very similarly.

4. We all share an evolutionary history.

5. Therefore, you (and other great apes and other species too) are conscious.

The basic argument is that 'if it walks like a duck and quacks like a duck ...'. If something behaves in all respects as if it is conscious, and there's no good reason to believe otherwise, then it (almost certainly) *is* conscious.

But doesn't this beg the question? Since we don't have direct access to other people's minds, our belief that others are conscious remains no more than an assumption (this is one of J.B. Watson's – the founder of behaviourism – arguments against the possibility of the scientific study of consciousness).

> ## Time for reflection
> A second argument against the view that specifically non-humans are conscious is that anyone who adopts it is guilty of **anthropomorphism**.
> - What do you understand by this term?
> - Can you think of any counter-arguments?

As we noted in Box 4.2, Searle (2007) claims that if it consciously appears to me that I am conscious, then I am conscious: we can never be mistaken (or deluded) about consciousness. Wise (2000) extends this argument to consciousness in non-human animals and, at the same time, argues against the anthropomorphism objection:

> *Most mammals and every primate act in ways that cause most reasonable people to think that they have minds of some kind ... It is circular thinking to dismiss this belief as mere anthropomorphism ... as some do. They begin by assuming that only humans are conscious, then label any contrary claim as anthropomorphic. Why? Because only humans are conscious.*

Although behavioural similarity is no guarantee of mental similarity:

> *... when animals who are closely related behave in a way that strongly suggests similarity in mental processes to ours, it seems reasonable and fair to shift the burden of proof to those who would argue that what we are seeing is not what we think we are seeing.* (Wise, 1999)

> ## Time for reflection
> - Can you think of any possible objections to Wise's position?
> - For example, is his extension of Searle's argument valid, i.e. even if you accept the 'appearance = reality' argument in relation to other people, does it inevitably apply to non-humans?

An evaluation of the 'argument from homology'

According to Allen and Bekoff (2007), similarity arguments for animal consciousness clearly have roots in commonsense observations (of our pets, for example). But they may also be bolstered by scientific study of behaviour and neurology, as well as considerations of evolutionary continuity (**homology**) between species. For example, the reactions of many animals, especially other mammals, to bodily events that humans would report as painful are easily and automatically recognised by most people as pain responses. High-pitched vocalisations, fear responses, nursing of injuries and learned avoidance are examples of responses to noxious stimuli that form part of the common mammalian heritage.

Again, as we noted in Chapters 1 and 3, all mammals share the same basic brain anatomy, and much is shared with vertebrates more generally. A large amount of scientific research that is directly relevant to the treatment of conscious human pain, including that on the efficacy of analgesics and anaesthetics, is conducted on rats and other mammals. The validity of this research depends on the similarity of the mechanisms involved; to many it seems arbitrary to deny that injured rats, who respond well to opiates, for example, feel pain. Similarly, much of the basic research relevant to understanding human visual consciousness has been conducted on the very similar visual system of monkeys (see Gross, 2010).

> ## Time for reflection
> - While the similarity arguments may be scientifically valid, is the use of animals for such (largely medical) research *ethically* acceptable?
> - Some researchers stress the dissimilarities between, say, rats and humans, leading them to question even the scientific validity of using these non-human mammals for such research.
>
> (For both issues, see Gross 2009, 2010.)

In Allen and Bekoff's view:

> *... Even when bolstered by evolutionary considerations of continuity between the species, the arguments are vulnerable, for the mere fact that humans have a trait does not entail that our closest relatives must have that trait too. There is no inconsistency with evolutionary continuity to maintain that only humans have the capacity to learn to play chess. Likewise for consciousness ...* (Allen and Bekoff, 2007)

A case, perhaps, of the whole being greater than the sum of its parts: while humans and other mammals, especially other great apes, might share a great deal (behaviourally, physiologically and morphologically), in humans these 'parts' simply produce a different 'whole' compared with other species.

Literature and consciousness

A different approach to demonstrating the existence of consciousness is taken by the novelist David Lodge (2002). He quotes Stuart Sutherland, who states (in the *International Dictionary of Psychology*, 1989) that 'Consciousness is a fascinating but elusive phenomenon; it is impossible to specify what it is, what it does, or why it evolved. Nothing worth reading has been written about it.' In making this claim, Sutherland was, inadvertently, dismissing the entire body of the world's literature, because literature is the richest and most comprehensive record of human consciousness we have. Some of those who work in cognitive science agree with Lodge – for example, Chomsky (in Lodge, 2002), who claims that 'it is quite possible ... that we will always learn more about human life and personality from novels than from scientific psychology'.

Lodge contrasts science's pursuit of universal explanatory laws with literature's description: '... in the guise of fiction the dense specificity of personal experience, which is always unique, because each of us has a slightly or very different personal history, modifying every new experience we have; and the creation of literary texts recapitulates this uniqueness ... (Lodge, 2002)

We saw in Chapter 1 that both science and literature demonstrate the *symbolic* nature of human beings. Both, in their very different ways, allow us to stand back from 'reality' to ask if things could have been different from how we experience them.

However, while Lodge emphasises literature's treatment of the uniqueness of personal experience with science's attempt to identify universal laws, other novelists (such as Ian McEwan) point out that great literature is great partly because it, too, deals with *universal* aspects of human experience. This is discussed further in Box 4.3.

Box 4.3 Literature, science and human nature (based on McEwan, 2006)

According to McEwan, when we read great novels such as *Anna Karenina* or *Madame Bovary*, '... Imaginary people appear before us, their historical and domestic circumstances are very particular, their characters equally so ...' And yet, '... By an unspoken agreement, a kind of contract between writer and reader, it is assumed that however strange these people are, we will understand them readily enough to be able to appreciate their strangeness ...'

It's our theory of mind (ToM) that enables us to get inside the minds of people living in historical and socio-cultural conditions that we've never ourselves experienced (see text below and Chapter 1). Through our ToM, we're able to appreciate what fictional characters all have in common – both with each other and with ourselves and other real people – namely, their individuality, which at the same time is one of the universals of human experience (see Chapter 8). As McEwan puts it: '... At its best, literature is universal, illuminating human nature at precisely the point at which it is most parochial and specific.'

Box 4.3 *Continued*

Also in the context of literature, Carroll (2006) argues that:

...What one senses in other people is not just the ineffable peculiarity of their unique individuality. What one senses is the common medium of common perception, common thought, common passion. If people were truly 'unique' in any very radical way, it would not be possible for ordinary empathy, ordinary insight into others' minds to take place ... the sense of individual uniqueness is itself one of those human universals that we all recognise in one another ...

In other words, part of our ToM is the recognition that every human being experiences the world from a unique position. But at the same time, this recognition is part of the shared, universal understanding of what it is to be a person.

McEwan gives the example of Saul Bellow's *Herzog* (1965). Standing in front of a mirror, the eponymous Herzog is wearing only a newly purchased straw hat and underpants. His mother,

... wanted [him] to become a rabbi and he seemed to himself gruesomely unlike a rabbi now in the trunks and straw hat, his face charged with heavy sadness, foolish utter longing of which a religious life might have purged him. That mouth! – heavy with desire and irreconcilable anger, the straight nose sometimes grim, the dark eyes! And his figure! – the long veins winding in the arms and filling in the hanging hands, an ancient system, of greater antiquity than the Jews themselves ... Bare legged, he looked like Hindu. (Saul Bellow, Herzog).

A reader may not understand from the inside every specific of Herzog's condition – a mid-twentieth-century Jewish American, a city dweller, divorcee, an alienated intellectual; nor might a young reader empathise with the remorse of early middle age. But we can all identify with a character who is scrutinising himself (and how many hours do young people spend in front of mirrors!), as well as recognise that our biology (here, the circulatory system) '... predates, and by implication, is even more of the essence of being human, than one's religion ... (McEwan, 2006)

Time for reflection

McEwan argues that, in contrast with great literature, greatness in science is harder for most of us to grasp.

● Can you think of reasons that would validate this claim?
● Can you think of exceptions to this general 'rule'?

McEwan claims that few of us have had the kind of intimate contact with science that would enable us to identify with great scientists (although we could probably make a list of such individuals). This partly reflects the objectifying, distancing nature of scientific activity, as well as the use of maths.

However, a notable exception is Darwin, whose scientific life can be read as a novel. McEwan believes that one of the factors that makes Darwin exceptional is that natural history in particular, and biology in general, is a *descriptive* science. His theory of evolution by natural selection is not, in its essentials, difficult to grasp, despite its enormous implications, formidable applications, and sometimes quite complex scientific consequences. Also, Darwin was intensely communicative, affectionate, intimate and honest. He also wrote many letters, and filled many notebooks.

McEwan (2006) concludes by saying:

> ... *That which binds us, our common nature, is what literature has always, knowingly and helplessly, given voice to. And it is this universality which science, now entering another of its exhilarating moments, is set to explore.*

The 'exhilarating moment' that McEwan refers to is the period following the sequencing of the human **genome** (see Chapter 2). He asks whose genome was this any way? What lucky individual was chosen to represent us all? Who is this universal person? In fact,

> ... *the **genes** of 15 people were merged into just the sort of composite, plausible, imaginary person a novelist might dream up, and here we contemplate the metaphorical convergence of these two noble and distinct forms of investigation into our condition: literature and science ...* (McEwan, 2006).

Consciousness and the vegetative state

Monti and Owen (2010) describe the case of Martha, a brain-injured patient whose eyes are now open. In medical terms, the return of alternating cycles of sleep and wakefulness mark her progression from coma (**comatose** state) to a **vegetative state** (**VS**) (Jennet and Plum, 1972). However, although her eyes are open and she gives the impression of 'seeing', in fact she does not. Visual information may well reach several centres of her brain dedicated to processing visual information, and her brain may even respond differently to different categories of objects. But this doesn't mean she can 'see' (i.e. is aware of what it is she's looking at).

Consciousness can be conceptualised as comprising two key components (Laureys, 2005):

1. level (i.e. wakefulness)
2. content (i.e. awareness).

Table 4.1 shows how these two components are typically present or absent in different normal and abnormal states/conditions.

Table 4.1 The appearance of level (wakefulness) and content (awareness) of consciousness as displayed in different normal and abnormal states/conditions (based on Monti and Owen, 2010)

	Consciousness	
Normal/abnormal states/conditions	**Level (wakefulness)**	**Content (wakefulness)**
Healthy (awake) individual	✔	✔
Comatose patient	✘	✘
Under general anaesthetic	Very low	Very low
From deep sedation/sleep ➜ wakefulness	✔	✔
Vegetative state (VS)	✔ (Apparent)	✘
REM ('dream') sleep and other oneiric (dream-related) experiences	✘	✔

Note that in Table 4.1, in between the healthy (awake) individual and comatose patient (which are at opposite ends of the spectrum), wakefulness and awareness typically appear to vary together (both very low during general anaesthesia, jointly returning as we progress from deep sedation/ sleep to wakefulness). However, in VS they seem to dissociate; VS patients appear to be awake but they are not aware. The reverse dissociation occurs naturally during **REM** (Rapid Eye Movement) **sleep**, and especially during **oneiric** experiences, where a subjective feeling of awareness is often present despite the individual not being awake.

Some VS patients will never make any significant recovery and will be diagnosed as in **permanent vegetative state** (permanent VS). (In the UK, such a diagnosis is made after at least six months for non-traumatic brain injury and 12 months for traumatic brain injury (Monti and Owen, 2010).) But other patients do regain some (transient) level of awareness, progressing to a **minimally conscious state** (**MCS**) (Giacino *et al.*, 2002).

How do we know that a patient has regained consciousness? Box 4.4 (based on Monti and Owen, 2010) provides some answers from the medical perspective.

Box 4.4 The medical assessment of consciousness (based on Monti and Owen, 2010)

In the absence of an agreed definition of consciousness and any means of quantifying it, we can only search for signs that may reveal its presence. In the medical setting, this translates into careful and repeated (albeit subjective) evaluations of the patient's spontaneous and elicited behaviour based on specifically developed scales. In particular, assessing the presence of consciousness, and thereby discriminating MCS from VS patients, requires finding evidence of:

1. awareness of the self or the environment

2. sustained, reproducible, purposeful or voluntary response to auditory, visual, tactile or noxious stimuli, or

3. language comprehension and/or expression.

If any evidence of such behaviour is apparent, then the patient is diagnosed MCS; conversely, where no such evidence is found, a VS diagnosis is made. However, according to Monti and Owen:

> ... *This approach ... suffers from a major flaw. A positive VS diagnosis ultimately relies on a negative result. Lack of evidence of consciousness is, in this situation, equated to evidence of lack of consciousness.*

Monti and Owen ask: What if a patient were conscious but couldn't produce any motor output? What if a patient could comprehend language, but were unable to speak or produce any other kind of response? How could such an individual ever be distinguished from a vegetative patient? In fact, on the basis of current clinical assessments, it isn't logically possible to do so: inasmuch as motor behaviour is required to signal a state of consciousness, an aware patient who cannot produce any behavioural output is *indistinguishable* from an unconscious one. Indeed, 40 per cent of (aware) MCS patients are misdiagnosed as VS.

Detecting consciousness via functional neuroimaging

In the past 10 years, an increasing number of research studies have highlighted the possibility that functional neuroimaging technology (such as **positron emission tomography (PET)** and

functional magnetic resonance imaging (fMRI)) can be used to look directly into the brain for indicators of consciousness. Monti and Owen (2010) cite two such studies which highlighted the fact that, despite severe brain injury, it is possible to retain relatively high-level brain activity. The crucial question with regard to patients is whether we can use brain activity to infer the presence of consciousness. Can brain activity be used as a substitute for voluntary motor behaviour in revealing the presence of consciousness? Does brain activity in response to pictures of faces imply that a patient is aware of them, that she can 'see' the faces? If a patient displays the same brain response to speech as healthy individuals, does this mean that she understands language?

The answer to these questions depends on the type of stimuli used, as well as what type of brain activity is elicited. Much sensory processing is rapid and automatic, and can happen in the absence of any conscious perception. Also, under normal circumstances a healthy individual cannot help seeing a face as a face. This means that '... while very revealing about the level of residual cognitive processing that is present, a simple brain response to stimulation cannot be taken as an unequivocal index of consciousness.' (Monti and Owen, 2010)

So, is it possible to distinguish the brain's automatic response to sensory stimulation from deliberate, voluntary processes (what Monti and Owen call 'wilful brain processing')? Imagine being shown the ambiguous picture given in Figure 4.2.

▲ **Figure 4.2** The reversible duck-rabbit

Time for reflection

- If you haven't seen the picture above before, what do you see?
- If you have seen it before, try to explain how you saw what you saw when you first looked at it.

This, and other reversible figures, demonstrate the important distinction between conception and perception (see Gross, 2010). Perception is a largely automatic process (we 'just see' a left-facing duck or a right-facing rabbit), but once we know what the two possibilities are (we might have seen both or had them pointed out to us), we can consciously select one or the other. While there is only a *single* pattern of light falling on the retina, at some level the two interpretations must entail *different* brain responses. If it were possible to demonstrate that a patient's brain response to a constant pattern of sensory stimulation can change at will, this would necessarily imply the role of awareness.

As Monti and Owen (2010) put it:

> ... in an experimental design in which two tasks are identical in terms of sensory stimulation and only differ according to the 'mind set' required, differential brain responses can demonstrate the ability to voluntarily adopt such 'mind sets', something that requires a state of awareness ...

Under these circumstances, then, voluntary brain activity can be viewed as a form of non-muscle-dependent behaviour which, like voluntary motor behaviour, implies the presence of awareness (Owen and Coleman, 2008). A striking application of this idea is described in Box 4.5.

Box 4.5 Playing tennis, walking and consciousness

A patient who failed to display any voluntary behaviour when tested at the bedside (and so was diagnosed VS), could voluntarily modulate brain activity by producing different kinds of mental imagery (Owen *et al.,* 2006). When tested with fMRI, the patient was asked to imagine playing tennis and, at a different time, to imagine walking around the rooms of her home. Importantly, while the patient was instructed to sustain the imagery for 30-second periods, the only sensory stimulation was a one-second-long aural cue instructing her to focus on one or other of the imagery tasks.

Strikingly, despite being unable to produce any type of wilful motor behaviour to demonstrate that she was conscious, the patient was able to produce wilful 'brain behaviour' by up-and-down modulation of her brain activity; this confirmed that she was engaging in the two imagery tasks.

When control participants (healthy individuals) were tested, it was found that unless they understood the task instructions and had decided to comply with them, no brain activity was observed (Owen *et al.,* 2007). This totally discounts the possibility that the patient's brain activity may have reflected an automatic response.

Monti *et al.* (2009) presented a listener with a series of emotionally neutral words, and alternately instructed them to either listen passively, or to count how many times a given target word was repeated. The types of words used, their number and repetition were all controlled. When a patient with severe brain injury was tested, the counting task revealed activation of the fronto-parietal regions typically associated with detecting targets and **working memory**. Unless the patient had understood the instructions, decided to cooperate, and retained a level of cognitive processing sufficient to perform the task, how could the same stimuli have led to systematically different activations?

According to Monti and Owen (2010), until we develop quantitative tools that can directly measure consciousness, we will have to continue to *infer* others' self-awareness 'by their appearance and by their acts'. But non-invasive neuroimaging techniques, such as those described in Box 4.5, are now beginning to allow us to redefine the meaning of 'appearance' and 'acts' to include non-muscle-dependent 'brain acts'. Indeed, functional neuroimaging can be used to allow aware, but non-responsive, patients to convey their state of consciousness without relying on muscle-dependent behaviour.

Time for reflection

Monti and Owen (2010) report that several recent studies have shown that what someone is viewing, recalling and even intending to do, can be ascertained solely by observing patterns of brain activity.

● While this kind of 'mind-reading' might allow non-responsive patients to express (some of) their thoughts and wishes, as well as prevent the misdiagnosis of VS, is there a worrying aspect to this kind of research? Could it be used (with both patients and healthy individuals) in a way that does not serve their best interests?

● What conclusions can we draw about the nature of consciousness from these research studies?

● What do they tell us about the importance for consciousness of having a body? (See Box 4.6 below.)

Box 4.6 Consciousness and the importance of having a body

According to Humphrey (1992), the subject of consciousness, 'I', is an embodied self. In the absence of bodily sensations, 'I' would cease: *Sentio, ergo sum* ('I feel, therefore I am' – this is a variant of Descartes' famous *Cogito, ergo sum*) 'I think, therefore I am' (see Chapter 1).

If there is something distinctive about human consciousness, where should we look for it? According to Eiser (1994):

> *Even if we could build a machine with a full capacity of a human brain [immensely interactive parallelism] we would still be reluctant to attribute to it the kind of consciousness, the sense of self, to which we ourselves lay claim ... To ask what is special about human consciousness, therefore, is not just a question about process. It is also to ask what is special about our experience of the world, the experience we have by virtue of physical presence in the world ...*

Any distinction we try to draw between mind and body (mind–body dualism) is, according to Eiser, objectionable precisely because it divorces mental from physical experience. The most continuous feature of our experience is our own body: *personal* identity (and that of others) depends on *physical* identity, we feel our body and we feel the world *through* it, and it provides the anchor and perspective from which we experience other things.

A similar position to those of Humphrey and Eiser is taken by the French phenomenologist Merleau-Ponty (1962, 1968). He distinguishes between 'one's own body' (the **phenomenal body**) and 'the **objective body**' (the body as object). Experience of our own body is not, essentially, experience of an object. In fact, most of the time we aren't aware of our body as such – it is, as it were, *transparent* to us. But without our body, we could not *be*.

Just as sense perception and motor skills function together (as do the different senses), so, for Merleau-Ponty, mind and body, mental and physical, are two aspects of the same thing, namely a person. The mind is embodied in that it can be identified with one aspect of something that has two aspects, neither of which can be reduced to (explained in terms of) the other (Teichman, 1988). The body provides us with a continuous patterned stream of input, and (simply from the fact that we cannot be in two places at the same time) imposes constraints on the information received by the brain about the outside world (Eiser, 1994). This, in turn, relates to the intentionality ('aboutness') of consciousness (see Box 4.2).

> **Time for reflection**
> - How do the views described in Box 4.6 impinge on the neuroimaging research described by Monti and Owen (2010) above regarding detecting consciousness in patients whose bodies are non-responsive?
> - What conclusions can we draw regarding the necessity of having a (working) body in order to display consciousness?
> - Eiser is arguing for the importance of having a body by focusing on our sense of self. How does this relate to Edelman's distinction above between primary and higher-order consciousness?
> - If Eiser is claiming that machines would need a body (as well as a human-like brain) in order to display consciousness, where does that leave non-human animals, especially those whose brains and bodies are most similar to our own (i.e. chimpanzees and other **primates**)?

Self-recognition: A way of assessing consciousness

> **Time for reflection**
> Look in a mirror.
> - What do you see?
> - How do you know it is you?
> - Do you ever look in the mirror and not recognise yourself?
> - If so, how do you account for such experiences?

Many non-human animals (including fish, birds, cats, chickens and elephants) react to their mirror image as if it were another animal – they don't seem to recognise it as their own reflection at all. But self-recognition has been observed in the higher primates – chimpanzees and other great apes. (See Povinelli (1993) for a review.)

In order to determine that an image in a mirror (or a person depicted in a photograph or on film) is oneself, particular knowledge seems to be necessary:

- At least a rudimentary knowledge of oneself as continuous through time (necessary for recognising ourselves in photographs or movies) and space (necessary for recognising ourselves in mirrors).
- Knowledge of particular features (what we look like).

Although other kinds of self-recognition exist (such as one's voice or feelings), only visual self-recognition has been studied extensively, both in humans and non-humans. Some of the earliest, and still the most cited research, was conducted by Gallup (1970, 1977), as described in Box 4.7.

Box 4.7 Mirror self-recognition in chimpanzees (Gallup, 1970, 1977)

▲ **Figure 4.3** Chimpanzees learn to use mirrors to explore parts of their bodies they cannot usually see

Gallup, working with pre-adolescent, wild-born chimps, placed a full-length mirror on the wall of each animal's cage. At first, they reacted as if another chimp had appeared – they threatened, vocalised or made conciliatory gestures. But this behaviour quickly faded out and after three days had almost disappeared. They then used their image to explore themselves. For example, they would pick up food and place it on their face, which they could not see without looking in the mirror (see the photographs opposite).

After 10 days' exposure, each chimp was anaesthetised and a bright red spot was painted on the uppermost part of one eyebrow ridge, and a second spot on the top of the opposite ear, using an odourless, non-irritating dye.

When it had recovered from the anaesthetic, the chimp was returned to its cage, from which the mirror had been removed. It was observed to see how often it touched the 'spotted' parts of its body. The mirror was then replaced and each chimp began to explore the spotted areas about 25 times more often than it had done before.

The procedure was repeated with chimps that had never seen themselves in the mirror: they reacted to the mirror image as if it were another chimp (they didn't touch the spots). When lower primates (monkeys, gibbons and baboons) were tested, there was no evidence of self-recognition.

A number of researchers (e.g. Lewis and Brooks-Gunn, 1979) have used modified forms of Gallup's technique with 6–24-month-old children. The mother applies a dot of rouge to the child's nose (while pretending to wipe its face) and the child is observed to see how often it touches its nose. The child is then placed in front of a mirror, and again the number of times it touches its nose is recorded.

While touching the dot in the mirror reflection was never seen before 15 months, between 15 and 18 months, 5–25 per cent of children did so, compared with 75 per cent of the 18–24-month-olds.

Interpreting Gallup's findings: Self-concept and mind-reading

> ### Time for reflection
> ● How would you interpret Gallup's findings?
> ● Does a chimp's ability to recognise itself necessarily mean the same as a child's ability to do so?
> ● What opportunities do chimps have in the wild to see their own reflection?
> ● What can we infer about the evolution of (primitive) self-consciousness from the findings using different primate species?

According to Mitchell (1997), while seeing itself in a mirror is not exactly an everyday experience for a chimp in the wild, opportunities do sometimes present themselves for self-reflection (such as when it looks into a pool of water). Success in self-recognition might be a sign not only that chimps can build up a conception of themselves when presented with the relevant visual evidence (i.e. their mirror-reflection), but that they have a *pre-existing* self-concept capable of accommodating the new data (i.e. their ability to interpret their own image may rest on their holding a pre-conception of their self).

Compared with monkeys, chimps appear to hold a concept that *self* is *me*. But what does 'me' mean? At the very least, me is not you, so perhaps mirror self-recognition in chimps is a sign of an ability to differentiate between oneself and other individuals. Here, 'oneself' becomes an object of one's own conscious attention, meaning that self and others are individuated.

> ... *This remarkable capacity might signal the dawning of consciousness about self as a sentient and thinking organism with a unique subjective experience, one that differs from other individuals. Hence, being able to recognise oneself in a mirror might be an important manifestation of a primitive and rudimentary conception of mind.* (Mitchell, 1997)

It's generally agreed that passing the mirror test is strong evidence that a chimp has a self-concept, and that only chimps, orang-utans and humans consistently pass it. However, Gallup (1998) infers much more than this. He claims that:

> ... *not only are some animals aware of themselves but ... such self-awareness enables these animals to infer the mental states of others. In other words, species that pass the mirror test are also able to sympathise, empathise and attribute intent and emotions in others – abilities that some might consider the exclusive domain of humans.*

In addition to claiming that 'Mirror self-recognition is an indicator of self-awareness' (Gallup *et al.*, 2002), Gallup believes that self-awareness (or self-consciousness) is the expression of some underlying process that allows organisms to use their experience as a means of modelling the experience of others. The ability to infer the existence of mental states in others (theory of mind (Baron-Cohen, 1995) or mental state attribution) is a by-product of being self-aware: 'If you are self-aware then you are in a position to use your experience to model the existence of comparable processes in others' (Gallup *et al.*, 2002). (This is similar to Humphrey's (1986, 1993) account of the evolution of human consciousness: see below.) This view is called the *mind-reading hypothesis* (MRH). What evidence is there to support Gallup's claim regarding the MRH?

Box 4.8 Evidence relevant to the relationship between self-consciousness and the MRH

- Gallup believes that the best support comes from the mirror studies discussed above. But doesn't this claim involve circular reasoning, in that (a) passing the mirror test implies self-awareness and, in turn, the ability to read others' minds; and (b) the best evidence for self-awareness and, in turn, the ability to read others' minds, is passing the mirror test? Is there any additional, independent evidence?

- Gallup's research also points to the right prefrontal cortex as the brain area that mediates self-awareness and mental states (such as deception and gratitude) – and this is the brain region that grows most rapidly between 18–34 months (see Chapter 3).

- As additional support for his MRH, Gallup cites studies by Povinelli and his colleagues involving chimps. These studies are often taken to show that chimps have a ToM, but, ironically, Povinelli (1998) himself disagrees with Gallup's interpretation. While agreeing that passing the mirror test indicates that chimps possess a self-concept, he disagrees that this means they also possess the deep psychological understanding of behaviour that seems so characteristic of humans.

If chimps *don't* genuinely reason about mental states, what can we say about their understanding of self based on the mirror test? Povinelli (1998) has tried to address this by shifting his attention from chimps to two-, three- and four-year-old children. Povinelli's studies are described in Box 4.9.

Box 4.9 Stickers, lies and videotapes (Povinelli, 1998)

In a series of experiments, children were videotaped while they played an unusual game. The experimenter secretly placed a large, brightly coloured sticker on top of the child's head. Three minutes later, they were shown either (a) a live video image of themselves, or (b) a recording made several minutes earlier, which clearly depicted the experimenter placing the sticker on the child's head.

Two- and three-year-olds responded very differently, depending on which video they saw. With the live image (equivalent to seeing themselves in a mirror), most reached up and removed the sticker from their head. But with the recording (the 'delayed self-recognition test'), only about one-third did so. However, this wasn't because they failed to notice the stickers (when the experimenter drew their attention to them and asked 'What is that?', most gave the correct answer). They also 'recognised' themselves in the recording: they all confidently responded with 'Me' and stated their name when asked 'Who is that?' But this reaction didn't seem to be much more than a recognition of facial and bodily features. When asked 'Where is that sticker?', they often referred to the 'other' child (e.g. 'It's on his or her head'), as if they were trying to say, 'Yes, that looks like me, but that's not me – she's not doing what I'm doing right now'. One three-year-old said, 'It's Jennifer' (her name), then hurriedly added, 'but why is she wearing my shirt?'

By about age four, a significant majority of the children began to pass the delayed self-recognition test. Most four- and five-year-olds confidently reached up to remove the stickers after watching the delayed video image of themselves. They no longer referred to 'him/her' or their proper names.

Autobiographical memory or kinaesthetic self-concept?

According to Povinelli (1998), these results are consistent with the view that genuine autobiographical memory (AM) appears to emerge in children between three-and-a-half and four-and-a-half (not the two-year mark favoured by Gallup). AM implies understanding that memories constitute a genuine 'past' – a history of the self leading up to the here and now. (AM is considered by many researchers to be one of the characteristics that distinguish human from non-human memory: see Chapters 1 and 7.) It also suggests that self-recognition in chimps – and human toddlers – is based on recognition of the self's *behaviour* and not the self's psychological states. When chimps and orang-utans see themselves in a mirror, Povinelli (1998) believes they:

> ... *form an equivalence relation between the actions they see in the mirror and their own behaviour. Every time they move, the mirror image moves with them. They conclude that everything that is true for the mirror image is also true for their own bodies, and vice versa. Thus, these apes can pass the mirror test by correlating coloured marks on the mirror image with marks on their own bodies. But the ape does not conclude, 'That's me!' Rather, the animal concludes, 'That's the same as me!'*

In short, chimps possess explicit mental representations of the positions and movements of their own bodies, which Povinelli calls the **kinaesthetic self-concept**.

Inconsistencies in findings from mirror test research

Interestingly, not all chimps and bonobos pass the mirror test. For example, Swartz and Evans (1991) found that only one of 11 chimps did so. Povinelli *et al.* (1994) reported that 26 per cent of 35 chimps (over the age of 16), 75 per cent (of twelve 8–15-year-olds), 20 per cent (of ten 6- and 7-year-olds) and just 2 per cent (of 48 one-to-five-year-olds) passed.

Wise (1999) suggests that these inconsistencies might be attributable to differences in rearing and socialisation, or individual differences in the animals being studied. It's also been suggested that they might be shy or embarrassed by the dot, as children sometimes are, and not touch it for this reason. Wise argues that just because (some) chimps don't actually display mirror self-recognition, we cannot necessarily infer that they lack this ability. He draws a comparison with gorillas' ability to make and use tools: while they don't display either skill in the wild, they often do in captivity. Based on Sober (1998), Wise argues that:

> ... *One hundred thousand years ago, human beings virtually identical to any reading this produced no known art, had no written, and perhaps spoken, language, and did not use agriculture. That we do all three today suggests that it would be a grave mistake to conclude that our ancestors of one hundred thousand years ago lacked the necessary cognitive capacities.*

Time for reflection
- While Sober's argument is consistent with the continuity approach (see Chapter 1), is it also valid to claim that even such a relatively basic form of consciousness as self-recognition has evolved in humans to become a much more reliable and distinctive ability compared with chimps and other apes?

The evolution of self-consciousness

As Mitchell (1997) points out, by documenting which species do and don't pass the mirror test, we can begin to build up a picture of approximately when the most primitive ingredients of self-consciousness evolved. Given that both chimps and humans are capable of mirror self-recognition, we can assume that the ancestor common to both species also had this ability (as a *homology*). This allows us to say that a primitive self-consciousness evolved at least 8 million years ago, since this is when chimps and humans diverged in their evolutionary development (see Chapter 1 and Figure 4.4 below).

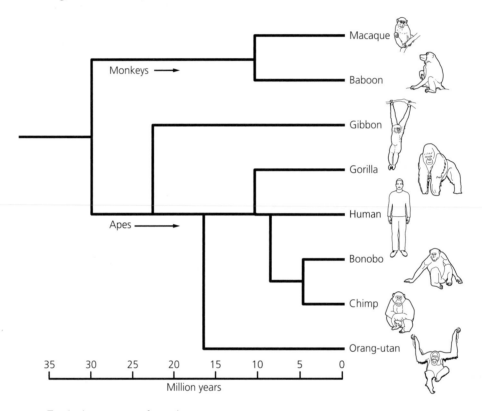

▲ **Figure 4.4** Evolutionary tree for primates

We can go further and place a limit on how far back self-consciousness first appeared. Monkeys, who branched off from apes almost 30 million years ago, show no evidence of mirror self-recognition (despite being able to use mirrors in other ways, such as reaching things seen only in reflection and turning around towards someone they have seen in a mirror). But could this be because monkeys find looking into a mirror threatening? Using cotton-top tamarins (small, tree-living monkeys with a spectacular tuft of white hair) Hauser (2000) replicated Gallup's mirror-test procedure, dying their tufts with bright pink, blue or green hair dye. He concluded that they did show mirror self-recognition after all, but this conclusion remains controversial (Blackmore, 2010).

If monkeys do lack self-consciousness, it's likely that the ancestor common to monkeys and apes also lacked this capacity; in other words, it would appear that self-consciousness evolved within the last 30 million years. We can be even more specific: orang-utans pass the mirror test, while gibbons don't, indicating that self-consciousness first appeared 15–20 million years ago (see Figure 4.3). But what about gorillas?

If orang-utans are capable of self-recognition, then we can infer that gorillas should also be capable of it, since these two species were linked by a common ancestor about 15 million years ago. However, gorillas show little aptitude for self-recognition (Gallup, 1998; Mitchell, 1997). How can we explain this anomaly?

- A famous exception to the general rule is Koko, a female gorilla which was taught American Sign Language in a study of non-human language (Patterson, 1978, 1980) (see Chapter 6). When asked what she saw in the mirror, she signed 'Me, Koko'. Koko may have behaved differently for the same reasons that some chimps – but not others – pass the mirror test (see above). As Povinelli (1993) puts it, the unusually stimulating social environment in which Koko was reared may have allowed her to resurrect a capacity for self-consciousness that lies dormant in most members of her species.

- This explanation, of course, begs the question as to why gorillas should have lost such a valuable faculty. Povinelli notes that the rate of maturation seems to have accelerated in gorillas relative to that in chimps. This could mean either that chimp development has slowed down or that gorillas have become precocious: gorillas are mobile at an earlier age and display other features of early maturity. Reaching maturity faster was, presumably, advantageous in their particular habitat. For example, for their young to be mobile from an earlier age would have been an advantage in the gorillas' more nomadic lifestyle (travelling further afield to forage for food). However, this speedier development might have actually involved a developmental short-cut in certain respects. Since such a sophisticated ability as self-consciousness requires a prolonged period of development, gorillas may have been denied the opportunity to acquire it. If the naturally fast development could be slowed down, then perhaps the gorilla's potential for self-consciousness could be realised; perhaps this is exactly what happened with Koko.

- Perhaps self-consciousness evolved *after* humans and chimps had split off from gorillas; this would mean that it developed about 8 million years ago in our own line of ancestry. If this were the case, we'd have to explain self-consciousness in orang-utans by proposing that the capacity evolved spontaneously and coincidentally. This would be an example of **evolutionary convergence**: the functional advantages of having self-consciousness promoted its development in two populations *independently* of one another (Mitchell, 1997).

Is it just apes that pass the mirror test?

Two major exceptions to the 'only apes display self-consciousness' rule are dolphins and whales. They're both extremely intelligent and communicative creatures, and some of them enjoy playing with mirrors (Blackmore, 2010). Using two captive bottlenose dolphins that were familiar with mirrors, Reiss and Marino (2001) marked them with either temporary black ink or just water on parts of their body they could not see. Both spent much more time twisting and turning in front of the mirror when the ink was used, and in ways that would help them see the otherwise invisible marks.

Elephants are also highly intelligent, social animals with large brains (see Chapter 3). Plotnik *et al.* (2006) gave three Asian elephants large mirrors; not only did they pass the mirror test, but they went through the familiar stages of mirror use (responding as if the image were another elephant, physically inspecting the mirror, testing it with their own behaviour, then finally apparently recognising themselves).

Corvid is the technical name for the crow family, a group of intelligent birds that include crows, magpies, ravens, rooks, jackdaws and jays. Prior *et al.* (2008) gave the mirror test to five European Magpies. After displaying the usual looking-for-another-animal-behind-the-mirror response (sometimes quite aggressively), three attempted to remove spots placed on their throats by looking in the mirror.

According to Blackmore (2010), what makes these findings so remarkable is that **corvids'** brains are quite different from those of great apes or elephants (see Chapter 3). The last common ancestor of mammals and birds lived almost 300 million years ago; as we saw in Chapter 3, bird brains are tiny compared with human brains and lack the convoluted cortex. However, as Blackmore notes, in all the species that have passed the mirror test, the brain weight/body weight ratio is very high.

> ## Time for reflection
> - What conclusions can we draw about self-consciousness from research using the mirror test?

The mirror test – conclusions

As we saw earlier, Gallup and Povinelli disagree about how to interpret the findings from studies using chimps. We have also seen that the failure of most gorillas to pass the test poses something of an evolutionary puzzle. Perhaps even more puzzling are the findings that crows, which are so far removed phylogenetically from chimps and humans, do pass. So, does passing the mirror test necessarily tell us the same thing regarding the animal's self-consciousness? For example, having a self-concept and a ToM are part of our concept of a person – but not of a crow or an elephant! But doesn't this beg its own fundamental question, reflecting the **human exceptionalism** argument? Perhaps a way forward is to break ToM down into some of its component parts, such as *deception*, and understanding *intention*.

Deception

Mitchell (1997) describes the 'remarkable' behaviour of a species of bird that feigns a broken wing when its nest is under attack from a predator. As the predator approaches the nest, the bird limps about elaborately nearby; the predator sees this as an easy kill and promptly pursues the bird, which then flies away with the predator in pursuit. When both are at a 'safe' distance from the nest, the bird flies away to safety and her chicks survive! Should we call this deception? In a human, we certainly would, but this bird's behaviour is highly automated, triggered by predator stimuli; these can be simulated under laboratory conditions. As Mitchell (1997) says:

> ... *Feigning a broken wing is not deception in the sense that we understand it, but rather it is an unthinking and automated response that is executed without any final goal or outcome in mind.*

Mitchell also gives examples of **learned deception**, such as the fox that is being pursued by hounds choosing one of two hollow trees, because it knows (i.e. it has learned) that in this particular tree is a burrow that leads the fox to safety. Superficially, it might appear as if the fox has the insight that the dogs believe (falsely) that it's inside the tree, while all the time escaping through the burrow. However, it's much more likely that a chance choosing of the burrow-tree in the past has led the fox to choose it this time (based on some form of operant conditioning): even if you aren't an arch behaviourist, you don't need to bring ToM into the explanation.

Insightful deception is different, however. It's performed in the absence of specialised genetic programming and without specific learning. According to Mitchell (1997):

> ... *It would require the calculation of the consequences of one's behaviour, especially how that behaviour would be interpreted by another individual. It would therefore require a conception of the future and a conception of other minds as observers and interpreters of the behaviour in question* ...

If apes have any sort of conception of mind, surely this would be apparent as an ability to deceive insightfully? Primatologists Byrne and Whiten (1987; Byrne, 1995) describe this ability (supporting their **Machiavellian intelligence** hypothesis (MIH)) (see Box 4.10 and Box 4.11).

Box 4.10 Mel and Paul: Machiavellian intelligence (Byrne and Whiten, 1987)

Mel dug furiously with her bare hands to extract the large succulent corm from the rock-hard Ethiopian ground. It was the dry season and food was scarce. Corms are edible bulbs somewhat like onions and are a staple during these long, hard months. Little Paul sat nearby and surreptitiously observed Mel's labours. Paul's mother was out of sight; she had left him to play in the grass, but he knew she would remain within earshot in case he needed her. Just as Mel managed, with a final pull, to yank her prize out of the earth, Paul let out an ear-splitting cry that shattered the peace of the savannah. His mother rushed to him. Heart pounding and adrenaline pumping, she burst upon the scene and quickly sized up the situation: Mel had obviously harassed her darling child. Shrieking, she stormed after the bewildered Mel, who dropped the corm and fled. Paul's scheme was complete. After a furtive glance to make sure nobody was looking, he scurried over to the corm, picked up his prize and began to eat. The trick worked so well that he used it several more times before anyone wised up.

Mel and Paul were Chacma baboons.

In 1983, Byrne and Whiten began noticing deceptive tactics among the mountain baboons in Drakensberg, South Africa. Catarrhine primates (which include the Old World monkeys, apes and humans) are all able to tactically dupe conspecifics (members of their own species). These behaviours are calculated, flexible and exquisitely sensitive to shifting social contexts (Smith, 2005). Based on these and other similar observations, Byrne and Whiten formulated their MIH, according to which the extraordinary explosion of intelligence in primate evolution was prompted by the need to master increasingly sophisticated forms of social trickery and manipulation. Primates had to get smart in order to keep up with the snowballing development of social gamesmanship. The MIH suggests that social complexity propelled our ancestors into becoming progressively more intelligent and adept at 'wheeling, dealing, bluffing and conniving' (Smith, 2005). This means that human beings are born liars: lying helps us facilitate social interactions, manipulate others and make friends.

More recently, Byrne and Corp (2004) have found that the size of the cortex is a good predictor of the degree of deception to be found in primate species (see Box 4.11).

Box 4.11 Neocortex size predicts deception rate in primates (Byrne and Corp, 2004)

Current variation in brain size among primates is largely a reflection of differences in the neocortex (Stephan *et al.,* 1981). Understanding the origins of this specialisation becomes a question of what selective pressure(s) favoured an enlarged neocortex during primate evolution. Although several theories have emphasised benefits in the form of environmental exploitation, Byrne and Corp claim that there's now some consensus that the chief benefits may be *social* ones: according to this 'social brain' hypothesis or MIH, the cognitive demands of intense social living select for increased social skill, mediated by neocortical enlargement (Byrne and Whiten, 1988; Dunbar, 1992; Humphrey, 1976; Seyfarth and Cheney, 2002).

Most monkeys and apes live in long-lasting groups, so that familiar conspecifics are major competitors for access to resources. This situation favours individuals that can offset the costs of competition by using manipulative tactics, and skilful manipulation depends on extensive social knowledge (Cheney and Seyfarth, 1990). Because competitive advantage operates relative to the ability of others in the population, an 'arms race' of increasing social skill results; this is kept in check by the high metabolic cost of brain tissue (see Chapter 3).

Byrne and Corp (2004) examined the relationship between neocortex size and a direct measure of social cognition, namely, how much species use behavioural deception to solve social problems. They measured both (a) absolute neocortex size/volume, and (b) the ratio of neocortex size to that of the rest of the brain.

Data were collected for 18 species for which both brain measurements and deception data were available (including four New World and seven Old World monkeys, and four ape species). The results showed quite clearly that the size of the neocortex (however this is measured) in a modern primate species predicts the extent to which individual members of that species use deceptive tactics for social manipulation. The typical size of a species' social group wasn't found to be a significant predictor of deception.

Laboratory studies of deception

Time for reflection

- How is the MIH related to Whiten's 'deep social brain account' (Whiten, 2007; Whiten *et al.*, 1999) (see Chapter 1)?

- The Machiavellian intelligence hypothesis is based almost exclusively on data collected from field studies (i.e. naturalistic observation of animals in the wild). Mitchell (1997) calls this evidence 'anecdotal'. What are the strengths and limitations of this method of data collection?

- What are the strengths and limitations of laboratory studies involving chimps and other non-human animals?

The pioneering experimental study of deception was conducted by Woodruff and Premack (1979), inspired by their earlier work with their chimp Sarah (see Chapter 6); she showed a preference for one trainer over another, even though both were well-intentioned. Woodruff and Premack contrived the situation such that one trainer was scripted to be nice in a very exaggerated way, while the other was overtly nasty; the latter wore sun-glasses and a cloth covered the lower half of his face so that he looked like a bandit.

After the four chimp subjects had got used to these behaviours, they took turns in being housed in a small cage within the laboratory. A person entered the laboratory with a tasty morsel of food, which he placed beneath one of two cups side-by-side. He then left, and one of the two trainers arrived. The chimp had the opportunity to obtain the food by informing the trainer where it was hidden. If the chimp gestured towards the cup containing the food, the trainer promptly and reliably looked there, found the food, then handed it to the chimp as a reward. If the chimp gestured towards the empty cup, the trainer would find nothing under the cup and then left without the chimp receiving anything. This is what happened with the 'nice' trainer.

When the 'nasty' trainer found the food under the cup, he gleefully gobbled it up himself! But if the chimp gestured towards the empty cup, the disappointed trainer would shuffle to the corner of the laboratory. At this moment, the chimp was released from his cage and allowed to search under the remaining cup and help himself to the food. In effect, the chimp was being rewarded for communicating dishonestly. Would the chimps deceive the 'nasty' trainer?

The answer is a qualified 'yes'. The four chimps did eventually differentiate between the two trainers in terms of the honesty of their gestures – but none discriminated systematically in fewer than 50 attempts. Initially, they gestured honestly to both trainers, before beginning to show a general reluctance to do so (but still without discriminating between them). Finally, after at least 50 trials, the chimps began to gesture dishonestly specifically to the nasty trainer.

Interpreting Woodruff and Premack's findings

As Mitchell (1997) points out, the difficulty in conducting experiments with chimps to assess their understanding of mind is that researchers are always going to be hampered by not being able to explain the rules or aim of a game verbally. Were the 50 trials necessary for the chimps to understand what the game was about? This is what might be expected from a study by Boysen (1993), which suggests that chimps have a strong natural tendency to point to a container with food, not so much as an act of communication but just as an *imperative gesture* ('I want that!'). Perhaps their extensive training was needed in order to overcome this natural tendency. Alternatively, chimps may simply not understand very much about mind and deception: their gestures may have been 'mindless' and simply about gaining food.

Another attempt at investigating the chimp's conception of mind, which Mitchell (1997) calls the most ingenious and convincing to date, was conducted by Povinelli *et al.* (1990) (see Box 4.12).

Box 4.12 Inferences about guessing and knowing in chimps (Povinelli *et al.*, 1990)

In the first part of the study, the chimp observed the trainer place a treat in a hiding place (one of two upturned cups (A and B)). A screen was erected between the chimp and the cups: although the chimp could infer that the trainer had hidden the food (the trainer's hands were empty), she couldn't tell which of the two cups had been used. The screen was then removed to reveal the two upturned cups and a second trainer arrived. Each trainer pointed to a cup (A or B) and the chimp was free to search under just one of the cups. The sensible strategy would be to search under the cup indicated by the trainer who hid the food: only he knew where it was. Presumably, the other trainer was just guessing, so he could be guessing incorrectly.

Initially, the chimps seemed to guess randomly. But their guessing slowly became more systematic: they adopted the sensible strategy. However, as in Woodruff and Premack's (1979) study, we need to explain why it took the chimps so long to begin working out what they needed to do to obtain the food: does it suggest that they didn't possess a deep understanding that this individual had *knowledge* of the food's location?

In a second phase, both trainers were present when the food was hidden by a third person. One trainer, who would later gesture, was a passive onlooker, while the other stood beside him with a bucket over his head, preventing him from seeing anything. Finally, the screen was removed to reveal the two upturned cups, and the two trainers pointed. As before, the passive onlooker trainer pointed to the cup where the food was hidden, while the 'bucket' trainer pointed to the empty cup.

The findings provided very strong support for the possibility that at least two of the four chimps had a deep understanding of knowledge and ignorance: they discriminated immediately between the two trainers, and allowed themselves to be informed exclusively by the informed trainer. All the chimps had already benefited from the training necessary to work out what they had to do: if they truly understood the relationship between seeing and believing, we'd expect all of them to search correctly in the place indicated by the trainer who saw it being hidden. However, a third chimp required a small amount of (additional) practice before she stopped choosing randomly, and the fourth required a lot more.

Povinelli and DeBlois (1992) repeated the Povinelli *et al.* (1990) experiment with young children. The children had previously observed that one of the assistants had witnessed the hiding, while the other had not (she had a paper bag over her head). From about three years onwards, children began to show that they inferred where the food was from following the lead of the assistant who'd observed it being hidden. Younger children tended to choose randomly. According to Povinelli (1993), children need to have developed an understanding of their own individual uniqueness/self-concept (as demonstrated by the mirror test), before they can understand that knowledge varies between people.

Interestingly, Povinelli *et al.* (1993) note a similar developmental trend in chimps. Not until 6–8 years do chimps pass the mirror test, and only those that have will be able to discriminate between a trainer who knows where the food is and one who doesn't.

... Unlike monkeys, perhaps apes and humans are able to appreciate the implications of recognition of one's own uniqueness. If I am unique in my mental life and subjective experiences, then that means that what I think, feel, want, know, hope, wish and intend is not necessarily shared with others ... mental life varies between people ... the faculty of self-awareness allows you to begin to speculate about the mental state of other individuals ... (Mitchell, 1997)

Understanding intention

Gallup's MRH relates to what Dunbar (2004) calls **second-order intentionality** (the capacity to reflect on the contents of someone else's mind). His research suggests that humans are limited to *fifth-order intentionality* ('I suppose [1] that you believe [2] that I want [3] you to think [4] that I intend [5] ...'). Chimps (and perhaps other great apes) may be capable of second-order, while monkeys stop at first order (along with most mammals and birds). Dunbar believes that these capacities are a linear function of the relative size of the frontal lobe: a large neocortex in general, and frontal lobes in particular, is a 'primate speciality' (see Box 4.11 and Chapter 3). However, he also argues that mind-reading is not a specialised (distinctive) primate or even human capacity: there's only a *quantitative difference* between species in the number of orders of intentionality they can travel (see Chapter 1).

Is there any evidence to support Dunbar's claims? In an earlier study involving their chimp, Sarah, Premack and Woodruff (1978) noted that she apparently enjoyed commercial television, which she seemed to find very absorbing. It's difficult to imagine what these programmes could offer Sarah (or any child or adult, for that matter), unless she had some understanding of the characters' psychology, including their emotion and intentions.

Premack and Woodruff presented Sarah with a selection of short videos that showed a character facing a problem, then gave her a series of cards, one of which showed an item relevant to what we might infer about the character's intention. (The rest of the cards were distracters.) For example, a man was shown unsuccessfully trying to leave a room, the door apparently locked. The three cards that followed all showed a key, but one was broken in the middle, and another was bent; only one was intact (see Figure 4.5). She reliably chose card 2 and was equally successful with other videos.

The findings don't show definitively that Sarah was able to infer the character's intention (she might have been successful just by focusing on the solution to the problem), but in order to identify the problem, she'd have needed to attribute some kind of purpose to the actor's behaviour.

A further study suggested that Sarah was genuinely attuned to the character's psychology. She watched a man in a cage trying to reach through the bars to get at some bananas located outside the cage. There was a box in his way, with bricks on top of it that prevented him from getting the fruit. As before, Sarah was shown a set of pictures and invited to choose one. On some trials she chose a picture that showed the man obtaining the bananas after having moved the box to one side. But under one particular condition (i.e. when Bill, one of two familiar trainers was the actor), she reliably chose a picture that showed the man lying on the floor with the bricks from the top of the box scattered over him, apparently the victim of an accident! Significantly, she did not get along with Bill! It was only when Keith, her preferred trainer, was the actor that she reliably chose the happy outcome. As Mitchell (1997) puts it, 'Evidently, she was not just oriented to solve the problem, but was also immersed in the psychology of the sketches that were acted out.'

Povinelli *et al.* (1992) designed a piece of apparatus in order to investigate the chimp's ability to exchange roles with another individual (see Figure 4.6). If the chimp was successful, it would strongly suggest that it had assimilated and understood the other individual's intention to communicate something meaningful.

▲ **Figure 4.5** Sarah was shown these three cards after watching a video of a man trying to leave a room whose door appeared to be locked. She reliably chose card 2.

The two players sit on either side of the apparatus, one playing the role of informant, the other playing the role of operator. One role would be played by a human, the other by a chimp (the roles assigned randomly). The chimps had already been trained to gesture imperatively by pointing ('I want that'), and to respond appropriately to another individual's imperative pointing (fetching an object when the trainer pointed to it).

When the chimp was the operator, his task was to pull a handle if and only if the informant pointed to it. Pulling the handle brought food within reach on either side of the apparatus, but only one food tray was baited (i.e. contained food). The chimp operator couldn't see which one it was: a mini-screen erected on one side of each tray blocked his view. But the food was in full view of the informant. This meant that the two players had to cooperate in co-ordinating their respective roles to obtain the food prize.

After extensive practice, both chimps and monkeys learned to perform well in both roles. However, more interesting was how easily they could swap roles: to do this they needed to have grasped that the informant was intending to communicate to the operator the whereabouts of the food in order to allow the latter to act appropriately. Three out of four chimps were easily able to swap roles from operator to informant, while monkeys found this extremely challenging (almost as if they had to be trained from scratch). Cheney and Seyfarth (1990) also concluded that monkeys don't have a ToM.

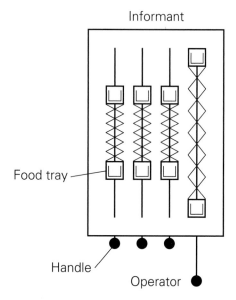

▲ **Figure 4.6** The apparatus used by Povinelli *et al.* (1992)

Conclusions: What can we say about the chimp's possession of a ToM?

According to Mitchell (1997): 'Chimps appear to have a remarkable understanding of mind, but it would be foolish to pretend that they match humans in this respect ...'

Povinelli and Eddy (1996b) conducted a major research programme to explore the extent of this 'gap' between ourselves and chimps. This built on the success of the earlier research, which showed that chimps regard the communication (pointing gesture) from a trainer who saw the hiding of a treat as more reliable than that of one who didn't see (see Box 4.12). Povinelli himself wondered whether, since the face of only one of the trainers was visible for the entire duration of the study, the chimps might have learned to trust him.

In the new study, Povinelli and Eddy (1996b) made use of a component of the chimp's natural repertoire of behaviour, namely, a begging gesture: the chimp assumes a distinctive posture, extending one hand with palm face-up. This request for food is spontaneous and requires no prior training. Povinelli and Eddy assumed that there wouldn't be much point in begging unless the other person could see you; in turn, this implies an understanding of the relationship between seeing and knowing (again, see Box 4.12). The Povinelli and Eddy (1996a and 1996b) study is described in Box 4.13.

Box 4.13 What do chimps know about seeing? (Povinelli and Eddy (1996a and 1996b))

Chimps were ushered into a testing chamber within the laboratory, where they obediently sat on a crate. In one control condition, a trainer sat in front of the chimp and had access to a food reward nearby; a transparent partition prevented the chimp from taking the food herself. But the partition had holes in it that allowed the chimp to extend her hand through in order to beg the trainer for food. Chimps did this quite readily and spontaneously, and the trainer obligingly handed over the food. In another control condition, there were two trainers: one held food while the other held a block of wood. The chimps easily discriminated between the two, directing their begging specifically at the food-holder.

Could the chimps discriminate according to who possessed *knowledge* of food and who could see its gesturing?

Food was then placed on the table adjacent to the trainers: one was facing forward and so could see both the food and the chimp, while the other sat with his back to the chimp. They begged specifically to the trainer who could see them, and this happened immediately.

While this implies that chimps understand the relationship between vision and knowledge, Povinelli and Eddy wanted to find out more precisely what chimps understand about the eyes in particular as a window of information about the external world. Chimps are able to calculate the target of another individual's line of sight, as well as recognising that solid opaque objects serve as obstacles to the line of sight (Povinelli and Eddy, 1996a). But would they understand that someone who hasn't perceived a critical fact must remain in a state of ignorance?

To test this, chimps were presented with two trainers, one wearing a blindfold over his eyes, the other wearing a gag over his mouth; there was no discrimination between the two. This was also the case when (a) one trainer covered his eyes with his hands and the other covered his ears; (b) one trainer had a bucket over his head, while the other held the bucket over his shoulder so that his view was unimpeded; and (c) both sat with their backs to the chimp, but one turned to look over his shoulder in the chimp's direction.

These findings imply that chimps don't appear to attach any particular significance to the eyes when deciding who does and doesn't know something. In turn, this reveals the chimp's limitations in understanding the relationship between seeing and knowing. However, with repeated testing they did begin to discriminate appropriately, yet this wasn't based so much on who could or could not see, but on whose face was visible or invisible. They first started to discriminate as in (b) and (c) above – but they still hadn't grasped the importance of the eyes and would beg from a trainer with his eyes closed as readily as from one with his eyes open.

How do children compare? This time, two experimenters both had access to prized stickers, and the children had to make a gesture to one or other in order to request a sticker. When one of the experimenters wore a blindfold (or for some other reason couldn't see, as described above), even 2-year-olds easily discriminated, directing their gestures toward the 'seeing' one.

Time for reflection
● What conclusions can we draw from these findings?

Rather than concluding from these findings that humans display understanding of the relationship between seeing and knowing (and from a very early age) and chimps don't, Mitchell (1997) prefers the view that this understanding is *relative* (not absolute). While monkeys seem to know *nothing* about the relationship and cannot learn anything about it, chimps are capable of learning about it. Only humans, it seems, are born with considerable knowledge of the seeing–knowing link – or, at least, an aptitude to learn about it easily. Viewed in this way, we can conclude that chimps have a well-developed conception of mind compared with monkeys, but they are no match for humans (Mitchell, 1997).

As we noted at the beginning of the section on intentionality, Dunbar (2004) reaches a similar conclusion. He observes (2007) that at around the age of four, children develop the capacity to reflect on other people's minds as well as their own (i.e. they now have a ToM). Crucially, once this capacity has developed, children can lie with conviction. Before this, they're what Dunbar calls 'good ethologists': they're good at reading observable behaviour, at noticing the correlations between events in the world, at learning how to manipulate the world to get what they want. Children know that if you say something with total conviction, adults will give you the benefit of the doubt most of the time – but they don't understand *why*. After age four, children begin to appreciate that other people have minds like their own, and that sometimes these other minds can have different beliefs about the world. As a result, they can begin to exploit those minds by feeding them false information in order to deliberately mislead them.

While there's still much to learn, 'the acquisition of theory of mind takes their mental world onto a new and higher plane' (Dunbar, 2007). Children display second-order intentionality: they *believe* that someone else *believes* (that something is the case), and those beliefs may sometimes be false (e.g. Baron-Cohen *et al.,* 1985; Gross, 2008).

Dunbar (2007) claims that there is no evidence to suggest that any non-human species possess a ToM. The evidence based on chimps (see above) he considers to be weak and open to dispute. But the evidence does suggest that chimps function at about the same level as 4–5-year-old children, who become more proficient as they get older (while chimps don't). While chimps are a 'cut above' the average monkey, lion, dolphin and rat, they're still a long way short of what adult humans can do. As we noted above, adult humans are capable of fifth-order intentionality; this is in a different and 'very grand league' compared with what chimps and human toddlers are capable of. Dunbar cites Shakespeare's *Othello* as illustrating both fifth-order intentionality (the audience *believes* that Iago *wanted* Othello to *suppose* that Desdemona *loved* Casio and that Casio, in turn, *loved* her – and hence that they planned to run away together) and a possible key to Shakespeare's genius, namely, his *intention* that the audience *believes* that Iago, etc. (this is *sixth-order intentionality*).

> *... So the lesson for us is that the flights of fancy that we engage in when dabbling in literature, even when just telling stories around the campfire, are far beyond the cognitive capacities of any other species of animal currently alive ... Only adult humans could ever intentionally produce literature of the kind that we associate with human culture ...* (Dunbar, 2007)

Time for reflection

Dunbar (2007) suggests that we can make exactly the same argument for religion (in the sense of communal commitment to dogma, mass worship and so on.

- Try to spell out how fifth-order intentionality might apply to religion in this form (i.e. organised, institutionalised, religion).

What is (self-)consciousness for?

According to Humphrey (1986), when we ask what consciousness does, what difference it makes to our lives, there are three possibilities that might more or less make sense:

1. *It might be making all the difference in the world:* it might be a necessary precondition of all intelligent and purposive behaviour, both in humans and non-humans.

2. *It might be making no difference whatsoever:* it may be a purely accidental feature that happens (at least) sometimes to be present in some animals and has no influence on their behaviour.

3. *It might, for those animals that have it, be making the difference between success and failure in some particular aspect of their lives.*

Time for reflection

- Which of Humphrey's three possibilities do you consider is the most likely to be true?
- Which corresponds to the commonsense view?

Humphrey believes that commonsense must back the first of these. Our everyday experience is that consciousness makes all the difference in the world (just as our experience tells us that we have free will: see Gross, 2009): we are either awake, alert and conscious or flat on our backs, and when we lose consciousness, we lose touch with the world (but see Table 4.1. and Box 4.4 above).

The cognitive unconscious

According to Frith and Rees (2007), perhaps the major development in consciousness research during the past 50 years has been the demonstration of unconscious, automatic, psychological processes in perception, memory and action (the **cognitive unconscious**: Kihlstrom, 1987). One major example is **blindsight** (Weiskrantz, 1986), which is described in Box 4.14.

Box 4.14 Blindsight: Can we see without really 'seeing'?

According to Humphrey (1986, 1993), there's increasing evidence that the higher animals, including humans, can demonstrate perception through their behaviour without being aware of what they're doing. During the 1960s, Humphrey worked with a monkey called Helen, who'd had her visual cortex removed (as part of a study of brain damage in humans), although her lower visual centres were intact. Over a six-month period following the operation, she began to use her eyes again, and over the next seven years many of her visual abilities returned.

At that time, there were no comparable human cases, but what relevant evidence existed suggested that people wouldn't recover their vision. Then, in 1974, Weiskrantz *et al.* reported the case of DB, a young man who'd recently undergone surgery to remove a tumour at the back of his brain. The entire right-side primary visual cortex had been removed, resulting in blindness in the left side of the visual field. So, for example, when he looked straight ahead, he couldn't see (with either eye) anything to the left of his nose. Or could he?

While there was no doubt that he was genuinely unaware of seeing anything in the blind half of his visual field, was it possible that his brain was nonetheless still receiving and processing visual input? What would happen if he could be persuaded to discount his own conscious opinion?

Weiskrantz asked him to forget for a moment that he was blind, and to 'guess' at what he might be seeing if he could see. To DB's own amazement, it turned out that he could locate an object accurately in his blind field and he could even guess certain aspects of its shape. Yet he continued to deny any conscious awareness. Weiskrantz (1986) called this phenomenon '"blindsight": visual capacity in a field defect in the absence of acknowledged awareness'. Other cases have since been described, and unconscious vision appears to be a clinical reality (Humphrey, 1986). As Weiskrantz (2007) says, 'Blindsight has made us aware that there is more to vision than seeing, and more to seeing than vision'.

However, despite the fact that perception (and other fundamental cognitive and behavioural processes) may not *require* consciousness, it remains true that these processes are very often *accompanied* by consciousness. If most other species lack the kind of consciousness that humans possess (see discussion above), isn't it reasonable to suppose that it evolved in humans for some purpose?

Humphrey (1986) asks us to imagine an animal that lacks the faculty of conscious or self-reflexive 'insight'. It has a brain that receives inputs from conventional sense organs and sends outputs to motor systems, and in between runs a highly sophisticated information processor and decision maker. But it has no picture of what this information processing is doing or how it works: the animal is 'unconscious'. Now imagine that a new form of sense organ evolves,

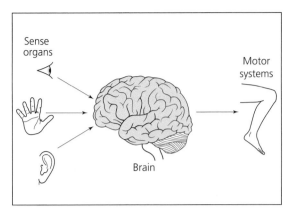

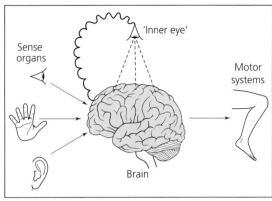

▲ **Figure 4.7** a) How an animal without insight works (from Humphrey, 1986)

▲ **Figure 4.7** b) How the addition of an 'inner eye' affects the animal (from Humphrey, 1986)

an 'inner eye', whose field of view is not the outside world *but the brain itself*. Like other sense organs, it provides a picture of the informational field (the brain) that is partial and selective, but, equally, like other sense organs it has been designed by natural selection to give a useful ('user-friendly') picture – one that will tell the subject as much as he or she needs to know: the animal is conscious. These two different types of animals are shown in Figure 4.7.

Suppose our ability to look in upon ourselves and examine our own minds at work is as much a part of human biology as our ability to walk upright or to perceive the outside world. Once upon a time there were animals – presumably our own ancestors – that couldn't do it but they gave rise to descendants who could. Why should those conscious descendants have been selected in the course of evolution? If Darwin's evolutionary theory is correct, the only answer is that, like every other natural ability and structure, consciousness must have come into being because it conferred some kind of biological advantage on those creatures that possessed it:

> *In some particular area of their lives, conscious human beings must have been able to do something which their unconscious forbears couldn't; something which, in competition with the other members of their species, distinctly improved their chances of survival – and so of passing on the underlying genetic trait for consciousness to the next generation.* (Humphrey, 1986)

If consciousness is the answer to anything at all, it must be to a biological challenge that human beings have had to meet. Could that challenge lie in the human need to understand, respond to and manipulate the behaviour of other human beings?

> *In evolutionary terms, I suspect that the possession of an 'inner eye' served one purpose before all: to allow our own ancestors to raise social life to a new level. The first use of human consciousness was – and is – to enable each human being to understand what it feels like to be human and so to make sense of himself and other people from the inside ...* (Humphrey, 1993)

This is, of course, a way of looking at people as *natural psychologists* (see Gross, 2009). It's no accident that humans are both the most highly social creatures to have evolved and are unique in their ability to use self-knowledge to interpret others. This view of people as natural psychologists is consistent with Whiten's (1999, 2007) **'deep social mind'** account (see Chapter 1).

Conclusions: The problem of causation

Part of the commonsense understanding of consciousness (Humphrey's (1986) 'it makes all the difference in the world' possibility: see above) is that conscious processing and the subjective experience of volition (i.e. having free will) do just what they seem to. In other words, we normally take our conscious decision to, say, get out of our chair and go into the kitchen, as the *cause* of those actions: it's 'I' who decides.

But what if it could be shown that my brain begins to become activated *before* I've made the (conscious) decision? Wouldn't this seriously detract from belief in free will and the causal properties of consciousness? Some very influential – and highly controversial – experiments by Libet (1985; Libet *et al.,* 1983) claim to have shown that:

- the conscious decision to act (in this case, flexing the finger or wrist) comes about 200 milliseconds (ms) (one-fifth of a second) *before* the action (consistent with the concept of free will); but

- the 'readiness potential' (i.e. gradually increasing electrical activity in the motor cortex) begins about 300–500 ms *before that* (i.e. 500–700 ms before the action – contrary to what belief in free will would predict).

(For a more detailed discussion of Libet's research, including a review by Banks and Pockett, 2007, see Gross, 2009.)

According to Velmans (2003), Libet's findings show that our conscious experiences typically occur 'too late to causally affect the processes to which they most obviously relate'. Rather than the conscious wish/decision causing the action, Velmans takes a feeling of volition to be an accurate representation of a *preconscious* voluntary decision. This is consistent with the general finding that consciousness often contains the *results* of cognitive processing, rather than the processing details (Mangan, 2007). In a much-cited article, Nisbett and Wilson (1977) argue that there's no direct access to cognitive processes at all; instead, there is access only to the ideas and inferences that are the outputs resulting from such processes. They claim that our commonsense, intuitive belief that we can accurately account for our own behaviour is *illusory*: what really guides our behaviour is unavailable to consciousness.

Similarly, Velmans (2003) argues that 'One is not conscious of one's own brain/body processing. So how could there be conscious control of such processing?' He asks us to consider 'hesitation pauses' in speech: if the causal efficacy hypothesis (the view that our conscious decisions are what cause our actions) were correct, we'd expect these pauses to contain experiences

> ... *associated with the formation of ideas ... [and] conscious planning of what to say ... But nothing is revealed of the processes that formulate ideas, translate these into a form suitable for expression in language, search for and retrieve words from memory, or assess which words are most appropriate.*

But according to Mangan (2007), we can certainly be ignorant of the details of a complex process and yet still have the power to initiate, influence or control it, especially in conjunction with a little feedback (such as driving a car, using a computer and making a baby). Higher levels of neural organisation control (but don't themselves contain) the information used to execute lower level functions. Indeed, Velmans himself seems to acknowledge later that the fringe component of a hesitation pause does represent *some* information about the underlying cognitive process (Mangan, 2007):

> *... We have a feeling of what we want to say before we say it and in this sense the feeling provides an implicit target. We also have a sense of whether our words fit our meaning, indicating whether they are 'on target' and so on ... the fringe of consciousness contains feelings and judgements about material at the focus of attention thereby providing context in a highly compressed form ...* (Velmans, 2003)

According to Mangan (2007), if there is sufficient information *in* consciousness in some form, (that is, relevant phenomenological contents) to support making volitional decisions, then consciousness *can* be a locus of volition (that is, consciousness does indeed do what commonsense assumes).

While it's difficult to deny that we sometimes need to choose a course of action (such as ducking to avoid an approaching missile) faster than could be achieved consciously (i.e. they're made preconsciously, as Libet has shown):

> *... the mechanisms of consciousness do still have a say: they are able to veto plans that would lead to disadvantage in the long run, and to permit only the beneficial ones to proceed. 'Free will' is thus expressed in the form of selective permission of automatically generated actions, rather than as the (Cartesian) initiation of action by an independent mind (Libet, 1985) ... Libet's (1994) philosophical conclusion is that consciousness exists as a dualistic mental field.* (Rose, 2006)

(Also see Chapter 1.)

Returning to the evolutionary argument, if consciousness evolved because of its survival value, could it have equipped human beings with such survival value unless it had causal properties (Gregory, 1981), that is, unless it could actually bring about changes in behaviour? There is no doubt that our subjective experience tells us that our mind affects our behaviour, that consciousness has causal properties.

Lodge (2002) quotes the physicist James Trefil, according to whom:

> *... no matter how my brain works, no matter how much interplay there is between my brain and my body, one single fact remains ... I am aware of a self that looks out at the world from somewhere inside my skull ... that is not simply an observation, but the central datum with which every theory of consciousness has to grapple. In the end the theory has to go from the firing of neurons to this essential perception.*

According to the neurobiologist, Colin Blakemore (1988), Humphrey's evolutionary theory raises two important questions:

- Why does consciousness use such strange symbolism? For example, the biological value of finding a partner obviously has to do with the nitty-gritty of procreation. But we feel we're in love, a sensation that tells us nothing about the crude necessity of reproduction: 'consciousness translates biological necessities into feelings of pain and pleasure, need and emotion'.
- Why does the inner eye see so little? It gives us only a tiny glimpse, and a distorted one at that, of the internal world (as we noted above in relation to the cognitive unconscious, much of what our brains do is entirely hidden from the 'spotlight' of consciousness.

For Blakemore, our only answers to these questions are in terms of the structure and organisation of the brain: 'to understand the organ that allows us to understand would be little short of a miracle. The human brain makes us what we are. It makes the mind.' (Blakemore, 1988). We discussed in Chapter 3 some of the distinctive features of the human brain's structure and organisation; perhaps the most distinctive feature of all is the (kind of) consciousness it produces. What that consciousness allows us to do, in conjunction with other special abilities such as language (see Chapter 6), is to try to understand the 'organ that allows us to understand'.

Chapter summary

- 'Consciousness' is an ambiguous term, denoting many different phenomena. The 'easy' problems are those that seem directly accessible to the standard methods of cognitive science (such as attention and sleep). The 'hard' problem is the problem of experience.

- Subjective experiences are known as qualia and this is the form in which consciousness manifests itself. For Edelman, Chalmers' 'hard' problem is the apparent discrepancy between subjective (involving a first-person account) and objective (involving science's third-person account).

- A famous attempt to protect first-person experience from reduction to third-person accounts is Nagel's 'What is it like to be a bat?' Not having an adequate language for describing subjective experience doesn't mean that it's not real.

- Searle identifies seven criteria for defining conscious states: they are qualitative, ontologically subjective, intentional, irreducible, experienced as part of a single, unified conscious field, have causal efficacy, and cannot be reduced to more fundamental neurobiological processes.

- Edelman distinguishes between primary consciousness (or sentience), which is likely possessed by all animals with a cortex, and higher-order consciousness (or self-consciousness), which involves direct awareness. With the possible exception of chimpanzees, only humans possess both types of consciousness.

- This primary/higher-order distinction is central to Edelman and Tononi's information integration theory (IIT) of consciousness. This helps explain how we can be conscious of being conscious.

- This primary/higher-order distinction is also sometimes presented as that between phenomenal consciousness and self-consciousness; the latter usually refers to an organism's capacity for second-order representations of its own mental states.

- Some modern philosophers (including Dennett, but not Block) would agree with Descartes' claim that language is necessary for what Block calls '**access consciousness**'.

- According to Wise, the strongest available argument that non-humans are conscious is 'by analogy', rejecting the anthropomorphism objection. This approach may be supported by considerations of evolutionary continuity or homology, as well as anatomical similarities between all mammals and vertebrates in general.

- Literature represents the most comprehensive record of human consciousness we have. While Lodge emphasises literature's treatment of the uniqueness of personal experience, McEwan and others observe that great literature also deals with universal aspects of human experience. This is related to our theory of mind (ToM).

- Consciousness can be conceptualised as comprising two key components: level (i.e. wakefulness) and content (i.e. awareness). In a comatose patient, wakefulness and awareness are both absent, while in patients in a vegetative state (VS), awareness is absent but they appear to be awake (there's a dissociation between level and content). A distinction is made between permanent VS and minimally conscious state (MCS).

- The reverse dissociation occurs naturally during REM sleep, and especially during oneiric experiences, where a subjective feeling of awareness is often present despite the individual not being awake.

- Inasmuch as motor behaviour is required to signal a state of consciousness, an aware patient who cannot produce any behavioural output is indistinguishable from an unconscious one. Indeed, 40 per cent of (aware) MCS patients are misdiagnosed as VS.

- An alternative means of detecting consciousness is through the use of functional neuroimaging technology (such as PET and fMRI). While it's possible to retain relatively high-level brain activity despite severe brain injury, the crucial question is whether we can infer the presence of consciousness from this activity; recent evidence involving a VS patient's use of mental imagery demonstrates that we can.

- According to Merleau-Ponty, our body is essential to our very being: mind and body, mental and physical, are two aspects of a person, neither of which can be reduced to the other.

- Gallup demonstrated mirror self-recognition in wild-born chimpanzees, and several researchers subsequently used his basic method with young children.

- It's generally agreed that passing the mirror test is strong evidence that a chimpanzee has a self-concept, and that only chimpanzees, orang-utans and humans consistently pass it. However, Gallup claims that it also supports the mind-reading hypothesis (MRH).

- Povinelli disagrees with Gallup's interpretation, arguing that self-recognition in chimpanzees (and children under four) is based on recognition of the self's behaviour and not the self's psychological states; more specifically, they demonstrate the kinaesthetic self-concept (rather than ToM).

- Since orang-utans pass the mirror test and gibbons don't, we can infer that self-consciousness first appeared 15–20 million years ago. But, surprisingly, gorillas usually fail the test (an exception being Koko), suggesting that self-consciousness evolved only after humans and chimpanzees had split from gorillas (about 8 million years ago).

- Elephants, dolphins and European Magpies have all demonstrated mirror self-recognition, raising doubts as to whether passing the mirror test tells us the same thing in different species.

- Mitchell distinguishes between learned and insightful deception, only the latter being a component part of ToM.

- Byrne and Whiten's claim that apes' ability to deceive insightfully reflects ToM is called the Machiavellian intelligence hypothesis (MIH).

- Byrne and Corp found that the size of the neocortex (however this is measured) in a modern primate species predicts the extent to which individual members of that species use deceptive tactics for social manipulation.

- The findings from Woodruff and Premack's pioneering experimental study of deception with chimpanzees suggested that they are capable of gesturing dishonestly. Consistent with this are Povinelli *et al*.'s findings that at least some chimpanzees have a deep understanding of knowledge and ignorance in human trainers.

- In studies of both chimpanzees and young children, it seems that an understanding of their own individual uniqueness/self-concept is a prerequisite for appreciating that knowledge varies between people.

- Gallup's MRH relates to what Dunbar calls second-order intentionality. While humans are limited to fifth-order intentionality, chimpanzees (and perhaps other great apes) may be capable of second-order.

- Premack and Woodruff's study involving Sarah, and Povinelli *et al*.'s chimpanzee experiments, support the claim that chimps have a ToM.

- Povinelli and Eddy also found evidence suggesting that chimpanzees understand the relationship between vision and knowledge, although they don't appear to attach any particular attention to the eyes when deciding who does/doesn't know something (unlike 2-year-old children). This species difference is merely quantitative.

- According to Humphrey, the commonsense view of consciousness is that it's a prerequisite for all human and non-human intelligent and purposive behaviour.

- Perhaps the major development in consciousness research during the past 50 years has been the demonstration of the cognitive unconscious (such as blindsight). However, perception and other fundamental cognitive and behavioural processes are very often accompanied by consciousness.

- According to Humphrey's 'inner eye' model, like every other natural ability and structure, consciousness must have evolved because it conferred a biological advantage on those creatures that possessed it, namely to enable each human being to understand what it feels like to be human (people as natural psychologists).

- Libet's finding that the 'readiness potential' begins 300–500 milliseconds *before* the conscious decision to act challenges the commonsense belief in free will and the causal properties of consciousness. Nisbett and Wilson argue that what really guides our behaviour is unavailable to consciousness.

- From an evolutionary perspective, it seems illogical that consciousness could have survival value unless it could actually produce changes in behaviour.

Suggested further reading

Blackmore, S. (2010) *Consciousness: An Introduction* (2nd edition). London: Hodder Education. An excellent textbook, written in a very accessible style, yet detailed and thorough. Blackmore examines a diverse range of topics, including the evolution of consciousness, the basic neuroscience of consciousness, and how subjective experiences can arise from objective brain processes.

Humphrey, N. (1986) *The Inner Eye*. London: Vintage. A brief but highly informative and thought-provoking discussion of the evolution of human consciousness, including its function in human social interaction. Also very relevant to Chapter 1.

Velmans, M. & Schneider, S. (eds) (2007) *The Blackwell Companion to Consciousness.* Oxford: Blackwell Publishing. An outstanding collection of 55 original essays, many by leading authorities (including Chris Frith, Allan Hobson, Richard Bentall, Lawrence Weiskrantz, Michael Gazzaniga, David Chalmers and John Searle), covering all major aspects of the philosophy and science of consciousness.

Selected websites

www.scholarpedia.org/article/vegetative_state

Sponsored by the Brain Corporation, this is a peer-reviewed, open-access encyclopedia, covering all aspects of consciousness. Other relevant articles (69 in total) include animal consciousness, blindsight, the functions of consciousness, the neural correlates of consciousness (see Chapter 3), time perception (see Chapter 7) and phenomenology (see Chapter 8).

www.consciousness.arizona.edu

Centre for Consciousness Studies, University of Arizona.

Chapter 5: Cognition: Hauser's hypothesis

Key questions

- What does Hauser mean by 'humaniqueness'?

- Are there different kinds of generative computation?

- How is recursion (or embededness) demonstrated in language?

- How do levels/orders of representation demonstrate recursion?

- What are the similarities and differences between language and music with respect to recursion, structure, areas of the brain that are implicated, and so on?

- How does tool use demonstrate generative computation?

- What evidence exists for the use and making of tools in non-human animals?

- What are the essential differences between human and non-human use and manufacture of tools?

- What is the relationship between language and (a) the 'promiscuous combination of ideas'; (b) mental symbols; and (c) abstract thought?

- How is imagery different from imagination?

- How is meta-representation related to pretend play, imagination and mind-reading?

Hauser's 'humaniqueness'

We noted in Chapter 1 that, in contrast with Darwin's (1871) view that the difference between human and non-human minds is 'one of degree and not of kind' (i.e. continuity), Hauser (e.g. 2009) believes there's mounting evidence that a 'profound gap' exists between them. While some of the 'building blocks' of human cognition have been found in other species (consistent with the evolutionary perspective), these building blocks constitute only 'the cement footprint of the skyscraper' of the human mind. Human cognition has evolved so far beyond other species' abilities that it has become *qualitatively* different. Hauser (2009) argues that: 'If we scientists are ever to unravel how the human mind came to be, we must first pinpoint exactly what sets it apart from the minds of other creatures ...'

Although humans share the vast majority of their **genes** with chimps, evidence suggests that small genetic shifts that occurred in the human lineage since it split from the chimp line produced massive differences in computational power (see Chapter 2). This rearranging, deleting and copying of universal genetic elements (there are no specifically human genes: see Chapter 2) created a brain with special properties. This 'deep chasm' (**human exceptionalism**) argument is captured in Hauser's term '**humaniqueness**', which denotes the key ingredients of the human mind. The four major ingredients of humaniqueness are:

- **generative computation**
- promiscuous combination of ideas

- mental symbols
- abstract thought.

Generative computation

Generative computation refers to the ability to create a virtually limitless variety of 'expressions' (such as arrangements of words, sequences of notes, combinations of actions or strings of mathematical symbols). Generative computation encompasses two types of operation: *recursive* and *combinatorial*.

Recursion

Recursion is the repeated use of a rule to create new expressions. For example, a short phrase can be embedded within another phrase, repeatedly, in order to create longer, richer descriptions of our thoughts.

Time for reflection

In Chapter 4, we considered examples of levels/orders of representation in relation to theory of mind (ToM) (Dunbar, 2004, 2007).

- Find examples of different levels/orders of representation that illustrate this principle of recursion (or embededness).

According to Jackendoff (1993), recursion is an example of a *pattern* in the mind, which, along with words and their meanings, overcomes the limitations of human memory (we couldn't possibly store all the sentences we're likely to hear or want to use). Recursion prepares us for any sentence we might encounter (most of which we've never heard before in that exact form and so, which are countless): we seem to know what the *possibilities* are. This is how the brain seems to achieve expressive variety.

Time for reflection

For each group of sentences below, try to identify the *pattern* (really, a sort of abstract rule) which generated them (and so which could generate an infinite number of similarly-structured sentences). (The examples are taken from Jackendoff, 1993; they include several that are absurd but nonetheless acceptable, *syntactically* correct sentences in English.)

(1) Amy ate two peanuts.
 Amy ate three peanuts.
 Amy ate four peanuts.

 ...

 Amy ate forty-three million, five hundred and nine peanuts.

 ...

 ...

---

(2) A numeral is not a numbskull.
A numeral is not a nun.
A numeral is not a nunnery.

...

A numbskull is not a numeral.
A numbskull is not a nun.
A numbskull is not a nunnery.

...

A nun is not a nursery.

...

An oboe is not an octopus.

...

(3) Since a numeral is not a numbskull, a numbskull is not a nun.
Since a numeral is not a numbskull, a numbskull is not a nunnery.
Since a numeral is not a numbskull, a numbskull is not a nuptial.

...

Since a numeral is not a nursery, a numbskull is not a nun.

...

Since an oboe is not an octopus, a numeral is not a numbskull.

...

The pattern for (1) is 'Amy ate N peanuts' (N = a specific number); the pattern for (2) is 'An X is not a Y' (X and Y = any kind of noun); and the pattern for (3) is 'Since an X is not a Y, a Z is not a W' (X and Y, and Z and W = different combinations of the nouns in (2)).

> ... *With such patterns, plus a list of words to insert into them, we can specify a large number of possibilities at minimal cost in storage. Moreover, such a system is prepared for novelty: it can recognise or create examples of the pattern on the spur of the moment, whether or not they have been encountered before.* (Jackendoff, 1993; (emphasis in original).)

Another pattern corresponds to the different levels/orders of representation (see above) which characterise ToM:

(4)

(a) Bill thinks that Beth is a genius.

(b) Sue suspects that Bill thinks that Beth is a genius.

(c) Charlie said that Sue suspects that Bill thinks that Beth is a genius.

(d) Jean knows that Charlie said that Sue suspects that Bill thinks that Beth is a genius,

This sequence can be extended *indefinitely* – we can always add one more element (or level/order of representation). But recall that, according to Dunbar (2004, 2007), most adult humans are limited to five (with Shakespeare, as the author of *Othello*, displaying an exceptional six). Jackendoff (1993) points out that, unlike the sentences in (1) – (3) above, those in (4) cannot be specified by a single pattern: rather, each example has to come from a different pattern, and the patterns get longer and longer. The sentences in (5) below show the first three of these patterns: the term 'Verbs' stands for one of the words 'thinks', 'suspects', 'knows', and so on.

(5) X Verbs that Y is a Z.

W Verbs that X Verbs that Y is a Z.

T Verbs that W Verbs that X Verbs that Y is a Z.

What all these examples show is the important relationship between language and memory (see Chapter 7). Another term for 'novelty' in the quote from Jackendoff above is **creativity/ productivity**; this is one of the criteria used to define language and to assess attempts to teach language to chimps and other non-humans (see Chapter 6).

These patterns form part of **mental grammar**. The notion of a mental grammar stored in the brain of a language user is *the* central theoretical construct of modern linguistics. The basic parameters underlying a theory of language ability were first laid out by Chomsky in the late 1950s and early 1960s (Jackendoff, 1993). According to Chomsky (e.g. 1957, 1979), in order for children to acquire language, they must construct a mental grammar on the basis of an interaction between input from the environment (nurture) and their own innate resources (nature). These innate resources consist of a **language acquisition device** (LAD), which enables them to identify the features shared by all languages (**linguistic universals**) and which represents a distinct mental module (or 'organ') (see Chapter 6). '... As a result, the apparently wide differences among languages of the world – even sign languages – actually turn out to be relatively constrained variations on a theme.' (Jackendoff, 1993)

Up until very recently, recursion has been included in the list of linguistic universals. But (as we noted in Chapter 1), this claim has been challenged (e.g. Evans and Levinson, 2009; Everett, 2009a and 2009b: again, see Chapter 6).

Generative computation and music

As we saw above, Hauser's definition of generative computation extends beyond language, to include, among other things, music. Jackendoff (1993) suggests that perhaps we can analyse music (musical notation) in a similar way to how linguists analyse language. Jackendoff claims that, like language, music is a uniquely human activity; at the very least, they are both human universals (Williamson, 2009).

> ### Time for reflection
> ● In what ways – and to what extent – can music be thought of as a (kind of) language?

Similarities and differences between music and language

● Both speech and music are complex auditory sequences that unfold over time (Williamson, 2009).

● Both language and music have a 'particulate' or 'combinatory' nature (a way of referring to generative computation), i.e. they're both composed of small elements (syllables or notes) that can be assembled in an apparently infinite number of combinations (sentences or melodies) using hierarchical structural rules or syntax (Patel, 2008). In language, these rules are (collectively) called grammar; in music, they can be tonality, harmony or form.

- According to Patel's (2003) *shared syntactic integration resource hypothesis* (SSIRH), while representations of language and music are likely to be stored independently in the brain, we use similar neural networks to integrate evolving speech and music sounds. In other words, while the ingredients may be different, the way we build structure from language and music is very similar. In support of the SSIRH, music has been found to excite brain regions involved in understanding and producing language, including **Broca's** and Wernicke's **areas** (Schrock, 2009) (see Chapter 3). 'Thus, musical syntax – for instance, the order of chords in a phrase – could have arisen from the mechanisms that evolved to organise and understand grammar' (Schrock, 2009). A relevant study is described in Box 5.1.

Box 5.1 Language, music, meaning and the brain

Steinbeis and Koelsch (2008) used an **affective priming paradigm** to investigate whether music meaning could influence subsequent processing of language meaning, and vice versa. In other words, if the music/language you hear leads you to expect a pleasant sound in the other domain (e.g. the word 'love' or a consonant chord), does your processing slow down when you hear an unpleasant sound ('hate' or a dissonant chord)?

What the researchers found was that people's responses were faster when the prime matched the target. They also found evidence for similar brainwave patterns associated with inconsistent/incongruous pairings (i.e. pleasant + unpleasant sounds in the two domains). This suggests that meaning of language and music may trigger comparable brain responses. But the fMRI (brain imaging) data they collected suggested that the processing of language and music meaning *didn't* occur in identical neural structures.

However, Steinbeis and Koelsch also argued against a generalised emotion explanation for the similarities: the brain activity they identified occurred outside those areas traditionally associated with emotion conflict.

Again, while some evidence exists for musical and linguistic processing taking place in separate brain areas (based on neuroimaging: Peretz and Zatorre, 2005), other neuroimaging studies have identified common activation for tasks that involve language and music memory (Koelsch *et al.,* 2008).

Like language, music has the kind of structure that's easily learned and understood by the human mind. Research has demonstrated a number of striking similarities in the way that children come to learn about language and music. Just as very young infants have already picked up certain structural regularities of spoken language, so similar research shows they know something about the structure of music (Sloboda, 1999). This can be explained partly by the concept of infant-directed speech (IDS), which is discussed in Box 5.2.

> **Box 5.2** Infant-directed speech (IDS): the 'musicality' of baby talk
>
> Research has revealed a number of striking similarities in the way that children come to learn about language and music. **Infant-directed speech (IDS)** or 'motherese' *(or baby-talk register)* refers to the way that adults quite automatically adjust their speech when interacting with babies and young children. They do this by using a higher-pitched voice, an exaggerated use of pitch and contour (the patterns of ups and downs), and slower pace (see Gross, 2003). These features of IDS seem to be fairly universal, despite the variations in world languages (Trainor and Desjardins, 2002) and this suggests that it may be the original starting point for both music and language.
>
> According to Mithen (2005), language and music both evolved from a musical proto-language used by our hominid ancestors. Neanderthals and other extinct human ancestors appear to have had vocal chord structures which suggest they could sing – or at least hum. Ancient humans certainly played instruments: archaeologists have unearthed bone flutes that are tens of thousands of years old.
>
> The musical aspects of IDS, in particular the pitch range, may help to communicate to babies the overall emotion and intention of speech before knowledge of direct meaning develops (Trainor *et al.,* 2000). But the musical aspects may also play a more direct role in helping babies acquire language, by helping them to identify important syllable and word boundaries in speech (Trainor and Desjardins, 2002).

Sloboda (1985) found that children as young as seven can consciously choose between well-formed and ill-formed musical sequences (taken from Western tonal music, a tradition of scale structure and harmony that emerged in European music during the Renaissance: Williamson, 2009).

According to McMullen and Saffran (2004), there's an aspect of *statistical learning* to both language and music that necessarily suggests a high level of overlap in the underlying processes that may be involved. This may explain why babies show little preference for either their native language or their culture's musical conventions early in life (Trehub *et al.,* 1999). At this stage babies are still gathering information about these sounds and internalising the patterns and structures that they hear regularly. It's only later that they develop a preference for the sounds (speech or music) that they're regularly exposed to.

Our preference for musical structures also helps explain why we find it difficult to listen to music from other cultures, where different rules apply (e.g. Javanese gamelan or Japanese gagaku). It also explains why many people find it difficult to listen to atonal music, where the rule book is 'thrown out of the window' (Williamson, 2009) and processing is severely disrupted (Sloboda, 1999).

Williamson (2009) has investigated the similarities between verbal and musical short-term memory, using predictions from Baddeley and Hitch's (1974) working memory (WM) model (see Gross, 2010). For example, she has found evidence that getting people to move their articulators (i.e. whispering) can disrupt both verbal *and* musical recall. It was previously believed that the use of articulatory suppression (requiring participants to utter speech sounds in order to interfere with/prevent speech-production processes) impacted only on memory for language (probably because it occupies the speech-motor planning system of the brain that we use to rehearse speech sounds). The finding that it can also influence memory for music suggests that this system of mental rehearsal is actually involved in maintaining aspects of both speech and music sounds in memory (Williamson, 2009).

While language is a *referential* form of communication (i.e. we use it to describe/denote things in the real world, as well as images and knowledge of those things), music is largely *a-referential*. The 'floating intentionality' of music (Cross, 1999) is at the heart of its ability to engage different emotions and meanings in people (Williamson, 2009). Music clearly isn't a language in the *technical* sense and is more appropriately treated as a form of communication (Jackendoff, 1993), but studying the interactions and overlaps between music and language can tell us more about the way we engage with our auditory environment than we can ever learn from studying either in isolation. '... Continuing to explore how and why we come to employ language and music will add another important dimension in our quest to learn more about what it means to be human.' (Williamson, 2009)

Combinatorial generative computation

This second type of generative computation refers to the mixing of discrete elements to produce new ideas, which can be expressed as novel words ('Walkman') or musical forms, among other possibilities (Hauser, 2009).

Time for reflection
- Try to identify examples of **combinatorial generative computation**.

Generative computation and tool use

Hauser (2009) claims that generative computation by humans, but not other animals, is reflected in the use of tools. He gives the example of an orang-utan using a large, single leaf as an umbrella; this is typical of non-humans making implements from a single material and for a single purpose. By contrast, humans routinely combine materials to form tools and often use a given tool in a number of ways (they are multi-purpose). Hauser's example is the No. 2 pencil (see Box 5.3).

▲ **Figure 5.1** Orang-utan using leaf as umbrella

Box 5.3 The No.2 pencil: Drawing on human versatility

▲ **Figure 5.2** No. 2 pencil

Hauser (2009) describes the No. 2 pencil as one of our most basic tools, used by every test taker (in America, anyway): it 'illustrates the exceptional freedom of the human mind as compared with the limited scope of animal cognition'.

You hold the pencil's painted wood, use the lead for writing and drawing, and erase with the pink rubber held in place by a metal ring: four different materials, each with a particular function, all wrapped up into a single tool. Although that tool was designed as a writing implement, it can also be used to pin long hair up into a bun, as a bookmark, or to stab an annoying insect. By contrast, animal tools – such as the stick chimps use to fish termites out from their mounds – consist of a single material, designed for a single purpose, and never used for any other. None has the combinatorial properties of the pencil.

Hauser gives another example of a human tool, this time one that demonstrates *recursion*, namely, the telescopic, collapsible cup found in many a camper's gear. To make this device, the manufacturer need only programme in one simple rule: add a segment of increasing size to the last segment and repeat until the desired size is reached. As we saw above in relation to language and music, humans use recursive operations like this in all aspects of mental life, as well as the generation of a limitless range of movements with our legs, hands and mouths.

Hauser argues that the only evidence of any kind of recursion in non-humans comes from watching their motor systems in action: 'All creatures are endowed with recursive motor machinery as part of their standard operating equipment.' To walk, they put one foot in front of the other, over and over again; to eat, they may grasp an object and bring it to their mouth repeatedly until the stomach sends the signal to stop. In animal minds, this recursive system is locked away in the brain's motor regions, closed off from other brain areas. This suggests that:

> *... a critical step in acquiring our own distinctive brand of thinking was not the evolution of recursion as a novel form of computation but the release of recursion from its motor prison to other domains of thought. How it was unlocked from this restrictive function links to ... promiscuous interfaces ...* (Hauser, 2009)

This is a way of referring to the promiscuous combination of ideas (see below).

Tool use and causal understanding

According to Wolpert (2007), causal understanding is unique to humans. There are, of course, similarities between human and mammalian (and especially primate) cognition: **primates** remember their local environment, take novel detours, follow object movement, recognise similarities and have some insight into problem solving. They also recognise individuals, predict their behaviour (see Chapter 4) and form alliances (see Chapter 9). However, they have little understanding of the causal relationships between inanimate objects.

> ... *They [primates] do not view the world in terms of underlying 'forces' that are fundamental to human thinking. They do not understand the world in intentional or causal terms (Povinelli, 2000; Tomasello, 1999). Non-human primates do not understand the causal relation between their acts and the outcomes they experience ...* (Wolpert, 2007)

In one of Povinelli's experiments (Povinelli, 2000), chimps could choose one of two rake tools to obtain a food reward: dragging food along a solid surface (the 'successful' choice) or dragging it over a large hole into which the food would fall. Only one of six chimps was successful, and the solitary success may have been due to chance at the first trial (although they all eventually learned the correct choice by **trial and error**). They also did badly with an inverted two-prong rake that could not move the food and on tests with flimsy tools. Again, when required to obtain a banana by pulling on a rope, they couldn't distinguish between (a) a rope that just lay on, or very close to, the banana; and (b) a rope that was actually tied to the banana. They showed no appreciation of physical connections as distinct from mere contact.

In another series of key experiments, chimps were set the task of using a stick to push food out of a clear tube. The tools were of various sizes, some being too short, too thick, or too flexible. An understanding of 'basic forces' should enable an individual to choose the right tool, and chimps managed to do this, but only after considerable trial and error. In another test, there was a small trap under part of the tube and to get the food, the chimp had to push the food from the end of the tube that avoided the trap. During 70 trials, the chimps performed no better than chance. Once they'd eventually learned how to avoid the trap, the tube was rotated through 180 degrees. Although the trap was now irrelevant as far as getting the food was concerned, the chimps continued to push the food away from the trap. By contrast, two- to three-year-old children understood what to do from the earliest trials.

Chimps' use of tools in the wild

In the experiments described above, chimps were being presented with human-made tools for use in contrived, artificially created tasks in an unnatural environment. What do observations of chimps in the wild tell us about their ability to both use and create tools?

The photograph in Figure 5.3 of the chimp extracting termites by using a stick is one that makes a lasting impression. An equally iconic image is that of 'cavemen' making stone tools and weapons for hunting.

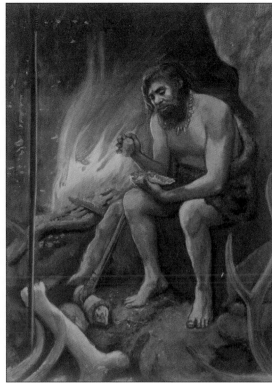

▲ **Figure 5.4** Early humans making stone tools

▲ **Figure 5.3** Chimpanzee using a stick to extract termites

One human exceptionalism argument (see Chapter 1), 'Man the toolmaker', was proposed by Kenneth Oakley of the Natural History Museum in London and was popular during the 1940s and 1950s: the making and using of stone tools (not weapons for fighting other humans) provided the impetus for human evolution. Significantly, during these decades the world was enthralled by the magic and power of technology (Leakey, 1994).

Leakey goes on to say that while chimps are adept tool *users* (e.g. using sticks to harvest termites, leaves as sponges, and stones to crack nuts):

> *... so far, at any rate – no chimpanzee in the wild has ever been seen to* manufacture *a stone tool. Humans began producing sharp-edged tools 2.5 million years ago by hitting two stones together, thus beginning a trail of technological activity that highlights human prehistory.*
> (Leakey, 1994 (emphasis added).

Perhaps we need to separate the two strands of this exceptionalism argument: (a) humans are the only tool-*making* species; and (b) it is the making of *stone* tools that is distinctive about human beings.

Tool using

Much of what we now know about chimps' use (and manufacture: see below) of tools is the result of the pioneering field work of Jane Goodall during the 1960s and 1970s (e.g. 1988) in Gombe National Park, Tanzania. For example, she describes a two-year old chimp, Merlin, who picked up a thin twig and, holding it rather like a human infant first holds a spoon, prodded with it at the surface of a termite heap. A year later, his tool-using ability had improved (but was still far from efficient): he almost always chose grasses or twigs that were too short (about two inches long compared with the 8–12 inch length used by adults. He also manipulated his tiny tools clumsily and incompetently: he pushed them quite carefully into termite passages but then almost instantly yanked them out, so any termite that might have been clinging on would almost certainly have been thrown off. Once he pushed a thick piece of straw firmly into a hole – but it got stuck and he couldn't pull it out!

Tool making

Over a period of time, Goodall observed two other, older chimps, David Graybeard and Goliath (who spent a lot of time together), scratching open the sealed-over entrances to termite passages with a thumb or forefinger. They bit off the end of their stick-tools when they became bent, or used the other end, or discarded them in favour of new ones. Goliath once moved at least 15 yards from the termite mound to select a firm-looking piece of vine; both males often picked up three or four stems while they were collecting tools and put the spares next to them on the ground until they needed them.

> *Most exciting of all, on several occasions they picked small leafy twigs and prepared them for use by stripping off the leaves. This was the first recorded example of a wild animal not merely using an object as a tool, but actually modifying an object and thus showing the crude beginnings of tool*making. (Goodall, 1988) (emphasis in original).

As we have already noted, humans had traditionally been regarded as the only tool-making animal. Indeed, one of the clauses within the widely accepted definition of *Homo sapiens* was that he was a creature who 'made tools to a regular and set pattern'. Clearly, as Goodall admits, her chimps had *not* made their tools to any set pattern: '... but, then, prehistoric man, before his development of stone tools, undoubtedly poked around with sticks and straws, at which stage it seems unlikely that he made tools to a set pattern, either.' (Goodall, 1988)

According to Goodall, the ability to use an object as a tool, on its own, doesn't necessarily indicate any special intelligence in the animal concerned. The fact that the Galapagos woodpecker finch uses a cactus spine or twig to probe insects from crevices in the bark of a tree is a fascinating phenomenon, but it doesn't make the bird more intelligent than a genuine woodpecker that uses its long beak and tongue for the same purpose.

> *The point at which tool-using and toolmaking, as such, acquire evolutionary significance is surely when an animal can adapt its ability to manipulate objects to a wide variety of purposes, and when it can use an object spontaneously to solve a brand-new problem that without the use of a tool would prove insoluble.* (Goodall, 1988)

This sounds very much like Hauser's generative computation, which, he claims, is only demonstrated through human tool use and tool making. But does Goodall provide any evidence that chimps also display generative computation?

Box 5.4 Do chimps demonstrate generative computation?

▲ **Figure 5.5** Sultan demonstrating insight learning and tool making

Goodall (1988) observed chimps using objects for many different purposes. They use stems and sticks to capture and eat insects and, if the material chosen is not suitable, then it's modified. They use leaves to mop up water they cannot reach with their lips; first they chew on the leaves, thereby increasing their absorbency. One individual used a similar sponge to clean out the last smears of brain from the inside of a baboon skull. They have also been seen using handfuls of leaves to wipe dirt from their bodies, to dab at wounds, and sometimes as toilet paper (after a bout of diarrhoea). They sometimes use sticks as levers to enlarge underground bees' nests. Sticks may also be used as weapons. As we noted earlier, leaves are stripped from a stem to make a tool suitable for termite-fishing; the edges of a wide blade of grass may be stripped off in order to make an appropriate tool.

Goodall also notes that chimps in captivity often use objects as tools quite spontaneously. She cites Wolfgang Kohler's (1925) famous studies of Sultan and other chimps, who used sticks to try to prise open box lids and to dig the ground for roots. Like wild chimps, they wiped themselves with leaves or straw, scratched themselves with stones and poked straws into columns of ants in order to eat them just as wild chimps fish for termites. They, too, often used sticks and stones as weapons during aggressive encounters. Sometimes, they used bread as bait to lure chickens close to their enclosure, whereupon they would suddenly prod the birds with sharp sticks – apparently for fun!

Kohler's research is better known for chimps' display of 'insight' learning (as opposed to trial and error learning) when trying to solve problems (usually involving obtaining bananas that were out of arm's length: see Gross, 2010). For example, Köhler suspended, out of reach, a bunch of bananas from the ceiling of Sultan's cage, which contained several items that could be used to reach the bananas (such as sticks of different length and empty boxes) – but none on its own was sufficient. Eventually, Sultan solved the problem by stacking empty boxes on top of each other and climbing onto them (as shown in Figure 5.5).

Later, Köhler allowed Sultan to see a box being placed in the corridor leading to his cage. He was then taken to his cage where, again, bananas were suspended from the ceiling. Sultan's first strategy was to remove a long bolt from the open cage's door. But then, quite suddenly, he stopped, ran down the corridor, and returned with the box which was again used to retrieve the bananas. For Köhler (one of the pioneering Gestalt psychologists), Sultan's behaviour was a result of sudden **perceptual reorganisation** (or insight), as distinct from trial-and-error learning (which is what is often taken to be the basis of operant/instrumental conditioning: see Gross, 2010).

Tool making and causal understanding

Wolpert (2007) cites the case of Kanzi, one of the bonobos studied by Sue Savage-Rumbaugh in the context of language acquisition (see Chapter 6). *Bonobos* (or pygmy chimps) are slightly smaller than common chimps (*Pan troglodytes*), more vocal and communicative through facial expressions and gestures, and generally more 'intelligent'. Kanzi has shown remarkable skills, such as learning to create and use stone tools to gain access to food, cutting a rope, and making stone flakes and evaluating them after observing a human striking two rocks together. On his own, Kanzi produced flakes by throwing one rock onto another on the ground, suggesting that he may indeed have a concept of force (unlike common chimps).

> ### Time for reflection
> ● To what extent does the evidence described above suggest that, contrary to Hauser's claim that only humans demonstrate generative computation, chimps are capable of this cognitive ability as shown in their tool use and tool making?

While common chimps do appreciate that contact is necessary in using a tool to get food, they focus on the contact and ignore the force it generates on the target object. If a chimp sees the wind blowing and shaking a branch till the fruit falls, it will never learn from this to shake the branch to get the fruit (Wolpert, 2007).

In the tropical forests of West Africa, chimps have been observed spending hours using stone or wooden hammers to break open the shells of nuts by first placing them on a stone (the anvil). However, there's no evidence of any real tool making, or of selection of stones according to the material they are made of; only the weight of the stone appears to have been taken into account. However, chimps have been seen to make the anvil level by placing a stone underneath it at the low end; this demonstrates a physical causal understanding. The nut-cracking technique of the Tai chimp requires about ten years of practice to master in the wild (Wolpert, 2007).

It's not only great apes that display causal understanding. A commonly cited example of a non-primate species displaying this ability is the New Caledonian crow, which manufactures and uses several types of tools, including straight and hooked sticks, and complex stepped-cut flat tools made from leaves which are used for extracting insects (Chappell and Kacelnik, 2002). These tools have some of the hallmarks of complex tool manufacture: form is imposed on the raw material with control of various shapes. A skilled tool-making technique is involved, and there's even standardisation of the shape of the finished tools. The birds show evidence of causal belief (Wolpert, 2007). Wolpert concludes his review of the evidence by saying:

> *... while primates and some birds use simple tools there is an almost total absence of causal beliefs in animals other than humans ... they [animals like crows and monkeys] have a very limited capacity for refining and combining objects to make better tools. The tools chimpanzees use have a narrow range of functions and there is little evidence that they can think up new functions for the same tool. Compare this with the way humans use a knife for a whole variety of purposes ...* (Wolpert, 2007)

Tools, evolution and technology

Perhaps the most critical difference of all (although arguably *not* part of Hauser's concept of generative computation – and going beyond it), is that chimps (unlike humans) have never been observed using one tool to make another (i.e. tools that were made by the use of another tool: *secondary tools*) (Goodall, 1988; Wolpert, 2007). Even simple stone tools require a hammer stone. It may be that stone hammers, like those used by chimps to break hard-shelled fruits or nuts, were later used by our hominid ancestors to shape rocks for cutting tools. Our tool-making ancestors also had to be competent field geologists in recognising which rocks were suitable for tool making. Some two million years ago, humans had acquired the skill needed for making stone tools – yet even for a modern human this takes several hours to master (Wolpert, 2007).

According to Wolpert (2007), one cannot make a complex tool without a concept of cause and effect. By 'complex' he means a tool that has a well characterised form for the use it will be put to; even more importantly, it describes any tool made out of two pieces put together (such as a spear and a stone head). In evolutionary terms, the advantage of causal beliefs is how they are related to the making of complex tools: '… It is only with causal beliefs that technology became possible, and it was technology – the ability to physically interact with the environment – that made life easier. Just consider things as simple as the basket and the wheel.' (Wolpert, 2007)

According to Schick and Toth (1993):

> It is the technological path that we humans took that has separated us most profoundly from our primate ancestry and from our extant primate relatives. Our technological adaptation has been shaping our evolutionary trajectory in crucial ways for the past several million years.

More recently, Kelly (2010) has claimed that technology is an extension of evolutionary life, a selfish system with its own urges and desires (such as diversity, beauty and complexity: see Chapter 9).

Time for reflection

Kelly defines technology in the broadest way, embracing all 'inventions' (including language and culture).

- Do you consider this to be an appropriate way of defining technology?
- Is it appropriate – or logically meaningful – to describe technology as a 'selfish system'?
- He compares the invention of the internet with the invention of language? How would you assess his claim?

(See Box 5.5 on page 112.)

Promiscuous combination of ideas, mental symbols and abstract thought

It's useful to consider the other three components of Hauser's 'humaniqueness' in the context of his discussion of the differences between human language and animal communication; these other three components are described in Box 5.5.

Box 5.5 Other components of Hauser's 'humaniqueness'

The second component of Hauser's 'humaniqueness' is the *promiscuous combination of ideas*. According to Hauser (2009):

> We routinely connect thoughts from different domains of knowledge, allowing our understanding of art, sex, space, causality and friendship to combine. From this mingling, new laws, social relationships and technologies can result, as when we decide that it is forbidden [moral domain] to push someone [motor action domain] intentionally [folk psychology domain] in front of a train [object domain] to save the lives [moral domain] of five [number domain] others.

The third component is *mental symbols*: we can spontaneously convert any sensory experience – real or imagined – into a symbol that we can either keep private or share with others through language, art, music or computer code.

The fourth component is *abstract thought*: unlike animal thoughts, which are largely anchored in sensory and perceptual experiences, many human thoughts are not. 'We alone ponder the likes of unicorns, nouns and verbs, infinity and God.'

Like other animals, humans have a non-verbal communication system that expresses their emotions and motivations to others. But humans alone have a system of linguistic communication based on the manipulation of mental symbols, with each example of a symbol falling into a specific and abstract category (such as noun, verb, and adjective):

> Although some animals have sounds that appear to represent more than their emotions, conveying information about objects and events such as food, sex and predation, the range of such sounds pales in relation to our own, and none of them falls into the abstract categories that structure our linguistic expressions. (Hauser, 2009)

Time for reflection

- Might the differences that Hauser describes be ones of degree rather than of kind (quantitative versus qualitative, respectively)?
- Hauser himself alludes to the possibility that animal vocabularies appear small because researchers simply do not understand animal communication well enough. Could this partially explain why we see human language as beyond the reach of other species?

(These issues are discussed in greater detail in Chapter 6.)

Animals' use of symbols

According to Hauser, even if the famous honeybee's waggle dance (which 'informs' the hive of the precise location of a pollen source) *symbolically represents* that location, and the putty-nosed monkey's alarm call *symbolically represents* different predators, these uses of symbols differ from ours in five fundamental ways:

1. They are triggered only by real objects or events, never imagined ones.
2. They are restricted to the present (see Chapter 7).
3. They are not part of a more abstract classification scheme, such as that which organises our words into nouns, verbs and adjectives.
4. They are rarely combined with other symbols and when they are, the combinations are limited to a string of two, with no rules.
5. They are fixed to particular contexts.

Another remarkable difference between human language and animal communication is that language operates equally well in the visual and auditory modes: a deaf person using sign language can convey anything that a hearing person can communicate via speech: they're equally expressive and structurally complex. But if a songbird loses its voice and a honeybee its waggle, their ability to communicate would be eradicated.

The 'promiscuous combination of ideas'

To illustrate the 'promiscuous combination of ideas', Hauser observes that our linguistic knowledge, along with the computations it requires, also interacts with other domains of knowledge/systems of understanding in fascinating, and uniquely human, ways. He asks us to consider the ability to quantify objects and events, a capacity that we share with other animals. A wide variety of species have at least two non-linguistic counting abilities: (a) one is precise and limited to numbers less than four; (b) the other is unlimited in scope, but is approximate and limited to certain ratios for discrimination. An animal that can discriminate one from two, for example, can also discriminate 2 from 4, 16 from 32, and so on. (a) is anchored in a brain region involved in keeping track of individuals; while (b) is anchored in brain regions that compute magnitudes.

Hauser describes a recently identified third counting system in rhesus monkeys, which may help to explain the origins of the human ability to mark the difference between singular and plural. This system operates when individuals see sets of objects (such as food items) presented at the same time (as opposed to serially/sequentially): they discriminate one from many, but not many from many. In Hauser's experiment, a rhesus monkey was shown one apple, which was then placed in a box. The same monkey then saw five apples and all five at once were put into a second box. Given a choice, the monkey consistently picked the second box with five apples. Then two apples were put into one box and five into the other. This time, the monkey did not show a consistent preference. Humans do essentially the same when we say 'one apple' and 'two, five or one hundred apples'.

But what happens when the human linguistic system connects up with this more ancient conceptual system?

> ### Time for reflection
> - For the numbers 0, 0.2 and −5, add the most appropriate word: 'apple' or 'apples'.
> - Which word would you select for 1.0?

If you are like most native English speakers, you opted for 'apples'. Hauser says it's good if you're surprised by this. If you think about it rationally, 'apple' (i.e. singular) is the correct choice, so we couldn't have learned this as a grammatical rule in school. It's part of the universal grammar we are born with. The rule is simple but abstract: anything that's not 'one' is pluralised.

This apple example demonstrates how different systems – syntax and the concept of sets – interact to produce new ways of thinking about or conceptualising the world. But the creativity process in humans doesn't stop there: we apply our language and number systems to cases of morality (saving five people is better than saving one), economics (if I'm given £10 and offer you £1, that seems unfair, and you'll reject the £1), and taboo trade-offs (in Western Europe and the US, selling our children, even for lots of money (or especially for lots of money?) isn't acceptable) (Hauser, 2009).

Mental symbols and abstract thoughts

Almost by definition, domains of knowledge/systems of understanding are *abstract*, that is, the terms we use to refer to them (e.g. economics, morality, language, grammar) don't denote anything that is tangible or perceptible in any other way: they're collective, 'higher-level' representations of real individual objects, events, activities and so on. But even here, things are far from straightforward. In that list given in the previous sentence, the terms all refer to abstract categories. For example, while we can visualise a specific object (say, a vase), we cannot visualise the category of 'object' (not, at least, without trying to picture a *particular* object). The category 'object' embraces an enormous range of things (e.g. cars, food, furniture, cleaning products, electrical goods), and each of these examples itself illustrates another abstract concept (but at a lower level in the mental hierarchy made up of all these concepts). Go into any supermarket and you'll see how 'food' (and, increasingly, other 'products') is separated into categories (e.g. the large signs above each aisle, then smaller labels on the shelves within each aisle). Similarly, within department or DIY stores, or 'specialist' music, computer or electrical goods stores. The aim is to help customers locate a specific item without them having to literally look at every single available product (or ask the invariably invisible member-of-staff).

Imagine how chaotic (and time-consuming) it would be if these stores weren't organised in this way. Now imagine how chaotic a place our minds would be if they weren't also organised in this way. However, while both stores and minds need to be organised, it's only minds that are/need to be organised *hierarchically*, and it's *language* that makes this possible. The crucial point here is that the world doesn't come naturally categorised or 'cut up' in this way: it's something that the human mind creates or constructs out of the 'raw material' of sensory experience. But just as human languages themselves differ (as well as sharing many fundamental attributes), so different cultures create different categories and concepts (see Chapter 9). As we've seen, language frees us from the here-and-now, our immediate environment, allowing us to explore what *could* be (or might have been) through the use of imagination.

Humans as symbolic creatures

As we saw in Chapter 1, Tattersall (2007) sees human beings (unlike other primates) as *symbolic* creatures, with language the ultimate symbolic activity. The world we occupy isn't the one presented to us directly by nature, but rather the one we've created in our heads through the use of language. Similarly, Dunbar (2007) claims that what makes humans unique is their ability to step back from the real world and ask how things could be different from how they experience it. Literature and science both, in their very different ways, try to address this question, and both are deeply symbolic activities.

A number of philosophers have based a human exceptionalism approach on the use of symbols in human life. For example, Ritchie (1936) argued that: '... As far as thought is concerned, and at all levels of thought, it [mental life] is a symbolic process. It is mental not because the symbols are immaterial ... but because they are symbols ... The essential act of thought is symbolisation ...'

According to Langer (1951), '... symbolism is the recognised key to that mental life which is characteristically human and above the level of sheer animality. Symbol and meaning make man's world far more than sensation ...' Similarly, Cassirer (1944) claims that:

> ... in the human world we find a new characteristic which appears to be the distinctive mark of human life. The functional circle of man is not only quantitatively enlarged; it has also undergone a qualitative change. Man has, as it were, discovered a new method of adapting himself to his environment. Between the receptor system and the effector system, which are to be found in all animal species, we find in a man a third link which we may describe as the symbolic system. This ... transforms the whole of human life. As compared with the other animals man lives not merely in a broader reality; he lives, so to speak, in a new dimension of reality ... (emphasis in original.)

And again: '... No longer in a merely physical universe, man lives in a symbolic universe. Language, myth, art, and religion are parts of this universe. They are the varied threads which weave the symbolic net, the tangled web of human experience ...' (Cassirer, 1944)

Both Langer and Cassirer cite the cases of Helen Keller and Laura Bridgman, both of whom were blind and deaf-mute, and so deeply reliant on the sense of touch. According to Langer (1951), despite these disabilities, both women were capable of 'living in a wider and richer world than a dog or an ape with all his senses alert'. Their cases are described in Box 5.6.

Box 5.6 Helen Keller (1902, 1908) and Laura Bridgford (Lamson, 1881)

Helen Keller's teacher, Mrs Sullivan, wrote:

> ... something very important has happened. Helen has taken the second great step in her education. She has learned that everything has a name, and that the manual alphabet is the key to everything she wants to know.

> ... This morning, while she was washing, she wanted to know the name for 'water'. When she wants to know the name of anything, she points to it, and pats my hand. I spelled 'w-a-t-e-r' and thought no more about it ... [Later on] we went out to the pump house, and I made Helen hold her mug under the spout while I pumped. As the cold water gushed forth,

---

Box 5.6 *Continued*

filling the mug, I spelled 'w-a-t-e-r' in Helen's free hand ... She dropped the mug and stood as one transfixed. A new light came into her face. She spelled 'water' several times. Then she dropped on the ground and asked for its name and pointed to the pump and the trellis and suddenly turning round she asked for my name. I spelled 'teacher'. All the way back to the house she was highly excited, and learned the name of every object she touched, so that in a few hours she had added thirty new words to her vocabulary. The next morning she ... flitted from object to object, asking the name of everything ... Everything must have a name now. Wherever we go, she asks eagerly for the names of things she has not learned at home ... her face grows more expressive each day. (Mrs Sullivan in Cassirer, 1944).

Helen Keller (who was seven at the time of these events) had previously learned to combine a certain thing or event with a certain sign of the manual alphabet: a fixed association had been established between these things and particular tactile impressions. But a series of such impressions, even if repeated and amplified, still doesn't imply an understanding of what human speech is and means: what's needed is the understanding that *everything has a name* – 'that the symbolic function isn't restricted to particular cases but is a principle of *universal* applicability which encompasses the whole field of human thought' (Cassirer, 1944). As usually happens some years earlier, Helen had come to use words as symbols – rather than mechanical signs or signals.

Laura Bridgman was greatly inferior to Helen Keller, both in intellectual ability and development. Yet, despite the absence of dramatic events as in Helen's case, Laura also suddenly reached the point where she began to understand the symbolism of human speech (having learned to use the finger alphabet), so there's a surprising parallel between the two cases (Cassirer, 1944).

According to Cassirer (1944):

The principle of symbolism, with its universality, validity, and general applicability, is the magic word, the Open Sesame! giving access to the specifically human world, to the world of human culture. Once man is in possession of this magic key further progress is assured. Such progress is evidently not obstructed or made impossible by any lack in the sense material ...

Cassirer goes on to point out that the case of Helen Keller, who reached a very high degree of intellectual development, shows 'clearly and irrefutably that a human being in the construction of his human world is not dependent upon the quality of his sense material' (i.e. the 'raw material' that reaches the brain via the sense organs). If *sensationalist* theories were correct in claiming that every idea were merely a faint copy of an original sense impression, then 'the condition of a blind, deaf, and dumb child would indeed be desperate'. Such a child would be an 'exile from reality'. But Helen Keller's case shows this not to be true: while speech may confer great technical advantages compared with a tactile language (the finger alphabet):

... The free development of symbolic thought and symbolic expression is not obstructed by the use of tactile signs in the place of vocal ones. If the child has succeeded in grasping the meaning of human language, it does not matter in which particular material this meaning is accessible to it ... (Cassirer, 1944)

In other words, meaning can be conveyed in different ways, in different forms, and speech (spoken language) is just one way, one form. Again, it's not the raw material that matters, but the 'finished article':

> ... *The thing of vital importance is not the individual bricks and stones but their general function* as architectural form. *In the realm of speech it is their general symbolic function which vivifies the material signs and 'makes them speak'. Without this vivifying principle the human mind would indeed remain deaf and mute. With this principle, even the world of a deaf, dumb, and blind child can become incomparably broader and richer than the world of the most highly developed animal.* (Cassirer, 1944)

Time for reflection

● What are the implications of Cassirer's arguments for the claim, based on attempts to teach language to non-humans (especially chimps), that language isn't a human species-specific behaviour? (See also Chapter 6.)

Cassirer's arguments are highly relevant to the claims made regarding non-human animals' capacity to *acquire* language. Their lack of speech clearly doesn't automatically disqualify them from acquiring language in some other form (such as American Sign Language), but at the same time their ability to use sign language doesn't necessarily imply that they grasp the *meaning* of those signs. One contentious issue in this area of research relates to the understanding that 'everything has a name' (see above and Chapter 6).

Cassirer points out that symbols aren't only *universal*, but, as a complementary characteristic, they're extremely *variable*: the same meaning can be expressed in different languages, and even within the limits of a single language, a particular thought or idea can be expressed in quite different ways. By contrast, a sign or a signal is related to the thing it refers to in a fixed and unique way. Cassirer gives the example of the unconditioned/conditioned stimuli in Pavlov's (1927) famous classical conditioning experiments with dogs (see Gross, 2010).

Unlike signs and signals, a genuine human symbol is versatile, not rigid or inflexible but mobile and dynamic. However, Cassirer observes that the full *awareness* of this mobility seems to be a rather late achievement in human intellectual and cultural development:

> ... *In primitive mentality this awareness is very seldom attained. Here the symbol is still regarded as a property of the thing like other physical properties. In mythical thought the name of a god is an integral part of the nature of the god. If I do not call the god by his right name, then the spell or prayer becomes ineffective. The same holds good for symbolic actions. A religious rite, a sacrifice, must always be performed in the same invariable way and in the same order if it is to have its effect ...* (Cassirer, 1944)

Langer (1951) regards the *need for symbolisation* as a basic – and uniquely – human need:

> ... *The symbol-making function is one of man's primary activities, like eating, looking, or moving about. It is the fundamental process of his mind, and goes on all the time. Sometimes we are aware of it, sometimes we merely find its results, and realise that certain experiences have passed through our brains and have been digested there.*

Imagery, imagination and meta-representation

Imagery typically comprises a *mental representation* (a picture in your head) of something in the outside, physical world. It can either be produced by sensory input or it can occur 'spontaneously' (as in dreaming or merely thinking). Mental images, typically, are faithful, accurate representations (they have 'truth relationships' to the outside world) (Baron-Cohen, 2006).

According to Leslie (1987), *imagination* basically involves three steps:

1. Take a 'primary' representation (an image that has truth relations to the outside world).

2. Then make a *copy* of this primary representation (a 'second-order' representation).

3. Then introduce some *change* to this second-order representation, playing with its truth relationships to the outside world but without jeopardising the important truth relationships the original image needs to preserve. This third step might involve *deleting* features from the original image, and/or *adding* features, then *fusing* two second-order representations together. For Leslie, when you use your imagination, you leave your primary representation untouched (you put it 'in quarantine'), but once you have a 'photocopy' of this image, you can do pretty much whatever you like with it.

Time for reflection

● Using Leslie's three-step process, describe how you might imagine a mermaid (example taken from Baron-Cohen, 2006).

As important as an image's truth relationships to the outside world may be for survival (as when our image of a dangerous animal is produced by a real lion waiting to pounce),

> ... the human brain ... can be ratcheted up to do more than just represent the outside world veridically, and modifying second-order representations opens up a world of new possibilities. It allows the brain to think about the possible, the hypothetical, about currently untrue states of affairs. (Baron-Cohen, 2006)

Imagination can produce 'hybrids', an image of something that doesn't actually exist, but which deletes from, adds to, then fuses together, features of things that do. Children's pretend play allows them to imagine hypothetical worlds, arguably a prerequisite for the serious enterprise of planning and engineering, as well as art or science (Baron-Cohen, 2006).

While any animal with a sensory system (such as vision, which includes the sense organ, the eye and a neural connection (the optic nerve) to a specialised brain area – the visual cortex) can produce an image (a primary representation), there's a lively debate about whether any non-human animals can produce second-order representations.

Mind-reading

Time for reflection

Leslie (1987) called steps 2 and 3 described above the 'meta-representational capacity', a mechanism that lies at the heart of the human ability to mind-read.

- Look back at research into **theory of mind** (**ToM**) involving chimps and other primates in Chapter 4. What conclusions could you draw from this research regarding non-humans' possession of imagination?

In what sense might a meta-representational capacity be essential for **mind-reading**? According to Leslie, when you mind-read (put yourself in someone else's shoes, imagine their thoughts and feelings), you need to 'quarantine' your primary representations (just as the child needs to do this in its pretend play).

Time for reflection

- Again using Leslie's three-step process, describe how you might believe ('imagine') that 'Mary believes that "John is having an affair with his colleague"'.

'John is having an affair with his colleague' is a primary representation of an external situation, and is true if John is actually having the affair. But when we mind-read, we again take the primary representation (step 1), *copy* it so that it becomes a secondary representation (step 2), and can then, if we wish, *add* a prefix such as 'Mary believes that' to the second-order representation to give 'Mary believes that "John is having an affair with his colleague"' (step 3).

Such second-order representations have a unique logical property: what philosophers of mind call **referential opacity**: 'Mary believes that "John is having an affair with his colleague"' is true if Mary believes it, regardless of whether John is really having an affair. Similarly, 'Pretend that "this tea-cup is hot"' is true, irrespective of whether the tea-cup is really hot. (Indeed, the child might be pretending that a (real) doll's shoe is a (pretend) tea-cup.). So, according to Leslie, both mind-reading and imagination involve such second-order representations. As Baron-Cohen puts it:

> ... *To mind-read, or to imagine the world from someone else's different perspective, one has to switch from one's own primary representations (what one takes to be true of the world) to someone else's representation (what they take to be true of the world, even if this could be untrue). Arguably, empathy, dialogue and relationships are all impossible without such an ability to switch between our primary and our second-order representations.* (Baron-Cohen, 2006)

For Leslie, the capacity for meta-representation involves a special module in the brain, which humans possess and that possibly no other species does:

> ... *In the vast majority of the population, this module functions well. It can be seen in the normal 14-month-old infant, who can introduce pretence into their play; in the normal four-year-old child, who can employ mind-reading in their relationships and thus appreciate different points of view; or in the adult novelist, who can imagine all sorts of scenarios that exist nowhere except in her own imagination, and in the imagination of her reader.* (Baron-Cohen, 2006)

121

Meta-representation and the autistic spectrum

As Baron-Cohen (2006) points out, this special module can sometimes fail to develop normally. Children with Asperger's Syndrome have degrees of difficulty with mind-reading, while those diagnosed with severe or extreme (classic) autism may never develop mind-reading to any degree (see Gross, 2008). Asperger's Syndrome and classic autism are both sub-groups of the 'autistic spectrum'. Some, including Baron-Cohen (2003), argue that this spectrum is caused by *genetic* factors affecting brain development; this implies that the capacity for meta-representation itself may depend on genes that can build the relevant brain structures that allow us to imagine other people's worlds (see Chapters 2 and 3).

Children with classic autism may end up with an exclusive interest in the real – physical – world, with no interest at all in either mind-reading, pretending or fiction. They may enjoy making patterns with real objects, or watching how real objects behave, but it never occurs to them to consider how someone else might be feeling or thinking. Imagination is also a non-starter. Children with Asperger's Syndrome may eventually manage to mind-read to a limited extent, but as adults they may still find empathy challenging. They may show a preference for reading factual material over fiction, or for documentaries over fictional films (Baron-Cohen, 2006).

Conclusions: meta-representation and metaphor

While Hauser doesn't explicitly use the term 'meta-representation', much of what he says regarding humaniqueness could be summarised using that concept. If, as Leslie (1987) claims, meta-representation lies at the heart of mind-reading, could it perhaps also be a central feature of human thought in general?

As we've seen, Baron-Cohen (1995, 2003, 2006) argues that individuals who fall on the autistic spectrum think about, and interact with, the world largely at the primary representational level; putting this another way, they understand the world (including other people) in a very *literal* way. As we saw in Chapter 4, asked where someone who doesn't know that an object has been moved from place X to place Y would look for it, autistic individuals would answer 'place Y', that is, where the object actually – and currently – is. To mind-read, you have to put yourself in the person's shoes: since this person believes the object is (still) in place X, this would be the correct answer and this involves a meta-representation, a step removed from the concrete, literal, reality of the situation.

In a similar way, much of our use of language involves meta-representation. When describing Leslie's (1987) three-step account of imagination above, we noted that when you use your imagination, you leave your primary representation untouched (you put it 'in quarantine'), but once you have a 'photocopy' of this image, you can do pretty much whatever you like with it. The use of 'quarantine' and 'photocopy' here illustrates the use of *metaphor*: the use of words in a non-literal (meta-representational) way, based on their literal (primary representational) meaning. The idea is that we can better understand something (in this case, a largely private, internal psychological process, which is also an abstract concept) by likening it to something concrete, tangible, physically and publicly real.

Perhaps a crucial aspect of what it means to be a symbolic creature is captured in this concept of metaphor. Although we make the important distinction between literal and metaphorical use of language, there may be something essentially metaphorical about *all* language, in the sense that, by definition, symbols (such as words) bear no intrinsic, inherent relationship to what they represent/stand for. But our thinking becomes so 'saturated' (another metaphor!) with the particular symbols we happen to use in our native language, that they appear to take on a concrete, literal reality that, in truth, they don't have. Perhaps this helps explain why it is so difficult to learn a second language (at least, as an adult): we have to 'photocopy' the list of symbols we're used to, and 'quarantine' it before we can start to use another list. Another language is like a meta-representation of our own beliefs about the world derived from all the years of thinking in our native tongue. Maybe *all* language use is metaphorical – but some uses are more metaphorical than others!

According to Langer (1951), thought starts out as metaphor before becoming more literal: at least as far as new ideas are concerned, the meta-representational *precedes* the primary representational:

> *Metaphor is our most striking evidence of* abstractive seeing, *of the power of the human mind to use presentational symbols. Every new experience, or new idea about things, evokes first of all some metaphorical expression. As the idea becomes familiar, this expression 'fades' to a new literal use of the once metaphorical predicate, a more general use than it had before ... The use of metaphor can hardly be called a conscious device. It is the power whereby language, even with a small vocabulary, manages to embrace a multimillion things; whereby new words are born and merely analogical meanings become stereotyped into literal definitions ...* (Langer, 1951) (emphasis in original)

Perhaps what this demonstrates is that we can only understand something new in terms of what we already know and understand. While this begs fundamental questions as to how we acquire understanding of *anything* in the first place, there's little doubt that language is the major symbolic tool that humans use for understanding the world. Language is discussed in Chapter 6.

Chapter summary

- Hauser believes that there's increasing evidence for a qualitative difference between the cognitive abilities of humans and non-humans. His deep chasm/exceptionalism argument is captured in the term 'humaniqueness.'
- 'Humaniqueness' denotes four major ingredients of the human mind, namely generative computation, promiscuous combination of ideas, mental symbols and abstract thought.
- Two types of generative computation are recursive and combinatorial.
- Jackendoff describes recursion as an example of a pattern in the mind; this overcomes the limitations of human memory, preparing us for any sentence we might encounter.
- In addition to mental patterns that generate an infinite number of syntactically correct sentences, other patterns correspond to the different levels/orders of representation which characterise theory of mind (ToM).
- These patterns form part of mental grammar, assumed to be stores in the brain of a language user. Chomsky argues that in order for children to acquire language, they must construct a mental grammar based on an interaction between environmental input and an innate language acquisition device (LAD).

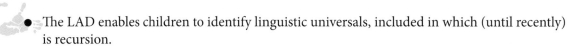

- The LAD enables children to identify linguistic universals, included in which (until recently) is recursion.

- Hauser's definition of generative computation extends beyond language, to include, among other things, music.

- Jackendoff suggests that musical notation can be analysed in a similar way to how linguists analyse language; like language, music is uniquely human.

- There are a number of similarities and differences between music and language. For example, according to Patel's shared syntactic integration resource hypothesis (SSIRH), while representations of language and music are likely to be stored independently in the brain, we use similar neural networks to integrate evolving speech and music sounds.

- In support of the SSIRH, music has been found to excite brain regions involved in understanding and producing language, including Broca's and Wernicke's areas. However, evidence also exists that musical and linguistic processing takes place in separate brain areas.

- Research has demonstrated a number of striking similarities in the way children come to learn about language and music. This can be explained partly by the concept of infant-directed speech (IDS) ('motherese' or baby talk register).

- Mithen claims that language and music both evolved from a musical proto-language used by our hominid ancestors.

- Babies show little preference for either their native language or their culture's musical conventions early in life. At this stage they're still gathering information about these sounds and internalising the patterns and structures they hear regularly.

- Based on Baddeley and Hitch's working memory (WM) model, Williamson's finding that articulatory suppression can influence both verbal and musical recall suggests that this form of mental rehearsal is involved in maintaining aspects of both speech and music in memory.

- Hauser claims that generative computation by humans – but not other animals – is reflected in the use of tools. Human tools are often multi-purpose (as in the case of the No.2 pencil), demonstrating combinatorial generative computation.

- Wolpert claims that only humans show understanding of the causal relationship between inanimate objects, or between their actions and the outcomes they produce. Povinelli has conducted experiments that support this claim.

- Goodall's research with wild chimpanzees helped explode the myth regarding the uniqueness of humans as tool users and makers. But she also argues that the ability to use an object as a tool, on its own, doesn't necessarily indicate any special intelligence.

- The evolutionary significance of tool using and tool making is the ability to manipulate an object to a variety of purposes and using an object spontaneously to solve a brand-new problem. This describes generative computation.

- Goodall's observational studies support the claim that chimpanzees display generative computation, as do Köhler's studies involving Sultan and other chimpanzees in captivity and Savage-Rumbaugh's language studies involving Kanzi the bonobo.

- A much-cited example of a non-primate species that manufactures and uses a variety of tools is the New Caledonian crow. But Wolpert argues that this, and the tools made and used by chimpanzees, has a very narrow range of functions compared with the versatility of human tool use. Perhaps the critical difference is that chimpanzees have never been observed using one tool to make another.

- While humans share with other animals a non-verbal communication system, only humans possess a system of linguistic communication based on the manipulation of mental symbols. These symbols make abstract thought possible.

- Symbols used in animal communication, compared with human language, are triggered only by real objects/events, are restricted to the present and to particular contexts, don't form part of a more abstract classification scheme, and are rarely combined with other symbols.

- Only human language operates equally well in the visual and auditory modes.

- The interaction between syntax and the concept of sets produces new ways of conceptualising the world; this illustrates the 'promiscuous combination of ideas'.

- By definition, domains of knowledge/systems of understanding are abstract; language enables the human mind to be organised hierarchically and to explore possibility through the use of imagination.

- According to Cassirer and others, human beings live in a symbolic universe, aspects of which include language, art, myth and religion.

- The cases of Helen Keller and Laura Bridgford demonstrate both the power of understanding that everything has a name and that we create our human world of meaning independently of the raw material that reaches the brain via our sense organs.

- Langer regards the need for symbolisation as a basic and uniquely human need.

- Imagery typically comprises a mental representation of something in the external world. While mental images may have truth relations to the outside world (a 'primary' representation), through imagination we can modify a copy of this primary representation (a 'second-order' representation). This allows the brain to consider the possible, the hypothetical, and the simply untrue.

- Leslie called the combination of second-order representation and use of imagination 'meta-representational capacity', which is at the core of mind-reading.

- Leslie believes that the capacity for meta-representation involves a special module in the brain, but this may fail to develop normally in children with Asperger's Syndrome or extreme (classic) autism.

- A crucial aspect of what it means to be a symbolic creature is captured in the concept of metaphor. According to Langer, thought starts out as metaphor before becoming more literal: at least as far as new ideas are concerned, the meta-representational precedes the primary representational.

Suggested further reading

Goodall, J. (1988) *In the Shadow of Man* (revised edition). London: Phoenix. Just one of Jane Goodall's accounts of her pioneering field research with chimpanzees in Africa, with informative discussions of language/communication, and tool use and manufacture.
Well illustrated, with an Introduction by S.J. Gould.

Jackendoff, R. (1993) *Patterns in the Mind: Language and Human Nature.* Hemel Hempstead: Harvester Wheatsheaf. Explores the question as to what the human mind must be like in order to make language possible in the light of research in linguistics and psychology. Also very relevant to Chapter 6.

Leakey, E. (1994) *The Origins of Humankind.* London: Weidenfeld and Nicolson. Part of the *Science Masters* series, an extremely lucid account of human evolution, including tool use and manufacture, language and art.

Selected websites

www.youtube.com/watch?v=2oMvtw4aeEY

Excellent Library of Congress Lectures in the 'Music in the Brain' series. The immediate link is to Anirddth Patel, author of *The Music of Language and the Language of Music.* Also relevant to Chapter 6.

http://www.janegoodall.org.uk/

The Jane Goodall Institute website. Includes video on the 50th anniversary of her pioneering research (including an interview with her). Also relevant to Chapters 6 and 9.

Chapter 6: Language: Do only humans have it?

Key questions

- What are the major differences between human language and animal communication?
- What makes spoken language (speech) so special?
- How, when and why did human language evolve?
- What is the relationship between the emergence of language and the evolution of the human brain?
- What is the relationship between the development of language in the child and brain development?
- Did language evolve as a distinct ability in its own right, or is it just a side-effect of other evolved abilities?
- What evidence is there for the role of genetic factors in human speech?
- What conclusions can we draw from attempts to teach language to non-human animals?

Human language and non-human communication: Key differences

What makes language special?

As we saw in Chapter 1, Whiten (1999, 2007) argues that language and communication (along with mind-reading, culture and cooperation) constitute part of the '**deep social mind**'. Whiten states that what makes language special is that it enables us to transmit to other human minds our intentions, ideas and knowledge. These, in turn, form the basis for cultural transmission, a tool through which mind-reading and cultural transmission operate (see Chapters 4, 5 and 9).

For Whiten, it is the *combination* of these four characteristics that is distinctively human. But for many others, language itself represents a uniquely human ability (see Chapter 1). According to Leakey (1994):

> *There is no question that the evolution of spoken language as we know it was a defining point in human prehistory. Perhaps it was* the *defining point. Equipped with language, humans were able to create new kinds of worlds in nature: the world of introspective consciousness and the world we manufacture and share with others, which we call 'culture'. Language became our medium and culture, our niche ...* (emphasis in original.)

Similarly, Bickerton (1990) claims that 'Only language could have broken through the prison of immediate experience in which every other creature is locked, releasing us into infinite freedoms of space and time.'

Leakey (1994) believes that the claims made by those who adopt **human exceptionalism** and continuity approaches (see Chapter 1) are most passionately debated with regard to the nature and origin of language. As Leakey says, 'the vitriol hurled by linguists at ape-language researchers undoubtedly reflects this divide (see below, pages 156–165).

According to Gibson (1992, in Leakey, 1994), the view that human language is unique '... fits firmly within a long Western philosophical tradition, dating at least to the authors of Genesis and to the writings of Plato and Aristotle, which holds that human mentality and behaviour [are] qualitatively different from that of animals.'

As a result of this tradition, the anthropological literature has for a long time been littered with behaviours that were considered uniquely human, including tool making (see Chapter 5), the ability to use symbols (see Chapter 5 and below, pages 130–131), mirror recognition (see Chapter 4), and language. According to Leakey (1994):

> ... Since the 1960s, this wall of uniqueness has steadily crumbled, with the discovery that apes can make and use tools, use symbols, and recognise themselves as individuals in a mirror. Only spoken language remains intact, so that linguists are effectively the last defenders of human uniqueness ...

According to Rose (2005):

> ... It is difficult to imagine effective social organisation or the spread of new technologies without language, or the possession of language without a concept of self, and at least a rudimentary theory of mind. Are minds possible without language, or language without minds? It would seem that neither can do without the other any more than proteins can do without nucleic acids and vice versa ...

However, as shown in Chapters 4 and 5, 'mind' seems to be a matter of degree, rather than something you either have or don't have. Some have argued that the same applies to the possession of language (see below, pages 156–165).

The importance of grammar

Grammar, the complex and yet intuitive understanding needed to make sense of any sentence we might hear and the complementary ability to produce such sentences, is what sets our language apart from other forms of non-human animal communication. While many other species communicate to conspecifics,

> ... only human language has the sophistication to combine purely abstract signals (words) in new ways to produce new meanings. Grammar is what makes language infinitely creative. There is truly no limit to the way words can be combined to express new ideas ... (Eliot, 1999)

The comparative approach

Hauser *et al.* (2002) point to a peculiar difference between the universality of the genetic mechanism based on DNA (see Chapter 2) and the species-uniqueness of all communication systems, which are apparently meaningful only to conspecifics. They also describe non-human communication systems as *closed* – unlike human speech they lack the expressive and open-ended power of human language. They claim that even the gestural communications of chimps and gorillas are essentially *signals*, not symbols. As Rose (2005) puts it:

... Communicative signals may be systematic and coded to support a variety of different instructions or intentions, but they are used strictly as indices, whereas symbols demand intersubjectivity. Symbols are conventional, resting on a shared understanding that any particular symbol is a token representing a particular feature of a particular referential class. Unlike a signal, which can be regarded as an instruction to behave in particular ways, a symbol guides not behaviour but understanding ...

Signals can only be used in relation to the immediate context or situation, whereas human language is essentially infinite: there's no obvious limit to the types of meaningful sentences that can be constructed, and this distinguishes it from all known non-human forms of communication.

But what if certain non-humans, such as chimps, could be shown to communicate about aspects of the environment in a way that not only conveyed information to other conspecifics, but also took account of how others might interpret the information being conveyed? Slocombe's research (described below) suggests that chimps, both captive and wild, may be capable of **functionally referential communication**, that is, using vocalisations to 'pick out' specific aspects of the external world and direct others' attention to it.

According to Slocombe (2008), '... Language is one of the most intricate and complex behaviours, and is one of the few that clearly distinguishes humans from the rest of the living world.' However, finding an evolutionary explanation for the origins of human language is an extremely difficult challenge: spoken language has left no fossil remains and very few clues as to when and how it emerged (Leakey, 1994; Slocombe, 2008). But both recent genetic evidence and archaeological evidence suggests that humans had an incredibly short time in which to evolve such a complex capacity as modern spoken language (see below). One powerful claim is that many of the underlying cognitive capacities involved in language processing are much older than language itself, with their phylogenetic roots deep in the **primate** lineage (Hauser *et al.*, 2002).

... Thus, a promising empirical approach to understanding the origins of human behaviour, including language, has been to examine the capacities of extant primates, whose phylogenetic relationships to modern humans are known ... (Slocombe, 2008)

Time for reflection

- What does 'phylogenetic' mean? (See Chapter 1.)
- What do we know about the genetic relationship between humans and chimpanzees? (See Chapter 2.)
- Why is the *comparative approach* important: what can it tell us about the evolution of human language?

This comparative approach is vital for identifying the elements of language that appear to have evolved gradually from a common primate ancestor and those that have no clear evolutionary path, which may be the 'novel' elements that caused human language to evolve into its current uniquely complex state (Hauser and Fitch, 2003).

Chimpanzees are the closest extant (living) approximation to the common human-chimpanzee ancestor (McGrew, 1991), and as such are one of the most informative models for the comparative approach (Lieberman, 2000). By studying vocal communication in chimps,

Slocombe (2008) aimed to identify prerequisites and elements of language that humans and chimps share, and those that they don't.

What can chimps communicate?

The global aim of Slocombe's research was to assess whether chimps are capable of communicating about events and objects in the external world. This type of communication has been found in several monkey species. Most famously, Seyfarth *et al.*, (1980) showed that vervet monkeys give different calls for different predators. When the alarm calls were played back in the absence of the predator, listeners responded as if they'd seen the predator themselves. This led to the conclusion that these calls functioned to refer to different types of predator, in a roughly equivalent way to how humans attach labels to events and objects.

What about chimps? Goodall (1988) observed that they have a wide range of calls, which certainly serve to convey different types of information. Some examples are given in Box 6.1.

Box 6.1 Chimpanzees' vocal communication (Goodall, 1988)

- When a chimp finds good food he utters loud barks; other chimps in the vicinity instantly become aware of the food source and hurry to join in.

- An attacked chimp screams and this may alert his mother or a friend, either of whom may hurry to his aid.

- A chimp confronted with an alarming and potentially dangerous situation utters his spine-chilling *wraaa* – again, other chimps may hurry to the spot to see what's happening.

- A male chimp about to enter a valley or charge toward a food source, utters pant-hoots – and other individuals realise that another member of the group is arriving and can identify which one.

- To our human ears, each chimp is characterised more by its pant-hoots than by any other type of call. This is significant, because the pant-hoot in particular is the call that serves to maintain contact between the scattered groups of the community. Yet the chimps themselves can certainly recognise individuals by other calls; for example, a mother knows her offspring's scream, and probably a chimp can recognise the calls of most of its acquaintances.

Goodall (1988) concludes that while chimps' calls serve to convey basic information about some situations, 'they cannot for the most part be compared to a spoken language':

> *... Man by means of words can communicate abstract ideas; he can benefit from the experience of others without having to be present at the time; he can make intelligent cooperative plans. All the same, when humans come to an exchange of emotional feelings, most people fall back on the old chimpanzee-type of gestural communication – the cheering pat, the embrace of exuberance, the clasp of hands. And when on these occasions we also use words, we often use them in rather the same way as a chimpanzee utters his calls – simply to convey the emotion we feel at that moment ...*

An example which demonstrates our tendency to use words in the same way a chimpanzee utters his calls is when we're surprised we utter inanities such as 'Golly', 'Gosh', or 'Gee whiz!' When we're angry, we may express ourselves with swear words and other more-or-less meaningless phrases.

'... This usage of words on the emotional level is as different from oratory, from literature, from intelligent conversation, as are the grunts and hoots of chimpanzees.' (Goodall, 1988)

But do any of the communicative acts described in Box 6.1 display the 'functionally referential' communication of the vervet monkeys? Apparently building on Goodall's field studies, but, strangely, not acknowledging it, Slocombe (2008) reports on her observational studies of the vocal communications of habituated individuals from the wild population of chimps in the Budongo forest in Uganda and captive individuals at Edinburgh zoo. Her findings are described in Box 6.2.

Box 6.2 'Functionally referential' communication in wild and captive chimps (Slocombe, 2008)

Chimps often produce calls ('rough grunts') when encountering food. Slocombe constructed a food-preference hierarchy by providing the captive chimps with a choice of two food types and recording their responses. Using this method, nine common food types were grouped into high, medium and low, and the rough grunts produced on discovery of the different foods were recorded.

- The rough grunts were acoustically different according to the value of the food encountered (Slocombe and Zuberbühler, 2006). High-value food triggered long, high-pitched grunts which graded into short, low-pitched, noisy grunts elicited by low-value food. So, chimps reliably produced grunts that reflected the value of the food they were eating.

- Slocombe and Zuberbühler then examined whether chimp calls could have a greater degree of referential specificity by acting as unique labels for specific food types. First, they needed to control for the effect their preference had on the acoustic structure of the rough grunts: did the grunts given in response to the three food types included within each value group differ in acoustic structure? While there was no evidence for this in low- and medium-value foods, within the high-value category the grunts given to bread, mango and banana were acoustically distinct. The grunts given to bread and bananas remained stable across different feeding situations, suggesting they could indeed function as labels for individual food types.

- The rough grunts made by wild chimps in response to three medium-high preference foods were comparable to those given by captive chimps in terms of their acoustic structure; this gives the results for the captive chimps a degree of ecological validity. However, Slocombe and Zuberbühler failed to replicate the finding that different food types elicited acoustically distinct grunts.

- In order for a call to be classified as a functionally referential signal, we must be able to show that listeners understand the meaning of the call and what it refers to. Slocombe and Zuberbühler (2005a) conducted a playback study with the captive chimps. Based on data collected from one individual (a six-year-old male, called Liberius), the researchers concluded that he understood that his group members' grunts referred to foods of different value and used this information to aid his own search for food. This was the first experimental evidence that any ape species uses its vocalisations in a referential manner (Slocombe and Zuberbühler, 2005b).

- As far as **agonistic screams** are concerned (i.e. those produced in aggressive encounters), Slocombe and Zuberbühler (2005a) found subtle but consistent differences in acoustic structure between the screams of 14 wild chimps – in the roles of both victim and aggressor. Moreover, victim screams varied in acoustic structure as a function of the severity of the aggression

---

Box 6.2 *Continued*

(Slocombe and Zuberbühler, 2007). Victims of severe aggression gave longer bouts of screams in which each call lasted longer and was of a higher frequency compared with screams produced by mild aggression. Recent playback experiments have shown that listening chimps can meaningfully distinguish between mild and severe victim screams (Slocombe *et al.*, 2010). This suggests that individuals out of sight of a fight can infer the nature of the fight simply by hearing the screams. This suggests that agonistic screams can be classed as functionally referential.

● In addition, victims of severe aggression were sensitive to the composition of the listening audience; they modified the acoustic structure of their screams accordingly. So, if there was an individual of equal or higher status than the aggressor (an individual who could effectively challenge the aggressor) nearby, then the victim produced screams that were acoustically consistent with extremely severe aggression. This vocal exaggeration only occurred when the victims most needed aid, that is, their screams functioned to recruit aid (Slocombe and Zuberbühler, 2007).

Time for reflection

● What conclusions can you draw from Slocombe and Zuberbühler's (2007) findings regarding victim chimps' exaggeration of the level of aggression depending on the status of the listener?

This raises the possibility that chimps are capable of intentional deception – exaggerating the level of aggression in order to affect the high-ranking chimps' understanding of the event, thus increasing their chances of receiving aid (Slocombe, 2008). It also suggests that wild chimps are capable of mind-reading (see Chapter 4).

In the later playback studies, Slocombe *et al.* (2010) broadcast sequences of agonistic calls that were either congruent or incongruent with existing social dominance hierarchies (that is, the screams either violated or didn't violate those hierarchies). Listeners looked significantly longer at *incongruent* sequences, despite them being acoustically less salient (fewer call types from fewer individuals). The researchers concluded that chimps categorised an apparently simple acoustic signal into victim and aggressor screams, and used their existing knowledge of the expected social interactions of the call producers regarding their social standing in the group to form inferences about third-party interactions they couldn't see:

> *... Further research into chimpanzee vocal behaviour may provide more evidence for continuity between elements of monkey and human vocal communication with considerable relevance for theories of language evolution.* (Slocombe et al., 2010)

These theories are discussed below.

Time for reflection

● In terms of the distinction made above between signals and symbols, how would you classify the rough grunts and agonistic screams described by Slocombe?
● Is it possible that they represent something in between, or a blend of the two?

While signals often involve a biologically determined act of communication (such as grunts and screams), symbols (as in language) refer to arbitrary, conventional labels for objects in the world and bear no relationship to those objects. While grunts and screams are biologically determined, they can be used *selectively* depending on the object (such as food type) or behaviour (such as mild or severe aggressive threat) and the individuals thought to be listening (lower or equal/higher status). This suggests that perhaps the signal/symbol distinction is a false dichotomy.

However, the neurophysiological evidence suggests that non-human primates have little if any cortical control over vocalisation, which is critical to speech (Gentilucci and Corballis, 2007).

The special nature of speech

As we saw in Chapter 1, Gentilucci and Corballis (2007) claim that it isn't language as such that distinguishes *Homo sapiens* from other hominids, but rather the conversion from a primarily visual (i.e. gestural) form of language to one that's conveyed largely through the medium of sound.

While humans can generate 50 discrete sounds (phonemes), chimps have about 12. But it is not so much the number that matters as the human ability to combine and recombine them endlessly:

> ... *They [phonemes] can be arranged and rearranged to endow the average human being with a vocabulary of a hundred thousand words, and those words can be combined in an infinity of sentences. As a consequence, the capacity of* Homo sapiens *for rapid, detailed communication and richness of thought is unmatched in the world of nature.* (Leakey, 1994) (emphasis in original)

Humans are able to produce a wide range of sounds because the larynx is situated low in the throat; this creates a large sound-chamber (the pharynx) above the vocal cords. Based on studies of the vocal tract in living animals and human fossils, Laitman (1984) claims that the expanded pharynx is the key to producing fully articulate speech. In all mammals, except humans, the larynx is high in the throat, which allows the animal to breathe and drink at the same time; but the small pharyngeal cavity limits the range of sounds that can be produced (see Figure 6.1, page 132). This means that most mammals rely on the shape of the oral cavity and lips to modify the sounds produced in the larynx. In fact, the larynx in mammals is often inserted into the nasal passage, creating a sealed nasal airway, which is how humans begin life: a newborn baby can breathe through its nose while swallowing milk through its mouth – without choking. But the larynx gradually descends over the next 3–4 years, making this feat no longer possible (Fitch, 2010).

Fitch (2010) cites two lines of evidence that cast doubt on the belief that we can put a date on the emergence of language by studying the position of the larynx in ancient fossils.

1. The reconfigured human vocal tract allows the free movement of the tongue; this is crucial to making the huge variety of human speech sounds. However, humans aren't unique in having a permanently descended larynx: lions, tigers, koalas and Mongolian gazelles all have a descended larynx, making it a *convergent trait* (similar traits have evolved independently without being present in a common ancestor). Since none of these species produces anything vaguely speech-like, such anatomical changes cannot be sufficient for speech to have emerged (see below).

2. X-rays of vocalising mammals show that dogs, monkeys, goats and pigs all lower the larynx during vocalisation. This ability to reconfigure the vocal tract appears to be a widespread and probably *homologous* feature of mammals. (Different species might display the same features simply because a common ancestor had the trait, which then persisted throughout the course of evolution; such traits are called homologies.) With its larynx retracted, a dog or a monkey has all the freedom of movement needed to produce many different vocalisations; the key changes must have occurred in the brain instead (see below: Fitch, 2010).

How and why did speech evolve?

According to Rose (2005), the ability to communicate in speech requires two distinct capacities on the part of the speaker. The first of these is essentially mechanical: to have the relevant muscular and neural control over vocalisation, the larynx, mouth and tongue need to be able to articulate a variety of distinctive sounds, a skill which human children need to develop as they learn to speak. Vocalisation depends on midbrain structures, especially a midbrain region called the **periaqueductal grey**; this is located close to the ventricles, is rich in hormone receptors and communicates with the amygdala and hippocampus (see Chapter 3).

Deacon (1997) argues that the move from generalised vocalisation to the ability to speak is related to an upwards shift in hominid evolution during which the periaqueductal grey came increasingly under cortical control. Given that this had already taken place in chimps, and that their control over tongue and facial movements and their neural representation is quite similar to those in humans, and that they have adequate auditory perceptual skills, Rose (2005) asks why can't – or won't – chimps speak – or even imitate human speech sounds in the way that parrots can and do? According to Savage-Rumbaugh *et al.* (1998), the problem is merely mechanical: because of the vertical position of the human head above the spinal column, our vocal tract curves downwards at a 90-degree angle at the point where the oral and pharyngeal cavities meet, whereas the chimp's vocal tract slopes gently downwards. This means that in humans the larynx and tongue are lower and the nasal cavity can be closed off, allowing lower-pitched, vowel-like sounds to be produced (see Figure 6.1).

The fact that non-human primates have little if any cortical control over vocalisation implies that the common ancestor of humans and chimps was much better pre-adapted to develop a voluntary communication system based on visible gestures rather than sounds (Gentilucci and Corballis, 2007). Ploog (2002) identifies two neural systems for vocal behaviour: a cingulate pathway and a neocortical pathway. In non-human primates, vocalisation is largely, if not exclusively, dependent on the cingulate pathway; the neocortical pathway progressively developed for voluntary control of manual movements, including relatively independent finger movements, from monkeys to apes to humans, and which is indispensable for voluntary control. Only in humans is the neocortical pathway developed for precise voluntary control of the muscles of the vocal cords and tongue.

The second requirement for linguistic communication, according to Rose (2005), is cognitive: the ability to use vocalisations to symbolise objects, processes and attributes (see Box 6.2 above). This, in turn, requires that the receiver of the communication possesses the relevant auditory perceptual apparatus for hearing and discriminating vocalisations, and shares a common understanding of their referents in the external world. But what's also needed is the ability to compute and categorise these sounds, an ability that must depend on brain structures distinct from those involved in the mechanics of sound production.

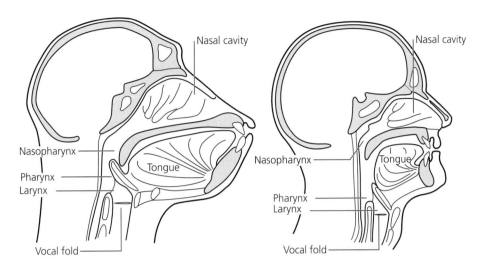

▲ **Figure 6.1** The vocal tracts of the chimpanzee and human being

Time for reflection

● What is it that makes the human brain distinctive compared with those of other mammals? (See Chapter 3.)

The gestural theory of speech

Monkeys make extensive use of facial expressions for communication, but these are more obviously gestural than language-like (Van Hooff, 1962, 1967). The most successful attempts to teach language to non-human primates have involved manual signs (as well as recognising specially devised symbols) (see below), as opposed to anything resembling vocal language. This is further evidence that voluntary control is more highly developed manually than vocally in our closest primate relatives. The human equivalents of primate vocalisations are probably emotionally based sounds, such as laughing, crying, grunting and shrieking, rather than words (see Goodall's research above): '... With the emergence of **bipedalism** in the hominid line some 6 million years ago, the hands were freed from locomotion, providing a potential boost to the evolution of manual communication.' (Gentilucci and Corballis, 2007)

According to the *gestural theory*, language evolved from manual gestures rather than from vocalisations. This theory is discussed further in Box 6.3.

Box 6.3 The gestural theory of language

The *gestural theory* of language dates at least to eighteenth-century philosopher, Condillac (1971/1756), but many forms of the theory have been proposed since (e.g. Donald, 1991; Gentilucci and Corballis, 2006; Rizzolatti and Arbib, 1998; Ruben, 2005).

Unlike spoken words, manual actions can provide more obvious iconic links with objects and actions in the physical world. In the course of evolution, 'pantomimes' of actions might have incorporated gestures that are analogue representations of objects or actions (Donald, 1991). Over time, these gestures may have lost the analogue features and become abstract. The shift from iconic gestures (which 'mimic' the object or action) to arbitrary symbols is called **conventionalisation** and appears to be common to both human and non-human communication systems; it represents a more economical communication system.

But how do we explain the switch that was needed to move from a visual language to an audible one (Burling, 2005)?

According to Gentilucci and Corballis (2006, 2007), the switch was a gradual one, and even today speech is typically accompanied by manual gestures that help convey the speaker's full meaning. Goldin-Meadow (1999) proposes that the imagistic and analogue gestures that accompany speech reflect the speaker's/gesturer's thought and knowledge that's often not expressed in other more codified forms of communication, such as speech. Again, gesture is a 'way-station' on the road to language over both ontogenetic (development of the individual) and phylogenetic (evolutionary) time. Similarly, Corballis (2002) argues that hand gestures and spoken language are integrally linked in human evolution. He claims that language developed from and within gesture systems rather than from vocal calls.

Nevertheless, the capacity to convey the major part of the message entirely through the vocal medium seems to have evolved only in *Homo sapiens* and may explain the 'human revolution' that has allowed our species to dominate the planet (see Chapter 1). It may also explain the demise of the Neanderthals, who in other respects seem to have been the cognitive equals of *Homo sapiens*.

Consistent with the gestural theory, there is a clear development in the use of gesture in children as they acquire language. Some examples are given in Box 6.4.

Box 6.4 Infants' use of gesture

- Infants first use pointing to request (around 10–12 months) and then later (around 18 months) to comment on objects and events (Doherty-Sneddon, 2008).

- Infants use gesture plus word combinations to form two-item strings (e.g. 'give' + point to a cup = 'give cup'). The use of these two-item gesture/word strings is predictive of the development of two-word strings (Bates *et al.*, 1979). Capirci *et al.* (1996) report that 16- to 20-month-old Italian children produced many gesture + word combinations (mostly complementary, where a single referent is singled out by a deictic gesture (e.g. 'flowers' + point to flowers). Combinations of two gestures were rare, and two representational gestures were never seen. This may be because babies are rarely exposed to representational gestures and probably never witness combinational sequences of representational gestures.

Box 6.4 *Continued*

● In hearing infants taught key-word signing, this pattern is extended: there are more gesture + gesture combinations before the occurrence of two-word utterances. They're also more likely to be representational gestures rather than just deictics in baby signers (Doherty-Sneddon, 2008).

● Deaf children born into hearing families don't have an external language model as they cannot hear the spoken language around them and their parents cannot use sign language (Goldin-Meadow, 1999). She reports data showing that children develop their own system of homesigns, i.e. gestures that stand for words. These are formed into 'sentences' with structure comparable to that of spoken languages.

Further support for the gestural theory comes in the form of the discovery of **mirror neurons**. These were first described by Rizzolatti and his colleagues in the mid-1990s (Dobbs, 2006). They are found in various parts of the brain, including area F5 in the ventral premotor cortex, and centres for language, empathy and pain. Mirror neurons were first observed in monkeys in relation to relatively simple actions, such as picking up a peanut: certain neurons in the monkey's motor cortex fired in the same way when it observed one of the researchers pick up a peanut as when the monkey itself picked it up. This pattern of neural activity associated with the observed action was a true representation in the brain of the action itself – regardless of who was performing it (Rizzolatti *et al.*, 2006). In both monkeys and humans, the mirror neurons are able to read another person's *intentions*.

By extension, mirror neurons seem to help us 'read' other people's *emotions*: such a mirror mechanism provides for the first time a functional neural basis for some of the basic aspects of complex social behaviours (Rizzolatti *et al.*, 2006). These effects are largely automatic and unconscious; this is illustrated by two recent experiments described in Box 6.5.

Box 6.5 The automatic mirroring of other's emotions and experiences

● Using brain-scanning techniques, Blakemore *et al.* (2005) found that, as expected, touching participants on the face or neck activated areas of the brain concerned with the sense of touch (primary and secondary somatosensory cortex). The exciting new result was that precisely the same areas were activated when the participants saw someone else being touched on the face or neck. But the vast majority of people don't consciously feel touch when they see another person being touched: with a few exceptions, most of us share the experience without even knowing it (Frith, 2010).

● Liepelt *et al.* (2009) used a standard choice reaction-time paradigm. Participants had to lift their first or second finger in response to the cue '1' or '2' appearing on the screen in front of them. The novel feature of the experiment was that these cues appeared superimposed on a picture of a hand. In one condition, all the fingers in the photo of a hand were free; in another condition, the first and second fingers in the photo were held down by metal clamps. The striking result was that the participants' reaction time was slowed down simply by seeing a hand whose fingers were clamped – even though their own were completely free.

Time for reflection

- How might you interpret Liepelt *et al.*'s findings?

The results from Liepelt *et al.*'s experiment shows that our actions are automatically affected by the situations of the other people we are with. The experiments described in Box 6.5 are just two of many recent studies that show we're much more embedded in the social world than we realise. These automatic and unconscious processes make us more socially oriented and less selfish, but they're probably quite independent of the processes that allow us to perform **theory of mind (ToM)** tasks (see Chapter 4). Exploring the precise relationship between mirroring and ToM is currently a 'hot' topic in **social cognitive neuroscience** (Frith, 2010).

Both neurophysiological recordings in primates and functional brain imaging in humans have identified a more general mirror system, involving temporal, parietal and frontal regions that are specialised for the perception and understanding of biological motion (Rizzolatti *et al.*, 2001). In monkeys, this system has been shown primarily for reaching and grasping movements, although it also maps certain movements (such as tearing paper or cracking nuts) onto the sounds of these movements (Kohler *et al.*, 2002). This suggests that the mirror system was also pre-adapted in the primate brain for cross-modal mapping. Although there's no clear-cut evidence from non-human primates for the mapping of the production of vocalisations onto the perception of vocalisations, this mapping is implicit in humans: according to the *motor theory of speech perception* (Liberman *et al.*, 1967), we understand speech in terms of how it's produced rather than its acoustic properties. This raises the possibility that vocalisation was incorporated into the mirror system *after* the split between the ape and hominid lineages (Gentilucci and Corballis, 2007).

Single-neuron recording studies have shown not only that F5 neurons code specific actions (such as grasping, holding or tearing), but also that many of them code specific types of hand shaping (such as the precision grip). As Gentilucci and Corballis (2007) point out, hand shape is an important feature of human signed languages. F5 neurons also often fire when the grasping action is performed with the mouth as well as with the hand (e.g. Rizzolatti *et al.*, 1988). From an evolutionary perspective, they may have been instrumental in the transfer of the gestural communication system from the hand to the mouth.

Because the mirror system is activated when observing and performing the same hand action, we can consider it to be involved in understanding the action *meaning* (Gallese *et al.*, 1996). It might, therefore, have provided the link between actor and observer that also exists between sender and receiver of messages. Rizzolatti and Arbib (1998) propose that the mirror system was used as an initial communication system in the evolution of language. Indeed, a comparable mirror system has also been inferred in present-day humans, based on evidence from studies using the **electroencephalogram** (Muthukumaraswamy *et al.*, 2004), **transcranial magnetic stimulation (TMS)** (Fadiga *et al.*, 1995), and fMRI (Iacoboni *et al.*, 1999) (see Gross, 2010). Area F5 is also considered to be the homologue of **Broca's area** (Rizzolatti and Arbib, 1998), and the mirror system in general corresponds quite closely with the cortical circuits (usually in the left hemisphere) involved in language – spoken or signed (see Chapter 3). According to Gentilucci and Corballis (2007):

... The perception and production of language might therefore be considered part of the mirror system, and indeed part of the more general system by which visuo-motor (and audio-motor) integration is used in the understanding of biological motion.

Given that newborns can imitate actions (such as sticking out the tongue), it is highly likely that mirror neurons are present – and active – at birth. According to Ramachandran (in Dobbs, 2006), mirror neurons may help explain how humans took a 'great leap forward' about 50,000 years ago, acquiring new skills in social organisation, tool use (see Chapter 5) and language that made human culture possible (see Chapter 9).

Is speech itself fundamentally gestural?

A key insight involved in the claim that vocal language evolved from gesture is that *speech itself is fundamentally gestural.* This idea is captured by Liberman *et al.*'s (1967) motor theory of speech perception (see above), and by what has more recently become known as **articulatory phonology** (Browman and Goldstein, 1995). According to Browman and Goldstein, speech isn't so much a system for producing sounds as a system for producing articulatory gestures, through the independent action of the six articulatory organs – the lips, velum (the soft palate behind the hard palate), larynx, and the blade, body and root of the tongue.

This approach derives from the discovery that phonemes do not exist as discrete units in the acoustic signal (Joos, 1948) and cannot be detected as discrete sounds in mechanical sound recordings, as in a sound spectrograph (Liberman *et al.*, 1967). The acoustic signals corresponding to individual phonemes vary widely, depending on the contexts in which they are embedded (such as other, neighbouring phonemes). Yet we can perceive speech at remarkably high rates (up to at least 10–15 phonemes per second), which seems at odds with the idea that there needs to be some complex, context-dependent transformation. Even relatively simple sound units, such as tones or noises, cannot be perceived at comparable rates; this suggests that a different principle underlies speech perception;

... The conceptualisation of speech as gesture *overcomes these difficulties, at least to some extent, since the articulatory gestures that give rise to speech partially overlap in time (co-articulation), which makes possible the high rates of production and perception...*
(Gentilucci and Corballis, 2007) (emphasis in original.)

MacNeilage (1998) has drawn attention to the similarity between human speech and primate sound-producing facial gestures, such as lipsmacks, tonguesmacks and teeth chatters. Ferrari *et al.* (2003) found evidence of activity both in mirror neurons in monkeys during the lipsmack (the most common facial gesture in monkeys), and from other mirror neurons in the same area during mouth movements related to eating. These findings suggest that nonvocal facial gestures may indeed be transitional between visual gesture and speech. In **echo phonology**, mouth movements parallel hand movements. For example, the mouth may open and close in synchrony with the opening and closing of the hand (Woll, 2002). Woll and Sieratzki (1998) have suggested that echo phonology might provide the link between gesture and speech.

As we've seen, the monkey mirror system is related to both arm (Gallese *et al.*, 1996; Rizzolatti *et al.*, 1996) and mouth movements (Ferrari *et al.*, 2003). This suggests that gestures of the mouth might have been added to the manual system to form a combined *manuofacial gestural system.* So far, a mirror system has been identified only for arm and mouth actions; the anatomical closeness of hand and mouth neurons in the premotor cortex may relate to the involvement of the hand and mouth in common goals, such as food acquisition. Area F5 of the monkey premotor cortex also includes a group of neurons that are activated when the animal grasps an object either with the hand or the mouth (Rizzolatti *et al.*, 1988). Gentilucci *et al.* (2001) infer a similar neuronal system in humans. When participants were asked to open their mouths while grasping an object, the size of the mouth opening increased with the size of the grasped object; conversely, when they opened their hands while grasping objects with their mouths, the size of the hand opening also increased with the size of the object.

> ... *In the evolution of communication, this mechanism of double command to hand and mouth could have been instrumental in the transfer of a communication system, based on the mirror system, from movements of the hand to movements of the mouth.*
> (Gentilucci and Corballis, 2007)

Gentilucci and Corballis go on to say that, early in language evolution, communication signals related to the meaning of actions (such as taking possession of an object by grasping, and bringing an edible object to the mouth) might have been associated with the activity of particular masticatory (i.e. chewing) organs of the mouth that were later co-opted for speech.

The strict relationship between representations of actions and spoken language is supported by neuroimaging studies, which show that Broca's area is activated when representing meaningful arm gestures (e.g. Gallagher and Frith, 2004). Motor imagery of hand movements has also been shown to activate both Broca's area and left premotor ventral areas (Gentilucci and Corballis, 2007).

When did language evolve?

If the last section was concerned with the 'how' and 'why' of language evolution, this one focuses on 'when'. According to Leakey (1994), there are two major views regarding the evolutionary source of language:

1. Language is a unique human trait, an ability that arose as an incidental consequence of our enlarged brain. In this case, language arose rapidly and recently, as a cognitive threshold was passed. The Canadian linguist Noam Chomsky has been a champion of this model.

2. Spoken language evolved through natural selection acting on various cognitive capacities – including but not limited to communication – in non-human ancestors. In this so-called continuity model, language evolved gradually in human pre-history, beginning with the evolution of the genus *Homo*. Steven Pinker, an American linguist, is the most well-known advocate of this view.

According to the Chomskian view, we needn't look to natural selection for the origins of language, because it arose as an accident of history: 'We have no idea, at present, how physical laws apply when 10^{10} neurons are placed in an object the size of a basketball, under the special conditions that arose during human evolution.' (Chomsky, 1988)

Pinker (1994) believes that Chomsky 'has it backwards'. The brain is more likely to have increased in size *as a result* of the evolution of language, rather than the other way round. As Pinker argues, 'it is the precise wiring of the brain's circuitry that makes language happen, not gross size, shape, or neuron packing' (see Chapter 3). He cites considerable evidence in favour of a genetic basis for spoken language, which supports its evolution by natural selection (see below, pages 148–150).

Consistent with Whiten's (1999, 2007) 'deep social mind' hypothesis (see above and Chapter 1) is Dunbar's (e.g. 1996) claim that the ability to recognise and groom a large number of conspecifics may be associated with a large brain. Language may have evolved as an energetically cheap means of social grooming (language-as-social-grooming hypothesis: see Chapter 1).

Disagreeing with Dunbar, and consistent with Pinker, we saw in Chapter 1 that Oppenheimer (2007) argues that it's much more likely that our hominid ancestors were already communicating 'usefully and deliberately' 2.5 million years ago: it was this that drove brain growth, rather than brain growth reaching some threshold size which 'miraculously' made speech possible.

Like Oppenheimer, Leakey (1994) believes that language emerged early in the evolution of *Homo*, followed by a gradual enhancement (rather than appearing recently and suddenly). Many anthropologists favour a recent, rapid origin of language, principally because of the abrupt change in behaviour seen in the **Upper Paleolithic Revolution** (see Box 6.6).

Box 6.6 The Upper Palaeolithic Revolution (based on Leakey, 1994)

The appearance of the genus *Homo* coincides roughly with the beginning of the **archaeological record** (the appearance of the first, very simple, stone tools), some 2.5 million years ago. Soon after the appearance of *Homo erectus*, 1.4 million years ago, stone tools became more complex (such as a simple hand axe), but little change occurred for more than a million years. The biological novelty in the anatomy of the archaic *sapiens*, including the Neanderthals, was clearly accompanied by a new level of technological competence (involving as many as 60 tools).

Little changed after this until between 10,000 and 40,000 years ago, but when change did come, it was dazzling. This period is referred to as the *Upper Palaelothic* (in Europe) (or the Late Stone Age in Africa). People began making tools of the finest form, fashioned from delicately struck stone blades. For the first time, bone and antler were used as raw material for tool making. Tool kits now comprised more than 100 items, including implements for making crude clothing, engraving and sculpting. For the first time, tools became works of art: antler spear throwers, for example, were adorned with lifelike animal carvings. Beads and pendants appear in the fossil record.

> *... And – most evocative of all – paintings on the walls of deep caves speak of a mental world we readily recognise as our own. Unlike previous eras ... innovation is now the essence of culture, with change being measured in millennia rather than hundreds of millennia ... this collective archaeological signal is unmistakable evidence of the modern human mind.* (Leakey, 1994)

According to White (1985), evidence of various forms of human activity earlier than 100,000 years ago implies 'a total absence of anything that modern humans would recognise as language'. Anatomically modern humans hadn't yet 'invented' language in a cultural context. This would come much later: 'By 35,000 years ago, these populations ... had mastered language and culture as we presently know them.' (White, 1985)

White lists seven areas of archaeological evidence that, in his view, point to dramatic enhancement of language abilities during the Upper Palaeolithic period:

1. Deliberate burial of the dead, which almost certainly began in Neanderthal times but became refined, with the inclusion of grave goods, only in the Upper Palaeolithic.

2. Artistic expression, which included image making and bodily adornment, began only in the Upper Palaeolithic.

3. A sudden acceleration in the pace of technological innovation and cultural change (see Box 6.6 above).

4. For the first time, regional differences in culture appeared – an expression and product of social boundaries.

5. Strong evidence of long-distance contacts, in the form of the trading of exotic objects.

6. Living sites significantly increased in size and language would have been necessary for such a degree of planning and coordination.

7. Technology moved from the predominant use of stone to include other raw materials, such as bone, antler and clay, indicating a complex manipulation of the physical environment which is unimaginable in the absence of language (again, see Box 6.6).

White and other anthropologists (such as Binford, 1981, 1985) are convinced that this cluster of 'firsts' in human activity is underpinned by the appearance of complex, fully modern spoken language. Binford sees no evidence of planning and little capacity for predicting and organising future events and activities among pre-modern humans. The great step forward was language; this, and, specifically, symbolising, make abstraction possible (see Chapter 5).

However, Falk's studies in the 1980s of the evolution of the human brain (cited in Leakey, 1994) led her to argue that language developed early: what else were hominids doing with their 'autocatalytically increasing brains?' Similarly, Deacon (1989), based on studies of modern rather than fossilised ones, claims that: 'Language competence evolved over a long period (at least 2 million years) of continuous selection determined by brain–language interaction'.

Based on comparisons of the differences in neuronal connectivity between the chimp and human brain, Deacon points out that the brain structures and circuits that changed the most in the course of human brain evolution reflect the unusual computational demands of speech.

The anatomical evidence

The expansion of the human brain began more than 2 million years ago with the appearance of the genus *Homo* and continued steadily (see Box 1.2, page 14). By 500,000 years ago, the average brain size among *Homo erectus* was 1,100 cm^3, which is close to the modern average. These increases surely reflected enhanced cognitive capacities. If brain size is also related to language capabilities, then the history of brain-size increase during the past 2 million years suggests a gradual development of our ancestors' language skills (Leakey, 1994). Deacon's (1989) comparison of the anatomy of chimp and human brains suggests that this is likely. After the initial 50 per cent increase from *Australopithecine* to *Homo*, there were no further sudden large increases in the size of the prehistoric human brain.

According to Jerison (1991), language is the engine of brain growth; he dismisses the notion that manipulative skills provided the evolutionary pressure for bigger brains, as implied by the 'man the toolmaker' hypothesis (Oakley, 1949, in Leakey, 1994). But Oakley, a British anthropologist, was also among the first to propose that the emergence of modern humans was triggered by the 'perfection' of language to the level we experience today: in other words, modern language made modern man. Jerison rejects the 'man the toolmaker' account on the grounds that tool-making can be achieved with very little brain tissue, while the production of simple, useful speech 'requires a substantial amount of brain tissue' (Jerison, 1991).

The brain architecture underlying language is much more complex than once thought. There appear to be several language-related areas, scattered throughout many regions of the human brain. Unfortunately, the anatomical evidence from the brains of extinct humans is restricted to surface contours: fossil brains provide no clues to internal structure. However, Broca's area, which is related to both language and tool use, is visible on the surface of the brain: a raised lump located near the left temple (in most people). If we could find evidence of Broca's area in fossil human brains, this would indicate the possibility of emerging language ability (Leakey, 1994). A second possible indicator is the greater size of the left hemisphere (see below and Chapter 3).

Holloway (1983) examined the shape of the brain of skull 1470, a fine example of *Homo habilis* found near Lake Turkana in 1972 and determined it to be almost 2 million years old (see Box 1.2, page 14). He detected not only the presence of Broca's area, but also a slight asymmetry in the left-right configuration of the brain; this indicated that *Homo habilis* communicated with more than the pant-hoot-grunt repertoire of modern chimps (see Box 6.1 and Box 6.2). While it's impossible to prove when or how language began, it's likely that its origins extended 'far back into the palaeontological past' (Holloway, 1983). Leakey (1994) believes that no form of spoken language appeared before the evolution of *Homo habilis*; like Bickerton (1990), Leakey suspects that this was a sort of *proto-language*, simple in content and structure, but a form of communication beyond the capacity of apes and **Australopithecines**.

A second major source of anatomical evidence comes from the vocal apparatus: the larynx, pharynx, tongue and lips (discussed above; see Figure 6.1). At birth, the human larynx is high in the throat (as in other mammals); this allows babies to drink and breathe simultaneously, which they must do during nursing. After about 18 months, the larynx begins to migrate down the throat, reaching the adult position by about age 14.

Laitman *et al.* (1984) realised that if they could determine the position of the larynx in the throats of human ancestral species, they could deduce something about these species' capacity for vocalisation and language. Although the vocal apparatus is constructed from soft tissues (cartilage, muscle and flesh), which don't fossilise, the shape of the bottom of the skull (or *basicranium*) provides a vital clue: in the basic mammalian pattern, this is essentially flat, while in humans it is distinctly arched. In the Australopithecines, the basicranium was basically flat (as they are in chimps); also like chimps, their vocal communication must have been limited. For example, they'd have been unable to produce some of the universal vowel sounds characteristic of human speech patterns. According to Laitman *et al.*, the earliest time in the fossil record that you find a fully arched basicranium is about 300,000 to 400,000 years ago in early *Homo sapiens*. It's unlikely that a fully modern language appeared before the appearance of anatomically modern humans (Leakey, 1994).

The change in the shape of the basicranium can be seen in the earliest-known *Homo erectus* specimen (skull 3733 from northern Kenya), dating from almost 2 million years ago. This suggests that this *Homo erectus* individual would have been able to produce certain vowels (such as in 'boot', 'father', 'feet'). Laitman *et al.* calculate that the position of the larynx in early *Homo erectus* would have been equivalent to that of a modern six-year-old.

143

Box 6.7 The Neanderthal basicranium and language

Leakey (1994) points out an apparent contradiction: judging by their basicrania, the Neanderthals had *poorer* verbal skills than those of other archaic *sapiens* that lived several hundred thousand years *earlier*. Did the Neanderthals regress, becoming less articulate than their ancestors? A more likely explanation is to be found in the anatomy of their face and cranium. As an apparent adaptation to cold climates, the Neanderthal midface protruded to an extraordinary degree, resulting in large nasal passages, where cold air can be warmed and moisture in exhaled breath can condense. These adaptations may have affected the shape of the basicranium *without* significantly diminishing their language capacity.

The archaeological evidence for tool technology and artistic expression

While the anatomical evidence overall indicates an early evolution of language, followed by gradual improvement of linguistic skills, the archaeological evidence for tool technology and artistic expression suggests a much later – and more sudden – appearance of language. As we saw in Box 6.6, the Upper Palaeolithic revolution marks a dramatic change in tool-making.

Some, like Isaac (1976), take this pattern of technological diversity and change as implying some form of spoken language. However, there are differences of opinion regarding what degree of spoken language earlier tool-makers had – if any (Leakey, 1994). Wynn and McGrew (1989) believe that the cognitive capacity of *Homo erectus,* based on their tool production, was equivalent to that of a seven-year-old modern human. Children of this age have considerable linguistic skills, including reference and grammar, and are close to being able to converse without having to point and gesture (Leakey, 1994: see below).

If artistic expression is taken as the only reliable indicator of spoken language, then language not only became fully modern recently but was also initiated recently. According to Davidson and Noble (1989), 'The making of images to resemble things can only have emerged prehistorically in communities with shared systems of meanings.' 'Shared systems of meaning' are mediated, of course, through language. Davidson and Noble argue that artistic expression was a medium through which referential language developed – *not* that art was made possible by language: art had to *predate*, or at least emerge in parallel with, language. The appearance of the first art in the archaeological record, therefore, indicates the first appearance of spoken, referential language.

Leakey (1994) concludes:

> ... *Those who wish to maintain humans as special will welcome evidence that points to a recent and abrupt origin of language. Those who are comfortable with human connection to the rest of nature will not be distressed by an early, slow development of this quintessentially human capacity. I conjecture that if ... populations of* Homo habilis *and* Homo erectus *still existed, we would see in them gradations of referential language. The gap between us and the rest of nature would therefore be closed by our own ancestors.* (emphasis in original)

Language and the brain

> **Time for reflection**
> ● What roles are played by the pre-frontal cortex (PFC) and the orbitofrontal cortex (OFC)? (See Chapter 3, pages 49–50.)

Language development and the brain

According to Gerhardt (2004), once the OFC is established, with its growing ability to manage feelings, the right and left sides start to knit together, linking the expression and management of feelings. There's a general shift from right hemisphere dominance towards development of the left brain, which is specialised for sequential processing (one message at a time) and language. At the same time, the brain becomes more stable and less open to change. The left hemisphere monitors the organised self that has emerged from the right hemisphere, asserts the self and expresses that self to other people.

Sometime after these changes, the **dorsolateral prefrontal cortex** (**DPFC**) starts to develop. This is where we play around with our thoughts and feelings, where we think about them; it's the main site of 'working memory' (see Chapter 7 and Gross, 2010).

The child's second year is notable for the increasing linguistic ability, based in the left hemisphere. Both the DPFC and the recently developed **anterior cingulate cortex** (which surrounds the amygdala and hypothalamus) are linked and are involved in speech production and verbal fluency.

Where do we 'do' language?

As we saw in Chapter 3, the human brain is no longer considered to be unique in displaying **functional lateralisation** (or hemispheric asymmetry); the brains of several other species (including birds and (other) mammals) also display this property (MacNeilage *et al.*, 2009). But human brains are unique in having two areas (always found in the left hemisphere, regardless of handedness) which are specialised for language – Broca's and Wernicke's areas. These are noticeably larger than the corresponding right hemisphere regions.

The French neurologist Paul Broca was the first modern researcher to attribute a specific function to an area of the brain based on a lesion in that area in a patient who'd lost the power of speech (one form of **aphasia**) and whose vocabulary was essentially limited to the sound 'tan'. After the patient's death, examination of his brain revealed a left hemisphere lesion, in a region just above the left ear (since known as Broca's area). Behind this lies Wernicke's area, and between them is the primary auditory cortex. Wernicke's area is responsible for language *comprehension* (rather than *production*). (See Box 6.8 and text below.) Damage to this area causes a different type of aphasia. The fact that chimps' brains are also asymmetrical suggests that the brain regions required for speech were already present prior to its emergence (Rose, 2005).

While the left hemisphere is undoubtedly dominant, this doesn't mean that the right hemisphere plays no role at all in language. Consistent with its more emotional character, the right hemisphere is responsible for **prosody**, the inflection and overall musical quality that lend important emphasis to verbal communication (see the description of 'motherese' in Box 5.2, page 103). Language is further localised to a broad central wedge of the left hemisphere, the **perisylvian cortex** (so-called because of the way it surrounds the Sylvian fissure, the deep horizontal 'canyon' that separates the temporal from the frontal and parietal lobes (see Figure 6.2).

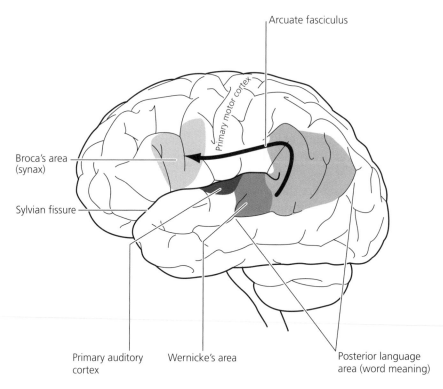

▲ **Figure 6.2** Language centres of the brain. Dots and Xs show brain areas activated during verb and noun use, respectively

How does linguistic processing happen in the brain?

> **Time for reflection**
> - What do you understand by 'grammar', '**phonology**', 'semantics' and 'syntax'?
> - How are these different aspects of language related?
>
> (See Gross, 2010.)

The 'classical' model of how the brain processes language is based on clinical case studies of patients with damage to either Broca's or Wernicke's area; this is described in Box 6.8.

Box 6.8 The 'classical' model of language processing in the brain (based on Eliot, 1999)

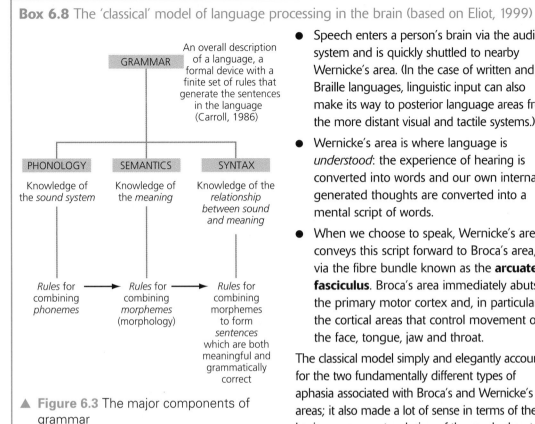

▲ **Figure 6.3** The major components of grammar

- Speech enters a person's brain via the auditory system and is quickly shuttled to nearby Wernicke's area. (In the case of written and Braille languages, linguistic input can also make its way to posterior language areas from the more distant visual and tactile systems.)

- Wernicke's area is where language is *understood*: the experience of hearing is converted into words and our own internally generated thoughts are converted into a mental script of words.

- When we choose to speak, Wernicke's area conveys this script forward to Broca's area, via the fibre bundle known as the **arcuate fasciculus**. Broca's area immediately abuts the primary motor cortex and, in particular, the cortical areas that control movement of the face, tongue, jaw and throat.

The classical model simply and elegantly accounted for the two fundamentally different types of aphasia associated with Broca's and Wernicke's areas; it also made a lot of sense in terms of the basic sensory-motor design of the cerebral cortex.

However, although these two areas are still distinguished, they're no longer considered to be responsible for speech production and comprehension respectively. Rather, they're now seen as dividing language up by **semantics** and **syntax** (see Figure 6.3).

Left posterior areas are activated during tasks involving the meaning of words (semantics), while the left frontal cortex is more specifically activated during tasks involving grammatical processing. For example, Broca's area 'lights up' when participants compare two sentences whose meaning is identical but that differ in word order (syntactic structure). But the left temporal-parietal area (including Wernicke's area and a large area above and behind it) is activated more by tasks that tax one's understanding of individual words, as when hearing the unusual sentence 'We bake cookies in the zoo'. In other words, the posterior language centre is where word meanings are stored, rather like a mental dictionary, whereas the frontal centre functions more like a grammar textbook, where we work out the significance and appropriateness of word order – the classic syntactic problem of who's doing what to whom (Eliot, 1999).

Because of the way different parts of speech work, verbs are processed in the frontal lobe and nouns in the left temporal-parietal region. Verbs, more than any other part of speech, are the central components in grammar. They determine the relationship between subject and object and are the most often modified part of speech (such as by adding 'ed', 'ing' and 's') to convey tense, person and other conditional features of a sentence (Eliot, 1999).

According to this new theory, people with damage to their Broca's area are impaired in using grammar, not in producing language. Their broken, **telegraphic speech** typically lacks verbs, as well as most of the small connectors ('of', 'to', 'and', 'in', 'the') that glue sentences together. But they can understand language because verbs are much less essential for inferring meaning (i.e. nouns convey relatively much more of the meaning of a sentence). Wernicke's aphasics are much worse off: although they retain the rules for connecting words (verb tenses, prepositions, conjunctions), they simply don't have enough words left in their damaged mental dictionaries to say (or understand) anything substantial.

As Eliot (1999) also points out, the segregation of syntax and meaning also makes sense in terms of the brain's division of other sensory and cognitive functions. Wernicke's area is located near the junction of three important senses – hearing, vision and touch; this makes it a good place for the brain to store the associations between the sound of words and the physical entities (people, places and things) they represent. Syntax, by contrast, fits more comfortably in the frontal lobe, where other cognitive skills involving planning, sequencing, logic and rule-learning are carried out.

Brain anatomy and language development

The **pre-linguistic stage** (0–12 months) consists largely of babbling (the production of phonemes). While babbling changes during this stage, the sounds that babies produce have no meaning (hence, 'pre-linguistic'). The **one-word stage** typically lasts from 12–18 months when babies produce their first articulate sounds, 'a systematic matching of form and meaning' (Scollon, 1976). Between 18–30 months (**stage 1 grammar**), children begin to put two-word sentences together, but their speech is telegraphic (much like that of Broca's aphasics): only those words that convey the most information are used (what Brown (1973) called *contentives*). Children will gradually begin to include the purely 'grammatical' terms (**functors**), such as the verb 'to be', plurals and possessives during **stage 2 grammar** (from 30 months to about four or five years). (For a more detailed account, see Gross, 2010.)

This gradual progression from word-learning to grammatical speech is mirrored by what is known about the relative maturation of Broca's and Wernicke's areas. Wernicke's area and the rest of the posterior language centre appears to develop *in advance* of Broca's area. As measured by the number of synapses formed (that is, the number of connections between neurons), a peak is reached in the left temporal-parietal region between 8–20 months, compared with 15–24 months in left frontal areas. Broca's area only reaches maturity at four years of age. Another developmental measure is **myelination**: the formation of myelin sheaths around the axons of neurons which aids the transmission of electrical impulses to neighbouring neurons. Broca's area myelinates much later than Wernicke's (at age 4–6 years compared with age 2 years). The arcuate fasciculus (which connects the two areas) is especially late to myelinate, thereby limiting the speed with which young children can put meaningful utterances into grammatical context (Eliot, 1999).

Brain plasticity and language acquisition

As we noted in Chapter 3, the human brain, especially the immature human brain, is remarkably 'plastic', that is, flexible, adaptable and able to repair itself. This plasticity helps explain why young children are so good at absorbing language. According to Eliot (1999), 'language offers the most dramatic illustration we have of early brain plasticity.' Unlike adults, in whom damage to the left perisylvian area can cause irreparable aphasia, children with comparable brain damage are capable of incredible language recovery. A child can even have its entire left hemisphere removed (which is occasionally the only treatment for certain intractable brain disorders) and still learn to talk, read and write – provided the surgery takes place early in the critical period, ideally, before the age of four or five. Children whose hemispheres are removed before age four or five recover almost completely, while those who undergo surgery at or after puberty lose all language ability.

What such cases show is that the language circuits of the brain, though genetically biased for the left hemisphere, can put themselves together remarkably well in the right hemisphere – provided such circuits begin to form fairly early in life. But not all circuits are equally plastic: in every case of severe language deprivation, whether through social isolation (as in the case of Genie: see Curtiss, 1977; Rolls, 2010), early brain damage or congenital blindness, the capacity for grammar (i.e. syntax) has been found to be much more vulnerable than the ability to learn word meaning (semantics). The development of Broca's area is much more sensitive to experience compared with Wernicke's: people who learn a second language later in life (such as English for deaf individuals already fluent in American Sign Language (ASL) show deviant frontal-lobe activity during syntactical processing, while activity in the temporal-parietal area in response to English words is relatively normal (Eliot, 1999).

Speech and the brain

Motor neurons that control the muscles involved in vocalisation – the lips, tongue and larynx – are located in the brainstem (see Chapter 3). After decades of painstaking research, we now know that humans have direct neural connections between the motor cortex and these brainstem neurons which non-human primates lack (Fitch, 2010). Could these direct neural connections explain our enhanced ability to control and coordinate the movements necessary for speech? Fortunately, we can test this hypothesis with the help of other species that display complex vocal learning.

If direct neural connections are necessary for vocal learning, then we can predict that they should appear in other vocal learning species. For birds, at least, this prediction appears to hold true: parrots and songbirds have the connection that chickens and pigeons lack. But we don't know about many other vocal learning species, including whales, seals, elephants and bats, because their neuroanatomy hasn't yet been fully investigated (Fitch, 2010).

While direct neural connections may be necessary, they aren't sufficient: complex vocal control in humans also relies on our ability to control the different articulators in the correct, often complex, sequences. The discovery of the **FOXP2 gene** has provided insights into the origins of this ability (see below and Chapter 2). Several studies have shown that the gene seems to be crucial for memory formation in the basal ganglia and cerebellum, which are involved in coordinating the patterns of movements that are essential for our complex vocalisations. Recently, fossil DNA recovered from Neanderthals has shown that they shared the modern variant of *FOXP2,* suggesting that they already possessed complex speech. However, speech is just one component of language, and similar questions must be asked about syntax and semantics before we can hope to understand the evolution of language as a whole (Fitch, 2010).

The genetics of language and the 'mental organ' view of language

Is there a 'language gene'?

In Chapter 2, we asked the question: Are there any exclusively, uniquely human genes? Given that so many psychologists, neuroscientists and philosophers whose views we've considered in this and earlier chapters believe that language is what ultimately distinguishes us from chimps (and all other non-humans), it wouldn't be altogether surprising if a uniquely human gene turned out to be involved in language.

Based on the study of the KE family (see Box 2.3, page 31), the *FOXP2* gene was identified as a possible 'language gene'. As we saw in Box 2.3, Gopnik (1990) claimed that the gene is involved in *morphosyntax* (understanding of the internal structure of words – morphology – and how words are put together to form phrases and sentences – syntax). Pinker (1994) went as far as calling *FOXP2* the 'grammar gene' – although he has more recently acknowledged that other genes probably also played a part in the evolution of grammar (Gentilucci and Corballis, 2007). The claim that a genetic basis for human linguistic capacity had been discovered was clearly a much oversimplified interpretation (Enard *et al.,* 2002).

We also noted in Chapter 2 that *FOXP2* is not a uniquely human gene, making the case for it being a language gene much more problematical. As Rose (2005) observes, *FOXP2* is found in gorillas and chimps, differing only in a couple of amino acids, and, with a few more variations, in mice. Whether these minor variations are enough to contribute to the profound difference in linguistic capacity between mice, chimps and humans remains to be resolved, but it doesn't seem intuitively very likely:

> *... It must be assumed that many of the genetic changes relevant to constructing a chimpanzee rather than a human phenotype are likely to lie in complex regulatory mechanisms rather than in the structural proteins which comprise the bulk of both chimpanzee and human brains and bodies ...* (Rose, 2005)

In some ways, a more serious blow to the language-gene hypothesis came when it was discovered that the core deficit in members of the KE family with a faulty *FOXP2* gene is one of articulation (i.e. speech), with grammatical impairment a secondary problem (Watkins *et al.,* 2002). According to Lai *et al.* (2001), the KE family's specific language impairment (SLI) involves the inability to make certain subtle, high-speed facial movements needed for normal human speech – despite possessing the cognitive ability required for processing language.

Is language an innate human ability?

While the genetic evidence may be weak, there are other versions of the view that language is an *innate* human capacity. According to Chomsky (1979), an innate language ability exists independently of other innate abilities, because the mind is constructed of 'mental organs', which are '... just as specialised and differentiated as those of the body ... and ... language is a system easy to isolate among the various mental faculties.'

Chomsky's view is echoed in the more recent claims of evolutionary psychologists, such as Pinker (who is primarily a linguist). Unlike earlier generations of genetic determinists, evolutionary psychologists argue that behaviours (such as language) aren't so much the direct product of gene action, but of the evolutionary sculpting of the human mind. Drawing heavily on artificial intelligence, they argue that the mind is a cognitive machine, an information-processing device (see Gross, 2010). But rather than being a general-purpose computer, the human mind consists of a number of specific modules (of which a language module is one).

The case for the modularity of mind was first proposed by the psychologists Jerry Fodor in 1983 (in a book by that title). While modularity doesn't necessarily imply innateness, Pinker's (1994) *The Language Instinct: How The Mind Creates Language* claims that language, like all the various mental modules, has evolved more or less independently during the evolution of *Homo sapiens* and has persisted unmodified throughout historical time. The archaeologist Steven Mithen (1996) counters Pinker's claim by arguing that, whereas in non-human species the modules were and are indeed distinct, the characteristic of human mentality is the ability to *integrate*. Rather than functioning in a modular way drawing from a toolkit of autonomous specialised functional units, like a Swiss army knife (the analogy favoured by Tooby and Cosmides, e.g. 1990), the human brain is like a general-purpose computer.

While neither Chomsky nor Pinker indicates which areas of the brain might 'house' the language organ or module, their claim is supported by the evidence discussed above for specialised language areas. Eliot (1999) likens this brain circuitry to an extra chip that evolution has inserted into the human computer. She also points out that language can be specifically impaired by certain types of brain injury or disease – without affecting a person's general intellectual functioning. Conversely, language can be specifically *preserved*, as in a particular type of mental retardation known as *Williams syndrome*; this is discussed in Box 6.9.

> **Box 6.9** Williams syndrome
>
> Adults with this rare genetic disorder (in which a small piece of chromosome 7 is missing) have very low IQs (intelligence quotients), usually in the 50s (with 100 being the average), meaning that their overall intelligence is extremely low (the mild category of mental retardation). Some of their major deficits include spatial cognition, number and problem solving (Rose, 2005). Yet these individuals are surprisingly skilled when it comes to language, as well as face-processing and social interaction. They have large and varied vocabularies and astutely recognise many subtle grammatical errors. Although their brains show many abnormalities, the areas that control language production and comprehension – the same areas damaged in aphasic patients – are mysteriously intact (Eliot, 1999).
>
> This relative sparing of specific faculties is, it's argued, evidence for a distinct 'language module' in the brain, such as Pinker's (1994) claim that 'The mind is likely to contain blueprints for grammatical rules … and a special set of genes that help wire it in place.' However, Annette Karmiloff-Smith (2000) challenges this conclusion. Far from linguistic and face-processing abilities being straightforwardly preserved in Williams syndrome, children with the syndrome are in fact impaired in quite subtle ways. As a result, as they grow up they develop alternative strategies for overcoming their deficits, thereby recovering some functions. As adults, they give the impression of possessing a specific 'language module'.

> **Box 6.9** Williams syndrome
>
> *... subtle differences in developmental timing, numbers of neurons and their connections, transmitter types and neural efficiency are likely to be the causes of dissociations in developmental outcomes. Such subtle initial differences may have a huge but very indirect impact on the resulting phenotype, ultimately giving rise to domain-specific impairments after the process of post-natal brain development.* (Karmiloff-Smith, 2000)

Interestingly, despite Chomsky's claim that language constitutes a distinct 'mental organ', he denies that it's been shaped by natural selection. Rather, he proposed that the language organ evolved for some other purpose and was 'co-opted' for its current purpose. This is similar to what Gould (2002) calls **exaptation**: the take-over of structures or processes originally evolved as an adaptation to one function for use in a totally different way. Chomsky and his colleagues (Hauser *et al.*, 2002) extended the 'co-opting' idea by distinguishing between 'the faculty of language in the broad sense' (FLB) and in the narrow sense (FLN). These are explained in Box 6.10.

> **Box 6.10** Language in the broad and narrow sense
>
> ● *Language in the broad sense* (FLB) refers to what we commonly call language (verbal communication) and includes all the cognitive operations that support it (such as auditory perception and planning). It also includes all the biological apparatus required to perform it.
>
> ● *Language in the narrow sense* (FLN) refers to only those features of language that are specific to language itself. Collectively, these features are called **linguistic universals**, and a major example is *recursion* (see Chapter 5 and the text below). FLN also refers to an internal abstract computational system that generates internal representations (mental language) and maps them onto sensory-motor outputs. However, they don't specify what brain regions might be involved in these processes.

Chomsky is adamant that only humans possess language (in either sense), which implies that 'it arrived as one giant step for hominidkind relatively recently' (Rose, 2005) (see the discussion above, pages 138–142). The alternative view, that language evolved slowly and incrementally through hominid evolution, is supported by the findings of Savage-Rumbaugh and her colleagues (e.g. Savage-Rumbaugh *et al.*, 1998) from their attempts to teach chimps ASL. If we accept their conclusions regarding the linguistic abilities of Kanzi, a bonobo, then they have demonstrated evidence of an evolutionary preparedness (Gould's 'exaptation'):

> *... Speech thus only awaits the human context, and the fortuitous alterations in the position of the human larynx, itself a consequence of upright bipedal locomotion rather than knuckle-walking as employed by our fellow apes ...* (Rose, 2005)

Chomsky's 'universal grammar' and the language acquisition device (LAD)

Central to Chomsky's (1957, 1965) theory of **transformational grammar** (TG) are *phrase-structure rules*, which specify what are acceptable/unacceptable utterances in a speaker's native language. When applied systematically, these rules generate sentences in English or any other language. However, phrase-structure rules don't specify all important aspects of language.

According to Chomsky, children are equipped with the ability to learn the rules for transforming **deep structure** into various **surface structure** items (see Box 6.11).

Box 6.11 Deep and surface structure and transformational grammar (TG)

- A sentence's *surface structure* refers to the actual words or phrases used in the sentence (its *syntactical structure*), while the *deep structure* more or less corresponds to the *meaning* of the sentence.

- Chomsky argues that when we hear a spoken sentence, we don't 'process' or retain its surface structure, but transform it into its deep structure.

- Transformational grammar (TG) is knowing how to transform a sentence's meaning into the words that make it up – and vice versa. This knowledge is an innate language acquisition device (LAD) and is what enables us to produce an infinite number of meaningful sentences.

- A single surface structure may have *more than one* deep structure, as in the sentence, 'The missionary was ready to eat'. This could be interpreted either as 'The missionary is ready to consume a meal' or 'The missionary has been prepared for consumption by others'.

- Conversely, different surface structures can have the *same* deep structure (as in the sentences 'A small boy helped the girl' and 'The girl was helped by a small boy').

Time for reflection

Try a Chomsky-type analysis on the following:
- Cleaning ladies can be delightful.
- Shaving men can be dangerous.

Chomsky claims that children are equipped with the ability to learn the rules for transforming deep structure into various surface structures. They do this by looking for certain kinds of linguistic features common to all languages, such as the use of consonants and vowels, syllables, modifiers, nouns and verbs, recursion and so on (see Box 6.10). Collectively, these linguistic features are called *linguistic universals* (or *universal grammar*): they provide the deep structure. They must be universal, because any child can acquire any language he or she is exposed to. As we saw in Box 6.11, the inborn LAD consists essentially of TG.

Linguistic diversity and linguistic universals

Chomsky's basic hypothesis emphasises what all languages have in common (they're all basically the same). LAD enables the child to extract these shared features in the particular mother tongue he or she is exposed to. This idea has dominated work in linguistics, psychology and cognitive science for 50 years: to understand language, we must sweep aside the dazzling diversity of languages and find the common human core (Kenneally, 2010).

But what if it's the very diversity of languages that provides the key to understanding human communication? This is the hypothesis proposed by Evans and Levinson (2009), in an article entitled 'The myth of language universals: Language diversity and its importance for cognitive science'. Everett (2009b) describes the article as 'a watershed in the history of linguistic theory'. According to Evans and Levinson, language *doesn't* share a common set of rules. Rather, its sheer variety is a defining feature of human communication – something not seen in non-humans (see above). They go further and argue that language diversity is the 'crucial fact for understanding the place of language in human cognition'. While it might be generally agreed that human thinking influences the form that language takes, what Evans and Levinsons claim implies that language in turn shapes our brains. This suggests that humans are more diverse than we thought, with our brains showing differences depending on the language environment we grow up in. According to Kenneally (2010), this leads to the disturbing conclusion that every time a language becomes extinct, humanity loses an important piece of diversity.

Exceptions to universal grammar

Since Chomsky first proposed his theory of linguistic universals, linguists have identified important exceptions to the rules of language.

- Some languages use 11 distinct sounds (phones or phonetic segments) with which to make words, while others use as many as 144. English uses 46 (Solso, 1995). As sounds that were once thought impossible are discovered, the idea that there's a fixed set of speech sounds is being rejected (Kenneally, 2010).

- Some languages use a single word where others need an entire sentence. For example, in English you might say 'I cooked the wrong meat for them again', while in the indigenous Australian language Bininj Gun-wok you'd say 'abanyawoihwarrgahmarneganjginjeng'. The more we know about language processing, the less likely it seems that these two structures are processed in the same way.

- Even plurals aren't straightforward. The Kiowa people of North America use a plural marker that means 'of unexpected number'. Attached to 'leg', the marker means 'one or more than two'; attached to 'stone', it means 'just two'.

- Some major word classes aren't found in all languages. For example, English lacks 'ideophones' where diverse feelings about an event and its participants are crammed into one word, such as 'rawa-dawa' from the Mundari language (of the Indian subcontinent), meaning 'the sensation of suddenly realising you can do something reprehensible, and no one is there to witness it'.

- It was once believed that no language would have a syllable that begins with a vowel and ends with a consonant (VC), if it didn't also have syllables that begin with a consonant and end with a vowel (CV). In 1999, it was found that Arrernte, spoken by Indigenous Australians from the area around Alice Springs in the Northern Territory, has VC syllables but no CV syllables.

- Since 1990, it's been shown that several languages lack an open class of adverbs. This means that, unlike in English where you can turn any word into an adverb (e.g. 'soft' into 'softly'), the number of adverbs is limited. Others, such as Lao, spoken in Laos, have no adjectives. More controversially, some linguists argue that a few languages, such as Straits Salish, spoken by indigenous people from north-western regions of North America, don't even have distinct nouns or verbs. Instead, they have a single word class to encompass events, entities and qualities.

● Exceptions have been found even to apparently fundamental and indisputable universals such as *recursion* (see Box 6.12).

Box 6.12 Recursion: universal or not?

As we saw in Chapter 5, recursion is a form of **generative computation** which Hauser (2009) believes is unique to human beings. In the context of language, recursion refers to the repeated use of a rule to create new expressions (embedding phrases/clauses within others to make theoretically infinitely long sentences). Recursion is widely considered to be a characteristic that sets human language apart from non-human communication.

However, according to Everett (2009b), instead of saying 'The man, who was tall, came into the house', Pirahas (who live in the Amazonian rainforest in Brazil) say 'The man came into the house. He was tall'. Everett believes that the Piraha lack of recursion derives from 'the immediacy of experience principle': Pirahas have little interest in what they cannot directly verify, so they communicate through a sequence of simple declarative assertions, removing the need for embedded clauses.

Evans and Levinson (2009) believe that the idea of universal grammar has sent researchers down a blind alley. But if languages don't obey a single set of shared rules, then how are they created? Evans and Levinson believe that instead of universals, what you have are 'standard engineering solutions' that languages adopt again and again, with the inevitable 'outliers' (i.e. exceptions). This is because any given language is a complex system shaped by many factors, including culture, genetics and history. There are no absolutely universal language traits, only *tendencies*: it's a mix of strong and weak tendencies that characterises the 'bio-cultural' hybrid we call language.

The *strong tendencies* explain why many languages converge on common patterns. Various factors, such as the structure of the brain, the biology of speech and the efficiencies of communication, tend to push language in a similar direction. Widely shared linguistic elements may also build on a particularly human kind of social reasoning. For example, the fact that before we learn to speak we see the world as a place full of things causing actions (agents) and things having actions performed on them (patients) explains why most languages make use of these categories. The *weak tendencies* are explained by the idiosyncrasies of different languages.

Evans and Levinson aren't the first to question the universal grammar hypothesis, but their arguments have generated widespread support. For example, the developmental psychologist, Michael Tomasello claims that 'Universal grammar is dead' (in Kenneally, 2010). Pinker (in Kenneally, 2010) agrees with many points made by Evans and Levinson, including (a) the fact that the criteria for defining 'universal' haven't been precise enough; (b) that language arises from the co-evolution of genes and culture; and (c) that it's very important to document the diversity of language. However, Pinker maintains that all humans share an innate set of mechanisms for learning language. While he accepts that the extent to which different languages use these mechanisms may be shaped by that culture's history, he still believes there are many universals that underlie all languages (Kenneally, 2010).

Linguistic diversity and the human mind

> **Time for reflection**
> ● What might the implications be of linguistic diversity for what we understand by the mind?
> ● More specifically, what might it suggest about the relationship between language and thought?
> (See Gross, 2010.)

Clearly, a belief in universal grammar and the LAD that embodies it (complemented by the evidence for specialised brain areas for language) emphasises what both languages and minds have in common: languages reflect the innate ability of language users to infer linguistic universals and apply them to particular languages, and our knowledge and understanding of the world reflect linguistic categories. But a focus on the diversity of languages, such as Evans and Levinson provide, suggests that culture may play a relatively greater role in how both language and the mind are shaped.

Consistent with this view, Everett (2009a and 2009b) proposes that there's a much stronger symbiosis between language and culture than many modern linguists and psychologists might have imagined. His research with the Piraha people suggests that the mind is more plastic and less modular than, say, Chomsky or Fodor would have us believe. There may be common mental properties, with language 'emerging' from their interaction with cultural constraints and general constraints on the nature of communication. Despite the absence of recursion, the Piraha can put into words (probably) any thought they entertain: this means that human **creativity** lies in human thought, rather than in human language. Even more problematic for Chomsky's theory, Piraha – and other languages – seem to lack phrase structure altogether.

Everett's research, however, also throws up some basic questions about other kinds of universals – not linguistic ones, but those concerning some basic human characteristics thought to distinguish us from non-humans. As we noted in Chapter 1, some believe that what makes humans unique is mental time travel (MTT) – the ability to transcend time (Corballis and Suddendorf, 2007). They propose that MMT may lie at the heart of language and that these probably co-evolved. This is consistent with the distinction between signals (the essence of non-human animal communication) and symbols (the essence of language) (see the discussion at the beginning of this chapter). The crucial finding from Everett's research relevant here is that the Pirahas seem to have no creation myths, no stories about heaven, hell or similar concepts beyond current experience: they live predominantly in the here and now (as non-humans are believed to do) (Everett, 2009b).

Linguistic diversity and communication

The diversity of human language is one of its major distinguishing characteristics compared with the communications systems of all other species. These tend to be the same for any group belonging to the same species regardless of where on the globe they live. While there's some evidence of regional variation among songbirds and higher primates, so that they display a range of learned expressions from one population to another (see Chapter 9), none is remotely as diverse as human language. Evans and Levinson (2009) attribute our linguistic 'exuberance' to the plasticity of the human brain (see Chapter 3) and believe that it changes how we should think about human thought.

The standard modern metaphor for cognition is the 'toolbox', with humans sharing some tools with other species, while possessing others that are exclusively ours (the continuity and human exceptionalism views, respectively: see Chapter 1). For Evans and Levinson (2009), cognition is more like 'a machine tool, capable of manufacturing special tools for special jobs … like calculating, playing the piano, reading right to left, or speaking Arabic'. According to this view, a child's brain is not pre-programmed with abstract linguistic rules, its initial setting is much simpler. Its first job is to build a more complicated brain, which it does by using any input it receives, including language. This could mean that speakers of very different languages have quite different brains (see above and Chapter 3), with the Piraha being a case in point.

Similarly, the linguist Guy Deutscher (2010), in *Through the Language Glass*, contradicts the view that language is wholly a product of nature. Instead, he promotes the much neglected view that language takes colour and value from culture and society. Our mother tongue affects how we think and perceive the world, a striking example being what he calls the 'language of space' – how we describe the arrangement of objects around us. Box 6.13 describes some fascinating exceptions to this rule.

Box 6.13 'The child is north of the tree'

Take the sentence 'the child is standing behind the tree': you would imagine that all languages would represent this description of space in the same or a similar way. It's almost inconceivable that there would be languages that don't use such concepts at all. For centuries, philosophers and psychologists have had us believe that spatial concepts such as 'in front of', 'behind', 'left' and 'right' are the universal building blocks of language and cognition.

But Deutscher (2010) cites the remote aboriginal language, Guugu Yimithirr from north Queensland (famous for giving us the word 'kangaroo'). Native speakers have a way of talking about space that seems incredibly odd to us, because they don't use any spatial concepts like 'behind' at all. Instead of saying 'the child is behind the tree', they would say 'the child is north of the tree'. They also say things such as 'there is an ant on your northern foot', and 'I left the pen on the southern edge of the western table in your northern room in the house'. They might also say, 'There is a fly to the north of your nose'. According to Deutscher, Guugu speakers aren't unique: other peoples around the globe, from Mexico to Indonesia, speak in a similar way.

If Guugu speakers are presented with an arrow pointing to their left, they'll later draw it pointing to the left only if they are still facing in the direction in which they saw the arrow originally. But if they turn round, they'll draw it pointing to the *right* – that is, in the same *absolute direction* as the original arrow (Ross, 2004: see Chapter 9, page 277).

According to Deutscher (2010), growing up with such a language essentially develops in your brain a sort of GPS system, an unfailing sense of orientation. If from the age at which you start speaking you have to be aware of the cardinal directions every second of your waking life in order to understand the most trivial things that people say around you, then your language trains you to pay constant attention to your orientation at all times. Because of this intense drilling, the sense of direction becomes second nature. If you ask Guugu speakers how they know where 'north' or 'south' is, they look at you in amazement – just as you would if you were asked how you know where 'in front' of you or 'behind' you is. In Ross's (2004) terms, these examples illustrate how linguistic categories can mould thought and behaviour.

As we noted earlier, children tend to go through the same stages of language development in a fairly regular and predictable sequence – and at fairly predictable ages (although there are always important individual differences). Not only does this reflect the maturation of the brain, but it is consistent with the universal grammar/LAD hypothesis. For example, Chomsky (e.g. 1979) believes that newborns' ability to make *phonetic discriminations* represents the first linguistic universal the baby discovers. However, it's been found that in some languages there are certain aspects that aren't mastered until later in life, such as the triangular kin terms of the Indigenous Australian language, Bininj Gun-Wok. These situate the speaker, listener and a third party relative simultaneously. For example, 'al-doingu' means 'the one who is my mother and your daughter, you being my maternal grandmother'. There are hundreds of such structures in the language, which native Bininj speakers only begin to acquire in their twenties (Evans and Levinson, 2009).

Each of the world's 7,000 or so languages contains its own unique clues to some of the mysteries of human existence. 'Observations about animal species, distinctness, behaviour and ecological relationships which are captured in the vocabulary of some languages distill millennia of close observations by the speakers of those languages' (Evans, in Kenneally, 2010). For example, some languages spoken in Arnhem Land, in Australia's Northern Territory, have words for five species of bee not yet described by science.

In the diversity of the world's languages we find facts about ancient human history, the path of languages through time, and deep knowledge of the planet. Seen in this light, languages and their speakers offer a scientific bonanza to anyone trying to understand human evolution, behaviour and cognition. (Kenneally, 2010)

Teaching language to non-humans

As we've seen, Chomsky believes that language is unique to human beings. Similarly, Lenneberg (1967) claims that it represents a *species-specific* behaviour, common to all humans and found only in humans. But if non-humans can be taught to use language, then they must have the *capacity* for language. The obvious subjects for such language training are our closest evolutionary relatives, chimps and other great apes.

Criteria for defining language

In order to be able to evaluate any attempts to teach language to chimps and gorillas, we need to define language appropriately. Based on 13 'design features' proposed by Hockett (1960) (see Figure 6.4), Aitchison (1983) proposed a list of 10 criteria, of which four are especially important:

1. **Semanticity:** use of symbols to mean or refer to objects, actions, etc. (what we called 'functionally referential' communication above: see Box 6.2).
2. **Displacement:** reference to things not present in time or space.
3. **Structure dependence:** the patterned nature of language/use of 'structured chunks, such as word order (see above, page x).
4. **Creativity:** the ability to produce/understand an infinite number of novel utterances (a feature of language highlighted by Chomsky; what Brown (1973) called productivity).

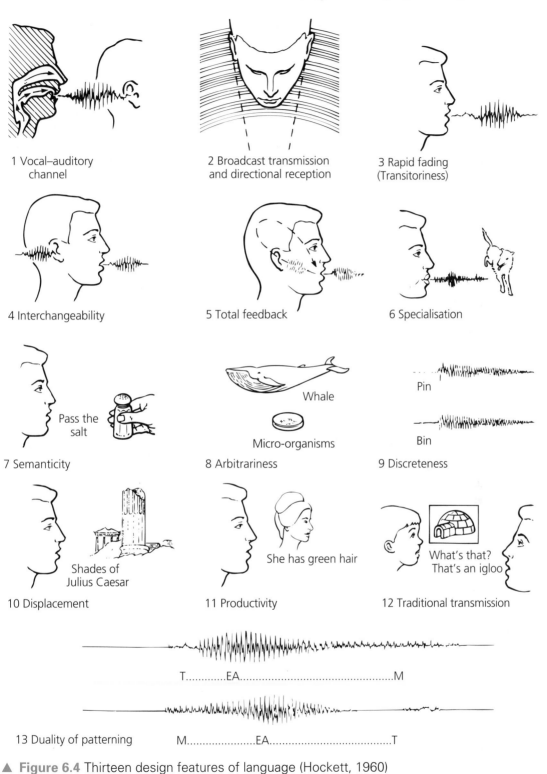

▲ **Figure 6.4** Thirteen design features of language (Hockett, 1960)

According to Fitch (2010), linguists define language as

> *... any system which allows the free and unfettered expression of thoughts into signals, and the complementary interpretation of such signals back into thoughts ...*

Note that Fitch uses the term 'signals', which we contrasted above with 'symbols'. However, the crucial part of his definition seems to be the use of 'free and unfettered'. He goes on to say that what sets human language apart from all other animal communication systems is that the latter can only express 'a limited set of signals'. What creativity/productivity conveys is an *unlimited* set (of signals, utterances, etc.). So, for example:

> *... A dog's bark ... may provide important information about the dog (how large or excited it is) or the outside world (that an intruder is present), but the dog cannot relate the story of its puppyhood, or express the route of its daily walk.* (Fitch, 2010)

What makes non-humans' communication systems limited is that they are *innate* – and yet this is what Chomsky, Pinker and others claim for human language! Fitch gives the example of the vervet monkey predator-related calls (see page 128), which are truly 'signals' in the sense that they are designed to trigger appropriate *behaviour* in conspecifics (running for cover in response to an 'eagle' call signal, or scaling trees in response to a 'leopard' call signal). By contrast, what is innate in humans is universal grammar. This is necessary precisely because of the *diversity* of human language. More importantly, perhaps, the symbols that comprise language are at least as much designed to convey *meaning* as to affect behaviour.

Production-based studies

As we have seen, the vocal apparatus of chimps is simply not designed for speech, so early attempts to teach chimps to speak (Kellogg and Kellogg, 1933; Hayes and Hayes, 1951) were doomed to failure. However, this doesn't rule out the possibility that chimps may still be capable of learning language in some non-spoken form; this is precisely what several psychologists have tried to demonstrate since the 1960s in what have come to be called **production-based studies**. As shown in Table 6.1, three of these have used some form of American Sign Language (ASL), which is particularly well-suited to chimps' natural manual dexterity. Others have used either small plastic symbols or a special typewriter controlled by a computer.

Table 6.1 Major studies which have attempted to teach language to non-human primates

Study	Subject	Method of language training
Gardner and Gardner (1969)	Washoe (female chimp)	American Sign Language (ASL or Ameslan). Based on a series of gestures, each corresponding to a word. Many gestures visually represent aspects of the word's meaning.
Premack (1971)	Sarah (female chimp)	Small plastic symbols of various shapes and colours, each symbol standing for a word; they could be arranged on a special magnetised board; e.g. a mauve △ = 'apple'; a pale blue ◇ = 'inert'; a red □ = 'banana'.
Rumbaugh *et al.* (1977)/ Savage-Rumbaugh *et al.* (1980)	Lana (female chimp)	Special typewriter controlled by a computer. Machine had 50 keys, each displaying a geometric pattern representing a word in a specially devised language ('Yerkish'). When Lana typed, the pattern appeared on the screen in front of her. ◇ 'Lana' ◎ 'Eat'
Patterson (1978, 1980)	Koko (female gorilla)	ASL
Terrace (1979)	Nim Chimpsky (male chimp)	ASL

An evaluation of production-based studies

One way of evaluating the studies summarised in Table 6.1 is to ask whether chimps' and gorillas' use of language is qualitatively different from that of children.

As far as *semanticity* is concerned, is the correct use of signs to refer to things sufficient? Savage-Rumbaugh *et al.* (1980) seriously doubt whether any of the apes (including their own, Lana) used the individual elements of their vocabularies as words. Terrace (1987) argues that the deceptively simple ability to use a symbol as a name required a cognitive advance in the evolution of human intelligence at least as significant as the advances that led to grammatical competence.

The function of much of a child's initial vocabulary is to inform another person (usually an adult) that it has noticed something (MacNamara, 1982). A child often refers to the object spontaneously, showing obvious delight from the sheer act of naming. (See the account of Helen Keller, Box 5.6, page 116.) This hasn't been observed in any of the ape studies. MacNamara believes that no amount of training could produce an ape with such an ability: the act of referring

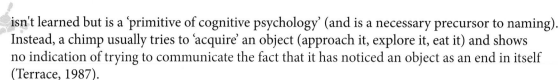

isn't learned but is a 'primitive of cognitive psychology' (and is a necessary precursor to naming). Instead, a chimp usually tries to 'acquire' an object (approach it, explore it, eat it) and shows no indication of trying to communicate the fact that it has noticed an object as an end in itself (Terrace, 1987).

Several critics have claimed that the linguistic abilities of chimps amount to a wholly 'instrumental use' of symbols. Referring to Savage-Rumbaugh's work with the bonobo Kanzi (see below), Seidenberg and Petitto (1987) claim that Kanzi 'may not know what the symbols mean', but only 'how to produce behaviours that others can interpret'. However, Gauker (1990) proposes that this may be essentially what *human* understanding of words involves. Wise (1999) cites many examples from production-based studies (including Gardner and Gardner (1969) and Terrace (1987)) of chimps spontaneously signing in order to name something just because it had been observed; this contradicts both Terrace's own conclusions and MacNamara's claim regarding the 'primitive of cognitive psychology'.

Other criticisms are based more directly on the *methodology* of these production-based studies, in particular the reward-based system (i.e. the use of operant conditioning to reinforce correct use of signs/symbols).

Time for reflection

- Can you think of any limitations to studies that use a reward-based system for teaching language to non-humans?

Joel Wallman (1992), a linguist and philosopher, points out the pitfalls of trying to teach any form of language to an ape exclusively by a training process. It can delude the trainers: what they often perceive as a meaningful response from the chimp isn't strictly language at all. With a reward system in operation, the exchanges between trainer and chimp are more like those between human and dog where the dog is asked to 'roll over' or 'play dead' for a reward. The chimp will be reacting to a visual cue in the same way as the dog is reacting to a verbal one. Just as it would be incorrect to say that the dog's movements showed that it understood the English instructions, so would it be mistaken to deduce that from the chimp's movements that it understood and responded appropriately to what was signed. Wallman compares the signing of chimps with the impressive, but nevertheless random and non-specific vocabulary of a parrot. Instead of conversation, what was taking place was a pattern of behaviour based around a stimulus (the trainer's sign), the chimp's reaction, and its reward (fruit or some other tid-bit). However, Wallman's comparison with a parrot isn't necessarily the most valid or helpful one he might have chosen, as demonstrated in Box 6.14.

> **Box 6.14** Alex: the African grey parrot (Irene Pepperberg, 1998)
>
> Parrots are famous for their uncanny ability to mimic human speech, but it is widely believed that this mimicry is just that, i.e. meaningless. However, beginning in 1977, Pepperberg's research with Alex has convinced her that grey parrots (*Psittacus erithacus*) can be taught to use and understand human speech. Greys inhabit dense forests and forest clearings across equatorial Africa, where vocal communication plays an important role. They use whistles and calls that they most likely learn by listening to adults.
>
> Laboratory studies conducted during the 1940s and 50s showed that parrots were capable of learning symbolic and conceptual tasks often associated with complex cognitive and communication skills, such as the representation of number/quantity. But other researchers found that they were unable to learn referential communication (see text above and Box 6. 2). Pepperberg wondered if this failure might reflect the inappropriate use of traditional conditioning techniques. Partly inspired by non-traditional (i.e. non-production based) methods being used with chimps (see text below), she designed a new technique involving two humans who teach other about the objects at hand while the parrot watches (**model/rival (M/R) protocol**).
>
> In a typical training session, Alex watched the trainer pick up an object and ask the human student a question about it, such as 'What colour?' If the student answered correctly, he or she received praise and was allowed to play with the object as a reward; if an incorrect answer was given, the trainer scolded the student and temporarily removed the object from sight. The second human thus acts as a *model* for Alex and a rival for the trainer's attention. The humans' interactions also demonstrate the consequences of an error: the model is told to try again or to talk more clearly. The training session is then repeated with the roles reversed; this shows Alex that communication is a two-way process and that each vocalisation is not specific to an individual.
>
> Using this and other techniques (such as **referential mapping**, which assigns meaning to vocalisations that Alex produced spontaneously, and **intrinsic reinforcement**, where the reward for a given vocalisation is the object the vocalisation refers to), Alex mastered tasks once thought to be beyond the capacity of all but human and certain great apes. Not only could he produce and understand labels describing 50 different objects and foods, but he could also categorise objects by *colour* (rose, blue, green, yellow, orange, grey, purple), *material* (wood, wool, paper, cork, chalk, hide, rock) and *shape* (objects having from two to six corners). Combining labels for these categories, Alex could identify, request and describe more than 100 different objects with about 80 per cent accuracy.
>
> Alex also seemed to understand that a single object can possess properties of more than one category (such as a green triangle being *both* green *and* three-cornered), and the abstract concepts of 'same' and 'different'. His understanding matched that of chimps and dolphins. The evidence strongly suggests that Alex wasn't merely mimicking his trainers but acquired an impressive understanding of some aspects of human speech.

An interim conclusion

When Terrace (1979) first evaluated his results from 'Project Nim' (see Table 6.1), he was encouraged: Nim seemed able and willing to mimic the signs demonstrated by his trainers. But did Nim's signing constitute language? Many researchers, including Terrace himself, thought not: the product of his training programme were various forms of 'habituated behaviour'. In an attempt to please his trainers, Nim would often produce a 'word salad' of signing – long strings of random, unconnected, repetitive and, ultimately, meaningless signs.

However, Terrace's conclusions are based on production-based studies. According to Phillips (1997), Terrace's admission that his approach was a *cul-de-sac* was a less sweeping claim than that often attributed to him, namely, that all current and future ape language studies, regardless of the methodology, would necessarily produce the same disappointing results. This stronger, more pessimistic claim is widespread among contemporary linguists and philosophers, with Chomsky being their 'guiding light'. While Chomsky agrees that if any of our fellow creatures did possess a language capacity we'd expect it to be our genetic cousins, he argues that if they indeed had such a capacity it would have manifested itself by now. Since it hasn't, we can only conclude that they don't (Chomsky, in Golden, 1991).

Both Chomsky and Wallman adopt a 'syntax as criterion' position: chimps cannot possess language skills because they don't possess a syntax, the defining feature of a language. According to Wallman (1992): 'It is beyond all dispute that all natural languages are predicated on rule systems ... involving elements grouped into nested categories of increasing abstraction ...'

'Nested' seems to denote 'embedded' or recursive, which, as we saw above, turns out not to be characteristic of all human languages after all. One of Wallman's examples is the concept of reference (the semanticity criterion: see above):

> *Reference, the use of the word to indicate the focus of one's attention, is neither present congenitally nor evident within the first year, but it appears soon after in all (human) children with an inevitability suggesting that it appears not to be learned; it is, indeed, hard to imagine how it could be learned. Reference seems to be part of the endowment of the species. Evidence for its natural occurrence elsewhere, on the other hand, is quite limited.* (Wallman, 1992)
> (emphasis in the original.)

But not completely absent! (See Box 6.2). This quote from Wallman mirrors MacNamara's (1982) observations discussed above, and it's undeniable that only humans display true language *naturally*. But is Wallman correct to deny the very *possibility* of language competence to apes (Phillips, 1997)? To answer this question, we turn to recent studies by Sue Savage-Rumbaugh with, in particular, Kanzi, the bonobo chimp, at the Yerkes Regional Primate Centre in Atlanta, USA.

Helping chimps be more like children: Comprehension versus production

Since the 1980s, Savage-Rumbaugh has been working with chimps in a way that's much more like how children acquire language. Instead of putting the chimps through rote learning of symbols (training), gradually building up a vocabulary a symbol at a time, Savage-Rumbaugh aimed to use a large vocabulary of symbols from the start, using them as language is used around human children. This represents a move away from an emphasis on grammatical structure (at least in the beginning) and towards *comprehension*.

This new approach was applied on a limited scale with Austin and Sherman, two common chimps (*Pan troglodytes*). But it really got going with some pygmy chimps or bonobos (*Pan paniscus*), which are slightly smaller than common chimps, and more vocal and communicative through gestures and facial expressions. Work began in 1981 with Matata, a wild bonobo, who, six months earlier had kidnapped a newborn infant, Kanzi, and kept him as her own. Instead of ASL, Savage-Rumbaugh used an extensive 'lexigram', a matrix of 256 geometrical shapes on a board. Instructors touch the symbols, which represent verbs and nouns, to create simple requests or commands. At the same time, the sentence is spoken, with the aim of testing comprehension of spoken English. When the chimp presses a symbol, a synthesised voice from the computer 'speaks' the word.

Although clearly intelligent in many ways, Matata was a slow learner; she was shown how to use the lexigram keyboard while her instructors spoke in English to each other and to Matata, but this proved ineffective. Even after a system of pairing lexigrams with rewards was introduced, Matata failed to use lexigrams as symbols. However, and amazingly, the benefit of the work with Matata showed up not with Matata herself, but with Kanzi. Kanzi had been with Matata for the first two years of her language instruction (from ages six months to two-and-half years), and, despite no attempt being made to teach Kanzi anything, he was allowed to observe his mother's instruction.

When Kanzi was two-and-a-half, Matata was removed from the research temporarily (for breeding purposes). In order to minimise a potentially traumatic separation, the researchers decided to maintain Kanzi's daily routine, which included spending the same amount of time in the laboratory. Kanzi began to use the lexigram keyboard of his own accord. On the first day, he used the keyboard on no fewer than 120 occasions (Savage-Rumbaugh and Lewin, 1994). One of the first things Kanzi did that morning was to press the 'apple' lexigram and then the 'chase' lexigram: he immediately picked up an apple, looked directly at Savage-Rumbaugh, and then ran away grinning and playful. This represented just the tip of the iceberg of Kanzi's potential. He had acquired a remarkable amount of linguistic knowledge merely by association. Several times on that first day, he selected specific food items on the computer and, when taken to the refrigerator, selected those same foods items: he was using specific lexigrams to request and name items and to announce his intentions on each particular occasion.

Box 6.15 Kanzi: 30 years of language acquisition

From this first day, Kanzi began using the lexigram keyboard in a purposeful way. For example, if he was presented with an array of objects including one whose corresponding lexigram he had pressed, he'd take only the 'requested' object; this indicates that he was able to use the symbols to refer to specific entities. He could also 'name' objects he was shown by pressing the appropriate lexigram. Also, as soon as he was using the keyboard regularly, Kanzi began to produce lexigram *combinations* – not only to respond to requests made of him (such as naming objects), but to make requests of his care givers, without prompting. Within four months, Kanzi's vocabulary rose from the original eight symbols (acquired from Matata) to more than 20; after 17 months, this had risen to almost 50.

More important than the size of his vocabulary, Kanzi produced multi-word utterances that were *spontaneous* (unlike those of Nim Chimpsky: Terrace, 1987): they weren't a response to instructors' requests, nor imitations of their utterances. For example, 'Matata group room tickle' was a request that his mother be allowed to join in a game of tickle in the group room. Many of his utterances had this character of novelty and functioned to suggest completely new actions and alternatives to the usual way of doing things. Also, again in contrast with Nim Chimpsky, each time Kanzi added more elements to his utterances, the information content increased. According to Savage-Rumbaugh and Lewin (1994):

Box 6.15 *Continued*

Of Kanzi's three-word utterances, the most interesting – and significant – were those in which he indicated someone other than himself as the agent or recipient of an action. Most of his three-item combinations involved the initiation of play, such as grab, chase and tickle. Some of these games involved Kanzi directly, but others were intended for his teachers. For instance, Kanzi might indicate 'grab chase' at the keyboard, and then take one person's hand and push it toward a second person: the chaser and the pursued. Statements of this sort were Kanzi's inventions, as none of us suggested we play with each other leaving Kanzi as spectator.

By age ten (1991), Kanzi had a vocabulary of some 200 words. But what's truly impressive is what the words apparently meant to him. He was given spoken requests to do things, in sentence form (none of them practised and all different), by someone out of his sight. The assistants in the same room with Kanzi wore headphones, preventing them from hearing the instructions and thereby cueing Kanzi, even unconsciously. 'Can you put the raisins in the bowl?' and 'Can you give the cereal to Karen?' posed Kanzi no problems; nor did 'Can you go to the colony room and get the telephone?' (There were four or five objects in the colony room which weren't usually there.)

More testing still was the instruction 'Go to the colony room and get the orange' when there was an orange in front of Kanzi; this confused him about 90 per cent of the time. But if asked to 'Get the orange that's in the colony room', he did so without hesitation: the syntactically more complex phrase seemed to produce better comprehension than the simple one (Savage-Rumbaugh, in Lewin, 1991). Kanzi showed this level of understanding when he was nine, but not before he was six. He also showed understanding of the syntactic rule that in two-word utterances, action precedes object. Significantly, he went from a random word-order initially to a clear, consistent preference.

An evaluation of Savage-Rumbaugh's 'comprehension' approach

As we noted earlier, Kanzi initially began to use the symbols that Matata had learned, but without any attempt to teach him the symbols – he picked them up entirely through *observational exposure*. This is comparable to how human children acquire language, and production-based language training can be seen as disrupting the 'normal course' of language acquisition (Savage-Rumbaugh, 1990). From that point onwards, an even greater effort was made to place language learning in a naturalistic context. Kanzi 'acquired' a sister, Mulika, when he was two-and-a-half and they grew up together.

Three other chimps (two bonobos and one common) have also learned symbols without training, so Kanzi's achievements are neither unique to him nor to his species. Chimps learn where one word ends and the next begins, that is, what the units are, through the learning of routines which emerge out of daily life that has been specially constructed for them (Savage-Rumbaugh, 1990).

According to Phillips (1997), what's revolutionary about the work undertaken with Kanzi is that it avoids so many of the standard objections that were levelled at the production/training-based studies. For example, Kanzi's ability isn't the result of habituated behaviour based on a reward system; nor is it confined to responses to a set of cues by his instructors. Using his computer keyboard, Kanzi also demonstrates understanding of English sentences and of imperatives, questions and references. Very few of these responses are linked to the mere satisfaction of wants: Kanzi often initiates a conversation for no other reason than that he wants to – for the sake of it!

At the age of nearly 30, Kanzi's grammatical comprehension was officially assessed as exceeding that of a two-and-a-half-year-old child, and he understood about 2,000 words. His 25-year-old sister, Panbanisha, has a vocabulary of at least 3,000 words, and Nyota, Panbanisha's son, is learning faster than his mother and uncle. It seems that the researchers' expectations were higher for those who came after Kanzi (Cohen, 2000).

Conclusions: Is language unique to humans?

Does Kanzi use 'language'? According to neo-Chomskians such as Wallman (1992), the answer is 'no'. The 'communicative situation' in which the supposed language-use takes place is largely irrelevant. The one defining criterion of language in Kanzi's case is the presence (or absence) of syntax in his lexigram utterances. According to Wallman (1992):

> *The testing of Kanzi's sentence comprehension, in summary, demonstrates that he is able to put together the object or objects and the action mentioned in the way that is appropriate given the properties of the objects involved, what he typically does with them, or both ... His (Kanzi's) performance provides no evidence, however, that he was attending to even so simple a syntactic feature as word order.*

Wallman (and other like-minded linguists) regard syntactic word order as the ultimate 'adjudicator' in deciding whether utterances deserve to be called 'language'. But according to Phillips (1997):

> *The Chomskian understanding of the concept of language is a technical one; but technical terms are legitimate only in explanatory models that do not do violence to the facts and are useful, or at least, edifying in some way. But in this case, Chomsky's notion of an 'innate' ability as a set of syntactical rules nested within a 'language organ' is no more than a carpet under which we can sweep the entire messy business of explanation.*

According to Aitchison (1983), the apparent ease with which children acquire language, compared with apes, supports the claim that they are innately programmed to do so. Similarly, although these chimps have grasped some of the rudiments of human language, what they've learned, and the speed at which they learn it, are *qualitatively* different from those of human beings (Carroll, 1986).

Aitchison and Carroll seem to be talking for a majority of psychologists. As we saw in Chapter 1, belief in human exceptionalism is especially powerful – and widely held – in relation to language. But we've seen here that most of the 'standard' criticisms of ape studies are based on the earlier, production-based studies. Savage-Rumbaugh's more naturalistic, comprehension-based studies have led her to conclude that the difference between ape and human language is merely *quantitative*. Responding to criticism by Terrace that Kanzi still uses his symbols only in order to acquire and to ask for things, rather than to share his perception of the world, Savage-Rumbaugh (1990; Savage-Rumbaugh and Lewin, 1994) observes that so do young children: in fact, normal children's predominant use of symbols is 'requesting'.

> **Time for reflection**
> - Do you consider it valid to ask whether chimps are capable of 'language'?
> - Is it ethically acceptable to use chimps and other apes for this kind of research?
> - Is it right that they are treated as if they were human when they are not?

Jackendoff (1993) believes that asking whether apes have language or not is a 'silly dispute, often driven by an interest either in reducing the distance between people and animals or in maintaining this distance at all costs' (see Chapter 1). Jackendoff prefers to ask: do the apes succeed in *communicating*? He thinks the answer is undoubtedly yes. He also believes that they appear to successfully communicate *symbolically*.

> *... But, going beyond that, it does not look as though they [apes] are capable of constructing a mental grammar that regiments the symbols coherently (... maybe there is a little, but nothing at all near human capacity.) In short, Universal Grammar, or even something remotely like it, appears to be exclusively human.* (Jackendoff, 1993)

According to Jackendoff, we're left with an embarrassing question: why can apes learn to use symbols at all?

> *... It's as though evolution has provided them with a necessary precursor for language, but it's something they have no use for in their normal environment. Is it just a lucky accident? Or is it a by-product of some other cognitive capacity that is of more palpable survival value to the species? ...*

His answer? We are not in a position to say at this time.

Kanzi's capacity for comprehension far outstrips his capacity for producing language using the lexigram. This makes him extremely frustrated, at which times he often becomes very vocal, making high-pitched squeaks. Is he trying to speak? If Kanzi were to talk, maybe the first thing he would say is that he's fed up with Terrace claiming that apes don't have language (Lewin, 1991). What is beyond dispute is that attempts to teach language to non-human primates have raised some fundamental *ethical* issues. Wise (1999), an American lawyer, argues that bonobos and other chimps deserve basic legal rights: he rejects the idea of human superiority.

Let's give the final word to Jane Goodall, whose pioneering work with wild chimps was discussed above and in Chapter 5. When asked in a recent interview what sets the human mind apart from the chimp mind, she answered 'The explosive development of intellect'.

> *... You can have very bright chimps that can learn sign language and do all kinds of things with computers, but it doesn't make sense to compare that intellect with even that of a normal human, let alone an Einstein. My own feeling is that the evolution of our intellect quickened once we began using the kind of language we use today, a language that enables us to discuss the past and to plan the distant future.* (Goodall, 2010).

Chapter summary

- While the belief that language is unique to humans is consistent with a long Western tradition, research showing that 'mind' is a matter of degree has led some researchers to argue that the same applies to the possession of language.

- Grammar is what sets human language apart from other forms of non-human animal communication, making it infinitely creative.

- Hauser *et al.* describe non-human communication systems as closed, lacking the expressive and open-ended power of human language; even the gestural communications of chimpanzees are essentially signals as opposed to symbols.

- Language is one of the few complex behaviours that clearly distinguishes humans from other species and recent genetic and archaeological evidence suggests that it evolved very quickly. Hauser *et al.* claim that many of the underlying cognitive abilities involved in language processing have their roots deep in the primate lineage.

- Seyfarth *et al.* showed that vervet monkeys give different calls for different predators, and Goodall observed that chimpanzees have a wide range of calls that convey different types of information.

- Slocombe's research suggests that both wild and captive chimpanzees may be capable of functionally referential communication. While rough grunts and **agonistic screams** are biologically determined, they can be used selectively depending on the object or behaviour and the individuals thought to be listening.

- While the signal/symbol distinction may be a false dichotomy, the neurophysiological evidence suggests that non-humans have little if any cortical control over vocalisation.

- According to Gentilucci and Corballis, speech, rather than language as such, is what distinguishes *Homo sapiens* from other hominids.

- Humans can produce 50 phonemes (compared with chimpanzees' 12) because the larynx is situated low in the throat, creating a large sound-chamber (pharynx) above the vocal cords.

- Fitch cites evidence of convergent traits and homologies in non-humans that cast doubt on the belief that we can date the emergence of language by studying the position of the larynx in ancient fossils.

- According to Deacon, the move from generalised vocalisation to speech is related to an increase in hominids' cortical control of the periaqueductal grey.

- In non-human primates, vocalisation is largely, if not exclusively, controlled by the cingulate pathway. Only in humans is the neocortical pathway developed for precise voluntary control of the muscles of the vocal cords and tongue.

- Voluntary control in chimpanzees is more highly developed manually than vocally.

- With the emergence of bipedalism, the hands were freed from locomotion; this provides a potential boost to the evolution of manual communication.

- According to the gestural theory of speech (of which there are several forms), language evolved from manual gestures rather than from vocalisations.

- Consistent with the gestural theory, there is a clear development in the use of gesture in children as they acquire language. Examples include pointing to request and then to comment on objects/events, the use of two-item gesture/word strings, and the development of homesigns among deaf children born into hearing families.

- The gestural theory also finds support in the form of mirror neurons, first identified in monkeys' motor cortex. In humans, they're found in various brain regions, including F5 in the ventral premotor cortex, and centres for language, empathy and pain.

- Mirror neurons help us 'read' other people's intentions and emotions; these effects are largely automatic and unconscious. Exploring the relationship between mirroring and theory of mind (ToM) is being actively investigated in social cognitive neuroscience.

- According to the motor theory of speech perception, we understand speech in terms of how it's produced rather than its acoustic properties. This raises the possibility that vocalisation was incorporated into the mirror system after the split between the ape and hominid lineages.

- Area F5 is also considered to be the homologue of Broca's area and the mirror system in general corresponds quite closely with the cortical circuits (usually in the left hemisphere) involved in language – spoken or signed.

- Browman and Goldstein claim that rather than being a system for producing sounds, speech is a system for producing articulatory gestures through the independent action of the six articulatory organs.

- Echo phonology, in which mouth movements parallel hand movements, might provide the link between gesture and speech.

- Chomsky supports the view that language arose rapidly and recently, as an incidental consequence of our enlarged brain. Opposed to this view is the continuity model, advocated by Pinker, which claims that language evolved gradually, beginning with the evolution of the genus *Homo*.

- Many anthropologists favour a recent, rapid origin of language, mainly because of the abrupt change in behaviour that occurred in the Upper Paleolithic Revolution (in Europe) (or the Late Stone Age in Africa).

- White and others argue that a cluster of 'firsts' (such as artistic expression, deliberate burial of the dead and a sudden acceleration in the pace of technological innovation and cultural change) was underpinned by the appearance of complex, fully modern spoken language.

- Deacon's comparison of the anatomy of chimpanzee and human brains suggests a gradual development of our ancestors' language skills during the past 2 million years.

- Holloway's detection of Broca's area and a slightly increased left hemisphere in *Homo habilis* suggests the presence of a language ability greater than that of chimpanzees, but this have been a structurally and content-simple proto-language.

- The earliest documented fully arched basicranium (a human characteristic) is about 300,000 to 400,000 years ago; it's unlikely that a fully modern language appeared before the appearance of anatomically modern *Homo sapiens*.

- Broca's and Wernicke's areas are uniquely human, specialised for language and always found in the left hemisphere (regardless of handedness). They're noticeably larger than the corresponding right hemisphere regions.

- The 'classical' model of language processing in the brain accounted well for the two types of aphasia associated with damage to Broca's or Wernicke's area (language production and comprehension, respectively).

- However, the two are now seen as dividing language up by semantics and syntax: damage to Broca's area causes impairment in using grammar (not in producing language), while Wernicke's aphasics do not have enough words left in their damaged mental dictionaries to say (or understand) anything substantial.

- The young child's progression from the one-word stage, through stage 1 and stage 2 grammar is mirrored by the relative maturation of Broca's and Wernicke's areas.

- According to Eliot, language provides the most dramatic illustration of the brain's plasticity. While adults who suffer damage to the left perisylvian area can experience irreparable aphasia, children with comparable brain damage display amazing language recovery.

- Humans have direct neural connections between the motor cortex and brainstem neurons that control the lips, tongue and larynx; non-human primates lack these neurons.

- Since the *FOXP2* gene is found in gorillas and chimpanzees, as well as mice, it's most unlikely to be a language or grammar gene. The KE family's core deficit is one of articulation, with grammatical impairment only a secondary problem.

- Chomsky, like Pinker, regards language as one of the mind's independently evolved organs or modules (the Swiss army knife analogy). Against this view, Mithen stresses the mind's integrative ability; the human brain is like a general-purpose computer.

- The existence of specialised language areas in the brain supports Chomsky and Pinker, as does the case of Williams syndrome, in which language is apparently preserved but overall intelligence is very low.

- Central to Chomsky's theory of transformational grammar (TG) are phrase-structure rules and the ability to transform deep structure into various surface structures. Children's innate LAD enables them to extract the linguistic universals (or universal grammar) from any native language to which they happen to be exposed.

- While Chomsky argues that all languages are basically the same, Evans and Levinson argue that it's the very diversity of languages that holds the key to understanding human communication. Instead of linguistic universals, there are only strong and weak tendencies.

- Linguists have identified important exceptions to the rules of language, ranging from the number of phones/phonetic segments used to the use of recursion.

- Based on his research with the Piraha people, Everett claims that there's a much stronger symbiosis between language and culture than many modern linguists and psychologists might have imagined.

- The diversity of human language compared with the communication systems of all other species has been attributed to the plasticity of the human brain. One implication of this is that speakers of very different languages could have quite different brains.

- Research with speakers of Guugu and other remote languages demonstrates how linguistic categories can mould thought and behaviour.

- The main criteria for defining language that have informed attempts to teach language to chimpanzees and other great apes are semanticity, displacement, structure dependence, creativity/productivity and syntax.

- Pepperberg's research with Alex, an African grey parrot, using referential mapping and intrinsic reinforcement, showed that his understanding of various concepts matched that of both chimpanzees and dolphins. He also acquired an impressive understanding of some aspects of human speech.

- Production-based studies, using either American Sign Language (ASL) or small plastic symbols or a special computer-controlled typewriter, have been criticised on both methodological grounds and in terms of the criteria used to define language. While these studies may have failed to demonstrate that apes possess language, they don't necessarily rule out the possibility of language competence. This was demonstrated by Savage-Rumbaugh's research involving the bonobo Kanzi and other chimpanzees, using a comprehension-based approach,

- At the age of 30, Kanzi's grammatical comprehension was officially assessed as exceeding that of a two-and-a-half-year-old child. While for Savage-Rumbaugh this represents merely a quantitative difference, Wallman, Aitchison, Goodall and others contend that humans display a qualitatively different language competence from chimpanzees and other non-humans.

Suggested further reading

Chomsky, N. (author), Belletti, A. & Luigi, R. (eds) (2002) *On Nature and Language.* Cambridge: Cambridge University Press. One of the more recent accounts of language and linguistics by this hugely influential and amazingly prolific theorist. Chomsky develops his thinking on the relationship between language, mind and brain, integrating current research in linguistics with neuroscience. Includes a lucid introduction by the editors.

Everett, D.L. (2009) *Don't Sleep, There are Snakes: Life and Language in the Amazonian jungle.* London: Profile Books. A fascinating account of Everett's stay with the Piraha in the Amazonian jungle, which not only represents a brilliant piece of ethnographical research but challenges some of the 'received wisdom' regarding the nature of human language.

Pinker, S. (2004) *The Language Instinct.* New York: Morrow. According to *Nature*, this is a 'dazzling' book. Pinker's big idea is that language is an instinct as 'natural' to humans as flying is to geese. According to *The Independent*, it's a marvellously readable book, illuminating every aspect of human language: its biological origin, uniqueness to humans, acquisition, grammatical structure, speech production and perception, and the pathology of language disorders.

Savage-Rumbaugh, S. & Lewin, R. (1994) *The Ape at the Brink of the Human Mind.* New York: John Wiley. The remarkable story of Kanzi, a 'talking' bonobo, who has challenged the assumption that language is a uniquely human ability. Savage-Rumbaugh is one of the world's leading ape-language researchers.

Selected websites

http://www.budongo.org

The website of the Budongo Conservation Field Station, Budongo Forest, Uganda, home to 600–700 chimpanzees. Its key aim is to study and conserve local chimpanzee populations.

http://www.tinytalk.co.uk/

The website of TinyTalk, which claims to be the biggest and best baby-signing classes in the UK, Ireland and Australia (where it's known as TinySign).

http://anthro.palomar.edu/language/language_5.htm

A discussion of language and thought and their interrelationship.

http://ase.tufts.edu/cogstud/papers/rolelang.htm

Dennett, D. (1994) 'The role of language in intelligence.' In J. Khalfa (ed.) *What is Intelligence?* The Darwin College Lectures. Cambridge: Cambridge University Press.

www.youtube.com/watch?v=mLWSC5p1VE

Video of talk by Chomsky (2008). Links to several related videos.

www.davidmswitzer.com/apelang.html

Language in Apes: How Much Do They Know and How Much Should We Teach Them? By D. Switzer (1995, 1999).

www.ted.com/talks/susan_savage_rumbaugh_on_apes_that_write.html

Video of talk by Sue Savage-Rumbaugh (filmed 2004, posted 2007). Links to several related videos.

www.youtube.com/watch?v=LxmbjLoUnhk

Video of Sue Savage-Rumbaugh testing Kanzi's ability to understand spoken language. Links to several related videos.

Chapter 7: Memory and the perception of time

Key questions

- Are there different ways of defining 'time'?
- Does time objectively exist?
- What's the difference between biological clocks and 'mind (or 'brain') time'?
- Is the perception of time unique to humans?
- What's the relationship between the brain and our perception of time?
- How can we account for the experience of time speeding up as we get older?
- How can we explain the finding that the accuracy of estimations of time intervals is related to the size of the intervals?
- How can we account for the experience of time speeding up or slowing down in different situations?
- What's the relationship between memory and the ability to estimate time?
- Are there different types of memory?
- Are there any types of memory that are unique to human beings?
- What is meant by 'déjà vu' and how can we account for it?

The nature of time

Time for reflection
- What do you understand by 'time'?
- Does time exist objectively?
- How do you experience time?
- How do you determine what is 'past', 'present' and 'future'?
- Can you imagine a world in which time didn't exist?

As you read this sentence, you probably think that this moment – right now – is what is happening. The present moment feels special. It is real. However much you may remember the past or anticipate the future, you live in the present. Of course, the moment during which you read that sentence is no longer happening. This one is. In other words, it feels as though time flows, in the sense that the present is constantly updating itself. We have a deep intuition that the future is open until it becomes present and that the past is fixed. As time flows, this structure of fixed past, immediate present and open future gets carried forward in time. This structure is built into our language, thought and behaviour. How we live our lives hangs on it.
(Callender, 2010)

As natural as this way of thinking is, however, it's not what physicists understand by time. According to Callender (2010), the equations of physics don't tell us which events are occurring right now – they're like a map without the 'you are here' symbol. The present moment doesn't exist in them, so neither does the flow of time. According to Albert Einstein's theories of relativity, not only is there no single special present but all moments are equally real: fundamentally, the future is no more open than the past.

The gap between the scientific and our everyday understanding of time has troubled thinkers throughout history and has widened as physicists have gradually stripped time of most of the characteristics we commonly attribute to it. Callender (2010) believes that

> ... the time of physics and the time of experience is reaching its logical conclusion, for many in theoretical physics have come to believe that time fundamentally does not even exist.

But how could this be? Everything we do, we do in time: the world is a series of events strung together by time. We observe change, which, by definition, takes time to occur. But if, as some physicists are claiming, time doesn't exist, how is change possible?

Time for reflection

- How can we 'square' the solidity of a table as part of our immediate perceptual experience of it with the physicist's understanding of a table as a swarm of particles composed mostly of empty space?
- These two 'realities' don't usually compete with each other in the 'truth stakes', but according to *reductionists*, the physicist's version represents the 'ultimate' truth. What's meant by 'reductionism' and how are the two realities related to different levels of description or *universes of discourse?* (See e.g. Gross (2010), Chapter 49.)
- What do you understand by an **'emergent property'**?
- Can you give some examples from psychology? (See, for example, Chapter 4 and Gross (2010), page 805.)

Although time may not exist at a fundamental level, it may arise at higher levels – just like the solid feel of the table: solidity is a collective, or *emergent*, property of the particles. Time, too, could be an emergent property of whatever the basic ingredients of the world are. Einstein believed that the key step forward in developing his relativity theory was his reconceptualisation of time (Callender, 2010).

Superimposed onto the 'flow' of time (or perhaps more accurately, drawn 'through' the flow) is the idea of the 'arrow of time'. The famous physicist Sir Isaac Newton (1687) proposed that the world comes equipped with a master clock, which uniquely and objectively carves the world up into instants of time. In addition, Newton believed that time flows and that this flow gives us an arrow telling us which direction is the future. His concept of 'time' (the master clock) brings the concepts of order, continuity, duration, simultaneity, flow and the arrow together (Callender, 2010), and this is reflected to a large extent in our commonsense understanding of 'time'. However, Einstein's (1905) special theory of relativity dispensed with the idea of absolute simultaneity: what events are happening at the same time depends on how fast you're going. The true arena of events isn't time or space, but their union: spacetime. Two observers moving at different speeds disagree about when and where an event occurs – but they agree on its spacetime location. Then in 1915, Einstein's general theory of relativity extended special relativity to situations that involve the operation of the force of gravity. Gravity distorts time: the passage of a second here may not mean the same as a second's passage there. Consequently, we cannot generally think of the world as unfolding, tick by tick, according to a single time parameter (Callender, 2010).

Box 7.1 Who needs time? (Based on Callender, 2010.)

Time is a way of describing the pace of motion or change, such as the speed of a light wave, how fast a heart beats or how frequently a planet spins:

- Light travels at 300,000 km per second.
- The (average) adult heart beats 75 times per minute.
- The earth rotates on its axis once per day (24 hours).

However, these processes could be related directly to one another without making any reference to time at all: a single heart beat is equivalent to light travelling 240,000 kilometres, while there are 108,000 heart beats per rotation of the earth.

Based on this sort of example, some physicists argue that time is a common currency, making the world easier to describe but without any independent existence. Measuring processes in terms of time could be like using money to buy things rather than exchanging goods (with no money changing hands).

According to the French phenomenological philosopher Maurice Merleau-Ponty (whose idea regarding the mind–body relationship we discussed in Chapter 4), time itself doesn't really flow: our tendency to believe that it does is the result of forgetting to put ourselves and our connections to the world into the picture. He was discussing our subjective experience of time, and until recently no one ever guessed that **objective time** might itself be explained in terms of those connections. Only by breaking the world into subsystems, looking at what ties them together, and detaching ourselves from everything else, can the concept of physical time emerge (Callender, 2010).

Different kinds of time

The subjective experience of time flowing, and the related sense of time as an arrow (that is, it travels in a straight line and in only one direction – from past, through present, to future) refers to 'mind' (or 'brain') time. But there's much more to mind time than just these subjective representations of time: it can be manifested in various ways, such as the experience of time speeding up as we get older (Draaisma, 2004), the greater accuracy of time estimations the smaller the intervals we're trying to estimate (e.g. Weardon, in Fox, 2009), the speed at which time seems to pass in different situations (for example, the slow-motion experience reported by people undergoing extremely stressful or traumatic events (Eagleman, in Fox, 2009), and the experience of having been somewhere or done something before when it's in actual fact happening for the first time (*déjà vu*, e.g. Wolfradt, 2005).

As we noted in Chapter 1, Corballis and Suddendorf (2007) believe that what makes human beings unique is mental time travel (MTT) – the ability to transcend time – which is, clearly, an integral part of mind time. While other species react to what's happening here and now (i.e. what's in their immediate environment), humans are able to remember the past and think about the future.

Corballis and Suddendorf claim that language and MTT probably co-evolved. In turn, these are both related to memory (with *déjà vu* representing a case of 'false' or 'mistaken' remembering).

As you'd expect, mind time is what psychologists and neuroscientists are mainly interested in and forms the major part of this chapter.

Callender's discussion above of the physics of time is concerned with 'objective time' in the ultimate sense of whether or not time 'exists'. But outside the context of theoretical physics, 'objective time' is usually taken to mean 'clock time' (see Box 7.1). As we shall see, experimental research into mind time uses clock time as the objective measure against which subjective (mind) time is gauged.

There's yet a third basic kind of time: **biological time**. This refers to the various biological 'clocks', which control the *periodicity* of basic physiological processes over the course of a 24-hour period, the part of that period when we're asleep, a month, a year, or even an individual's lifetime. While all species display various biological clocks, mind time seems to be uniquely human.

Biological (or body) time

The late biologist John Gibbon described time as the 'primordial context' (Wright, 2006): a fact of life that has been felt by all organisms in every era. In the human body, biological clocks keep track of days, months and years; cellular chronometers (or 'time-pieces') may even determine when we die. (As we shall see below, there's one kind of biological clock in the brain that marks much shorter time spans of seconds to hours. Because this so-called 'stopwatch' is related to our *experience* of time under different conditions, we'll discuss it in relation to 'mind time').

According to the neurophysiologist, Colin Blakemore (1988):

> *For all the advances of modern society, we cannot afford to ignore the rhythms of the animal brain within us, any more than we can neglect our need to breathe or eat. Without the biological clocks in our brains, our lives would be chaotic, our actions disorganised. The brain has internalised the rhythms of Nature, but can tick on for months without sight of the sun.*

Box 7.2 describes the most important **bodily rhythms**.

Box 7.2 Bodily rhythms

- A bodily rhythm is 'a cyclical variation over some period of time in physiological or psychological processes' (Gross *et al.*, 2000).
- Many human activities take place within a cycle of about 24 hours; these are called **circadian rhythms** ('circa' = 'about', 'diem' = 'a day').
- Rhythms that have a cycle longer than 24 hours are called **infradian rhythms;** an example is the human menstrual cycle.
- **Circannual rhythms** are yearly rhythms and are a subset of infradian rhythms.
- **Ultradian rhythms** last less than 24 hours, a major example being the 90–120 minute cycle of human sleep stages (see Gross, 2010).
- Environmental factors such as light–dark cycles, noise and clocks that provide clues to these internal rhythms are called **exogenous** (i.e. external) **zeitgebers** (German for 'time-givers'). In the absence of any zeitgebers, behaviours that show rhythmical alternation/periodicity are controlled by internal timing devices – internal biological clocks (or **endogenous pacemakers**).

Circadian rhythms

Most animals display a circadian rhythm, which tunes our bodies to the cycles of sunlight and darkness caused by the earth's rotation. It helps to program the daily habit of sleeping at night and waking in the morning. During a 24-hour period, there's a cycle of several physiological functions (heart rate, breathing rate, body temperature, hormonal secretion, urine excretion, immune function, alertness and so on). These tend to reach maximum values during the late afternoon/early evening, and minimum values in the early hours of the morning.

This internal clock is as reliable as most manufactured ones – the rhythm deviates by no more than a few minutes over several months. It runs without the need for a stimulus from the external environment (zeitbegers), as demonstrated by Siffre's (1975) underground cave study. Siffre, then a young French cave explorer (and now a chronobiologist, studying humans' internal clocks), spent seven months underground with no clues as to the time of day. Circadian patterns are expressed in every cell of the body: confined to a petri dish under constant lighting, human cells still follow a 24-hour cycle of **gene** activity, hormone secretion and energy production. The cycles are hardwired, varying by as little as one per cent – just minutes a day (Wright, 2006).

While light isn't required to establish a circadian cycle, it *is* needed to synchronise the phase of the hardwired clock with natural day and night cycles. Like an ordinary clock that runs a few minutes slow or fast each day, the circadian clock needs to be continually reset to stay accurate (Wright, 2006). So, how is the internal (biological) clock reset each day to the cycle of the real world, and where is the 'clock' to be found?

The clock is believed to be a tiny cluster of about 3,000 neurons, the **suprachiasmatic nucleus (SCN)**, located in the medial hypothalamus (see Figure 7.1). Damage to the SCN in rats produces complete disappearance of the circadian rhythm: the sleep–wake cycle, eating and drinking, hormone secretion and so on, become completely random during the course of a 24-hour period. Most of what's known about the SCN is based on experiments with non-humans using *ablation* (surgically removing parts of the brain), and we cannot make direct electrophysiological recordings from the human brain. But anatomical studies have shown that humans have an SCN (Empson, 1993). The SCN's function is to synchronise all the bodily functions that are governed by the circadian rhythm.

The SCN is situated directly above the optic chiasma (the junction of the two optic nerves en route to the brain). A tuft of thin nerve fibres branches off from the main nerve and penetrates the hypothalamus above, forming synaptic connections with cells in the SCN. This anatomically insignificant pathway is the link between the outside world and the brain's own clock (Blakemore, 1988). So, the retina (at the back of the eye) projects directly onto the SCN, which ensures that the sleep–wake cycle is tuned to the rhythm of night and day; if this connection with the retina is cut, the cycle goes 'haywire'.

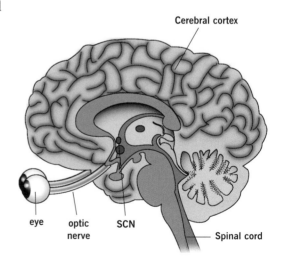

▲ **Figure 7.1** The human brain, showing the location of the suprachiasmatic nucleus (SCN)

The SCN also tells the brain's **pineal gland** (what Descartes believed was the point at which mind and body 'meet' or the 'seat of the mind': see Chapter 1), which is situated near the corpus callosum (see Chapter 3) to release melatonin (the 'sleep hormone'). Melatonin promotes sleep in humans and is secreted only at night. In response to daylight, the SCN emits signals that stop the **paraventricular nucleus** from producing a message that would ultimately result in the release of melatonin.

Mind time

> *The idea of our body – and the related concept of space – might seem to be the most deeply 'plumbed-in' concept we have. But in fact there is another concept that is even more taken for granted by humans: that of time. Like space, it seems absurd to think of time as an idea. It seems just to be. But if that were the case – if time proceeded at its stately pace without any conceptual input – it would pass at the same pace for each of us, whatever our circumstances and whatever the conditions of our brains. And that is not the case ...* (Carter, 2006) (emphasis in original.)

Carter is describing *mind time*. As she says, and we have indicated above, our experience of time depends on a number of factors, including age, the nature of the situation and the state of our brains. The latter can denote both abnormalities (caused through disease or accident) and the way that the normal, intact, brain functions.

Consciousness and the perception of time

According to Damasio (2006):

> *... 'Mind time' has to do with how we experience the passage of time and how we organise chronology. Despite the steady tick of the clock, duration can seem fast or slow, short or long. And this variability can happen on different scales, from decades, seasons, weeks and hours, down to the tiniest intervals of music – the span of a note or the moment of silence between two notes. We also place events in time, deciding when they occurred, in which order and on what scale, whether that of a lifetime or of a few seconds.*

Complementing these different examples given by Damasio is a distinction made by Frankenheuser (1959) between (a) *perception of time*, which relates to the experience of brief intervals of time, grasped as a single perceptual unit, and relatively unaffected by memory; and (b) *retention of time*, which denotes the experience in retrospect of longer time intervals assumed to be affected by memory.

Discrete visual frames

Perhaps the most fundamental question being investigated by neuroscientists is whether our perception of the world is continuous or a series of discrete snapshots, like frames on a film strip. If we understand this, then perhaps we'll be able to explain how the healthy brain works out the chronological order of the mass of events that bombards our senses (Fox, 2009).

Some of the first hints that we may perceive the world through discrete 'frames' arrived with studies of the well-known '**wagon wheel illusion**'.

Time for reflection

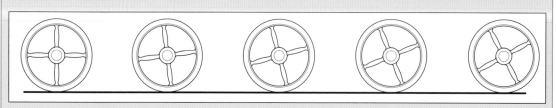

▲ **Figure 7.2a** The wagon wheel illusion

- If these frames were played in succession, which way would the wheel appear to be rolling – clockwise or anticlockwise? (See page 181.)

In the wagon wheel illusion, the wheels of a forward-moving vehicle appear to slow down or even roll backwards. The illusion was first noted during the playback of old Westerns and is produced by the fact that the camera takes a sequence of snapshots of the wheel as it rotates: if the speed of rotation is right, it can look as if each spoke has rotated a small distance *backwards* with each frame, when in actual fact they have moved *forwards*. Typically, each frame captured by the camera shows the wheel after just under a quarter of a revolution. This effect isn't confined to the movies; people also report experiencing it in real life. If these observations could be reproduced in the laboratory, it would suggest that the brain naturally slices our visual perception into a succession of snapshots (Fox, 2009).

VanRullen *et al.* (2008) recreated the illusion in their laboratory and found that when the wheel was spun at particular speeds, all the participants reported seeing it turn the 'wrong' way. This suggests that the continuity of our perceptual experience is itself an illusion. The researchers proposed a visual frame rate of 13 frames per second. What in the brain determines this rate? Research by VanRullen *et al.* (2008) throws light on this question and is described in Box 7.3.

Box 7.3 Discrete visual frames and the right inferior parietal lobe (VanRullen *et al.*, 2008)

VanRullen *et al.* measured participants' brain waves using an **electroencephalogram** (EEG) and found a specific rhythm (a 13-hertz wave) in the right inferior parietal lobe (RPL). This is normally associated with perception of visual location. It seemed plausible that as this wave oscillates (moves up and down), the RPL's receptivity to new visual information also oscillates, leading to something comparable to discrete visual frames.

To test this hypothesis, VanRullen *et al.* used transcranial magnetic stimulation, a non-invasive technique that can interfere with (and block) activity in specific areas of the brain, in order to disrupt the regular brain wave in the RPL. The effect of this disruption was to inhibit the periodic sampling of visual frames that's crucial for the wagon wheel illusion (the probability of seeing the illusion was reduced by 30 per cent). However, participants could still see the regular motion of the wheels, probably because other regions of the brain, which don't operate at the necessary 13 hertz, took over some of the motion perception. VanRullen *et al.* call the RPL the 'when' pathway: it plays a critical role in timing perceptual events relative to one another.

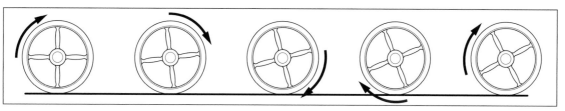

▲ **Figure 7.2b**

However, the case for discrete perception is far from 'proven' (Fox, 2009). Fox cites research by David Eagleman in which participants were shown a pair of overlapping patterns, both moving at the same rate. They often reported seeing one pattern reversing independently of the other, which suggests that they weren't taking frames of the world – otherwise, everything would have to reverse at the same time. However, VanRullen (e.g. Busch *et al.*, 2009) offers an alternative explanation: the brain processes different objects within the visual field independently of the other – even if they overlap in space. The RPL may well be taking the 'snapshots' of the two moving patterns at *separate* moments – and possibly at slightly different rates – making it plausible that the illusions could happen independently for each object. This implies that rather than a single 'roll of film', the brain possesses several separate streams, each recording a separate piece of information.

This way of dealing with incoming information may also apply to other forms of perception, such as object or sound recognition. To investigate this possibility, Busch *et al.* (2009) examined **near-threshold luminance detection**. Participants were exposed to flashes of light barely bright enough to see: the likelihood of them consciously noticing the flash depended on the phase of another wave in the front of the brain, which rises and falls about seven times per second. When this wave was near its trough (or fall), participants were more likely to see the flash; when it was near its peak, they were more likely to miss it. These findings suggest that there's a succession of 'on' and 'off' periods of perception: attention involves collecting information through snapshots.

If, as it appears, each separate neural process that governs our perception is recorded in its own stream of discrete frames, how might all these streams fit together to give us a consistent picture of the world? According to the neuroscientist, Ernst Poppel (2009), all the separate snapshots from the senses may feed into blocks of information (the 'building blocks of consciousness') within a higher processing stream; these building blocks underlie our perception of time.

The 'building blocks' of consciousness

> ### Time for reflection
>
> - Try to imagine what it would be like if we were unable to piece together a chronological order of sensory events.
> - For example, since light travels faster than sound, there's actually a miniscule gap (in the brain) between the visual stimulus of, say, a cup hitting the floor and breaking and hearing the sound of it breaking (Carter, 2006); without some sort of grouping system we might see the cup smashing before we hear it happen (Fox, 2009).
> - Again, consider what experience would be like if different moments of consciousness were discrete in such a way that what we experienced in each moment wasn't temporally connected to what we'd just experienced (Gallagher, 2007), that is, different moments were separated in time from each other/not continuous.

According to Poppel's building blocks of consciousness hypothesis, if two events fall into the same building block, they're perceived as simultaneous (they're different aspects of the *same* event). If they fall into consecutive building blocks, they're perceived as successive (two *different* events). Poppel believes that a space of 30–50 milliseconds is necessary to bring together the distributed activity within the neural system into a single time-window. In one experiment, Poppel and Logothetis (1986) analysed participants' reaction times (RTs) by measuring how quickly their eye moved to follow a dot jumping across a computer screen. Their RTs seemed to follow a 30-millisecond cycle: if the dot moved at any point within this cycle, it took until the end of the interval before any response occurred. A similar cycle has been observed when participants are asked to judge whether an auditory and a visual stimulus are simultaneous or consecutive (Fox, 2009).

Complementing this 30-millisecond cycle is a '**dopamine loop**'. According to Carter (2006), the notion of flowing time is encoded in a neural circuit fuelled by the transmitter dopamine. Each 'loop' of activity takes, on average, one-tenth of a second to complete (i.e. 100 milliseconds), and events registered by the brain within the duration of a single loop are experienced as a single occurrence. This, in turn, is related to our sense of 'the present' or 'now' (what William James (1890) called the 'saddle-back' of duration or the 'specious present'). Edelman's (1989) use of the term 'the remembered present' is intended to highlight the 'dynamic interaction ... that gives rise to consciousness'. While our subjective sense of the passing moment is unified, the neural mechanisms which carry out this feat are extremely diverse, complex, massively parallel and occupy many interacting loci in the brain, especially the thalamus and cortex. The dopamine loop is part of the concept of an interval timer (IT), which is discussed in more detail below.

In a more general way, Edelman's remembered present is described within 'a framework of past and future': human beings have evolved the ability to distinguish conceptual-symbolic models of the world from ongoing perceptual experience, which, in turn, allows a concept of the past to be developed. This frees the individual from the bondage of an immediate time frame or ongoing events occurring in real time (Edelman, 1992). This is related to Corballis and Suddendorf's (2007) MTT (see Chapter 1, page 8).

The 'ticking' of the internal clock

Our normal idea of the present moment corresponds to one of the 'temporal packets' or 'ticks' of the internal clock: about one-tenth to one-fifth of a second. Each tick is the time it takes for the electrical nerve impulse to travel around a loop of dopamine-producing neurons. All the information we process during that time-window is experienced as happening simultaneously. This allows us to perceive the breaking cup (see above) as a single incident. Carter (2006) calls this a 'smearing' of time, fleshing out the subjective moment by squashing into it all the events that fall into a particular time packet. However, the downside of this 'smearing 'or 'squashing' is that each of our moments is slightly blurred, sometimes literally:

> ... *When we watch the beating of a fly's wings, we cannot see each individual flap because several of them happen in each of our time windows. The result is that we see a fuzzy haze rather than a clear outline of a moving wing. If our subjective concept of time was more fine-grained, allowing us to split each moment into many more parts, we would see things more clearly ...* (Carter, 2006)

As Carter herself observes, we probably didn't evolve a more fine-grained sense of time because this would have produced information-overload. After all, what advantage is there to seeing the individual beats of a fly's wing?

> ... *The things we need to discriminate most clearly are those that happen in seconds (animals moving or, today, cars bearing down on us) – not milliseconds. Just as there is no need for us to experience all the visual details that our brains detect unconsciously, time experience is most usefully cast in relatively broad brushstrokes. Only when we are faced with a life-threatening situation, or one which is wildly exciting, can we afford to ignore everything in the past and future and concentrate on the present moment. And when that happens our brains oblige by breaking the moment into more parts so each one can be separately scrutinised and dealt with.* (Carter, 2006)

As conveyed by William James's (1890) concept of the stream of consciousness, consciousness has a changing yet continuous character. If different moments were separate and unconnected, although we may still perceive a world of stable objects, there would be no coherence to our experience:

> ... *we would experience a flash of existence at a time, and this flash would not be integrated with the previous moment or the next one. One might think that this discontinuous strobe-like existence would require that we remember from one moment to the next what we have experienced and make judgements that would somehow summarise or collate the succession of moments into a coherent object. But if consciousness were genuinely discontinuous, so would be our memory and our judgement ...* (Gallagher, 2007)

Gallagher (2007) likens such experience to James's (1890) 'blooming, buzzing confusion' (which was actually meant to describe a newborn baby's perceptual experience). For example, we'd be unable to experience a movement or a melody as it develops.

Husserl (1928/1991) worked out a description of how it's possible to actually hear a melody, see a movement or perceive identity over time. One moment of consciousness isn't disconnected from the previous one or the next. If things appear in a continuous or continually developing way, which they do in normal waking consciousness, then previous phases of experience must in some way be tied together with subsequent ones. Of course, some of the things we experience may themselves be disjointed events, but we still experience an integrated successive flow rather than a disjointed, stop-and-start progression. If experience weren't like this, then *all* events would appear disjointed.

But how exactly is one moment of consciousness interconnected with the previous and subsequent ones? Husserl's answer is a detailed account of the structure of what he calls **internal time-consciousness** (see Box 7.4).

Box 7.4 Husserl's (1928/1991) account of internal time-consciousness

As one moment of consciousness fades into the past, we don't call upon memory as a new cognitive act in order to somehow capture that moment. Indeed, even in remembering something our experience is structured as a connected streaming process. If we claimed that memory is responsible for retaining the past phases of memory, we'd get stuck in an *infinite regress*; in other words, for every act of remembering, there'd have to be another that allows us to remember the previous one – and so on *ad infinitum*. Rather, implicit in the very nature of consciousness (whether it involves perception, memory, imagination, a train of conceptual thought, etc.) is a binding of one moment to the next, which Husserl calls *retention* (in relation to past moments of consciousness) and *protention* (in relation to the future). According to Gallagher (2007):

> ... Husserl's model explains not only how the perception of a temporal object, such as a melody, is possible, given a changing stream of consciousness, it also explains how consciousness unifies itself *across time*. (emphasis in original.)

If we imagine a momentary phase of consciousness, abstracting it from the flowing continuum of consciousness, it appears to be structured by three functions:

1. *Primal impression*, which allows for the consciousness of an object (such as a musical note) that's simultaneous with the current phase of consciousness.

2. *Retention*, which retains the previous phase of consciousness and its intentional content (the just past note of the melody).

3. *Protention*, which anticipates experience that's just about to happen.

Since retention retains the entire just-past phase, which also includes retention of the previous phase, there's a retentional continuum that stretches back over prior experience; this maintains the sense of the past moments *in the present*.

Gallagher (2007) gives the example of speaking the sentence 'The cat is on the mat' to illustrate Husserl's account. When I reach the word 'on', I'm no longer saying the previous words, but I, and anyone who's listening to me, still retain a sense of the beginning of the sentence – otherwise the sentence would make so sense. Retention keeps the intentional sense of the words available even after the words are no longer being spoken. As I'm uttering the sentence, not only do I have a sense of the sentence as it develops, but I also have a sense that *I* am the one who's just spoken the words and is uttering the sentence. This sense of self is built into experience at the very basic level of the retentional function; indeed, it is the retentional structure of consciousness that makes it possible (Gallagher, 2007).

When saying the word 'on', I also have an anticipatory sense (protention) of where the sentence is going, or, at least, that the sentence is heading towards some kind of ending; some sense of anticipation seems essential to the experience I have of speaking in a meaningful way. '... More generally, this is a feature of all normal experience. We do not go blindly into the future; we have an experiential heading.' (Gallagher, 2007)

Another way of capturing the nature of 'now' has been proposed in Poppel's (e.g. 2004) concept of the subjective present and the related **three-second window** (or rule). This is described in Box 7.5.

Box 7.5. The subjective present and the three-second window

As we've seen, psychologists have been interested in 'the present' as a basic temporal phenomenon for more than a hundred years (e.g. James, 1890). According to Poppel (2004), we're now in a position to assess how long such a subjective present actually lasts: a number of different experiments all converge on the value of approximately 2–3 seconds.

What Poppel calls the three-second window was first described by various researchers in the mid-1800s. For example, in 1868 Karl von Vierordt dubbed this time interval the 'point of indifference': participants estimated that tones that were actually shorter than three seconds lasted longer, while those that actually lasted longer than three seconds were reported as being shorter. This three-second point of indifference has remained constant, despite technological and social revolutions and 'cultural speed-up', suggesting that it's hardwired into the brain (Wallisch, 2008).

Support for the three-second window comes from different domains, including temporal perception proper, speech, movement control, vision, audition and memory.

> *... All these observations suggest that conscious activities are temporally segmented into intervals of a few seconds ... providing a temporal platform for conscious activity ...* (Wallisch, 2008)

Time for reflection

- What do you see in Figure 7.3?
- If you've seen this before, you'll know that there are two different ways of interpreting the image: if you stare at it long enough, it will automatically switch to the alternative (and back again) – but usually this will take just three seconds.
- Try repeating out loud, as fast as you can, the following (meaningless) syllables 'ku-ba-ku'.
- What happens?
- What usually happens is that , eventually, you'll be saying 'kuba' or 'baku': these will start alternating every three seconds (beyond your control); one or other will 'take possession of conscious content' (Poppel, 2004).

▲ Figure 7.3

('Kuba' is likely to become 'Cuba'; Baku is in fact the capital of Azerbaijan: Wallisch, 2008.)

Gerstner and Fazio (1995) found that various species of higher mammals tend to segment their motor behaviour in the same temporal range as humans (i.e. 2–3 seconds). This suggests that we're dealing with a universal principle of temporal integration that transcends human cognitive and behavioural control (Poppel, 2004). Poppel also claims that it's impossible to perform two or three different tasks simultaneously with the same degree of concentration. Apparently simultaneous awareness and processing of information actually takes place within three-second windows, during each of which the brain takes in all the data about the environment *as a block*; subsequent events are then processed in the next window. This represents a major sticking point in our ability to *multi-task*.

> *What appears to be multitasking is thus more akin to channel surfing among different television stations. A person can concentrate on a conversation for three seconds, then for three seconds on a crying child and three on a computer screen. While one subject at a time occupies the foreground of consciousness, the others stay in the background until they, in turn, are given access to the central processor.* (Manhart, 2004)

What Manhart calls 'concentration', the foreground of consciousness, Poppel (1997) calls the singular 'state of being conscious' (or STOBCON).

> *... This universal integrative process is automatic and pre-semantic, i.e. it is not determined by what is processed, but it defines a temporal window within which conscious activities can be implemented. Because of the omnipresence of this phenomenon, it can be used as a pragmatic definition of the subjective present which is characterised by the phenomenal impression of 'nowness'. Temporal integration in the range of 2 to 3 seconds [also] ... defines ... the singular 'state of being conscious' or STOBCON ... The 3-second-window provides a logistic basis for conscious representation, a working platform for our phenomenal present.* (Poppel, 2004)

Access to this temporal operating platform is apparently controlled by independent neuronal mechanism, as suggested by phenomena such as **blindsight** (see Chapter 4). This form of unconscious cognition can be understood as involving a deficit in the operations that normally allow access to the temporal platform of conscious activity (Poppel, 2004)

The interval timer

The so-called *interval timer* (IT) (or 'stopwatch' in the brain) marks time spans of seconds to hours. The IT helps you to work out how fast you have to run to catch a ball, when to applaud your favourite song, and lets you sense how long you can stay in bed after the alarm has gone off (Wright, 2006). Interval timing enlists the higher cognitive powers of the cerebral cortex, which governs perception, memory and conscious thought (see Chapter 3).

Rao *et al.* (2001) used **functional magnetic resonance imaging (fMRI)** to identify the brain regions involved in interval timing. Participants were presented with two pairs of tones and had to decide whether the interval between the second pair was longer or shorter than the interval between the first pair. The fMRI scan records changes in blood flow and oxygen consumption once every 250 milliseconds: brain structures involved in the task consume more oxygen than those that aren't. The first structures that were activated were the *basal ganglia*, one area of which, the *striatum*, contains a number of conspicuously well-connected neurons that receive signals from other parts of the brain. The axons of these striatal cells are covered with 10,000–30,000 spines, each of which gathers information from a different neuron in a different location. If the brain acts like a network, then the striatal spiky neurons are critical nodes, where thousands of neurons converge on a single neuron.

Striatal spiny neurons are central to an *interval-timing theory* (e.g. Matell and Meck, 2000), according to which a collection of neural oscillators in the cerebral cortex fire at different rates (10–40 cycles per second) without regard to their neighbours' tempos or external stimulation. These cortical oscillators are connected to the striatum via millions of signal-carrying axons and this enables the striatal spiky neurons to 'eavesdrop' on all these de-synchronised 'conversations' taking place among the oscillators. When an external stimulus (such as a changing traffic light) grabs the attention of the cortical cells, they begin to fire simultaneously; this produces a characteristic spike in electrical output about 300 milliseconds later. The cortical cells then resume their disorganised oscillations.

However, the spike represents a distinct, reproducible pattern of neuronal activity; the spiny neurons monitor these patterns, helping them to 'count' elapsed time. At the end of a specified interval (for example, the traffic light turns red), a part of the basal ganglia called the *substantia nigra* sends a burst of dopamine to the striatum. This dopamine burst (or loop) induces the spiny neurons to record the pattern of cortical oscillations they receive at that instant, like a flashbulb exposing the interval's cortical signature on the spiny neurons' film. Once a spiny neuron has learned the time stamp of the interval for a given event, subsequent occurrences of the event trigger both the spike and the dopamine burst at the *beginning* of the interval. The dopamine burst now tells the spiny neurons to start tracking the patterns of cortical impulses that follow. When the spiny neurons recognise the time stamp marking the end of the interval, they send an electrical impulse from the striatum to the thalamus, which, in turn, communicates with the cortex; here memory, decision making and other higher cognitive functions, take over. Evidence relating to interval timing theory is discussed in Box 7.6.

Box 7.6 Factors affecting the interval timer (IT)

- If Matell and Meck's theory is correct, and dopamine bursts play an important role in framing a time interval, then diseases and drugs that affect dopamine levels should also disrupt the IT mechanism. This is what Meck and others have found (Wright, 2006).

- For example, patients with untreated Parkinson's disease release less dopamine into the striatum, and their internal clock runs slow: they consistently *underestimate* the duration of time intervals (Carter, 2006; Wright, 2006). If you ask most people to say (starting at a particular moment) when they think that a minute has elapsed, their answer, typically, will be to say 'now' after about 35–40 seconds. Untreated Parkinson's patients are likely to choose a far longer duration (Carter, 2006).

- Marijuana also lowers dopamine levels and slows down time, while recreational stimulants (such as cocaine and methamphetamine) *increase* the availability of dopamine, making the IT speed up – time seems to *expand*.

- Adrenaline and other stress hormones also make the clock speed up: a second can feel like an hour during stressful situations (Wright, 2006: see text below).

Box 7.6 *Continued*

- States of deep concentration or extreme emotion may flood the system or bypass it altogether: in such cases, time may seem to stand still or not exist at all. Because an attentional spike initiates the timing mechanism, people with attention-deficit hyperactivity disorder (ADHD) might also have difficulty gauging the true length of time intervals (Wright, 2006).

- Binofski and Block (1996) report the case of a 66-year-old man, who found one day as he drove to work that other traffic seemed to be rushing towards him at terrific speed; he simultaneously felt that his own car seemed to be going unusually fast. Even when he slowed down to walking pace, it seemed to be hurtling along beyond his ability to control it. He also found that he couldn't watch TV because things happened too quickly for him to keep up with them, and he seemed to be perpetually tired. When doctors gave him the '60-second' test, he waited almost five minutes before saying 'now'. A medical examination revealed that he had a growth in his prefrontal cortex.

- Damage to the basal ganglia and/or frontal lobes sometimes produces *catatonia*, in which people may become 'frozen', like living statues. Some such affected people have been paralysed in mid-action, their hand outstretched as though reaching for something, or contorted into strange postures which they may hold – despite what would normally be extreme discomfort – for days at a time. Although they don't appear to be conscious during these episodes, some patients have later reported that they could remember it, but that these recollections lacked any sense of passing time: their consciousness was completely still and devoid of possibilities. A sense of timelessness – though markedly *full* of possibility – is also reported by people in meditation or trance (Carter, 2006).

Distortions in the judgement of time

As we saw in Box 7.6, damage to various parts of the brain, as well as imbibing different drugs, can interfere with the normal judgement and perception of time. We also noted that different kinds of situation (such as very stressful ones or highly relaxed ones) can also influence how we experience the passage of time. In this section, we will consider some further examples.

'Mind time' has to do with how we experience the passage of time and how we organise chronology (the order in which things happen). It also involves the scale on which things happen, whether that of a lifetime or of a few seconds. Box 7.7 describes the relationship between time and memory.

Box 7.7 Time and memory: amnesia and mind time (Damasio, 2006)

People who sustain damage to regions of the brain involved in learning and recalling new facts develop major disturbances in their ability to place past events in the correct era and sequence. These amnesics also lose the ability to estimate the passage of time accurately at the scale of hours, months, years and decades. This occurs despite their biological clock often remaining intact, as well as their ability to judge brief intervals of a minute or less and to order them correctly (see text above). At the very least, the experiences of these patients suggest that the processing of time and certain types of memory must share some common neurological pathways.

Box 7.7 *Continued*

The association between amnesia and time can be seen most dramatically in cases of permanent brain damage to the hippocampus, a region that's crucial to memory, and to the nearby temporal lobe, through which the hippocampus holds a two-way communication with the rest of the cortex. Damage to the hippocampus prevents the creation of new memories (**anterograde amnesia**). The ability to form memories is an indispensable part of the construction of a sense of our own chronology: we build our time line event by event and connect personal happenings to those that occur around us. When the hippocampus is impaired, patients become unable to hold factual memories for longer than about one minute. A dramatic case of the effects of hippocampal damage is that of Clive Wearing, which is described in Box 7.8.

The memories that the hippocampus helps to create aren't actually stored there: they're distributed in neural networks located in parts of the cortex (including the temporal lobe) related to the material being recorded (areas dedicated to vision, sound, touch, etc.). These networks must be activated to both lay down and recall a memory; when they're destroyed, patients cannot recover long-term memories (**retrograde amnesia**). The memories most markedly lost in retrograde amnesia are precisely those that bear a time stamp: recollections of unique, personal events that happened in a particular context on a particular occasion (*episodic* or *autobiographical memory*: Tulving, 1972). The temporal lobe that surrounds the hippocampus is critical in making and retrieving such memories.

In patients with temporal lobe damage (through, for example, viral encephalitis, stroke or Alzheimer's disease), years and even decades of autobiographical memory can be permanently destroyed. Damasio describes a patient, who, at the age of 46, sustained damage both to the hippocampus and to parts of the temporal lobe; this resulted in both anterograde and retrograde amnesia. He inhabits a permanent present, unable to remember what happened a minute or 20 years ago. Indeed, he has no sense of time at all: he cannot say what the date or his age is (guessing as wildly as 1943 and 2013). If he has access to a window, he can guess time more accurately based on light and shadows. But without a watch or window, morning is no different from afternoon, or night from day: the body clock doesn't help. He knows that he was married (but his wife divorced him more than 20 years ago) with two children (he's actually a grandfather), but he cannot place himself in the time line of his family life.

Box 7.8 Clive Wearing (based on Baddeley, 1990; Blakemore, 1988)

Clive Wearing was the chorus master of the London Sinfonietta and a world expert on Renaissance music, as well as a BBC radio producer. In March 1985, he suffered a rare brain infection caused by the cold sore virus (*Herpes simplex*). The virus attacked and destroyed his hippocampus, along with parts of his cortex.

He lives in a snapshot of time, constantly believing that he has just woken up from years of unconsciousness. For example, when his wife, Deborah, enters his hospital room for the third time in a single morning, he embraces her as if they'd been separated for years, saying, 'I'm conscious for the first time' and 'It's the first time I've seen anybody at all'.

At first his confusion was total and very frightening to him. Once, he held a chocolate in the palm of one hand, covered it with the other for a few seconds, until its image disappeared from his memory. When he uncovered it, he thought he'd performed a magic trick, conjuring it up from nowhere. He repeated it again and again, with total astonishment, and growing fear, each time.

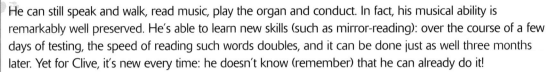

He can still speak and walk, read music, play the organ and conduct. In fact, his musical ability is remarkably well preserved. He's able to learn new skills (such as mirror-reading): over the course of a few days of testing, the speed of reading such words doubles, and it can be done just as well three months later. Yet for Clive, it's new every time: he doesn't know (remember) that he can already do it!

His capacity for remembering his earlier life is extremely patchy. For example, when shown pictures of Cambridge (where he'd spent four years as an undergraduate and had often visited subsequently), he only recognised King's College Chapel – the most distinctive Cambridge building – but not his own college. He couldn't remember who wrote *Romeo and Juliet* and he thought the Queen and Prince Philip were singers he'd known from a Catholic church.

According to Deborah, 'without consciousness he's in many senses dead'. In his own words, his life is 'Hell on earth – it's like being dead – all the bloody time'.

Fear and the slowing down of time

As commonly portrayed in TV and film, someone facing a frightening, potentially dangerous or even fatal situation, such as losing control of a car and heading for another vehicle or the edge of a cliff, experiences a dramatic slowing down of time – things seem to happen in slow motion.

Neuropsychologist David Eagleman experienced this apparent slowing of time as an eight-year-old when he fell off a roof and broke his nose. This phenomenon could either be related to memory, or it could be that the brain's processing speed accelerates under stressful conditions, making external events appear to slow down in comparison. Eagleman decided to replicate his childhood experience under carefully controlled conditions.

With his colleagues (Stetson *et al.*, 2007), Eagleman asked six psychology graduate students to take a thrill ride known as a 'suspended catch air device' which drops people from a 31 m (150 ft) scaffolding tower into a safety net below (see Figure 7.4).

To measure the speed of participants' perceptions, they wore a specially designed wrist-worn device (a perceptual chronometer). An LED array on the face of the device displayed a flickering single-digit number alternating with the negative of its image about 20 times per second, which is normally too quick for people to distinguish between the two images (you'd just perceive all the elements of the LED array to be shining simultaneously). However, if the perceptual clocks of the terrified participants speeded up even a little, the number should become visible. As predicted, the participants overestimated the time it took to drop into the net (they estimated over three seconds, compared with the actual 2.5 seconds). However, contrary to

▲ **Figure 7.4** 'Eagleman's tower': people are in free fall for 31 m until they reach a safety net below

predictions, they couldn't identify the flickering number on the display; this suggests that their perceptions hadn't actually speeded up.

According to Eagleman and Pariyadath (2009), the apparent slowing down of time is attributable to a trick of memory. An intense experience involving heightened fear or excitement focuses our attention and produces the firing of many neurons across the brain; this causes us to absorb more sensory details. Richer memories seem to last longer, because we assume that more time would have been needed to record so many details. This could account for other temporal illusions, such as the 'oddball effect'. When participants see the same things repeatedly (say, the image of a dog flashed on a computer screen) and then suddenly see something different (say, an image of Margaret Thatcher), the novel stimulus seems to last longer – even if all the images are in fact presented for the same duration. fMRI evidence shows a spike in brain activity when an unexpected stimulus is presented, suggesting that it causes a richer memory to be formed; this explains why the experience seems to last longer. In a reframed version of this explanation, Eagleman and Pariyadath (2010) propose that the experience of duration is a 'signature of the amount of energy expended in representing a stimulus – that is, the coding efficiency'.

According to John Wearden, a British experimental psychologist (in Cavanagh, 2000), the massively increased pace of the internal clock during stressful events may have adaptive advantage: the perceived slowing down of external events may provide a valuable opportunity for flight-or-fight decisions to be made. However, laboratory studies of the effect of arousal on subjective time haven't wholly supported this account. Experimental manipulations designed to moderately increase physiological arousal have little or no effect on subjective time estimates. Wearden suggests that the relationship between subjective time and arousal may be *non-linear*: changes in the pace of the internal clock may only be seen at *extreme* levels of arousal, which are difficult to induce under laboratory conditions.

> ## Time for reflection
> - Eagleman's tower experiment induced extreme levels of arousal (i.e. fear) in the participants. Even assuming that they gave their informed consent to participate, does the experiment raise any important ethical issues?
>
> (You may want to read the original journal article for details regarding consent/informed consent, right to withdraw and debriefing. Also, bear in mind that the participants were graduate psychology students.)

Can the brain's internal clock be speeded up?

While the participants in 'Eagleman's tower' failed to show any evidence of their internal clock speeding up, Weardon claims to have found a way of achieving this. When Wearden exposed participants to 10 seconds of fast clicks (about five per second) and then asked them to estimate the duration of a burst of light or a sound, they believed that the second stimulus lasted about 10 per cent longer than if they'd heard silence or white noise before the burst (Fox, 2009).

Had their central pacemaker actually speeded up, or could the results have simply been due to a distortion of memory? Ogden and Jones (2009) decided to test participants' rate of mental processing in a replication of Wearden's experiment. After exposing them to the clicks, they measured how quickly they could achieve three different tasks: basic arithmetic, memorising words and hitting a specified key on a computer keyboard. What Ogden and Jones found was that the clicks accelerated the participants' performance on all three tasks by 10–20 per cent. It was as if the drumbeat of their brain's internal slave galley had speeded up, compelling each neuron to row faster. White noise had no such effect. According to Wearden, if you speed up people's subjective time, they really do seem to have more time to process things, and the practical implications are enormous (such as allowing students to cram more work into less time). But there are also ethical issues involved, especially in a sports context (Fox, 2009).

The fact that there was no evidence of changes in participants' heart rate, skin conductance (galvanic skin response/GSR) or muscle tension, suggests strongly that the results weren't merely the result of an increase in autonomic arousal (as claimed by some critics, including Eagleman). So, how else might the clicks be changing time perception and information-processing speeds? According to Fox (2009), research by the neuroscientist Edward Large has found that rhythmic sounds can entrain gamma brain waves; this causes the beginning of each sound to be accompanied by a burst of several especially strong wave peaks. The clicks may also entrain other types of brain waves, perhaps including those that correspond to the discrete snapshots in our perceptions. Both VanRullen and Jones agree with this proposed explanation: faster oscillations produce more snapshots per second, making a given time seem to last longer. If this explanation is correct, the clicks are literally resetting the brain's frame-capture rate (Fox, 2009).

Speeding up and slowing down reversed

According to William James (1890): 'A day full of excitement is said to pass "ere we know it". On the contrary a day full of waiting, of unsatisfied desire for change, will seem a small eternity.'

According to the popular saying 'time flies when you're having fun', or whenever we're exposed to a large number of new, fast-changing or complex stimuli (such as playing an exciting video game), but it 'drags' when we're bored. Presumably, in the former situation our limited attentional resources are fully taken over by the demands of the fast-paced, changing stimulation (Wallisch, 2008).

While there's certainly anecdotal evidence to support these views of time perception, in retrospect these relations become *reversed*. The enjoyable holiday that seemed to fly by at the time seems, when we look back on it, to have 'lasted an age'. Yet the succession of dull days, during which time dragged, seems, in retrospect to have passed quite quickly (McKellar, 1968). Wearden (2005, in Wallisch, 2008) reported experimental findings which support this anecdotal evidence. He showed one group of participants a nine-minute clip from the movie *Armageddon*; a second group spent the same amount of time in a waiting room with nothing to do. As expected – and consistent with James's observation above – the first group reported that time passed much faster compared with the second group. However, when the participants were questioned some time later, the second group estimated the time they'd spent just waiting as 10 per cent *shorter* than those who'd watched the movie.

> *... In retrospect, an eventful period appears longer, phases of boredom shorter. What seems to be crucial is the quantity of amassed memory. Rich and varied memories are associated with long periods, less intense or similar memories with shorter ones. This neatly illustrates that the subjective experience of time arises from the interplay – some say as the by-product – of processes in attention and memory.* (Wallisch, 2008)

The elasticity of time

Damasio (2006) proposes that the elasticity of time is perhaps best appreciated when we are the spectators of a performance, whether this is a film, a play, a concert or a lecture. The actual duration of the performance and its subjective duration are different things.

He cites the example of Alfred Hitchcock's (1948) film *Rope*, a 'technically remarkable work' that was shot in continuous, unedited 10-minute takes. While others have used long continuous shots (such as Orson Welles in *Touch of Evil*, Robert Altman in *The Player* and Martin Scorsese in *GoodFellas*), no other film has used this technique as consistently as in *Rope*. Hitchcock invented this technique as an attempt to depict a story that had been told in a play occurring in continuous time. But he was limited by the amount of film that could be loaded into the camera, roughly enough for 10 minutes of action.

In an interview with Francois Truffaut in 1966, Hitchcock explained that the story begins at 7.30 pm and ends at 9.15 pm – 105 minutes later. Yet the film consists of eight reels of 10 minutes each: a total of 81 minutes (with credits added). Where did the missing 25 minutes go? Do we experience the film as shorter than 105 minutes? The answer is 'no': the film never seems shorter than it should, and a viewer has no sense of haste or editing. On the contrary, for many the film seems *longer* than its actual projection time.

Damasio identifies several aspects of the film that account for this perceived time.

1. Most of the action takes place in the living room of a penthouse in summer, and the skyline of New York is visible through a panoramic window. At the beginning of the film, the light suggests late afternoon; by the end, it is night. Our daily experience of fading daylight makes us perceive the real time action as taking long enough to cover the several hours of approaching darkness, when in fact Hitchcock artificially accelerates those changes in light.

2. Similarly, the nature and context of the depicted actions elicit other automatic judgements about time. After the proverbial Hitchcock murder at the beginning of the film's first reel, the story focuses on an elegant dinner party hosted by the two murderers and attended by the relatives and friends of the victim. The actual time during which food is served spans about two reels, but viewers attribute more time to that sequence because we know that neither the hosts nor the guests, who look calm, polite and unhurried, would get through dinner at such a pace (i.e. 20 minutes). When the action later splits – some guests chat in the living room in front of the camera, while others retire to the dining room to look at rare books – we sensibly attribute a longer duration to this off-screen episode than the few minutes it actually takes.

3. There are no 'jump-cuts' within each 10-minute reel: the camera glides slowly toward and away from each character. Yet Hitchcock finished most takes with a close-up of an object, in order to join each segment to the next. In most cases, the camera moves to the back of an actor wearing a dark suit and the screen goes black for a very brief interval; the next take begins as the camera pulls away from the actor's back. Although the black screen isn't meant to signal a time break, it may nonetheless contribute to the perception of the time being longer: we're used to interpreting breaks in the continuity of visual perception as a lapse in the continuity of time. Film-editing techniques (such as the dissolve and fade) often cause spectators to infer that time has elapsed between the preceding shot and the following one. In *Rope*, each of the seven breaks delays real time by a fraction of a second, but *cumulatively*, for some viewers at least, they may suggest that a longer interval has passed.

4. When we're uncomfortable or worried, we often experience time as passing more slowly because we focus on negative images associated with our anxiety (see Stetson *et al.*'s (2007) research above). Damasio's own research has shown that the brain generates images at faster rates when we're experiencing positive emotions (see the section on 'Speeding up and slowing down reversed' above). He refers to a recent experience of aircraft turbulence, which he experienced as 'achingly slow': his attention was directed to the negative aspects of the situation. Perhaps the unpleasantness of the situation depicted in *Rope* conspires to stretch time in a similar way.

By providing a significant discrepancy between real time and the audience's perception of time, *Rope* illustrates how the experience of duration is a *construct* (Damasio, 2006); that is, it demonstrates very dramatically the difference between mind time and objective ('real') time.

Mental disorder and the perception of time

McKellar (1957) describes the 'time discontinuity phenomenon' in relation to 'model psychosis experiments' with the hallucinogenic drug mescaline. In one such experiment, in which McKellar acted as the participant, he played chess with the experimenter (with whom he'd previously played). He experienced a number of paranoid delusions that focused on the tasking of his chess pieces: despite reasoning that he'd taken a substantial amount of mescaline as part of a scientific experiment, and having no reason to believe that his opponent would have cheated, he nonetheless inferred that this was what had in fact happened. Since McKellar had absolutely no memory of his pieces having been taken during the course of the game, this was the only explanation he could come up with for how he'd lost his pieces.

Interviews with several psychotic patients with persecutory delusions provided evidence of similar experiences of time discontinuity. Blank periods – periods of brief amnesia – can occur, but events do happen in them of which the patients have no awareness. The result can be alarming impressions of objects and people appearing and disappearing unpredictably, rather than moving about in the way we'd see them do so with normal and continuous experience of the passage of time:

> ... *Uncaused, unexplained, and frighteningly unexpected events provide excellent subject-matter for delusions, including the delusion that these happenings result from the activities of one's "persecutors".* (McKellar, 1968)

Such paranoid delusions are a common feature of (certain types of) schizophrenia, the most serious form of mental disorder. Could these delusions stem from a faulty internal clock? Schizophrenia certainly seems to affect people's perception of time. If someone with schizophrenia is shown a flash of light and a sound one tenth of a second apart, he or she typically has trouble telling which came first. These patients also estimate the passing of time less accurately than non-schizophrenics (Fox, 2009).

According to Fox, several studies have now shown that if you disturb the internal clocks of healthy people, you can create some of the symptoms associated with schizophrenia, including delusions. In one experiment, healthy participants learned to play a video game in which they had to steer a plane around obstacles. Once they'd got used to the game, the researchers modified it by inserting a 0.2 second delay in the plane's response to movements of the mouse: initially, performance on the game worsened, but they eventually adjusted to the delay so that the movements of the mouse and of the plane were perceived as simultaneous. However, when the researchers removed the delay (so that the timing was set back to normal), the participants now experienced the plane to be moving *before* they consciously steered it with the mouse. This is remarkably similar to how people with schizophrenia describe feelings that they're somehow being controlled by another being. There's also some evidence that schizophrenic brains are temporally inflexible: using a video game similar to the one involving steering a plane, Eagleman (in Fox, 2009) has found that people with schizophrenia (compared with healthy controls) find it more difficult to compensate for delays between their actions and the outcomes of their actions. During a broad range of mental tasks, people with schizophrenia display less activity in their cerebellum (Andreasen and Pierson, 2008).

> ## Time for reflection
> - Try tickling yourself. Does it work – can you make yourself laugh?
> - If not, try to explain this in terms of the timing of the stimulus (the tickling movements) and the response (laughing).
> - How might the timing relationship be changed in order to make it work?

We cannot normally tickle ourselves: somehow the intention to make the necessary movements also suppresses the response. But Fox (2009) cites an experiment in which participants were asked to brush the palm of their hand using a robotic probe which produced a 200-millisecond delay between the intended movements and the actual movements; under these conditions, participants experienced the same sensations as they would if someone else were tickling them.

In fact, voice-hearing psychotic patients display a greater ability to tickle themselves compared with non-psychotic controls (Blakemore *et al.*, 2001, in Bentall, 2007), Could it be that for people with schizophrenia there's some kind of delay between intention and response? Poor time-processing could explain many of the experiences of people with schizophrenia. For example, by muddling the order of thoughts and perceptions within your brain, you might move your hand before you are conscious of the decision, making it feel as if someone else is controlling your movements. When an advert appears on TV, your brain might picture the product before you consciously register seeing it on the screen; this could create the disturbing illusion that your thoughts are being broadcast on TV (Fox, 2009).

In relation to auditory-verbal hallucinations, some researchers have attempted to directly measure **source monitoring** – the capacity to distinguish between self-generated thoughts and externally-presented stimuli. One idea is that hallucinating patients have **dysfunctional metacognitive beliefs** (beliefs about their own mental processes) that lead them to make self-defeating efforts to control their thoughts: this makes the thoughts seem unintended – and, therefore, alien. A second idea is that source monitoring errors reflect a general failure to monitor one's own intentional states: hallucinating patients don't display the same dampening in the auditory perception areas of the temporal lobe seen during talking and inner speech (Ford and Mathlon, 2004, in Bentall, 2007).

Mental time lag and consciousness

While most of us don't have to grapple with the large gaps of memory or the chronological confusion as described in Boxes 7.6, 7.7 and 7.8, we do all share a strange mental time lag, a phenomenon first identified by neurophysiologist, Benjamin Libet (see Chapter 4). His research is described in Box 7.9.

Box 7.9 Libet's experiments on consciousness and free will

Libet (1985; 2004; Libet *et al.*, 1983) asked the question: when someone spontaneously and deliberately flexes his or her finger or wrist, what starts the action off? Is it the conscious decision to act, or is it some unconscious brain process? To find out, Libet asked participants to flex their finger/ wrist at least 40 times, at times of their own choosing, and measured the following:

1. The time at which the action occurred (M). This can be easily detected by using electrodes on the wrist (**electromyogram (EMG)**).

2. The beginning of brain activity in the motor cortex. This can also be detected through placing electrodes on the scalp (**electroencephalogram (EEG)**), which can detect a gradually increasing signal (the 'readiness potential'/RP).

3. The time at which the participant consciously decided to act (the moment of willing/W).

The key question is: which comes first?

W is the most difficult to determine. If you ask participants to shout or press a button or do anything else, there'll be another lag before this. Also, the decision to shout or press the button may interfere with the main decision being measured. Libet devised a special method for measuring W: he asked participants to note the position of a spot of light (moving around the circumference of a circular screen placed in front of them) at the moment they decided to act. They could then say, after the action was over, where the spot had been at that critical moment.

Libet found that W came about 200 milliseconds (ms) (one-fifth of a second) before the action (consistent with the concept of free will). But the RP began about 300–500 ms before that (that is, 500–700 ms before the action – contrary to what belief in free will would predict). In other words, there was activity in the brain for anything up to half a second before participants were subjectively aware of having made the decision: consciousness lagged behind brain activity.

Libet's results caused a storm of debate among philosophers, neuroscientists, psychologists and physiologists, which has been raging ever since (Banks and Pockett, 2007; Damasio, 2006). What was controversial was the blow they appeared to deal to our cherished belief in free will (see Gross, 2009). There are two other questions raised by Libet's findings: (1) Why aren't we aware of this delay between brain activity and consciousness? (2) How should we view or experience the present, the 'now'?

1. One attractive explanation of why we're not aware of the delay is that because we have similar brains and they work in similar ways, we're all 'hopelessly late for consciousness' and no one notices it. But perhaps more likely is that the brain can institute its own connections on the central processing of events, such that, at the microtemporal level, it manages to 'antedate' some events so that delayed processes can appear less delayed and differently delayed processes can appear to have similar delays (Damasio, 2006). This possibility may explain why we maintain the illusion of continuity of time and space when we move our eyes more quickly from one target to another: we notice neither the blur that accompanies the eye movements, nor the time it takes to move the eyes from one place to another. Yarrow *et al.* (2001) suggest that the brain predates the perception of the target by as much as 120 ms, thereby giving us all the perception of seamless viewing. 'The brain's ability to edit our visual experiences and

---

to impart a sense of volition after neurons have already acted is an indication of its exquisite sensitivity to time ...' (Damasio, 2006).

2. The delay, of up to half a second, in the appearance of awareness of a sensory event introduced a problem regarding how to define or understand 'the present moment' (Libet, 2004). However, the brain's ability to 'antedate' some events (see above), what Libet calls 'subjective referral backward in time' puts the *subjective* experience of the present back into the present:

> ... *So we have the strange situation in which actual awareness of the present is really delayed, but the* content *of the conscious experience is brought into alignment with the present. Subjectively, then, we do live in the antedated present, although in fact we are not aware of the present for up to 0.5 sec after the sensory signal arrives at the cerebral cortex.* (Libet, 2004) (emphasis in original.)

The philosopher, Ludwig Wittgenstein (1953) claimed that 'The present is neither past or future. To experience the present is therefore a phenomenon with timelessness.' But if our experience of a sensory stimulus is actually antedated after the 0.5 second delay, the experience is actually one of an event 0.5 seconds in the past: as the subjective 'present' is actually of a past sensory event, it cannot be 'timeless' (Libet, 2004).

Time estimation in the laboratory

McKellar (1968) describes a study of his own in which participants (undergraduate students) were given a routine task, interrupted at intervals, and then asked to estimate how long had elapsed since the task had begun. For a total clock time of 260 seconds, the average estimate was 398 seconds: the group as a whole produced an average positive error (overestimate) of 138 seconds in their verbal estimations. There were quite dramatic individual differences in participants' estimates, ranging from 98–720 seconds.

This 'method of verbal estimation' is one of the standard techniques for laboratory investigation of time. Another is the 'method of production', in which the experimenter decides on a time interval (say, a minute), asks participants to start estimating and then to stop when they think a minute has elapsed. Unlike verbal estimation, the method of production essentially assesses participants' concept of the specified time interval. Again, this method produces huge individual differences: McKellar (1968) reports, in the case of a minute, that individuals vary between 15 and over 90 seconds.

Loehlin (1959) found evidence for four factors underlying the verbal estimation of time:

1. An interest versus boredom factor: the more bored participants tended to give longer estimates (see above).

2. A filled time versus empty time factor: longer estimates tended to occur with filled than with empty time.

3. A repetition factor: estimates of the second of two periods of a repeated activity tended to be shorter.

4. An activity versus passivity factor: periods of passivity are estimated as longer than those of activity.

Does time really go faster as we get older?

Why Life Speeds Up As You Get Older is the title of a 2004 book by the Dutch psychologist, Douwe Draaisma. The subtitle is *How Memory Shapes Our Past*. The major kind of memory in question is autobiographical memory (AM). As we noted in Box 7.8, Clive Wearing's capacity for remembering major features of his past, including his knowledge of 'current affairs', was almost totally destroyed along with destruction of his hippocampus. However, other abilities were well-preserved, as was his ability to acquire new skills (although he couldn't recall that he'd acquired them). These apparent contradictions within his long-term memory (LTM) illustrate crucial distinctions between **episodic memory (EM)**, **semantic memory (SM)** (Tulving, 1972) and **procedural memory (PM)** (Tulving, 1985: see Box 7.10) and **declarative memory** versus *procedural memory* (Cohen and Squire, 1980: see Figure 7. 5).

Box 7.10 Episodic, semantic and procedural memory (Tulving, 1972, 1985)

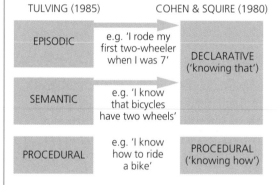

TULVING (1985)   COHEN & SQUIRE (1980)

EPISODIC	e.g. 'I rode my first two-wheeler when I was 7'	DECLARATIVE ('knowing that')
SEMANTIC	e.g. 'I know that bicycles have two wheels'	
PROCEDURAL	e.g. 'I know how to ride a bike'	PROCEDURAL ('knowing how')

▲ **Figure 7.5.** Distinctions between different kinds of LTM

- *Episodic memory (EM)* is an 'autobiographical' memory responsible for storing a record of our past experiences – the events, people, objects and so on which we have personally encountered. EM usually includes details about the particular time and place in which objects and events were experienced (they have a spatio-temporal context: e.g. 'Where did you go on your holiday last year?' and 'What did you have for breakfast this morning?'). EMs also have a subjective (self-focused) reality, but most could, in principle, be verified by others.

- **Flashbulb memories** are a special kind of EM, in which we can give vivid and detailed recollections of where we were and what we were doing when we first heard about some major public national or international event (Brown and Kulik, 1977).

- *Semantic memory (SM)* refers to our store of general, factual knowledge about the world, including concepts, rules and language, 'a mental thesaurus, organised knowledge a person possesses about words and other verbal symbols, their meaning and referents' (Tulving, 1972). SM can also be used without reference to where and when that knowledge was originally acquired. For example, we don't remember 'learning to talk' – we just 'know English' (or whatever our native language happens to be). But SM can also store information about ourselves (such as how many brothers and sisters we have, or how much we like psychology).

- *Procedural memory (PM)* refers to information from LTM which cannot be inspected consciously. For example, riding a bike is a complex skill which is even more difficult to describe. In the same way, native speakers of a language cannot usually describe the complex grammatical rules by which they speak correctly (perhaps because they weren't learned consciously in the first place: see Chapter 4). By contrast, both EM and SM are amenable to being inspected consciously, and the content of both can be described to another person.

According to Draaisma (2004), 'Our memory has a will of its own'; as Nooteboom (1983, in Draaisma) says, 'Memory is like a dog that lies down where it pleases'. Our autobiographical memory,

> *... is the chronicle of our lives, a long record we consult whenever someone asks us what our earliest memory is, what the house we lived in as a child looked like, or what was the last book we read. Autobiographical memory recalls and forgets at the same time ...* (Draaisma, 2004)

> *Autobiographical memory obeys some mysterious laws of its own. Why does it contain next to nothing about what happened before we were three or four? Why are hurtful events invariably recorded in indelible ink? Why are humiliations remembered for years on end with the precision of a charge sheet? Why is it invariably set in motion at sombre moments and during sombre events? ... Now and then we are taken by surprise by our own memory. A smell suddenly reminds us of something we haven't thought about for thirty years. A street we last saw when we were seven seems to have shrunk beyond all recognition. Memories of youth can seem clearer in old age than they were at the age of forty ...* (Draaisma, 2004)

The telescopy phenomenon

In 1955, the American statistician, Gray, identified a pattern in how people respond to items in questionnaires. For example, in response to questions such as, 'How often have you visited your general practitioner during the past two years?', participants tended to overestimate the frequency when their answers were checked: they included visits that fell just outside the two-year period. In other words, people in general tend to date events *more recently* than they actually occurred (the so-called **telescopy phenomenon** or *forward telescoping*).

The telescopy phenomenon is highlighted under certain conditions. Draaisma cites the work of the French academic, Jean-Marie Guyau, whose 1890 theory of time is based upon the basic analogy of space – not the geometric kind, but that used in perspective (i.e. space as manifested to the observer). The experience of time involves 'internal optics: memory orders experiences in time much like a painter orders space with the use of perspective'. Memories lend depth to consciousness: as soon as the order in our memory is broken, as happens during the imperceptible transitions between dream images, our sense of time also disappears. A number of factors influence the internal optics of mind time, including the intensity of our sensations and ideas, their alternation, number, and the tempo with which they succeed one another, how much attention we pay them, the effort required to store them in memory, and the emotions and associations they conjure up in us. However, these very same factors that can help us find our bearings in time can also lead to mistaken estimates. For example, focusing our attention works like a telescope: the detail this reveals produces the illusion that the object is close to us (far closer that it really is). Guyau borrowed this analogy from the English psychologist Sully, who, in his *Illusion* (1881) observed that a sensational event (such as an abduction or murder) is estimated as being much more recent than it actually was.

Although not mentioned by Sully, Guyau or Gray, *age* can be added to the list of variables thought to contribute to the telescop phenomenon and, in turn, to the explanation of the anecdotally common experience that time speeds up as we get older. While acknowledging that the subjective acceleration of time with age has been observed so often that it's probably true, Fraisse (1964) argued that it wouldn't be reflected in objective time judgements. Crawley and Pring (2000)

aimed to look for evidence that age would affect the ability to date public events, as well as evidence of gender differences. When personal incidents are involved (as in 'true' EM), it's often difficult to judge the extent of telescopy accurately. This problem is avoided in the cases of public events (closer perhaps to flashbulb memories than EM in general, although Crawley and Pring were interested only in participants' ability to *date* these public events: see Box 7.10).

Time for reflection

Try to identify the year in which each of the events listed below occurred:

a. The Chernobyl disaster

b. The Lockerbie disaster

c. Margaret Thatcher becoming British Prime Minister

d. The Argentine occupation of the Falkland Islands

e. The assassination of John Lennon

f. The assassination of Indira Gandhi

g. The Harrods bomb

h. The bombing of the Grand Hotel in Brighton

i. The Queen's Silver Jubilee

j. The fall of the Berlin Wall

Answers can be found at the end of this chapter.

The ten public events listed above formed just part of a longer list. In the first part of the study, Crawley and Pring (2000) investigated memory for public events over a seven-year period (1990–1996) and compared three age groups (18–21; 35–50; and 60 plus). The second part of the study took the two older groups and looked at an earlier period (1977–1989) to see if the effects of age became apparent only with longer retention periods.

A tendency towards forward telescoping was observed in the youngest age group when dating recent events, although this tendency lessened with increasing age. When recalling events further back, although the 35–50 age group was still dating too recently (thus confirming the telescopy found in earlier experiments), the over-60s (average age about 70) now dated *too distantly*. It was as if the older participants had turned the telescope round, thus extending the interval (Draaisma, 2004). Crawley and Pring failed to find a gender difference in dating accuracy (in favour of females), as Skowranski and Thompson (1990) had done earlier. However, this earlier study had involved recall of personal, as opposed to public events, so the two sets of results aren't directly comparable.

In terms of the original hypothesis, the results indicated that older people really do believe that more time has passed than is the case, which is why the years seem to 'fly by as we get older' (Crawley and Pring, 2000): time in the subjectively longer period must have passed more quickly. But Draaisma (2004) points out how difficult it is to interpret the results of time perception research: a case can be made for drawing the *opposite* conclusion.

... It is precisely those who think something happened three years ago when in fact it was five, who will claim 'Gosh, how time flies'. The speeding up of the years seems to be due to telescopy rather than to reverse telescopy. Crawley and Pring's theory can only be saved by the assumption of a reverse connection between the overestimate of the duration of a period of time and its subjective tempo. That does indeed manifest itself with the quickened pace of a week on holiday, which upon one's return home seems longer than an ordinary week. However, in that case, both telescopy and reverse telescopy will make us feel that time is rushing past, and that robs them of any explanatory value. (Draaisma, 2004)

The reminiscence effect

In addition to telescopy, Draaisma (2004) discusses two further explanations of the acceleration of the passing years: the *reminiscence effect* and *physiological clocks*. The reminiscence effect is described in Box 7.11.

> **Box 7.11** The reminiscence effect (RE) (based on Draaisma, 2004)
>
> As early as 1879, Sir Francis Galton, the English scientist (and cousin of Charles Darwin) identified what is called the **reminiscence bump**. If older participants (60 plus) are given cue words to help them recall personal events (the 'Galton cueing technique'), there's an undeniable concentration of memories from a period covering some ten years, with age 20 lying at the centre. The bump increases further in size when the participant is asked to describe three or four of his or her most vivid memories: there's now a solid peak at age 15. The RE becomes more prominent as age increases beyond 60.

McCormack (1979) used Galton's method to study the autobiographical memory of older participants (average age of 80), using cue words such as 'horse', 'river' and 'king'. He dated the memories these words triggered and showed that most of the memories stemmed from the first and (to a somewhat lesser extent) from the second quarter of life. For most participants, the third quarter (ages 40–60) showed a sharp drop. The same pattern, with small variations, has been found in dozens of other studies. Combining the results of a long series of experiments, Rubin and Schulkind (1997) established that the 'bump' is still absent in 40-year-olds, begins slowly in 50-year-olds, and becomes clearly visible in 60-year-olds.

The RE is a robust phenomenon and is evident even in patients with Alzheimer's disease. Fromholt and Larsen (1992) gave 30 healthy elderly participants and 30 Alzheimer's patients (all aged 71–89) 15 minutes to relate their reminiscences of events that were of significance to them. Although the Alzheimer's patients recounted eight such events, compared with the healthy group's 18, the distribution of these memories over the course of their life was similar: both groups had most to tell about their adolescence.

How can we explain the RE?

Draaisma (2004) identifies three accounts:

1. Neurophysiologically, memory may be at its peak in our twenties, so that what we experience then is retained without difficulty. We store more memories then compared with any subsequent period. This explains why, more than 50 years later, the likelihood of retrieving memories from that time is so much greater. However, if the quality of a memory were its most important

feature, then the reminiscence bump would have to occur some ten years earlier than it does: experiments show that memory has the greatest sticking power at that time.

2. Between the ages of 15–25, we normally experience more that's worth remembering. This is suggested by the experimental finding that when participants are asked to recount three or four of their most vivid recollections, there's a stronger RE than when cue words are used. So, this explanation emphasises the impact that the remembered event has made. As we might expect, these bump-related reminiscences are related to 'first times' of various types (Jansari and Parkin, 1996), such as 'the first time', the first kiss, the first menstrual period, the first public speaking engagement, the first holiday without our parents, our first driving lesson, our first dead body and our first day at work. Many of these have a flashbulb clarity (see Box 7.10). While 'firsts' aren't exclusive to this early part of our life, they become decidedly less common as we get older.

Time for reflection
- What are some of your 'firsts'?
- When did they happen?

---

3. During our youth and early adulthood, events occur that shape our personality, determine our identity and guide the course of our life. These are the 'turning points' or 'formative experiences' that we tend to recall. The similarities between the present-day self and the experiences that have helped shape that self lead the elderly to remember those events almost automatically; they form part of the individual's life history. Conversely, how we recount that history defines and demonstrates his or her own identity. In old age, people like to look back on their lives as a story that may hold surprises and unexpected changes, but which is nonetheless held together by the typical reactions of a stable central character. In the light of this stable self, much of what might have at first seemed new proves to be predictable, routine, repetition and 'in character' (Fitzgerald, 1992).

Whichever of the three explanations of the RE we consider to be the most valid (indeed, all three might contribute something to our understanding), several researchers have included the notion of *markers* in their accounts of time relationships in autobiographical memory. For example, Conway (1990) talks of 'reference points', and Shum (1998) uses the term 'temporal landmarks', which determine how long ago something happened, either before or after something else; these markers may even help us determine the precise date on which some event occurred.

As Draaisma (2004) notes, only at moments when we're having real difficulty in dating a memory can we see our own time markers at work: they allow the memory to bounce between two ever-closer end-points. According to Shum (1998), the RE is a consequence of the fact that a greater number of time markers become available for the period typically covered by it (see Box 7.11).

... A period that brings up many memories will expand when seen in retrospect and seems to have lasted longer than an equally long period comprising few memories. Conversely, time markers will become less numerous at about middle age and later, and in the void thus created time will speed up subjectively ... (Draaisma, 2004)

This account has much in common with James's (1890) view regarding the vivid and exciting memories of youth and the uniformity and routine of later years. But Shum has added the claim that the crucial factor might well be the *temporal organisation* of memories: if the network of time markers disappears (along with variety), then we've lost an important *access* to memories from that period (Draaisma, 2004).

Physiological changes and the perception of time

The third and final account of the speeding up of time with age relates to what we called biological/body time earlier in the chapter (see page 174). One relevant finding here concerns the SCN: depletion of SCN cells and of dopamine production, both of which occur in old age, may cause crucial problems in how we deal with time. According to the American neurologist, Mangan (1996), these physiological changes may underlie the results of experiments in which older people were asked to estimate how long it took for a three-minute interval to pass.

It was known from earlier research that children's ability to estimate time accurately increases with age, peaking at around age 20; the ability of elderly people drops to the level of young children. Mangan showed that older people invariably *overestimate* lapsed time intervals. He asked three age groups (19–24; 45–50; 60–70) to measure an interval of three minutes by counting off the seconds. The youngest group could do this extremely accurately: they overestimated by, on average, just three seconds, compared with 16 seconds for the middle group and 40 seconds for the oldest. This effect was even more marked when participants were asked to repeat the task, this time when engaged in a distracting task: the average overestimates were 46, 63 and 106 seconds, respectively.

Déjà vu

Time for reflection
- What do you understand by the term *'déjà vu'*?
- Can you describe a personal experience of *déjà vu*?

The *déjà vu* (French for 'already seen') experience, has been defined as 'any subjectively inappropriate impression of familiarity of a present experience with an undefined past' (Neppe, 1983), and has presented a tantalising puzzle for philosophers, physicians, poets, psychologists and mystics for centuries.

Various studies indicate that 50–90 per cent of us can recall having had at least one such experience in our lives (Wolfradt, 2005). Each lasts 10–30 seconds and is accompanied by surprise, a sense of mystery and sometimes confusion (Brown, 2004) and downright panic (Draaisma, 2004). We experience a vague sense of having encountered a situation before, identical in every detail, even though we cannot say when the original event took place – indeed, we may *know* that we haven't been there or done this before. Different attempts at explaining *déjà vu* involve different interpretations of just what kind of phenomenon it is – is it essentially to do with memory, time perception, temporal organisation, a confusion between dream content and perception of the external world, or a brain-related phenomenon?

1. One early interpretation was that *déjà vu* marks an intersection with a former life: your memory contains latent (dormant) recollections of that former life, which, thanks to the sudden coincidence with the present situation, begin to resonate and hence a sense of repeating the past. The *déjà vu* is bound up with the single moment at which the two lives intersect (Draaisma, 2004). While this hypothesis fits with what the *déjà vu* experience feels like, we'd expect it to have a more gradual course: we'd expect the sense of recognition to increase as the correspondence between the present and former lives becomes greater. But instead, a *déjà vu* has an all-or-nothing character and is too fleeting to hold onto. A variant on this interpretation is that a *déjà vu* is the 'crack in time' that suddenly grants us a glimpse of the external return of our own existence. But on this hypothesis, why don't we see our whole life as one protracted *déjà vu*? Wouldn't *déjà vu* have to be the *rule*, rather than the exception?

2. Instead of a memory of a former life, a second explanation proposes that a *déjà vu* is a memory of something that used to be (consciously) present in our mind, namely *dreams*. According to Sully (1881), for example, as soon as the similarity between some dream content and the situation we're currently in is strong enough, our current experience activates associations with what we dreamt: we then have the impression of familiarity. Dream and life briefly go hand in hand. For Sully, *déjà vu* was the *negative* of what Freud (1900) called the *day residue*, fragments from conscious, waking life that become incorporated into that night's dream.

   > ... The 'when' of the dream can no longer be recovered, which explains why a déjà vu feels as if it had occurred in some vague past. A déjà vu *is not an intersection between the present and the past, rather it is a brief form of parallelism with a vague trace in the memory.* (Draaisma, 2004)

   Some items (such as words, objects) that we encounter are registered in memory *implicitly*, outside of our conscious awareness (see point 4 below). This could perhaps explain the feeling that *déjà vu* experiences are *presaged* (foretold) in dreams. Maybe bits and pieces of our dreams stick in our unconscious memory, and a later waking experience contains elements resembling those dream fragments. When they connect to these latent dream memories, it automatically pulls them to the forefront of our consciousness, triggering a *déjà vu*. Or perhaps the odd feeling during *déjà vu* is similar to a dream state, leading us to believe that a dream memory is being duplicated (Brown, 2004).

3. For many psychologists, including some of Sully's contemporaries, this dream-related hypothesis was too sweeping. Couldn't it simply be that a *déjà vu* happens when something in the present resembles what we've actually experienced in the past (after all, this is what the term conveys)? William James (1890) had repeatedly managed to trace back the familiarity of his own feelings of *déjà vu* to genuine memories: if we concentrate hard enough, we can begin to spot differences between the two, with the original memory becoming fuller and the feeling of familiarity receding. Like James, the Swiss psychoanalyst Oskar Pfister claimed that feelings of *déjà vu* could be traced back to something actually present in the memory; significantly, while James believed that the pairing of the current experience and the memory was more-or-less accidental, Pfister believed it happened for a good reason (it was *functional*, part of our arsenal of defence mechanisms called upon in stressful situations: see Gross, 2010).

4. Research into **implicit memory** (IM) has repeatedly shown that aspects of our prior experiences unavailable to our conscious awareness can influence our current behaviour

(e.g. Schacter, 1987). So, for example, a match between an inaccessible childhood memory and a present experience may trigger a *déjà vu*. This tendency can be reinforced by the ease with which false information can be implanted in our memory: we may come to believe false stories told to us about our own childhood (e.g. Loftus and Pickrell, 1995: see Gross, 2010).

5. *Déjà vu* could also be triggered by *part* of the present experience that is familiar but which is unrecognised as such. Familiar objects, people, smells and sounds may be difficult to identify when removed from the setting in which we're used to encountering them (such as seeing your GP in the supermarket). In the case of *déjà vu*, we may *misattribute* familiarity to an entire situation when in fact only a single aspect of it is really familiar (Brown, 2004).

    Conversely, we might sometimes ignore something that is staring us in the face, because our attention is focused elsewhere (**inattentional blindness**: Mack and Rock, 1998): even though we're not consciously aware of a particular item, it still registers in our memory. For example, we 'see' someone while texting on our mobile phone, but this person doesn't register consciously. However, a second glance a few seconds later triggers (correctly) a sense of familiarity. When unable to connect this with the original distracted glance, we assume that the experience happened days or weeks earlier – producing a *déjà vu* (Brown, 2004).

6. The Dutch philosopher and psychologist, Gerard Heymans (1904, 1906, in Draaisma, 2004), investigated the possible link between *déjà vu* and **depersonalisation**, 'the sudden, generally quickly passing condition in which everything we perceive strikes us as being strange, new and dream-like rather than real; when the people to whom we speak give the impression of being machines, when even our own voice sounds as strange in our ears as that of somebody else, and when we have the feeling that we are not acting or speaking ourselves, but are observing our actions and words as passive spectators'. Heymans' questionnaire studies confirmed his theory that feelings of both *déjà vu* and of depersonalisation are based on a very specific kind of memory illusion (see Draaisma, 2004).

7. A great deal of research has focused on the possible link between *déjà vu* and epilepsy, especially in the pre-seizure aura of some temporal lobe patients. During the aura, the patient hears strange noises or has a strange taste in the mouth. This can be accompanied by a sensation of being lifted up unexpectedly or of seeing familiar shapes being stretched into bizarre dimensions. Hughlings Jackson (1888) described a 'dreamy state': shortly before the seizure, the normal sense of time seems to vanish, the patient has the feeling of being outside reality, he or she may have vivid hallucinations, and everything seems unusually familiar ('reminiscence' – or what we'd now call *déjà vu*).

    Although it's very difficult to locate precisely where in the brain the *déjà vu* experience originates, much of the evidence based on patients with epilepsy, as well as with brain tumours, suggests that it probably originates in the hippocampus and parahippocampal gyrus in the *right* hemisphere (Brown, 2004). One implication of these findings is that brain pathology could underlie *déjà vu*, but involve a harmless variety that we all experience. Spontaneous firing of neurons in our brain (seizures) happens occasionally (comparable to a hiccup or muscle cramp), going unnoticed; but if they occur in brain structures that process familiarity (such as the hippocampus), such a misfiring may create a feeling of intense familiarity apparently disconnected from the current experience (Spatt, 2002).

It's also worth noting that the medial temporal lobe is directly involved in our declarative, conscious memory (see above). The hippocampus, which helps to register perceptual events as episodes and which later enables us to recall them as if we are watching a movie, is also located within this area of the brain. The parahippocampus gyrus, rhinal cortex and amygdala, all also found in the medial temporal lobe, are all heavily involved in memory (Wolfradt, 2005).

8. Another brain dysfunction that could possibly produce *déjà vu* involves a brief disruption in the normal course of neural information transmission. Information is usually transmitted from our sense organs to the higher brain centres in a rapid and reliably regular way. But suppose that a very brief delay occurs along one of these neural pathways – a slight disruption at one synapse. Because our brain is used to a precise rhythm in its circuitry, any disturbance gets its attention: a slight neural hiccup changes our level of awareness, and we misinterpret this as familiarity (Brown, 2004).

The temporal gap interpretation

If we now extend this possibility to two neural pathways, each carries duplicate messages but follows different routes to the final destination in the higher brain centres where the two messages converge. If one pathway is delayed (even by milliseconds), this gap in the arrival of the two messages may make the late message appear to repeat the earlier one (Milner and Goodale, 1995). The brain usually merges these separate neural messages, but a small temporal gap creates the illusion of two separate experiences, leading to *déjà vu* (Brown, 2004).

This temporal gap interpretation may also explain the sense of *precognition* that occasionally accompanies *déjà vu*. If you focus on the *delayed* message, then there is the feeling that this has happened before (*déjà vu*); but if you focus on the *leading* message, then it triggers a sense of 'I know what will happen next' (precognition). Recent advances in brain imaging and electrical brain-recording techniques may soon allow us to track small changes in the electrochemical activity of very small brain areas. Technology also exists which allows us to present visual and auditory information *asynchronolously* to each hemisphere, providing an experimental laboratory analogue of the *neural delay theory* of *déjà vu* (Brown, 2004).

Conclusions: Time perception, *déjà vu* and existentialism

Time for reflection
● If you have seen *Groundhog Day* (1993), starring Bill Murray, what do you consider the film to *really* be about?

> **Box 7.12** *Groundhog Day:* the ultimate *déjà vu*?
>
> In the film, Bill Murray plays Phil Connors, a cynical, world-weary TV weatherman who makes the annual trip to a rural Groundhog festival: according to legend, the behaviour of a small rodent set free from a box indicates how soon winter will end and spring begin. The day is, as usual, a nightmare for him, but the real ordeal begins the following morning: Connors wakes to discover that, for some inexplicable reason, it's Groundhog Day again! Everything happens exactly as it did the previous day – but only he seems to be aware of this. The next day it happens again, and the day after that, and the day after that, and so on. Connors is trapped, forced to endure the worst day of his life over and over again.

According to Coniam (2001), the film works perfectly as existential allegory. The French existentialist novelist Albert Camus's (1942/2005) *The Myth of Sisyphus* likens the human condition to the Sisyphus of Greek legend, who was condemned by the gods to roll a huge rock up a hill, only to then see it roll down again, repeatedly, for all eternity. If the Greek myth speaks of the futility of human labour and toil, then Connors must endlessly endure a ritual he finds pointless and unpleasant, unable to share his pain with anyone. It's the existentialist picture of life in a Godless universe.

The second part of the film documents Connors's attempts to meet the existential challenges he faces. He passes through three stages (as described by the French existentialist philosopher, Jean-Paul Sartre). First, he's opportunistic, exploiting the advantages his situation offers him, such as financial gain, sexual encounters and (other) physical pleasure. But the realisation that whatever he gains is automatically removed the next day plunges him into pessimism. Connors makes various melodramatic attempts at self-destruction, but none can prevent him from waking fit and well the following day to experience the torture again. Finally, he faces up to the necessity of confronting the true nature of his existence, dealing with issues such as freedom, choice and responsibility.

While this makes for a 'happy ending' (along with the inexplicable return to 'normality'), Coniam (2001) finds this a disappointing conclusion. Camus concluded that we have to imagine Sisyphus as happy in his labours: values can be constructed and simple contentment found in the face of cosmic absurdity. The choice is either to give in to futility or to make the best of the less-than-perfect hand we've been dealt: '... However unsatisfying life may seem to one in the throes of existential despair, the prospect of death's oblivion usually makes it seem more palatable ...' (Coniam, 2001)

For many years now, existential despair and awareness of our mortality have been at the core of existentialist philosophy (with Sartre and Camus key twentieth-century figures). More recently, a growing number of research psychologists have started to bring experimental methods to bear on these same concerns that lie at the heart of the human condition. Their work is the subject of Chapter 8.

Chapter summary

- The commonsense 'arrow of time' concept reflects Newton's 'master clock' concept of time, but this isn't how modern physicists understand time. Einstein's special theory of relativity, for example, dispensed with the idea of absolute simultaneity.

- While some physicists have gone so far as to claim that time fundamentally doesn't exist, it could be an emergent property.

- According to Callender, time is a way of describing the pace of motion or change, such as how fast a heart beats. This is a view of time as a common currency, making the world easier to describe but without any independent existence.

- Outside the context of theoretical physics, objective time is usually taken to mean clock time.

- Biological time refers to various biological 'clocks' which control the periodicity of basic physiological processes over different time periods; this is displayed by all species, while mind time is uniquely human.

- Major bodily rhythms include circadian, infradian, circannual and ultradian.

- Environmental factors that provide clues to these internal rhythms are called exogenous (i.e. external) zeitgebers. In the absence of any zeitgebers, behaviours that show rhythmical alternation/periodicity are controlled by internal biological clocks (or endogenous pacemakers).

- The internal (biological) clock is believed to be the suprachiasmatic nucleus (SCN), located in the medial hypothalamus. Its function is to synchronise all the bodily functions that are governed by the circadian rhythm.

- Mind (or brain) time refers to the subjective experience of the passage of time and the related sense of time as an arrow. It can be manifested in various ways, such as mental time travel (MTT), and is what psychologists and neuroscientists are mainly interested in.

- Frankenheuser distinguished between perception of time, which relates to the experience of brief time intervals, grasped as a single unit, and retention of time, which denotes the retrospective experience of longer time intervals and so is affected by memory.

- Perhaps the most fundamental question being investigated by neuroscientists is whether our perception of the world is continuous or a series of discrete snapshots, like frames on a film strip. This would help us explain how the healthy brain works out the chronological order of the mass of events that bombards our senses.

- The 'wagon wheel illusion' (WWI) suggests that the continuity of our perceptual experience is itself an illusion.

- VanRullen *et al.* found that by blocking 13-hertz waves in the right inferior parietal lobe (RPL: the 'when' pathway), participants were 30 per cent less likely to experience the WWI; the periodic sampling of visual frames crucial for the WWI was inhibited.

- The brain might process different objects or (moving) patterns within the visual field independently of the other – even if they overlap in space. The RPL may well be taking 'snapshots' at separate moments, and possibly at slightly different rates.

- Busch *et al.*'s findings regarding near-threshold luminance detection suggest that there's a succession of 'on' and 'off' periods of perception; attention involves collecting information through snapshots.

- According to Poppel, all the separate snapshots from the senses may feed into information blocks (the 'building blocks of consciousness') within a higher processing stream; these building blocks underlie our perception of time.

- Poppel believes that a space of 30–50 milliseconds is needed to bring together the distributed activity within the neural system into a single time window.

- Complementing this 30 millisecond cycle is a 'dopamine loop', each taking an average of 100 milliseconds to complete. Events registered by the brain within the duration of a single loop are experienced as a single occurrence. This, in turn, is related to the 'specious present' (James) or 'the remembered present' (Edelman).

- Our normal idea of the present moment corresponds to one of the 'ticks' of the internal clock: about one-tenth to one-fifth of a second. Each tick is the time it takes for the electrical nerve impulse to travel around a loop of dopamine-producing neurons; all the information we process during that time-window is experienced as happening simultaneously.

- From an evolutionary perspective, it makes sense to usually perceive events that take seconds to occur rather than milliseconds. This prevents information overload (a 'blooming, buzzing confusion') and helps give coherence and continuity to our experience.

- According to Husserl's account of internal time-consciousness, implicit in the very nature of consciousness is a binding of one moment to the next, both in relation to past moments of consciousness (retention) and future moments (protention).

- Another way of capturing the nature of 'now' is Poppel's concept of the subjective present and the related three-second window (or rule). A number of different experiments all converge on the value of approximately 2–3 seconds as the duration of the subjective present.

- Gerstner and Fazio found that various species of higher mammals tend to segment their motor behaviour in the same temporal range as humans (i.e. 2–3 seconds). This suggests that we're dealing with a universal principle of temporal integration that transcends human cognitive and behavioural control.

- Apparently simultaneous awareness and processing of information actually takes place within three-second windows, during each of which the brain takes in all the data about the environment as a *block*; subsequent events are then processed in the next window. This represents a major sticking point in our ability to multitask.

- What Manhart calls 'concentration', the foreground of consciousness, Poppel (1997) calls the singular 'state of being conscious' (or STOBCON).

- The so-called interval timer (IT) (or 'stopwatch' in the brain) marks time spans of seconds to hours; it enlists the higher cognitive powers of the cerebral cortex.

- According to interval-timing theory (e.g. Matell and Meck), a collection of neural oscillators in the cerebral cortex are connected to the striatum via millions of signal-carrying axons. This enables striatal spiky neurons to 'eavesdrop' on all these de-synchronised 'conversations' taking place among the oscillators.

- When an external stimulus grabs the attention of the cortical cells, they begin to fire simultaneously; this produces a characteristic spike in electrical output about 300 milliseconds later. The spike represents a distinct, reproducible pattern of neuronal activity; the spiny neurons monitor these patterns, helping them to 'count' elapsed time.

- At the end of a specified interval, the substantia nigra sends a burst of dopamine to the striatum. This dopamine burst (or loop) induces the spiny neurons to record the pattern of cortical oscillations they receive at that instant. The dopamine burst tells the spiny neurons to start tracking the patterns of cortical impulses that follow.

- When the spiny neurons recognise the time stamp marking the end of the interval, they send an electrical impulse from the striatum to the thalamus, which, in turn, communicates with the cortex.

- Factors affecting the IT, thereby supporting interval-timing theory, include drugs and diseases that affect dopamine levels, and damage to the basal ganglia and/or frontal lobes.

- The association between amnesia and time can be seen most dramatically in cases of permanent brain damage to the hippocampus, a region that's crucial to memory. Such damage produces anterograde amnesia. A dramatic case of the effects of hippocampal damage is that of Clive Wearing.

- The memories most markedly lost in retrograde amnesia are precisely those that bear a time stamp: recollections of unique, personal events that happened in a particular context on a particular occasion (episodic or autobiographical memory). The temporal lobe that surrounds the hippocampus is critical in making and retrieving such memories.

- In patients with temporal lobe damage (through, for example, viral encephalitis, stroke or Alzheimer's disease), years and even decades of autobiographical memory can be permanently destroyed.

- As predicted, participants in 'Eagleman's tower' experiment overestimated the time it took to drop the 31 m into the safety net. This reflects an apparent slowing down of time associated with an intense experience of fear (or excitement).

- During such experiences, our focused attention produces the firing of many neurons across the brain, which causes us to absorb more sensory details. Richer memories seem to last longer, because we assume that more time would have been needed to record so much detail.

- Wearden suggests that the relationship between subjective time and arousal may be non-linear: changes in the pace of the internal clock may only be seen at extreme levels of arousal, which are difficult to induce under laboratory conditions.

- Evidence exists which suggests that the brain's internal clock/central pacemaker can be experimentally speeded up: a series of fast clicks might be literally resetting the brain's frame-capture rate.

- While there's anecdotal evidence to support the popular beliefs that time flies when we're having fun and drags when we're bored, in retrospect these relations become reversed. Weardon found experimental evidence for both the popular beliefs and their reversal.

- Damasio proposes that the elasticity of time is perhaps best appreciated when we're the spectators of a performance, such as a film. By providing a significant discrepancy between real time and the audience's perception of time, Hitchcock's *Rope* illustrates how the experience of duration is a construct.

- McKellar describes the time discontinuity phenomenon in relation to experiments involving mescaline, psychotic patients with persecutory delusions and schizophrenic patients.

- Controversially, Libet reported that when participants were asked to flex their finger or wrist, there was activity in the brain for up to half a second before they were subjectively aware of having made the decision: consciousness lagged behind brain activity.

- Not only do Libet's results challenge the commonsense idea of free will, but they also pose a difficulty regarding how to define/understand 'the present moment'. What Libet calls 'subjective referral backward in time' puts the subjective experience of the present back into the present.

- Major different forms of long-term memory (LTM) include episodic (or autobiographical) memory (EM), semantic memory (SM), and procedural memory (PM). EM and SM are both forms of declarative (as opposed to procedural) memory.

- Evidence suggests that people in general tend to date events more recently than they actually occurred (telescopy or forward telescoping). Sully found that sensational events are likely to be dated as much more recent.

- Crawley and Pring found evidence of forward telescoping when dating public events (such as the Lockerbie disaster), but older participants dated too distantly (i.e. reverse telescopy).

- Reverse telescopy is consistent with the popular belief that time speeds up as we get older. Two additional explanations for this phenomenon relate to physiological clocks and the reminiscence effect (RE), the latter originating with Galton's identification of the reminiscence bump. The RE is a robust phenomenon and is evident even in Alzheimer's patients.

- Draaisma discusses three explanations of the RE: (a) memory is neurophysiologically at its peak in our 20s; (b) we experience more 'first times' between age 15–25; (c) 'turning points' or 'formative experiences' occur during these years. Another explanation centres around the concept of time markers or 'temporal landmarks'.

- Different attempts at explaining *déjà vu* involve different interpretations of just what kind of phenomenon it is – is it essentially to do with memory, time perception, temporal organisation, a confusion between dream content and perception of the external world, or a brain-related phenomenon (such as epilepsy)?

- Technology exists which allows us to present visual and auditory information asynchronolously to each hemisphere, providing an experimental laboratory analogue of the neural delay theory of *déjà vu*.

Suggested further reading

Draaisma, D. (2004) *Why Life Speeds Up As You Get Older: How Memory Shapes Our Past.* Cambridge: Cambridge University Press. The book title is in fact the title of one of 17 fascinating chapters, which blend experimental data with autobiobraphical and historical accounts of the role of autobiographical memory in human life (including *déjà vu*). Draaisma is the author of the internationally acclaimed *Metaphors of Memory* (2001). Cambridge: Cambridge University Press.

Libet, B. (2004) *Mind Time: The Temporal Factor in Consciousness.* Cambridge, MA: Harvard University Press. Libet's own account of his ground-breaking experiments that have helped us see how the brain produces conscious awareness and which have challenged some of our basic assumptions regarding free will.

Rose, S. (2003) *The Making of Memory: From Molecules to Mind.* London: Vintage. Award-winning discussion of past and present memory research, including potential new treatments for Alzheimer's disease. Rose considers theoretical issues raised by this research, including reductionism.

Selected websites

http://www.bbc.co.uk/radio4/science/frontiers_20060517.shtml

A 30-minute radio programme on time perception.

http://sciencestage.com/v/952/free-fall-experiment-time-perception.html

Video of David Eagleman's 'free-fall' experiment.

http://memory.uva.nl/index_en

The Human Memory website of the University of Amsterdam.

www.exploratorium.edu/memory/index.html

Memory: details of the exhibition held at San Francisco's Exploratorium, 1998–89.

Answers to Time for reflection (page 197)

- The Chernobyl disaster (1986)
- The Lockerbie disaster (1988)
- Margaret Thatcher becoming British Prime Minister (1979)
- The Argentine occupation of the Falkland Islands (1982)
- The assassination of John Lennon (1982)
- The assassination of Indira Gandhi (1984)
- The Harrods bomb (1983)
- The bombing of the Grand Hotel in Brighton (1984)
- The Queen's Silver Jubilee (1977)
- The fall of the Berlin Wall (1989)

Chapter 8: Fear of death and other 'facts of life'

Key questions

- How are human consciousness and existentialist concerns, such as our fear of death, related?

- What is meant by 'existentialism'?

- How is existentialist philosophy relevant to psychology and psychotherapy?

- How has human awareness of mortality and fear of death been described by writers such as Becker and Yalom?

- What's meant by the 'givens of existence' (Yalom, 2008)?

- What are the basic principles and methods of experimental existential psychology (XXP)?

- What evidence exists to support terror management theory (TMT)?

- How valid is the mortality salience (MS) paradigm?

- Is human life inherently pointless?

- What role does religion play in helping us deal with any sense of meaninglessness?

- Is there a link between death terror and our desire to produce offspring?

Human consciousness, psychology and existentialism

Possessing the sort of consciousness that humans do is something of a mixed blessing. As we noted in Chapter 4, Edelman (1992) contends that humans and non-humans share *primary consciousness*, the state of being mentally aware of things in the world, of having mental images in the *here-and-now*. To be conscious in this sense doesn't necessarily imply any kind of 'I' who is aware and having mental images. What's unique to humans is **higher-order consciousness** – the recognition by a thinking subject of his or her own acts or affections, embodying a model of the personal, and of the past and future as well as the present. We're 'conscious of being conscious'. This, Edelman believes, puts human beings in a 'privileged position'.

However, there's a flip side to this privileged position. As the psychotherapist Rollo May observes in *Love and Will* (1969): '... It [consciousness] is the fearful joy, the blessing, and the curse of man that he can be conscious of himself and his world.'

Why a curse? Because we're the only species aware of the fact that we die, as well as having the capacity to question the purpose of what we do in and with our lives. As the existential psychotherapist Irvin Yalom (2008) puts it:

> *Self-awareness is a supreme gift, a treasure as precious as life. This is what makes us human. But it comes with a costly price: the wound of mortality. Our existence is forever shadowed by the knowledge that we will grow, blossom, and, inevitably, diminish and die.*

Yalom quotes from the 4,000 year-old Babylonian hero, Gilgamesh, reflecting on the death of his friend, Enkidu:'Thou hast become dark and cannot hear me. When I die shall I not be like Enkidu? Sorrow enters my heart. I am afraid of death.'

> *Gilgamesh speaks for all of us. As he feared death, so do we all – each and every man, woman, and child. For some of us the fear of death manifests only indirectly, either as generalised unrest or masqueraded as another psychological symptom; other individuals experience an explicit and conscious stream of anxiety about death; and for some of us the fear of death erupts into terror that negates all happiness and fulfilment.* (Yalom, 2008)

As Jones (2008) puts it, our 'cherished gifts' (our unique capacity for language, culture, abstract thought, conscious self-reflection, thinking about the future and our long-term goals) come at a price:

> *...Our self-awareness and unparalleled foresight mean that we humans, unlike other animals, realise that we will all shuffle off this mortal coil sooner or later. This poses a potentially devastating challenge to our psychological equanimity – the prospect of annihilation threatens to rob life of ultimate purpose, and render the pursuit of a meaningful life a futile effort.*

According to Deacon (1997), uniquely human awareness of mortality was a by-product of self-consciousness, which otherwise provides human beings with remarkable adaptive advantages (see Chapter 4). However, self-conscious creatures oriented toward survival in a threatening world but now burdened with awareness of their mortality, might be overwhelmed by debilitating terror to the point of cognitive and behavioural paralysis – at which point self-consciousness would no longer confer an adaptive advantage. From now on, only those humans who developed and adopted cultural worldviews that could keep death terror in check would enjoy evolutionary advantages offered by self-awareness. This is a fundamental assumption made by **terror management theory** (**TMT**) (e.g. Solomon *et al.*, 2004), which is discussed in detail below. Archaeological evidence, theory and research from evolutionary psychology, anthropology and cognitive neuroscience converge in supporting the claim that humans 'solved' the problems associated with realisation of their mortality by creating uniquely human cultural products, including art, language, religion, agriculture and economics (Solomon *et al.*, 2004).

▲ **Figure 8.1** Irvin Yalom

Experimental psychology has flourished for well over 100 years (indeed, a 2010 special edition of *The Psychologist* celebrated 150 years of experimental psychology), and existential ideas have made their way into the theories of clinically oriented theorists and therapists for most of the twentieth century (including May, Yalom and Viktor Frankl). However, these two approaches have traditionally been thought of as opposite ends of the very broad and typically finely defined field of psychology (Pyszczynski *et al.*, 2004).

...Experimental psychologists applied rigorous research methods to relatively simple phenomena, usually with the intention of discovering the most basic building blocks of human behaviour. Existential psychologists, on the other hand, speculated about the human confrontation with

very abstract questions regarding the nature of existence and the meaning of life – ideas that typically are considered far too abstruse and intractable to be fruitfully addressed by the scientific method... (Pyszczynski et al., 2004)

Pyszczynski *et al.* go on to point out that experimentalists and existentialists usually only acknowledged each other's existence when pointing to the fundamental absurdity of what the other was trying to achieve. For example, Yalom (1980) commented that in psychological research, 'the precision of the result is directly proportional to the triviality of the variables studied. A strange type of science.'

Time for reflection

- What do you understand by 'the scientific method'?
- Are there any *inherent problems* involved in applying the scientific method to the study of human behaviour and experience (as opposed to, say, aspects of the physical world)? (See Gross, 2009, 2010.)
- Drawing on mainstream experimental psychology, can you identify any examples of what Yalom might have in mind in his 1980 quote above? (See Gross, 2010.)
- Is it possible, at least in principle, that methods from experimental psychology could be applied to the study of existential issues – or are they mutually incompatible?

What is Existentialism?

According to the philosopher H.J. Blackham (1961),

The peculiarity of existentialism...is that it deals with the separation of man from himself and from the world...existentialism goes back to the beginning of philosophy and appeals to all men to awaken from their dogmatic slumbers and discover what it means to become a human being...

There cannot be any universal answers to the question of what it means to be human: there's an 'insurmountable ambiguity...at the heart of man and of the world' (Blackham, 1961).

Philosopher William Barrett (1958) defined **existentialism** as:

...a philosophy that confronts the human situation in its totality to ask what the basic conditions of human existence are and how man can establish his own meaning out of these conditions.' (emphasis in original.)

Another philosopher, John Macquarrie (1972), believes that part of the problem in defining existentialism is that what was intended as a serious philosophy has often been vulgarised to the level of a fad, so that 'existentialist' gets applied to all sorts of people and activities that are only remotely – if at all – connected with existentialist philosophy. However, there's also a kind of elusiveness built into existentialism itself. Agreeing with Blackham, Macquarrie notes that existentialist philosophers deny that reality can be neatly packaged in concepts or presented as an interlocking system. Our experience and our knowledge are always incomplete and fragmentary; only a divine Mind, if there is one, could know the world as a whole – and perhaps even for such a Mind there'd be gaps and discontinuities.

Because there's no common body of doctrine shared by all existentialists (unlike certain other schools of philosophy), Macquarrie prefers to talk of existentialism as a 'style of philosophising' rather than a 'philosophy'. As such, it can lead those who adopt it to very different conclusions regarding the world and human beings' place in it. This is evidenced by the three 'greats': Soren Kierkegaard (1813–55), the Danish philosopher, theologian and religious author; Martin Heidegger (1889–1976), the German philosopher, and Jean-Paul Sartre (1905–80), the French philosopher, novelist and playwright. Box 8.1 describes the existential style of philosophising.

▲ **Figure 8.2** Jean-Paul Sartre

Box 8.1 Doing philosophy the existentialist way (based on Macquarrie, 1972)

- Most obviously, it begins from the human being rather than from nature. It's a philosophy of the subject as distinct from the object. Not only is the person a thinking subject but also an initiator of action and a centre of feeling. It's this whole spectrum of existence, known directly and concretely in the very act of existing, that existentialism tries to express. This means that sometimes the existentialist appears anti-intellectualist, thinking with passion, as one who is involved in the actualities of existence.

- In stressing existence, it is also implied that one cannot identify a 'nature' or an 'essence' of the person; perhaps this, above all, gives existentialism, its somewhat elusive character. In Sartre's (1956) terms, man's existence precedes his essence:

  ...man first of all exists, encounters himself, surges up in the world – and defines himself afterwards. If man, as the existentialist sees him, is not definable, it is because to begin with he is nothing. He will not be anything until later, and then he will be what he makes of himself. (Sartre, 1956)

- Despite the lack of 'doctrine' it's possible to identify some recurring themes in existentialism, which distinguish it from other approaches/schools within philosophy. These include *freedom*, *decision* and *responsibility*, which constitute the core of personal being. The exercise of freedom and the ability to shape the future are what distinguish humans from all other creatures on the planet (see Chapter 1): it's through free and responsible decisions that we become authentically ourselves. This has been expressed in the concept of 'self as agent', in contrast with traditional Western philosophy's 'self as (thinking) subject' (especially since Descartes). The focus has very much been on the individual, whose quest for authentic selfhood concerns the meaning of personal being; this implies a view of the person as an isolated, if not dislocated, creature.

- Other recurring themes include *finitude*, *guilt*, *alienation*, *despair* and *death* (see text above and below).

Existentialism and the arts

Existential thinking can be traced back to one of the oldest known written documents, *The Gilgamesh Epic*, which Yalom (2008) quotes from (see above). Consideration of existential issues can also be found in the work of the great thinkers of the Western classical era, such as Homer, Plato, Socrates and Seneca, and continued through the work of theologians such as Augustine and Aquinas. Existential issues were also explored in the blossoming arts and humanities of the European Renaissance, as in the writing of Cervantes, Dante, Milton, Shakespeare and Swift. The arts became even more focused on these issues during the Romantic period of the nineteenth century, as in the poetry of Byron, Shelley and Keats; the novels of Balzac, Dostoyevsky, Hugo and Tolstoy; and the music of Beethoven, Brahms, Bruckner and Tchaikovsky. More recently, the arts have become even more focused on existential concerns, as in the plays of Beckett, O'Neill and Ionesco; the classical music of Mahler and Cage; the rock music of John Lennon and The Doors; and the surrealist paintings of Dali, Ernst, Tanguy and many others (Pyszczynski *et al.*, 2004).

> *...One could even say that virtually everyone who is widely considered a 'great artist' explored existential issues in his or her work in one form or another. Indeed, the expression of deep existential concerns may be the underlying commonality of all great artistic creation.* (Pyszczynski et al., 2004).

While the key existential thinkers (including the three 'greats' identified by Macquarrie above) approach existential questions from very diverse perspectives and sometimes draw dramatically different conclusions,

> *...all these thinkers addressed the questions of what it means to be a human being, how we humans relate to the physical and metaphysical world that surrounds us, and how we can find meaning given the realities of life and death. Most important, they considered the implications of how ordinary humans struggle with these questions for what happens in their daily lives. Thus, existential issues were not conceived of as material for the abstruse musings of philosophers and intellectuals but, rather, as pressing issues with enormous impact on the lives of us all.* (Pyszczynski et al., 2004).

Existentialism, phenomenology and existential psychology

Most existentialists are also phenomenologists (though there are many phenomenologists who aren't existentialists). **Phenomenology** seems to offer existentialists the kind of methodology they need for investigating human existence. Phenomenology is described in Box 8.2.

> **Box 8.2** Phenomenology (based on Ashworth, 2003; Giorgi and Giorgi, 2003)
>
> The founder of phenomenology as a philosophical movement, Edmund Husserl (1859–1938), was critical of both the introspectionism of Wilhelm Wundt, one of the pioneers of modern experimental psychology, and Watson's behaviourism (see Gross, 2010). However, his fundamental aim was to provide a firm foundation for *all* the disciplines – sciences, arts and humanities – by establishing the meaning of their most basic concepts. He believed that not only psychology, but all the academic disciplines, lacked a method that would establish the nature of their fundamental concepts (such as 'perception' in psychology). Phenomenology was intended to allow basic concepts to be framed in a rigorous way that would give a firm basis to each discipline.
>
> To achieve this, Husserl decided to begin with the problem of how objects and events appeared to consciousness: nothing could even be spoken about or witnessed if it didn't come through someone's consciousness (which included pre-conscious and unconscious processes). Husserl (1925/1977, 1931/1960, 1936/1970) advocated a *return to the things themselves*, as experienced. His core philosophical belief was a rejection of the presupposition that there's something 'behind' or 'underlying 'or 'more fundamental than' experience. Rather, what appears is to be taken as 'reality': we should begin our investigation with *what is experienced*, the thing itself as it appears (i.e. the 'phenomenon').
>
> While phenomenology was originally intended to apply to all disciplines, the infant science of psychology's concern with conscious thought, not surprisingly, soon became the most 'fertile' area for Husserl's approach. Contrary to the *positivist* approach that underlies mainstream experimental psychology (see Gross, 2010), Husserl maintained that human experience in general is *not* a lawful response to the 'variables' assumed to be in operation. Rather, experience comprises a system of interrelated meanings (or *gestalten*) that's bound up in a totality (the 'lifeworld') (Husserl, 1936/1970). In other words, the human realm essentially entails embodied, conscious relatedness to a personal world of experience. The natural scientific approach is inappropriate. Human meanings are the key to the study of lived experience, not causal variables. For phenomenology, then, the individual is a conscious agent, whose experience must be studied from the 'first-person' perspective. Experience is of a meaningful lifeworld. 'Existential phenomenologists', such as the early Heidegger (1927/1962), Merleau-Ponty (1962) and Sartre (1958) developed phenomenology in a way that emphasised the lifeworld (Ashworth, 2003).

Within psychology, a loosely defined existentialist movement began to emerge, initially as a reaction to orthodox psychoanalytic (Freudian) theory. In Europe, theorists such as Ludwig Binswanger, Medard Boss, and Viktor Frankl argued for the importance of basing our analyses of human behaviour in the phenomenological world of the subject. In Binswanger's (1956) words, 'There is not one space and time only, but as many spaces and times as there are subjects.' Otto Rank was perhaps the first theorist to incorporate existentialist concepts into a broad account of human behaviour: the twin fears of life and death play a critical role in the development of the child's self-concept and throughout the lifespan. Rank also discussed art and creativity, the soul and the will, all to be found in later existential psychological theorising ((Pyszczynski *et al.*, 2004).

Binswanger, Boss, Frankl and Rank, were not only influential theorists, but also all practising psychiatrists, psychoanalysts or both. This also applies to other major individuals with similar existentialist leanings, such as Karen Horney, who emphasised our conception of the future as a critical determinant of behaviour, and Erich Fromm, perhaps best known for his analysis of the pursuit and avoidance of freedom. Others include the two great 'humanistic' psychologists (sometimes referred to as 'humanistic-phenomenological'), namely Abraham Maslow, who described **self-actualisation** as the peak of the hierarchy of needs, and Carl Rogers, best known for his self-theory and client-/person-centred therapy.

More recent examples of existentialist practitioners/theorists include R.D. Laing's radical work on schizophrenia during the 1960s and 1970s (see Gross, 2010), Ernest Becker's discussion of 'death terror' (famously, in his classic *The Denial of Death*, 1973: see below), and Yalom's *Existential Psychotherapy* (1980) and *Staring at the Sun: Overcoming the Dread of Death*, 2008).

Yalom's 'givens of existence'

In his classic text on existential psychotherapy, Yalom (1980) described existential thought as focused on human confrontation with the fundamentals of existence. He viewed existential psychology as rooted in Freudian psychodynamics, in the sense that it explored the motivational consequences of important human conflicts. However, the fundamental conflicts of concern to existentialists are very different from those emphasised by Freud (namely, those involving 'suppressed instinctual strivings' or 'internalised significant adults'). The former focus on conflicts that flow from the 'individual's confrontation with the **givens of existence**'. In other words, existential psychology attempts to explain how ordinary human beings come to terms with the basic facts of life that we all have to contend with. These are deep, potentially terrifying issues, and consequently people typically avoid direct confrontation with them. Indeed, many people claim that they *never* think about such things. Nevertheless, Yalom argued that these basic concerns affect us all – whether we realise it or not. These 'givens of existence' are described in Box 8.3.

Box 8.3 The 'givens of existence' (Yalom, 1980)

- *Fear of death:* The consequences of awareness and fear of death is the best-studied of Yalom's four 'givens of existence'. The inevitability of death is a simple fact of life of which we're all aware. This inevitability in an animal that desperately wants to live produces a conflict that cannot be brushed aside.

- *Freedom:* The concern with freedom reflects the conflict between (a) a desire for self-determination/self-control and (b) the sense of groundlessness and ambiguity that results when we realise that much of what happens in our lives is really up to ourselves – and that there are few, if any, absolute rules to live by.

- *Existential isolation:* This refers to 'a fundamental isolation...from both creatures and world...No matter how close each of us becomes to another, there remains a final, unbridgeable gap; each of us enters existence alone and must depart from it alone'. Existentialist isolation is the inevitable consequence of the very personal, subjective and individual nature of human experience that can never be fully shared with another being.

- *Meaninglessness:* This is a result of the first three basic concerns/'givens of existence'. In a world where the only true certainty is death, where meaning and value are subjective human creations rather than absolute truths, and where one can never fully share one's experience with others, what meaning does life have? The very real possibility that human life is utterly *devoid* of meaning lurks just beneath the surface of our attempts to cling to whatever meaning we can

---

Box 8.3 *Continued*

find or create. According to Yalom, the crisis of meaninglessness 'stems from the dilemma of a meaning-seeking creature who is thrown into a universe that has no meaning' (see Chapter 1).

All these 'givens of existence' have become the focus of the (relatively) new sub-discipline of **experimental existential psychology** (or XXP), with fear of death by far the most widely investigated to date (see below). However, Yalom acknowledged that these four concerns were by no means a complete list. Indeed, a wide range of additional existential concerns are also being actively explored under the banner of XXP. These include questions of how we humans fit into the physical universe, how we relate to nature, and how we come to grips with the physical nature of our own bodies – questions about beauty, spirituality and nostalgia; others involve questions about the role of existential concerns in intrapersonal, interpersonal and intergroup conflict.

Another of these additional concerns is *identity*. We all feel the need to 'find ourselves' – to make sense of our diverse views and experiences of the world, and to integrate them into a coherent and consistent sense of who we are. Uncertainty about our identity can lead to defensive psychological moves, such as a more zealous defence of our attitudes (McGregor, 2006). 'Work on the self has told us a great deal about the malleability and multiplicity of identities, their socially constructed nature, and the desire to sustain a coherent sense of self over the lifespan – a story about the self, or self-narrative' (Greenberg, in Jones, 2008).

Time for reflection

- Does one of the 'givens of existence' and other existential concerns described above strike you as more fundamental – or have more personal significance for you – than any of the others?
- Try to identify the reasons for your choice.
- Are there any existential concerns that you think could/should be added to the list?

Becker and the terror of death

According to Pyszczynski *et al.*(2004), perhaps the one construct that pervades all existential concerns is that of self-awareness. Ernest Becker (1962), the American cultural anthropologist and award-winning academic author, argued (in *The Birth and Death of Meaning*) that self-awareness is the most important feature that distinguishes human beings from other animals, and that it's this capacity for self-awareness that sets the stage for the existential terror that led to the development of culture and humankind as we know it today. Related to this is the uniquely human problem of having both an animal body and a symbolic self – two ways of being that are not easily compatible. How the 'human condition' manifests itself in different types of mental disorder is discussed in Box 8.4.

> **Box 8.4** Neurosis, psychosis, and the human condition
>
> According to Becker (1973):
>
> > *The neurotic tries to cheat nature. He won't pay the price that nature wants of him: to age, fall ill or be injured, and die...We can see that neurosis is par excellence the danger of a symbolic animal whose body is a problem to him. Instead of living in the part way that nature provided for he lives in the total way made possible by symbols. One substitutes the magical all-inclusive world of the self for the real fragmentary world of experience.*
>
> Becker observes that it's impossible to live with the totality of life: 'Men aren't built to be gods, to take in the whole world: they are built like other creatures, to take in the piece of ground under their noses'.
>
> > ### Time for reflection
> > ● Is there a contradiction here with what he says about the 'human condition', i.e. the inherent incompatibility/incongruence between being an animal and being a symbolic creature (see Chapter 1)?
>
> By contrast, the psychotic shuts out even the fragments and withdraws into his fantasies, creating his own world in his head. Most of us, to some extent, are neurotic. We have to protect ourselves from being overwhelmed by endless possibilities, biting off only what we can chew. Some bite off more than they can digest. At the other end of the spectrum are those who are so fearful of life that they become almost incapable of action and look for safety in obsessions and phobias. Through their symptoms, they're trying hard to live, as if to step outside their well-organised rituals would be to risk death. But, in fact, both fears come together in the symptom (Becker, 1973).

In what is generally regarded as Becker's most influential work, *The Denial of Death* (1973), he claims that '...of all things that move man, one of the principal ones is his terror of death'.

> *...All historical religions addressed themselves to this same problem of how to bear the end of life. Religions like Hinduism and Buddhism performed the ingenious trick of pretending not to want to be reborn, which is a sort of negative magic: claiming not to want what you really want most. When philosophy took over from religion it also took over religion's central problem, and death became the real 'muse of philosophy' from its beginnings in Greece right through Hiedegger and modern existentialism.* (Becker, 1973)

Becker cites James's (1902) *The Varieties of Religious Experience*. Speaking for those who believe that fear of death is natural and is present in everyone, a fear from which no one is immune no matter how disguised it may be, James called death 'the worm at the core' of man's pretensions to happiness. He also cites the psychoanalyst, Gregory Zilboorg (1943), who claimed that most people think death fear is absent because it rarely shows its true face: underneath all appearances fear of death is universally present:

> *For behind the sense of insecurity in the face of danger, behind the sense of discouragement and depression, there always lurks the basic fear of death, a fear which undergoes most complex elaborations and manifests itself in many different ways...No one is free of the fear*

of death...The anxiety neuroses, the various phobic states, even a considerable number of depressive suicidal states and many schizophrenias amply demonstrate the ever-present fear of death which becomes woven into the major conflicts of the given psychopathological conditions...We may take for granted that the fear of death is always present in our mental functioning. (Zilboorg, 1943)

According to Zilboorg, arguing along Darwinian lines, this fear is actually an expression of the instinct of *self-preservation*, which functions as a constant drive to maintain life and to master the dangers that threaten life:

Such constant expenditure of psychological energy on the business of preserving life would be impossible if the fear of death were not as constant. The very term 'self-preservation' implies an effort against some force of disintegration; the affective aspect of this is fear, fear of death. (Zilboorg, 1943)

In other words, the fear of death must be present behind all our normal functioning, in order for the organism to be armed toward self-preservation. But the fear of death cannot be present constantly in one's mental functioning, otherwise the organism could not function (Becker, 1973).

If this fear were as constantly conscious, we should be unable to function normally. It must be properly repressed to keep us living with any modicum of comfort. We know very well that to repress means more than to put away and to forget that which was put away and the place where we put it. It means also to maintain a constant psychological effort to keep the lid on and inwardly never relax our watchfulness. (Zilboorg, 1943)

Time for reflection

- How convincing do you find Becker's argument regarding the universal – and inevitable – nature of fear of death?
- If Zilboorg (and Becker) are correct, we should never *consciously* experience fear of death: either repression works effectively to keep it out of consciousness on a minute-by-minute, day-by-day basis, or it becomes converted into one or other forms of mental disorder, where (conscious) fear of death is still not a preoccupation or even a symptom. Is this a case of the psychoanalytic 'heads I win, tails you lose' (e.g. Eysenck, 1985; Popper, 1959: see Gross, 2010)?
- Do you find the evolutionary argument any more convincing?

According to Becker, there's a fundamental paradox involved here: on the one hand, there's the ever-present fear of death, part of the normal biological functioning of our instinct of self-preservation. On the other hand, utterly oblivious to this fear in our conscious life.

...in normal times we move about actually without ever believing in our own death, as if we fully believed in our own corporeal immortality. We are intent on mastering death... A man will say, of course, that he knows he will die some day, but he does not really care. He is having a good time with living, and he does not think about death and does not care to bother about it – but this is a purely intellectual, verbal admission. The affect of fear is repressed. (Zilboorg, 1943)

Becker believes that the argument from biology and evolution is basic and must be taken seriously. In order to survive, animals have had to be protected by fear responses, in relation not only to other animals, but to nature itself. They have needed to see the real relationship between their limited powers and the dangerous world surrounding them. Reality and fear go together naturally. In the case of human infants, their state of helplessness and complete dependency suggests that their fear response would have become heightened compared with non-humans. Early humans who were most afraid were more realistic about their situation in nature: they would have passed this realism, which had a high survival value, onto their offspring. This resulted in human beings as we know them: a hyperanxious animal that constantly invents reasons for anxiety – even where there are none (Becker, 1973).

Compared with this evolutionary account, psychoanalytic accounts are less speculative and should be taken even more seriously (Becker, 1973). What we'd not previously realised was that the child's inner world is more filled with terror, the more the child differed from other species. While fear is programmed into the lower animals by ready-made instincts, human fears are fashioned from their perceptions of the world. So, what's unique about the human infant's perception of the world? See Box 8.5.

Box 8.5 The psychoanalytic view of the child's inner world (Becker, 1973)

Because of the infant's utter dependence on others, when its needs are met, it must seem that it possesses magical powers – real *omnipotence*. If it experiences pain, hunger or discomfort, all it has to do is to scream and its pain, etc., will be relieved: '...He is a magician and a telepath who has only to mumble and to imagine and the world turns to his desires.'

But there's a penalty to pay for such perceptions.

> *...In a magical world where things cause other things to happen just by a mere thought or a look of displeasure, anything can happen to anyone. When the child experiences inevitable and real frustrations from parents, he directs hate and destructive feelings towards them; and he has no way of knowing that malevolent feelings cannot be fulfilled by the same magic as were his other wishes...*

Psychoanalysts believe that this confusion is a major cause of guilt and helplessness in the child, who is too weak to take responsibility for all this destructive feeling and unable to control the magical execution of its desires (the child is said have an *immature ego*).

> *...he can't control his own activity; and he doesn't have sure command over the acts of others. He thus has no real control over the magical cause-and-effect that he senses, either inside himself or outside in nature and in others; his destructive wishes could explode, his parents' wishes likewise. The forces of nature are confused, externally and internally; and for a weak ego this fact makes for quantities of exaggerated potential power and added terror. The result is that the child – at least some of the time – lives with an inner sense of chaos that other animals are immune to.*

Box 8.5 *Continued*

This inner sense of chaos helps to explain the recurrent nightmares that are so typical of young children:

> *...In their tortured interiors radiate complex symbols of many inadmissible realities – terror of the world, the horror of one's own wishes, the fear of vengeance by the parents, the disappearance of things, one's lack of control over anything, really. It is too much for any animal to take, but the child has to take it, and so he wakes up screaming with almost punctual regularity during the period when his weak ego is in the process of consolidating things.*

If, as we've seen, the fear of death needs to 'disappear' as a conscious preoccupation if we're to be able to get on with life, then how does this happen? Becker's answer is through *repression*. He contends that, rather than repression being 'a magical word for winning arguments' (see the 'Time for reflection' below), it is a 'real phenomenon'. For Becker, *consciousness of death* is more strongly repressed than sexuality: '...*This* is what is creaturely about man, *this* is the repression on which culture is based, a repression unique to the self-conscious animal...' (Becker, 1973) (Italics in original.)

Related to repression is the process by which 'the complex symbol of death is transmuted and transcended by man – belief in immortality, the extension of one's being into eternity'. Religion is discussed later in this chapter.

Time for reflection

- Do you agree that the fear of death/death terror is so well repressed that we very rarely (or ever) experience it consciously and directly?
- How are (a) fear of death and (b) fear of dying different?
- In your own experience, are people likely to acknowledge one more than the other?
- How about yourself?

According to Carl Jung (1977), the founder of analytical psychology (and formerly one of Freud's 'disciples'):

> *When one is alone and it is night and so dark and still that one hears nothing and sees nothing but the thoughts which add and subtract the years, and the long row of those disagreeable facts which remorselessly indicate how far the hand of the clock has moved forward, and the slow irresistible approach of the wall of darkness which will eventually engulf everything I love, possess, wish for, hope for, then all our profundities about life slink off to some undiscoverable hiding place, and fear envelopes the sleepless one like a smothering blanket.*

Jung here describes a fear that many people will recognise, but some only occasionally. Those who habitually look into the nothingness of death and shudder may think that it's only they who are sane and that those who go through life without this awareness are neurotically repressing a truth they dare not face. Yet, strangely, they may find themselves being judged as morbid, whereas not to fear death is the way to be health-minded (Orbach, 1999). However:

I am inclined to regard healthy-mindedness as a manic defence against the darker side of reality. Those of us who are undefended need to learn how we can live, psychologically, religiously and existentially, with that 'wall of darkness' that Jung described and which it is impossible for us not to fear. (Orbach, 1999)

According to Feifel (1969):

Death is something that happens to each of us. Even before its actual arrival it is an absent presence...the notion of the uniqueness and individuality of each one of us gathers full meaning only in realising that we must die.

Feifel believes that the precariousness of twentieth century living has, with two world wars and the nuclear threat, brought death both closer and further from individual consciousness: closer because the means of destruction have increased so enormously, and further because the possibilities of wiping out all life on this planet are too terrifying to contemplate. It's in this threatening situation that the existentialist movement has developed:

It has accented death as a constitutive part rather than the mere end of life, and high-pointed the idea that only by integrating the concept of death into the self does an authentic and genuine existence become possible. The price for denying death is undefined anxiety, self-alienation. To completely understand himself, man must confront death, become aware of personal death. (Feifel, 1969)

Death is the ultimate human 'given' (i.e. it's one of the very few things we can be certain of). Death is always with us and life is unimaginable without it. Heidegger claimed that, if honestly confronted, death could become 'an integrating factor in an authentic existence' (Macquarrie, 1972). Paul Tillich (1974), a German-American theologian and Christian existentialist philosopher, believed in a 'courage to be' as self-affirmation despite the constant threat of non-being and the need to try and transcend ourselves through participating in 'being-itself', which 'means that every courage to be has, openly or covertly, a religious root'.

Philip Larkin's poem, *Aubade*, captures brilliantly the full horror of fear of death.

Existential experimental psychology (XXP)

Solomon *et al.* (2004) describe Becker's *The Denial of Death* as the 'most compelling book to emerge from the existential psychodynamic tradition in the 20th century'. However, they observe that Becker's work was rejected by orthodox psychoanalysts for straying from Freud's emphasis on sexuality, and by anthropologists and philosophers as tainted and intellectually compromised by crossing traditional disciplinary boundaries and incorporating ideas that were alien to them. Becker was also rejected, dismissed or entirely ignored by proponents of mainstream psychology (especially cognitive scientists) as beyond the scope of modern empirical science. But Solomon *et al.* saw in his work answers to two very fundamental questions that were not being given sufficient attention at that time:

1. *Why are people so intensely concerned with their self-esteem?* Despite it being one of the oldest (James, 1890, had noted its importance) and most common constructs in social psychological discourse, there'd been no serious efforts by experimental social psychologists to define self-esteem, how it's acquired and maintained, or its psychological function.

2. *Why do people cling so tenaciously to their own cultural beliefs and have such difficulty coexisting with people from different cultures?* In the early 1980s, there were only the beginnings of a dawning awareness among social psychologists of the importance of culture as a defining human characteristic (see Chapter 9).

The issues traditionally discussed by existentialist philosophers (such as Kierkegaard, Sartre and Heidegger) and novelists (such as Camus), existential psychotherapists (such as Yalom), and cultural anthropologists (such as Becker) in recent years have increasingly been subjected to the experimental techniques of modern psychology. The philosophers, novelists and cultural anthropologists have tended to rely on introspection and 'armchair rumination', as well as integrating and synthesising other thinkers' ideas and theories, while the psychotherapists have additionally drawn on 'data' from work with their patients. Only those researchers participating in the new subfield of *experimental existential psychology* (XXP) have used traditional methodologies taken from mainstream psychology.

According to Jones (2008), XXP crystallised out of a 2001 conference organised by psychologists Jeff Greenberg, Sander Kool, and Tom Pyszczynski. The *Handbook of Experimental Existential Psychology* was published in 2004. Since then, the field has continued to grow; hundreds of researchers around the world are exploring the 'human confrontation with reality'. As we noted earlier, this has required crossing many traditional academic boundaries, and a crucial factor in overcoming scepticism about the possibility of a psychology of existential concerns has been the development of rigorous experimental tools for probing these issues. The rise of XXP has coincided with, and drawn inspiration from, renewed interest in the role of non-conscious psychological processes in guiding attitudes and behaviour (see Gross, 2010). Indeed, a key tenet of XXP is that the effects of existential concerns are mediated by processes outside of conscious awareness (Jones, 2008) (see Chapter 4).

As we noted earlier, to date XXP has focused primarily on five key existential concerns: Yalom's (1980) original 'givens of existence' plus identity. Of these five, the fear of death has received by far the greatest attention. *Terror management theory* (TMT) represents a broad theoretical account of how we cope with this fundamental fact of life.

Terror management theory (TMT)

According to **terror management theory (TMT)** (e.g. Solomon *et al.,* 1991a,1991b, 2004), human beings, like all forms of life, are the products of evolution by natural selection, having acquired over extremely long periods of time (either gradually or in abrupt 'punctuated' moments: Gould, 2002) adaptations that rendered individual members of their species able to successfully compete for resources necessary to survive and reproduce in their respective environmental niches. Specific adaptations differ radically across species and include morphological, functional, biochemical, behavioural and psychological affectations (see Chapters 1, 2 and 3).

So, what are the distinctive human evolutionary adaptations? In many ways, this entire book is devoted to trying to answer this fundamental, highly complex – and controversial – question. One answer relates to our highly social nature, linked, in turn, to our vast intelligence.

> *...These attributes fostered cooperation and division of labour and led to the invention of tools, agriculture, cooking, houses, and a host of other very useful habits and devices that allowed our ancestral forbears to rapidly multiply from a small band of hominids in a single neighbourhood in Africa to the huge population of* Homo sapiens *that currently occupy almost every habitable inch of the planet.* (Solomon et al., 2004)

A major aspect of human intelligence is self-awareness (see above and Chapter 4). We're alive and know we're alive; this sense of 'self' enables us to reflect on the past and contemplate the future, which help us function effectively in the present. Knowing one is alive is tremendously uplifting and provides humans with the potential for unbridled awe and joy. However, we're also perpetually troubled by the concurrent realisation that all living things, ourselves included, ultimately die, and that death can occur for reasons that can never be anticipated or controlled (Kiergegaard, 1844/1944). Human beings, therefore, by virtue of our awareness of death and our relative helplessness and vulnerability to ultimate annihilation, are in constant danger of being incapacitated by overwhelming terror. This terror is compounded by our profound unease at being corporeal creatures (creatures with a body) (Rank, 1941/1958). Becker (1973) neatly captured this uniquely human existential dilemma like this:

> *Man...is a creator with a mind that soars out to speculate about atoms and infinity...Yet at the same time, as the Eastern sages also knew, man is a worm and food for worms.*

Homo sapiens solved this existential dilemma by developing *cultural worldviews*: humanly constructed beliefs about reality shared by individuals in a group that serves to reduce the potentially overwhelming terror resulting from death awareness.

> *...Culture reduces anxiety by providing its constituents with a sense that they are valuable members of a meaningful universe. Meaning is derived from cultural worldviews that offer an account of the origin of the universe, prescriptions of appropriate conduct, and guarantees of safety and security to those who adhere to such instructions – in this life and beyond, in the form of symbolic and/or literal immortality...* (Solomon et al., 2004)

Time for reflection

- What do you understand by 'symbolic immortality'?
- Can you give some examples?
- How can we achieve literal immortality?

Symbolic immortality can be obtained by perceiving oneself as part of a culture that endures beyond one's lifetime, or by creating visible testaments to one's existence in the form of great works of art or science, impressive buildings or monuments, amassing vast fortunes or properties, and having children. Literal immortality is achieved via the various afterlives promised by almost all organised religions. See Box 8.6.

Box 8.6 Is there more than one heaven?

Based on a 1994 poll, Panati (1996) reported that 77 per cent of the American public (a majority of which is Christian) believe that heaven exists and that 76 per cent feel they have an excellent chance of residing there one day. Of those who believe in its existence, 91 per cent see heaven as a peaceful place, free of stress, and with ample leisure time, and 70 per cent believe that they will be in God's eternal presence, meet up with family and friends, surrounded by humour and frequent laughter.

At least for male Muslims, heaven is an opulent and sensual paradise: 'the Islamic Heaven physically resembles the Garden of Eden, though it is no longer populated with only one man and one woman. There are many available young maidens in this male-oriented Paradise, which brims with an abundance of fresh figs, dates, and sweet libations' (Panati, 1996).

For Hindus and Buddhists, the ethereal existence promised in perpetuity is Nirvana.

So, all cultural worldviews provide a sense of enduring meaning and a basis for perceiving oneself as a person of worth within the world of meaning one subscribes to. By meeting or exceeding individually internalised standards of value, norms and social norms derived from the culture, people qualify for death transcendence and hence can maintain psychological equanimity/ composure – despite their knowledge of their own mortality. For TMT, *self-esteem* refers to the belief that one is a person of value in a world of meaning; its primary function is to buffer anxiety, especially anxiety resulting from the uniquely human awareness of death (Solomon *et al.*, 2004).

From this theoretical perspective, the *need* for self-esteem is universal: people everywhere need to feel that life has meaning and that they're valuable participants in the cultural drama they subscribe to. Self-esteem is, ultimately, a culturally based construction: it's derived from adhering to the individual's internalised conception of the standards of value that are prescribed by the culture. It follows that cultures can vary greatly in terms of the attributes and behaviours that confer self-esteem:

> ...*Pastoral herders derive feelings of self-worth by the number of cattle in their possession; traditional Japanese women by their gracious hospitality; Samurai warriors by their courage and ferocity; American males by the size of their penis and bank accounts; American women by the extent to which their figure approximates the shape of a piece of linguini.*
> (Solomon *et al.*, 2004)

...Given that all cultural worldviews are fragile human constructions that can never be unequivocally confirmed, and none of them are likely to be literally true, TMT posits (following Festinger, 1954) that social consensus is an utterly essential means to sustain culturally constructed beliefs. (Solomon et al., 2004)

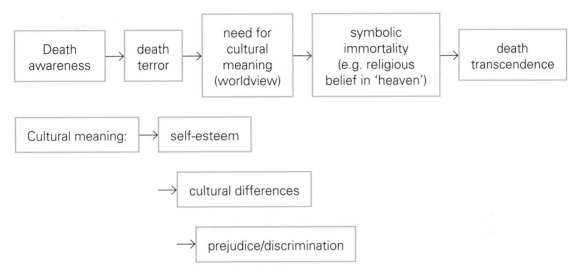

▲ **Figure 8.3** Summary of TMT

Time for reflection

- As you can see from Figure 8.3, one of the consequences of possessing cultural meaning is prejudice.
- Who or what do you think the target of such prejudice/discrimination might be?
- Explain how such a consequence could arise?

According to Solomon *et al.* (2004):

Because so many of the meaning and value-conferring aspects of the worldview are ultimately fictional, the existence of other people with different beliefs is fundamentally threatening. Acknowledging the validity of an alternative conception of reality would undermine the confidence with which people subscribe to their own points of view, and so doing would expose them to the unmitigated terror of death that their cultural worldviews were erected to mollify. People consequently react to those who are different by derogating them, convincing them to dispose of their cultural worldviews and convert to one's own (e.g. religious or political proselytising), absorbing important aspects of 'alien' worldviews into mainstream culture in ways that divest them of their threatening character...or obliterating them entirely...From this perspective, humankind's long and sordid history of violent inhumanity to other humans is thus understood as (at least in part) the result of a fundamental inability to tolerate those who do not share our death-denying cultural constructions.

Empirical assessment of TMT

Considerable research has been conducted in an attempt to test a number of interrelated hypotheses derived from TMT:

1. According to the *self-esteem as anxiety buffer hypothesis*, if self-esteem functions to buffer anxiety, then raising self-esteem (or dispositionally high self-esteem) should reduce anxiety in response to subsequent threats.

2. According to the **mortality salience hypothesis** (MS hypothesis), if cultural worldviews and self-esteem provide beliefs about the nature of reality that function to reduce anxiety associated with death awareness, then asking people to think about their own mortality (the **mortality salience paradigm (MS paradigm)**) should increase the need for the protection provided by such beliefs. In the MS paradigm, participants are reminded of their own mortality, typically by asking them to describe the emotions that the thought of their own death elicits or what they think will happen when they physically die (control participants are often asked about either a neutral topic, such as watching television, or an aversive but death-unrelated event, such as failing an exam or experiencing toothache). The dependent variable in such studies is measures on some attitudinal or behavioural scale.

3. The MS hypothesis is related, in turn, to **worldview defence** (Greenberg *et al.*, 1992b). If the function of adopting a particular cultural worldview and the beliefs it embodies is to protect us against the terror of the awareness of death, then MS should increase the need for such protection. This, in turn, should cause greater affection for, and agreement with, those who hold similar views to ourselves, as well as increased hostility towards those who hold dissimilar views ('worldview defence': Greenberg *et al.*, 1992b).

4. Self-esteem serves as a buffer against the negative effects of MS. If self-esteem serves to buffer anxiety, then worldview defence following MS should be significantly reduced (or eliminated) in individuals who have dispositionally ('naturally') high self-esteem or in whom it's situationally-induced.

5. If self-esteem serves to buffer death-related anxiety, then an MS induction should increase efforts to *acquire* self-esteem.

Other important hypotheses include the following:

6. Just as elevated self-esteem can militate against worldview defence, so can certain kinds of belief (such as *intrinsic religiosity*).

7. Based on evolutionary and other evidence, it's likely that one of the major motivations underlying the formation and maintenance of close (romantic) relationships is the human need to deny death terror, i.e. a terror management function (Mikulincer *et al.*, 2004). An extension of this hypothesis predicts that MS should promote the desire for offspring to the extent that it does not conflict with other self-relevant worldviews that also serve a terror management function (e.g. Wisman and Goldenberg, 2005).

● In a test of *hypothesis 1*, Greenberg *et al.* (1992a) found that (compared with control conditions) momentarily raising self-esteem (by false personality feedback or false feedback on a supposed IQ test) reduced both self-reported anxiety in response to graphic video footage of an autopsy/post-mortem examination and an electrocution and physiological arousal (assessed by galvanic skin response/GSR) in response to anticipation of electric shocks. Greenberg *et al.*(2003) also showed that momentarily raised or dispositionally high self-esteem, reduced vulnerability-denying defensive distortions.

- In a typical test of the MS hypothesis and worldview defence (*hypotheses 2 and 3*), after exposure to the MS paradigm as described above, participants were asked to rate individuals who either support or violate cherished aspects of participants' worldviews. For example, Greenberg *et al.* (1990, Study 1) had Christian participants evaluate Christian and Jewish targets (very similar demographically except for religious affiliation) after an MS or control condition. As predicted, MS participants reported a greater fondness for the Christian target and more negative feelings towards the Jewish target. No such differences were found in the control condition. An additional study replicated and extended this finding by showing that after an MS induction, American participants increased their affection for a pro-American author and increased their dislike of an anti-American author.

- Just as elevated self-esteem can militate against worldview defence, so too can certain kinds of belief. For example, Jonas and Fischer (2006) found that worldview defence following MS induction is reduced among religious believers, in particular those who score highly on **intrinsic religiosity** (a deep, heartfelt faith characterised by striving for meaning and value), as opposed to **extrinsic religiosity** (a more utilitarian approach that treats religion more as a means to an end, such as social acceptance or increased status).

- Solomon *et al.* (2004) cite other research which shows that asking participants to think about their own death does *not* typically induce self-reported anxiety and negative affect; in other words, MS induction produces quite specific, non-general, effects. This is consistent with research which shows that only certain operationalisations of MS will produce differences between experimental and control conditions. Those that *do* produce such differences include death anxiety scales, gory car accident footage and proximity to a funeral director's building. Those that don't include asking participants to ponder their next important exam, cultural values, speaking in public, general anxieties, meaninglessness, failure, being paralysed in a car crash, being socially excluded and dental or other physical pain (Solomon *et al.*, 2004).

- *Hypothesis 4* has been supported in a series of studies by Harmon-Jones *et al.* (1997) and Arndt and Greenberg (1999). In the former, individuals whose self-esteem was situationally elevated showed reduced MS-induction effects. Also consistent with this idea is research showing that (a) other self-esteem-related psychological resources, such as hardiness (Florian *et al.*, 2001) and secure attachment styles (Mikulincer *et al.*, 2003: see Gross, 2010) reduce the effects of MS; and (b) deficits in such resources, such as neuroticism (Goldenberg *et al.*, 1999) and depression, (Simon *et al.*, 1996) increase MS effects.

- Greenberg *et al.* (1992b) provided preliminary support for *hypothesis 5*: MS led liberals, who are committed to the principle of tolerance, to respond more favourably to someone who challenged their worldviews. A series of studies aiming to establish that MS intensifies self-esteem striving was based on the idea that MS will increase or decrease identification with entities that impinge positively or negatively upon self-esteem. Goldenberg *et al.* (2000) showed that MS increased identification with one's body as an important aspect of self among those high in body self-esteem and decreased monitoring of one's physical appearance among those low in body self-esteem (but who valued their physical attractiveness highly).

MS leads people to alter their levels of identification with their ingroups (gender, ethnic and school affiliation) to protect and enhance self-esteem (Arndt *et al.*, 2002; Dechesne *et al.*, 2000; Dechesne *et al.*, 2000). MS has also been shown to influence a variety of other behaviours likely to bolster self-esteem, including the desire to amass wealth and possessions (Kasser and Sheldon, 2000) and generosity toward favoured charities (Jonas *et al.*, 2002).

Time for reflection

- Self-esteem bolstering can also take the form of a *self-serving attributional bias*. What do you understand by this term? (See Gross, 2010.)
- Mikulincer and Florian (2002) found that MS increased the *self-serving attributional bias* and Dechesne *et al.* (2003) showed that MS leads to increased belief in the validity of positive information about the self, whether it came from horoscopes or personality tests.
- In another series of experiments, Dechesne *et al.* (2003) found that convincing individuals that there is scientific evidence of consciousness after death *eliminated* the tendency of MS to increase these self-serving biases. What conclusions can you draw from this finding regarding the function of self-esteem in relation to fears about death as the end of existence?

Mikulincer *et al.* (2004) analyse *hypothesis 7* as a whole into four basic, component hypotheses; these are described in Box 8.7.

Box 8.7 Component hypotheses relating to the terror management function of romantic relationships

1. Reminding people of their own mortality heightens their attempts to form and maintain close relationships in order to mitigate the terror of death awareness.
2. Whereas the formation and maintenance of close relationships provide a symbolic shield against death awareness, potential or actual threats to the integrity of close relationships, such as separation or loss, result in the upsurge of the awareness of one's existential plight.
3. The heightening of relational strivings in response to death reminders overrides the activation of other terror management devices.
4. The reliance on close relationships as a terror management mechanism depends on a person's inner resources, such as self-esteem and attachment security.

The terror management function of close relationships

Despite the impressive body of empirical evidence supporting the anxiety-buffering function of worldview validation and self-esteem (see above), some critics (Baron, 1997; Buss, 1997) claim that TMT has overlooked basic interpersonal processes, such as mate selection and parenting. These have evolved to promote actual survival and can shield against a wide variety of anxieties. According to Mikulincer *et al.* (2004), the human needs for communion, belongingness, affiliation, attachment, togetherness and intimacy are subordinate components of the fundamental need for self-preservation and then can serve as protective devices against death terror awareness. The maintenance of close relationships, which represents both a universal need for bonding to significant others and a culturally valued interpersonal behaviour (Baumeister and

Leary, 1995), fulfils major survival functions (Buss and Schmitt, 1993), has basic anxiety-reducing properties (Bowlby, 1969), meets cultural standards and expectations (Baumeister and Leary, 1995), is a primary source for the construction of high self-esteem (Leary and Downs, 1995), and offers the promise of symbolic immortality (Lifton, 1979). As a result, close relationships can be useful tools for mitigating death concerns and protecting the individual from death awareness.

Although TMT hasn't explicitly acknowledged the role of close relationships, the idea that they are an important source of protection, meaning and value can be found in the work of Rank and Becker. Rank (1934, 1944), for example, claimed that love relationships provide a basic sense of security and that they represent an important means of obtaining a sense of death transcendence. Similarly, Becker (1962, 1973) described the adult romantic solution, in which the romantic partner is a primary source of meaning, self-worth and death transcendence. Close relationships are a source of death transcendence in Western culture during the twentieth century, replacing the meanings and values formerly provided by religion (see later in this chapter).

Box 8.8 Death and sex

According to Rollo May (1969), in *Love and Will*, our twentieth-century obsession with sex serves to conceal our fear of death. We have fewer defences against this universal fear, such as the belief in immortality or any widely shared views regarding the purpose of life.

Like all obsessions, our preoccupation with sex 'drains off anxiety from some other area and prevents the person from having to confront something distasteful'. So, what is it that our sex obsession shields us from? May's answer is the fact that we must die: 'The clamour of sex all about us drowns out the ever-waiting presence of death'.

> *When I strive to prove my potency in order to cover up and silence my inner fears of impotence, I am engaging in a pattern as ancient as man himself. Death is the symbol of ultimate impotence and finiteness, and anxiety arising from this inescapable experience calls forth the struggle to make ourselves infinite by way of sex. Sexual activity is the most ready way to silence the inner dread of death, and through the symbol of procreation, to triumph over it.* (May, 1969)

May compares our repression of death and its symbolism with the way the Victorians repressed sex:

> *...Death is obscene, unmentionable, pornographic; if sex was nasty, death is a nasty mistake. Death is not to be talked of in front of the children, nor talked about at all if we can help it. We dress death up in grotesquely colourful caskets in the same way Victorian women camouflaged their bodies by means of voluminous dresses. We throw flowers on the casket to make death smell better...* (May, 1969)

Sex and death have in common the fact that they're the two biological aspects of the *mysterium tremendum*. Mystery – a situation in which the data impinge on the problem – has its ultimate meaning in these two human experiences. Both are related to creation and destruction; not surprisingly, they're interwoven in complex ways as part of human experience. '...In both [sex and death] we are taken over by an event; we cannot stand outside either love or death – and, if we try to, we destroy whatever value the experience can have.' (May, 1969)

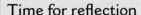

> **Time for reflection**
>
> - Can you identify the properties/characteristics of close relationships that enable them to protect us from death terror?

Mikulincer *et al.* (2004) identify six such properties.

1. Relationships have an evolutionary significance: they are a product of natural and sexual selection processes that have important survival and reproductive benefits (Buss and Schmitt, 1993). Close relationships provide the framework for sexual acts, thus increasing the chances of bearing offspring that will reach maturity and survive. Consistent with this characteristic is evidence of a connection between the desire for offspring and MS. Some relevant studies are described in Box 8.9.

2. Close relationships are a source of protection and security in threatening and dangerous situations (Bowlby, 1969; Schachter, 1959: see Gross, 2010). In optimal conditions, relationship partners become a safe haven, facilitating threat removal and distress alleviation, and a secure base, from which to explore the world. Staying close (proximity maintenance) to the supportive parent provides the infant with comfort and relief, a sense of basic trust and security, and reinforces its confidence in the anxiety-reducing efficiency of attachment figures. The attachment system is active over the entire lifespan and is manifested in thoughts and behaviours related to the formation and maintenance of close relationships (Mikulincer and Shaver, 2003). These anxiety-reducing properties also offer protection from death terror.

3. The formation and maintenance of close relationships are culturally valued behaviours. Many social institutions and rituals have evolved to promote and protect one's close interpersonal relationships (Baumeister and Leary, 1995; Goffman, 1972). People who fail to form or maintain close relationships are stereotyped as unhappy, problematic and dysfunctional (e.g. Peplau and Perlman, 1982), and aloneness is viewed as a personal deficiency and a deviant social state (e.g. Horney, 1943; Sullivan, 1953). In most cultures, the formation and maintenance of close relationships are important components of the cultural worldview; basic values that enhance their likelihood and stability are transmitted across the generations through the process of socialisation. Like other aspects of cherished worldviews, the formation and maintenance of close relationships can be a source of meaning, order and value.

4. Close relationships are an important source of self-esteem (e.g. Leary, 1999; Leary and Downs, 1995). Self-esteem reflects the extent to which we succeed in forming and maintaining close relationships; specifically, high self-esteem implies being accepted and valued by others, while low self-esteem reflects social rejection and failure to maintain close ties (e.g. Leary *et al.*, 1995).

5. Close relationships offer a symbolic promise of continuity and permanence and increase a person's sense of symbolic immortality (Lifton, 1979). Lifton and Olson (1974) emphasised the psychological equation between aloneness and death. Close relationships provide the framework for biological procreation: this allows us to transcend our biological existence and believe that we'll continue to live through our progeny (see Box 8.9). Such relationships also offer individuals the opportunity to feel part of a larger symbolic entity (such as couple or family group) that transcends their biological limitations and expands the boundaries of their own self (Aron *et al.*, 2001).

6. Close relationships can directly mitigate basic interpersonal death-related concerns. According to Florian and Kravetz (1983), different people may fear death for different reasons. These may include intrapersonal worries (e.g. lack of self-fulfilment) and interpersonal concerns. One of the basic interpersonal death-related concerns is the fear that no one will remember us after our death and that we won't leave any impression on the world (the *loss of identity* factor). According to Mikulincer *et al.* (2004), the formation and maintenance of close relationships can mitigate this interpersonal fear.

Box 8.9 MS and the desire for offspring

Wisman and Goldenberg (2005) predicted that mortality salience should promote the desire for offspring to the extent that it doesn't interfere with other self-relevant worldviews that also serve terror management. In three separate studies, Wisman and Goldenberg found that men, but not women, desired more children after MS compared with various control conditions. In support of their hypothesis that women's desire for offspring would be inhibited as a function of concerns about career success, the researchers found that career strivings moderated the effects of MS on a desire for offspring in female participants only. However, when the compatibility of having children and a career was made salient, female participants responded to MS with an increased number of desired children. Taken together, the findings suggested that a desire for offspring can function as a terror-management defence mechanism (Wisman and Goldenberg, 2005).

Fritsche *et al.* (2007) replicated previous German research and found increased desire for offspring following MS – in both men and women (Study 1). In an extension of previous research, they also found that following MS, not only was the accessibility of death-related thoughts increased, but also the accessibility of thoughts related to offspring (Study 2). Study 3 suggested that the MS effect on ingroup bias was eliminated under conditions of offspring salience. Taken together, these findings support the view that anticipated or actual offspring function as a buffer against existential anxiety (Fritsche *et al.,* 2007).

Mikulincer *et al.* (2004) reviewed a large body of research relating to four major aspects of the terror management function of close relationships. They draw the following conclusions from the findings:

1. When participants are reminded of their own mortality (MS induction), their motivation to form and maintain close relationships is increased.

2. Whereas the successful accomplishment of relational tasks tends to buffer death concerns and make the activation of other defences less necessary, the potential disruption of close relationships lead to an upsurge of death awareness.

3. The activation of relational defences in response to death reminders (MS induction) tends to override other culturally derived defences; participants seem to be prepared to pay the psychological price of securing close relationships.

4. Theoretically coherent individual differences (such as self-esteem and attachment style) have been found in how participants rely on relational defences. Overall, the use of close relationships as a terror management mechanism is characteristic of people who have developed a strong sense of self-worth and connectedness to the world.

Mikulincer *et al.* (2004)believe that these findings can deepen our understanding of basic existential concerns about love and death.

An assessment of TMT from an evolutionary perspective

As we saw at the beginning of the section on TMT, its authors claim that it's an *evolutionary* account. However, Kirkpatrick and Navarette (2006) argue that in several crucial ways it's entirely out of step with contemporary understandings of evolution by natural selection. It's unlikely that natural selection would have designed a 'survival instinct' or innate 'fear of death', nor an anxiety-reduction system in general, or worldview-defence system in particular, to counter such fears. These authors believe that the results of MS experiments are better explained as *by-products* of a psychological system of *coalitional computation* that evolved for a variety of functions, including defence against other humans, that's activated by certain kinds of death-related thoughts.

If fear of death were adaptive, a terror-management psychological system that reduced it artificially couldn't evolve without undermining its adaptive value. If it were maladaptive, it couldn't have evolved in the first place. The remaining logical possibility is that fear of death is adaptively *neutral*: in this case, there would be no adaptive problem to be solved (there would be no need for a terror-management system to have evolved to reduce it). But might such a system have evolved in order to relieve the discomfort associated with fear of death?

> *...In general, natural selection cannot be expected to design systems merely for the sake of making organisms feel good, happy, or secure. Natural selection is blind to purely internal psychological states or feelings except insofar as these lead to adaptive or maladaptive behaviour. Natural selection is not in the business of building happy organisms.*
> (Kirkpatrick and Navarette, 2006)

Religion and non-Western worldviews

In the context of symbolic immortality (see page 22), Kirkpatrick (1999, 2005) has argued that religion isn't an adaptation *in its own right*; rather, it emerges as a collection of by-products of several psychological systems evolved to solve everyday adaptive problems related to understanding the natural world (e.g. naive physics, naive biology) and negotiating functionally distinct forms of interpersonal relationships (e.g. attachment, coalitions, kin relations, social exchange).

Is maintenance and defence of shared worldviews really a fundamental, species-wide feature of human psychology? One obvious problem that doesn't require an evolutionary perspective to see is that worldviews obviously vary in the degree to which they effectively combat death anxiety. Many Christian beliefs, for example, address the problem directly in terms of beliefs about life and death, heaven as a wonderful place (see Box 8.6 on page 228), and so on. At the same time, beliefs about hell, which vary considerably across denominations, would seem to have precisely the opposite effect. God and Jesus appear in the New Testament as generally comforting, nurturing figures similar to parents or friends, while the Old Testament God or the God of the Apocalypse in the Revelation of John has a dangerous temper that leads followers to be 'God-fearing Christians' (Kirkpatrick and Navarette, 2006).

An examination of non-Western, non-Christian cultures casts even greater doubt on the claim that worldviews serve the terror management function proposed by TMT. The optimistic worldview of contemporary Christian beliefs is by no means typical as worldviews go:

> *...The anthropological record is replete with examples of belief systems in which misfortune is thought to befall individuals through no fault of their own, capricious supernatural entities murder children, crops fail because of witchcraft, the 'evil eye' of envy causes catastrophe to befall successful people, and so on...* (Kirkpatrick and Navarette, 2006)

Boyer (2001) gives the example of the Fang people of Gabon, who believe that an internal bodily organ can launch attacks against other people, drink their blood, and bring illness, harm or even death to the victims (Evans-Pritchard, 1937). Life among the Azande people of the Sudan has been described as rife with paranoia, fear and suspicion due to a worldview saturated with witchcraft beliefs. In each of these and numerous other cases, pain, suffering and death rain down upon people regardless of whether or not they live up to the standards of the given cultural worldview (Kirkpatrick and Navarette, 2006).

> *...The TMT perspective on belief systems is one developed in the context of a 20th Century post-war milieu where ideological beliefs of the White North American middle class have become sanitised, egoistic, and much more comforting than was true in the past, or is true in most cultures outside of the US today. Because TMT does not attend to the belief systems of non-Western societies...it provides a limited and ethnocentric approach to the function of worldviews. A North American Christian worldview of the later 20th Century is hardly an appropriate prototype in any theory that aims to describe a phenomenon which is purportedly ubiquitous across the panoply of cultures past and present.* (Kirkpatrick and Navarette, 2006)

Coalitional computation

In addition to threats of starvation, dehydration and disease, a key challenge to survival in ancestral environments (as it is today in many parts of the world) would have been the threat of harm from other people. Like our chimp cousins, *Homo sapiens* live in groups that defend territory and compete with other groups, sometimes violently. Within these groups, coalitions and alliances shift over time and provide the primary means of attaining status (in contrast to most other species where status is largely a matter of physical dominance). These coalitions also provide a primary defence against harm by outgroup or other ingroup members. In humans, shared worldviews provide an important symbolic means of identifying allies and enemies, ingroups and outgroups. For example, one central tenet of most religious belief and moral systems involves differentiating believers from heathens and other characterisations of us-versus-them (Kirkpatrick and Navarette, 2006).

Kirkpatrick and Navarette argue that the contemplation of death elicits increased endorsement of the ingroup's normative beliefs primarily because the likely common causes of death in ancestral environments (illness, disease, severe bodily injury, starvation) were conditions in which successfully acquiring increased social support (and, perhaps, avoiding outgroup members) would have had significant fitness (survival) consequences. They propose that the mortality salience phenomena reported by TMT researchers might be better explained as output generated by a system of adaptive mechanisms that promote the formation and maintenance of close relationships, coalitions and alliances.

Whereas adherents of TMT explicitly predict that worldview defence effects are uniquely caused by death-related thoughts (see above), Kirkpatrick and Navarette predict that the same effects can be produced by fitness-relevant stimuli unrelated to death – provided these stimuli contain content relevant to adaptive challenges that could be effectively dealt with through social support. In six studies conducted in the USA and Costa Rica (Navarette, 2005; Navarette *et al.*, 2004), participants who contemplated death, theft of resources, social isolation or soliciting help for a cooperative task all showed increased support of a pro-nationalist author over a societal critic, compared with control participants. In three separate experiments, MS failed to increase normative bias among Costa Rican participants. These results show that worldview-defence effects aren't produced exclusively by MS induction, as TMT would predict.

> ...while shared beliefs are important in determining group identity (i.e. who belongs and who does not), it is not the beliefs per se that are the relevant issue, but rather the group membership that is marked by a system of coalitional computation. Contrary to TMT claims, we hold that group identity does not function to assuage worldview defence needs, but rather, worldviews serve the purpose of facilitating intergroup and interpersonal relationships.
>
> ...From our coalitional perspective, because affiliation is itself the goal underlying worldview defence, if affiliation can be achieved directly then the need for worldview defence is reduced.
>
> (Kirkpatrick and Navarette, 2006)

Religion and the human predicament

As we noted in Chapter 1, religion represents one aspect of the symbolic nature of *Homo sapiens*. According to Dunbar (2007), our ability to ask if the world could have been otherwise than we experience it represents 'the basis for everything that we would think of as uniquely human'. One aspect of this imaginative ability is contemplation of alternative universes in the development of religious beliefs.

As we've noted earlier in this chapter, religious belief represents a major form of death terror management: the promise of (symbolic) immortality is a hard-to-beat defence against the prospect of ceasing to exist – for all eternity. For believers, their religion represents a fundamental, if not exclusive, feature of their worldview. Indeed, Batson and Stocks (2004) define religion as 'whatever a person does to deal with existential questions', which are those that arise from our awareness that we and others like us are alive and that we will die (the 'human predicament').

According to Yalom (2008):

> It's not easy to live every moment wholly aware of death. It's like trying to stare at the sun in the face: you can stand only so much of it. Because we cannot live frozen in fear, we generate methods to soften death's terror. We project ourselves into the future through our children; we grow rich, famous, ever larger; we develop compulsive protective rituals; or we embrace an impregnable belief in an ultimate rescuer.
>
> ...Death anxiety is the mother of all religions, which, in one way or another, attempt to temper the anguish of our finitude. God, as formulated transculturally, not only softens the pain of mortality through some vision of everlasting life but also palliates fearful isolation by offering an eternal presence, and provides a clear blueprint for living a meaningful life.

> **Time for reflection**
> - Briefly describe Maslow's (1954, 1970) 'hierarchy of needs' (see Gross, 2010).
> - Try to identify existential questions that might be raised by each need in the hierarchy.

From the bottom of the hierarchy upwards, the needs are: physiological, safety, love and belonging, esteem, cognitive and self-actualisation. Batson and Stocks (2004) take Maslow's hierarchy as a 'broad heuristic frame' on which to stretch their thinking about the psychological functions of religion. They propose that religion, in its various forms, can function to address each of Maslow's needs because each of these needs can raise existential questions. Table 8.1 presents examples of such existential questions. Note that self-actualisation is classified as a *conative* (motivational) need along with all the others, except for *cognitive needs*. Batson and Stocks also propose that religion can function to challenge the individual to transcend all of these needs through subjugation of oneself and one's personal needs to a higher purpose or cause.

Table 8.1 Basic psychological needs and resulting existential questions, which religion can function to address (adapted from Batson and Stocks, 2004)

Physiological needs arising from person–situation interaction	Existential questions raised by these needs
Conative needs	
Physiological needs – needs for food, drink, warmth, sex, etc.	How do I satisfy my hunger and thirst? What if the crop fails? How do I stay warm and dry? How do I deal with this injury or disease?
Safety needs – needs to keep oneself and one's possessions safe.	What can and should I do to protect myself? Are there powerful forces that I can and should appeal to for safety? How can I control the future?
Belongingness and love needs – needs to have a place in the social world, to be loved, and to love.	Where do I belong? Who are my people? Who loves me? Whom do I love? What is my responsibility to others?
Esteem needs – needs for a sense of strength and competence, as well as for reputation, status and appreciation.	Am I a person of worth? Am I valued by others? How am I to live with my shortcomings, mistakes and inabilities?
Need for self-actualisation – need to become everything one is capable of becoming, to express one's true nature.	What is my true nature? What will make me truly happy? How can I be fulfilled?

Physiological needs arising from person–situation interaction	**Existential questions raised by these needs**
Cognitive needs	
Need to know and understand – Need to have a sense of meaning and purpose in one's life.	What is the meaning and purpose of my life? What will happen to me when I die? What should I do, given my inevitable death?

The religious response to existential questions (based on Batson and Stocks, 2004)

1. As far as *physiological needs* are concerned, in early civilisations, when the food supply was uncertain, planting was a time for religious rituals, a time to ask God or the gods for a successful crop. Harvest was a time for religious celebrations and prayers of thanksgiving. If during the growing season rains did not come, people turned to priests and shamans to appeal for divine intervention (and prayers for rain are still offered today in many farming communities).

   For nomadic herders and early farmers living in arid areas of the Middle East, the Promised Land was often described as a 'a land flowing with milk and honey'; it was promised by Yahweh (the Hebrew God), the One who could provide manna in the desert (food that 'appeared from nowhere'). The Christian Lord's Prayer states: 'give us this day our daily bread', and 'grace before meals' is a common practice in many religions (and after meals in Judaism).

2. *Safety threats*, whether from nature, our peers or signs of illness, lead us to fear the future and wish for a world that is safe, reliable, predictable and controllable. As children, we may have assumed that our parents could and would protect us; once we begin to recognise their limitations, we may long to know that someone or something even more powerful is in control and is 'looking out for us'. We may look to God or gods.

   In *The Future of an Illusion* (1927/1964), Freud focused on religion as a source of safety: the first task of the gods is to 'exorcise the terrors of nature'. Similarly, Maslow (1954) suggested that religion often speaks to the desire to see the universe as organised, coherent and meaningful; this desire is partly motivated by basic safety needs. Gordon Allport (1966) made an important distinction between (a) an *extrinsic approach* to religion, where religion functions as an instrumental means to self-serving ends; and (b) an *intrinsic approach*, where it functions as an end in itself and 'strives to transcend all self-centred needs'. A sense of safety is one of the most important of the self-serving ends promoted by (a). In Kirkpatrick's (1994) application of attachment theory to religion, he noted that God often functions as a 'safe haven', much as the primary caregiver does for the securely attached child. In two longitudinal studies, he found that adults with insecure attachment styles were especially likely to turn to God as a substitute attachment figure (Kirkpatrick, 1997, 1998; see Gross, 2003).

3. For millennia, a core function of all the major world religions has been to respond to the need for *belongingness* and *love*. Judaism early on focused on the special relationship between the Israelites and their God, who was a 'jealous god', whom they should love with all their heart and exclusively; they, in turn, were God's 'Chosen People'. Six centuries later, Jesus repeated, elaborated and extended the command to 'love thy neighbour as thyself' – this applied not only to strangers but even to enemies. As Christianity spread into the Greek world, the

word used to denote God's love is *agape*, selfless attention to the welfare of others. Islam also offers the faithful an ever-present, compassionate and merciful God, as well as a sense of brotherhood of believers and a special place in the social order of this world – and the world to come. Buddhism places less emphasis on a loving relationship with God, stressing a loving, compassionate relationship with *all* living things.

4. According to Maslow (1970), *esteem needs* take two forms: (a) a need for strength, achievement, mastery and competence; (b) a need for reputation, prestige, status, recognition and appreciation. Satisfaction of these needs leads to a sense of self-confidence, worth, capability and value to the world. At least in the USA, feeling good about oneself and seeing oneself as a person of worth and value play a major role in much contemporary religion; historically, things are less clear-cut. On the one hand, religion has offered assurance of personal worth simply by virtue of being a person; it has also questioned the value of reputation. On the other hand, religion has provided an alternative set of standards of worth and so on – based on piety, devotion and service. Thus, one may be assured that he or she was created by and is valued by God.

    Most religious traditions disapprove of people who see themselves as especially worthy in God's eyes or who make a public show of their devotion (Allport's extrinsic approach: see above). False piety is condemned; humility is highly praised. Fortunately, one of the hallmarks of all major religious traditions is that they provide the means through which personal failures and shortcomings are forgiven: sacrifice, confession and penance.

    Consistent with the idea that active pursuit of esteem through religion is doomed to failure (Allport, 1950, 1966), research has shown that measures of extrinsic religion tend to be *negatively* correlated with measures of self-esteem; measures of intrinsic religion tend to correlate *positively*. However, rather than measures of intrinsic religion tapping authentic humility, with esteem as an unintended 'fringe benefit' (as Allport believed), the opposite may be true: measures of intrinsic religion may actually reflect an instrumental use of religion to enhance self-esteem – one's sense of oneself as a good, righteous person – even more than do measures of extrinsic religion (Batson *et al.*, 1993).

5. Historically the promotion of *self-actualisation* or expression of one's unique, individual nature hasn't been a function of religion: it's too self-centred. However, it has been central to the New Age mixture of Jungian and humanistic psychology that became popular in the last quarter of the twentieth century among some liberal Protestants in the USA (more popularly, the Hippie/'flower power' movement of the 1960s and 1970s).

    For Jung (1938), religion was perhaps the most effective means of achieving *individuality*:

    > In so far as 'individuality' embraces our innermost, last, and incomparable uniqueness, it also implies becoming one's own self. We could therefore translate individuation as 'coming to self-hood' or 'self-realisation'. (Jung, 1938)

    May (1953) and the psychoanalyst Erich Fromm (1950, 1960) express a similar idea. For example, Fromm (1960) believed that humanistic religion (as opposed to authoritarian religion) holds the key to 'overcoming the limitations of an egotistical self, achieving love, objectivity, and humility and respecting life so that the aim of life is living itself, and man becomes what he potentially is'. Maslow was suspicious of organised religion (equivalent to Fromm's 'authoritarian' religion), because he felt it provided little support for the pursuit of self-actualisation. However, he described self-actualised individuals as likely to have 'peak experiences' – non-traditional 'core-religious' experiences of a rather mystical nature, in which the individual has a sense of wholeness and integration both within the self and with the world, a sense of effortless and creative involvement in the here and now (Maslow, 1964). (This complements the 'time-travelling nature of human consciousness': see Chapters 1, 4, and 7.) The mystical aspects of such experiences seem to have much in common with the experiences of wholeness and integration in the meditative traditions of Buddhism, although Buddhism places much less emphasis on the self.

6. At one level, Maslow (1970) viewed *cognitive capacities* as a set of tools used in the service of the basic conative needs (see Table 8.1): 'acquiring knowledge and systematising the universe' seems to provide a sense of basic safety in the world, which serves the expression of self-actualisation. At another level, however, the desire to know and understand forms a *hierarchy of needs* in its own right:

> *Even after we know, we are impelled to know more and more minutely and microscopically on the one hand, and on the other, more and more extensively in the direction of a world philosophy, theology, etc. ...This process has been phrased by some as the search for meaning.* (Maslow, 1970)

Maslow cautioned against drawing a sharp distinction between cognitive and conative needs: (a) the desire to know and understand has a strong motivational character; it's often experienced as a passionate drive, a desperate longing for meaning and purpose – not merely as a philosophical puzzle; and (b) the two types of need are intertwined.

The meaning and purpose of life

Time for reflection
- 'What is the meaning of life?' 'Does life have a purpose?' Are these valid, meaningful questions to ask at all?
- If so, are they more appropriately posed by philosophers, theologians or psychological scientists?

Religion revisited

> *...Sharp and pressing existential questions arise from the clash between the desire to know and understand and two key characteristics of the human predicament – awareness of our individual existence and awareness of our mortality...* (Batson and Stocks, 2004)

Existential questions arise inevitably from the human condition, and religion is one of the oldest and, arguably, still one of the most effective solutions to these existential dilemmas. For many, the most salient core psychological function of religion is to provide a sense of meaning and purpose in life. Batson and Stocks (2004) cite the case of the great Russian novelist Leo Tolstoy, who asked:

...What will be the outcome of what I do today? Of what I shall do tomorrow? What will be the outcome of my life? Why should I live? Why should I do anything? Is there in life any purpose which the inevitable death which awaits me does not undo and destroy? (Tolstoy, 1904)

Religion provided the answers that eventually brought Tolstoy back from the brink of suicide.

The Polish cultural anthropologist Bronislaw Malinowski, described the role of religion in providing meaning and purpose in more general terms:

Into this supreme dilemma of life and final death, religion steps in, selecting the positive creed, the comforting view, the culturally valuable belief in immortality, in the spirit independent of the body, and in the continuance of life after death. In the various ceremonies at death, in commemoration and communion with the departed, and the worship of ancestral ghosts, religion gives body and form to the saving beliefs. (Malinowski, 1954)

James (1902), Freud (1927/1964, 1930/1961) and Jung (1964) all recognised the importance of religion as a source of meaning and purpose in life. Allport (1950) believed that mature (as opposed to immature) religion provides an overarching sense of meaning and purpose that integrates and orders the personality, allows the individual honestly to face the human predicament, and provides a master-motive for living. He later (1966) replaced mature/immature religion with the concepts of intrinsic and extrinsic respectively (see above). Batson (1976) proposed a third dimension of personal religion to complement Allport's intrinsic and extrinsic, namely, religion as a *quest*, a search for meaning (rather than a solution). Subsequent research has revealed that many of the *social* benefits that Allport believed were associated with an intrinsic approach to religion (such as reduced prejudice and increased concern for those worse off than oneself) are in fact associated with the quest dimension. *Personal* benefits, however, such as life satisfaction and reduced anxiety, are more likely to be associated with the clear sense of meaning and purpose reflected in an intrinsic approach than with a quest approach (Batson and Stocks, 2004).

▲ **Figure 8.4** Muslims at prayer

As far as TMT is concerned, religion is given a major role, both as a cultural institution and as a personal belief system. Solomon *et al.* (1991a) proposed that the motive underlying terror management is a primitive and basic one, namely, a tendency towards self-preservation (common to all life forms). However, as we noted earlier, TMT seems to rest on a mistaken view of the nature of evolution by natural selection (Kirkpatrick and Navarette, 2006). This also applies to its understanding of self-preservation.

> ...Rather than being a primitive and ancient motive shared with other species, our concern for self-preservation is almost certainly a recent evolutionary development. It is dependent on the cognitive capacities to (1) understand oneself as an existing person and (2) imagine the radically altered reality in which this person no longer exists. These capacities can, in turn, produce truly terrifying doubts...about the meaning and purpose of life... (Batson and Stocks, 2004)

Religion and self-transcendence

In addition to satisfying the needs identified in Maslow's hierarchy, which are needs of the person or individual, religion may also function to promote **self-transcendence**, that is, to place value outside oneself, to pursue some higher purpose or cause. Sometimes, this may involve focusing on meeting *others'* needs and trusting in God as a way of effectively satisfying one's own needs. Alternatively, it may involve a shift to a new set of values. A third route to self-transcendence is to discipline oneself to eliminate personal needs and desires; this is central to Taoism and various forms of Buddhism, where the eightfold path is Nirvana, a state of nothingness and oneness with the Universe without personal desire. Here, religion functions not to save oneself but to free oneself from oneself (Batson and Stocks, 2004).

Meaning without religion

In the context of the question 'What does it all mean?' (arguably the most vexing and difficult question that humans face in reflecting on their lives: Jones, 2008), the philosopher Thomas Nagel (1987) suggests that we have an 'incurable tendency' to take ourselves and our endeavours seriously, and to feel that what we do isn't just important to us personally, but important in some wider sense. This sense of seriousness and importance often fuels our ambitions and drives us forward:

> If we have to give this up, it may threaten to take the wind out of our sails. If life is not real, life is not earnest, and the grave is its goal, perhaps it's ridiculous to take ourselves so seriously. On the other hand, if we can't help taking ourselves so seriously, perhaps we just have to put up with being ridiculous. Life may be not only meaningless but absurd. (Nagel, 1987)

For some, such as the evolutionary biologist Richard Dawkins, there's really no riddle at all regarding the purpose of life. In *The God Delusion* (2006), he attacks *creationist* explanations of life, that is, the claim that the universe and everything in it was created by God (or some supernatural being): evolution can account for everything that exists, without having to bring God into it. Indeed, Dawkins claims that, at least from the perspective of a non-believer or atheist, the question 'What is the purpose of life?' is totally meaningless.

However, while the theory of natural selection should have convinced us that we don't need God to explain our creation, it has failed to do so. While many people don't believe in God, they still ask themselves about the purpose of life and cannot easily shake off their curiosity about this seemingly grand mystery (Bering, 2010). According to Bering (2010):

> *...For psychological purposes, we needn't concern ourselves over whether the 'whys' are good questions, bad questions, or non-questions. We just want to know why they're so cognitively seductive and so recalcitrant in the face of logical science.*

Bering cites Jean Piaget, the famous Swiss developmental psychologist. Piaget (1965)was sceptical of atheists' claims of entirely escaping a psychological bias of seeing the natural world in intentional terms. His concept of **artificialism** referred to young children's perception of the natural world as existing solely to solve human problems – or at least meant for human use (see Gross, 2010). Yet Piaget (1965) suspected that artificialist beliefs never really go away; rather, they'd continue cropping up in the non-believer's mental representations in very subtle ways. For example, 'A semi-educated man may well dismiss as "contrary to science" a theological explanation of the universe, and yet find no difficulty in accepting the notion that the sun is there to give us light' (Piaget,1965). (See Box 8.10.)

Box 8.10 Children's perception of purpose: teleo-functional explanations (based on Bering, 2010)

Bering (2010) cites recent studies which have found that children possess a more scientific understanding of natural events than Piaget claimed. However, one basic feature of his argument has continued to hold up under controlled conditions: children reason in terms of an inherent purpose when it comes to the origins of natural phenomena. Human minds are biased toward reasoning in this *teleo-functional* manner: we tend to believe that something exists for a purposeful reason, rather than because 'it's just there'. It is logical to say that a showerhead sprays clean, plumbed-in water over dirty bodies, because it's designed for exactly that purpose. But it would be bizarre to claim that a waterfall is 'for' anything in particular (or anything at all), although if you happened to be standing beneath one, it would do the same job as the showerhead:

> *...As an artefact, the shower is the product of human intentional design, and thus it has an essential purpose that can be traced to the mind of its creator. In contrast, the waterfall is simply there as the result of some naturally occurring geographical configuration.*
> (Bering, 2010)

Young children, however, attribute such natural, inanimate entities – waterfalls, clouds, rocks, etc., – with their own teleo-functional purposes. For example, when asked why mountains exist, seven-to-eight-year-olds overwhelmingly prefer teleo-functional explanations ('to give animals a place to climb') over mechanistic or physical, causal explanations ('because volcanoes cooled into lumps'). It is only around the age of nine that children begin to give scientifically more accurate accounts. However, without a basic science education, teleo-functional thinking remains a fixture of adult thought (e.g. Casler and Keleman's (2008) study of uneducated Romanian Romani adults. Even science-literate adults with Alzheimer's disease display this preference (Lombrozo *et al.,* 2007), indicating that **teleo-functional reasoning** is not so much replaced by degradable scientific knowledge as it is consciously overridden.

According to Bering (2010), findings like those described in Box 8.10 have obvious implications 'for our ability ever to truly grasp the completely mindless principles of evolution by random mutation and natural selection'. Creationist beliefs (**creationism**) are due in large part to the way our cognitive systems have evolved (Evans, 2000). Irrespective of their parents' beliefs, when five-to-seven-year-olds are asked where the first member of a particular animal species came from, they give either spontaneous *generationist* ('it got born there') or *creationist* ('God made it') responses. But by age eight, children from both secular and religious backgrounds give almost exclusively creationist answers. If not 'God', then 'Nature' is personified, seen as a deliberate agent that intentionally made the animal. It's at this age, then, that teleo-functional reasoning turns into a full-blown 'design stance': children envisage an actual mental agent as creating the entity in question for its own personal reasons. Only the oldest children, the 10-to-12-year-olds, that Evans studied, showed the impact of parental beliefs on their own explicit explanations.

> *All of this suggests strongly that thinking like an evolutionist is hard work because, ironically, it works against the grain of evolved human psychology. Evolutionists will probably never outnumber creationists since the latter have a paradoxical ally in the way natural selection has lent itself to our species' ability to reason about its own origins.* (Bering, 2010)

Even if we aren't particularly religious, we often attribute some vague purpose to human existence, such as 'to love one another'. But we often go one step further, displaying an extreme form of teleo-functional reasoning by claiming that individual members of our species exist 'for' a special reason (Bering, 2006); it's their 'destiny' to do what they do and become what they become.

Nagel (1979)suggests that, if we can accept that life may be not only meaningless but absurd, then perhaps 'We can approach our absurd lives with irony instead of heroism or despair' (see Nagel quote on p 243). Such reflections resonate with the ideas of existential psychology. According to Pyszczynski (in Jones, 2008):

> *... The value of humour in life is seriously underestimated by psychologists and other scholars, yet it can be easily seen in the popularity of humour that puts humankind in its place by pointing to the absurdity of much of what we do. Humour is one form of transformation in the way we view our lot in life and Nagel hits the nail on the head by pointing to its potential for not just distracting us from our daily concerns, but also transforming the way we go about living.* (Pyszczynski in Jones, 2008)

However, Greenberg (in Jones, 2008) calls for some qualifications:

> *The animal inside us is built to take things seriously and not to accept death or absurdity, and I suspect Nagel takes at least his own musings on absurdity seriously. Fully embracing reality, including absurdity and eventual non-existence, leads to only cowardly, desperate hedonistic grasping of total despair. The alternative, which I attribute to Camus, is to create meaning and take it seriously, even though one knows it is ultimately illusory ...* (Greenberg in Jones, 2008)

Perhaps the key is trying to strike a balance between seriousness and absurdity. But would we want to free ourselves of our existential concerns even if we could? If they are part of the human condition, then denying and avoiding them may cause as many problems as these defences are designed to solve. Indeed, could confronting our existential concerns help us achieve psychological growth and well-being?

Conclusions: The positive side of the human predicament

Along with many other writers, Yalom (2008) claims that however hard we try, we can never completely subdue death anxiety: '...it is always there, lurking in some hidden ravine of the mind...' It creates problems that may not at first seem to be directly related to mortality:

> *...Death has a long reach, with an impact that is often concealed. Though fear of dying can totally immobilise some people, often the fear is covert and expressed in symptoms that appear to have nothing to do with one's mortality.* (Yalom, 2008)

For Yalom, Freud's view regarding the relationship between psychopathology and the repression of sexuality is far too narrow; his clinical work has convinced him that '...one may repress not just sexuality but one's whole creaturely self and especially its finite nature'.

However, confronting death needn't result in despair that strips away all purpose in life. On the contrary, it can be an 'awakening experience to a fuller life'. One of the central themes of Yalom's *Staring at the Sun* (2008) is that '*though the physicality of death destroys us, the idea of death saves us.*' (Italics in original.) In the final chapter, he offers instruction to therapists, who, for the most part, avoid working directly with death anxiety. His existential therapy is designed precisely to help clients with their death anxiety, whether this is overt or more indirect.

> *I feel strongly – as a man who will himself die one day and in the not-too-distant future and as a psychiatrist who has spent decades dealing with death anxiety – that confronting death allows us, not to open some noisome Pandora's box, but to reenter life in a richer, more compassionate manner.* (Yalom, 2008)

In *Man's Search for Meaning* (1946/2004), Viktor Frankl, late professor of neurology and psychiatry in Vienna, and concentration camp survivor, explains the experience which led to his discovery of *logotherapy,* his own version of modern existential psychotherapy. In the preface to one edition of this classic work, Gordon Allport (2004) writes:

> *...As a longtime prisoner in bestial concentration camps he found himself stripped to naked existence. His father, mother, brother, and his wife died in camps or were sent to the gas ovens, so that, excepting for his sister, his entire family perished in these camps. How could he – every possession lost, every value destroyed, suffering from hunger, cold and brutality, hourly expecting extermination – how could he find life worth preserving?...*

What does a human being do when he or she suddenly realises that there's 'nothing to lose except his so ridiculous naked life'? Frankl describes a mixed flow of emotion and apathy. First to the rescue comes a cold detached curiosity concerning one's fate; swiftly, too, come strategies to preserve the remnants of one's life, though the chances of survival are slight. Hunger, humiliation, fear and deep anger at injustice are made tolerable by closely guarded images of loved ones, by religion, by a grim sense of humour and even by glimpses of the healing beauties of nature – a tree or a sunset.

However, these moments of comfort don't establish the will to live unless they help the prisoner to make larger sense out of his or her apparently senseless suffering. It's here that we encounter the central theme of existentialism: *to live is to suffer, to survive is to find meaning in the suffering.* If there is a purpose in life at all, there must be a purpose in suffering and in dying. Each individual has to find out for him or herself what this purpose is and must accept the responsibility that this discovery entails. Frankl is fond of quoting Nietzsche, who claimed that 'He who has a *why* to live can bear with almost any *how*' (italics in original).

In the concentration camp, every circumstance conspires to make the prisoner lose his hold; all the familiar goals in life are snatched away. All that remains is 'the last of human freedoms' – the ability to 'choose one's attitude in a given set of circumstances'. This ultimate freedom, recognised by the ancient Stoics as well as by modern existentialists, enables even 'average men' to rise above their outward fate.

Frankl's logotherapy is aimed at helping people to achieve this distinctively human capacity, to awaken in a patient the feeling of being responsible to life for something, however grim his or her circumstances may be. Unlike many European existentialists, Frankl is neither pessimistic nor antireligious. On the contrary, for a writer who experienced and witnessed such suffering and the forces of evil, he takes a surprisingly hopeful view of the human capacity to transcend our predicament and discover an adequate guiding truth (Allport, 2004).

A similar account of the human capacity for finding a reason to survive the most horrific circumstances is given by the late chemist and author Primo Levi in *If This Is A Man* (1958/1987). What emerges from his account of his time in Auschwitz is 'a sense of Man's worth, of dignity fought for and maintained against all the odds (Bailey, 1987):

Then for the first time we became aware that our language lacks words to express this offence, the demolition of a man. In a moment, with almost prophetic intuition, the reality was revealed to us: we had reached the bottom. It is not possible to sink lower than this; no human condition is more miserable than this, nor could it conceivably be so. Nothing belongs to us any more; they have taken away our clothes, our shoes, even our hair; if we speak, they will not listen to us, and if they listen, they will not understand. They will even take away our name: and if we want to keep it, we will have to find in ourselves the strength to do so, to manage somehow so that behind the name something of us, of us as we were, still remains. (Levi, 1958/1987)

▲ **Figure 8.5** Prisoners in a concentration camp

Prisoner 174517 somehow found the inner strength to retain something of Primo Levi. But he was initially shocked into finding it by the example of others. A key moment was observing his friend, Steinlauf, washing, without soap, without anything to dry himself with, but going through one of the routines of normal life. At first, Levi thought this a pointless exercise, especially as they were all about to die. However, what Levi learnt from watching his friend:

...was the sense, not forgotten either then or later: that precisely because the Lager [camp] was a great machine to reduce us to beasts, we must not become beasts; that even in this place one can survive, and therefore one must want to survive, to tell the story, to bear witness; and that to survive we must force ourselves to save at least the skeleton, the scaffolding, the form of civilisation...We must walk erect, without dragging our feet, not in homage to Prussian [German] discipline but to remain alive, not to begin to die. (Levi, 1958/1987)

Levi, who has confronted the unendurable, couldn't be persuaded that our short time on earth is just a matter of waste disposal (Bailey, 1987).

Chapter summary

- While higher-order consciousness is unique to human beings, it means that we're the only animals aware of our mortality.

- According to Solomon *et al.*, a wide variety of theory and evidence supports the claim that cultural products, including art, language and religion, were created as a solution to the problems associated with death awareness.

- Existentialism is notoriously difficult to define and lacks a common body of doctrine shared by all existentialists. Macquarrie prefers to talk of existentialism as a style of philosophising rather than as a philosophy as such. But some recurring themes which give it a distinctive character are freedom, decision and responsibility (which constitute the core of personal being), finitude, guilt, alienation, despair and death.

- Three of the 'greats' of existentialism are Kierkegaard, Heidegger and Jean-Paul Sartre, but existential thinking is evident in the Western classical era, the European Renaissance and Romantic periods, and many of the arts and popular culture of thetwentieth century.

- Most existentialists subscribe to phenomenology, which Husserl intended as a means of framing in a rigorous way basic concepts in the sciences, arts and humanities. His core philosophical belief was that what appears should be taken as reality: we should begin any investigation with how things are experienced (i.e. the phenomenon).

- Experience comprises a system of interrelated meanings (or *gestalten*) that's bound up in a totality (the 'lifeworld'). The human realm essentially entails embodied, conscious relatedness to a personal world of experience. The natural scientific approach is inappropriate.

- Important existentialist theorists within psychology include Binswanger, Boss, Frankl, Fromm, Horney and Rank, who were also all practising psychiatrists, psychoanalysts or both. Others include the two great 'humanistic' psychologists, Maslow and Rogers.

- More recent examples of existentialist practitioners/theorists include Laing's radical work on schizophrenia during the 1960s and 1970s, Ernest Becker's discussion of 'death terror' and Yalom'sexistential psychotherapy.

- For Yalom, existential psychology attempts to explain how ordinary human beings come to terms with the 'givens of existence', namely fear of death, freedom, existential isolation and meaninglessness.

- All these givens of existence have become the focus of the (relatively) new sub-discipline of experimental existential psychology (or XXP), with fear of death by far the most widely investigated to date. Other existential concerns explored by XXP include identity and questions of how we humans fit into the physical universe, how we relate to nature, and how we come to grips with the physical nature of our own bodies.

- According to Becker, self-awareness is the most important feature that distinguishes human beings from other animals. It's this capacity that sets the stage for the existential terror that led to the development of culture and humankind as we know it today.

- Becker discusses how the 'human condition' manifests itself in different types of mental disorder, including neurosis, such as obsessions and phobias, and psychosis.

- Both James and Zilboorg share Becker's view that the fear of death is universal; Zilboorg also argues that it is an expression of the self-preservation instinct.

- Becker observes that if this fear were constantly conscious, the individual couldn't function: to be able to get on with life, we have to repress it. Consciousness of death is more strongly repressed than sexuality.

- Becker's work addressed two fundamental issues that weren't being given sufficient attention at that time: (a) why people are so intensely concerned with their self-esteem; and (b) why people cling so tenaciously to their own cultural beliefs and have such difficulty coexisting with people from different cultures.

- Terror management theory (TMT), which is central to XXP, claims that both raising self-esteem (self-esteem-as-anxiety-buffer hypothesis) and the clinging to our own cultural beliefs (worldview defence) are ways of dealing with fear of death.

- From the TMT perspective, humankind's history of violent inhumanity to other humans is thus understood as (at least partly) the result of a fundamental inability to tolerate those who doesn't share our death-denying cultural constructions. This is another component of worldview defence.

- Culture provides its members with a sense of meaning, both in this life and beyond, in the form of symbolic and/or literal immortality. Self-esteem refers to the belief that one is a person of value in a world of meaning.

- Symbolic immortality can be obtained by perceiving oneself as part of a culture that endures beyond one's lifetime, or by creating visible testaments to one's existence in the form of great works of art or science, amassing great wealth and having children. Literal immortality is achieved via the various afterlives ('heaven') promised by almost all organised religions.

- A major experimental procedure used to test TMT in general, and specifically the mortality salience (MS) hypothesis, is the MS paradigm.

- Another important TMT hypothesis predicts that it's likely that one of the major motivations underlying the formation and maintenance of close (romantic) relationships is the human need to deny death terror. An extension of this hypothesis predicts that MS should promote the desire for offspring.

- Despite the impressive body of empirical evidence supporting the anxiety-buffering function of worldview validation and self-esteem, some critics claim that TMT has overlooked basic interpersonal processes, such as mate selection and parenting: these have evolved to promote actual survival and can shield against a wide variety of anxieties.

- According to Mukilincer *et al.*, the human needs for communion, belongingness, affiliation, attachment, togetherness and intimacy are subordinate components of the fundamental need for self-preservation and they can serve as protective devices against death terror awareness.

- The maintenance of close relationships fulfils major survival functions, has basic anxiety-reducing properties, meets cultural standards and expectations, is a primary source for the construction of high self-esteem, and offers the promise of symbolic immortality. As a result, close relationships can help protect the individual from death awareness.

- Although TMT hasn't explicitly acknowledged the role of close relationships, the idea that they're an important source of protection, meaning and value can be found in the work of Rank and Becker. Becker, for example, described the adult romantic solution, in which the romantic partner is a primary source of meaning, self-worth and death transcendence. Close relationships are a source of death transcendence in Western culture during the twentieth century, replacing the meanings and values formerly provided by religion.

- In their review of a large body of research into the terror management function of close relationships, Mikulincer *et al.* conclude that the use of close relationships as a terror management mechanism is characteristic of people with a strong sense of self-worth and connectedness to the world.

- While TMT claims to be an evolutionary theory, Kirkpatrick and Navarette argue that it's unlikely that natural selection would have designed a 'survival instinct' or innate 'fear of death', nor an anxiety-reduction system in general, or worldview-defence in particular, to counter such fears.

- Kirkpatrick and Navarette also believe that the results of MS experiments are better explained as by-products of a psychological system of coalitional computation that evolved for a variety of functions, including defence against other humans, that's activated by certain kinds of death-related thoughts.

- Different worldviews clearly vary in the degree to which they effectively combat death anxiety: an examination of non-Western, non-Christian cultures cast further doubt on the claim that worldviews serve the terror management function.

- Batson and Stocks propose that religion, in its various forms, can function to address each of the needs identified by Maslow's hierarchy of needs because each need can raise existential questions. Religion can challenge the individual to transcend all of these needs through subjugation of one's personal needs to a higher cause or purpose.

- For many, including Allport, Malinowski, James, Freud and Jung, the most salient core psychological function of religion is to give life a sense of meaning and purpose.

- Allport replaced his concepts of mature and immature religion with intrinsic and extrinsic, respectively. Batson proposed religion as a quest to complement the latter. Research has shown that the personal benefits of religion are more likely to be associated with a clear sense of meaning and purpose reflected in an intrinsic than a quest approach.

- While Dawkins rejects the question regarding the purpose of life as meaningless, many non-believers still ask themselves the question.

- Piaget believes that the child's artificialism survives in adult atheists' mental representations. Later research suggests that human minds (child and adult) are naturally biased toward teleo-functional reasoning. Paradoxically, our minds have evolved in a way that supports a creationist view of human origins.

- According to Yalom, confronting death can enrich our lives and make us more compassionate. Both Frankl and Levi describe the human capacity for finding a reason to survive the most horrific circumstances imaginable.

Suggested Further Reading

Becker, E. (1973) *The Denial of Death.* New York: Free Press. Pulitzer-prize-winning book, considered a classic of its type, which argues that terror of death is an innate fear which haunts us from birth. A challenging but potentially attitude-changing read.

Greenberg, J., Koole, S.L. & Pyszczynski, T. (eds.) (2004) *Handbook of Experimental Existential Psychology.* New York: The Guilford Press. A collection of 30 original chapters by the pioneers and leading researchers in the still relatively new field of XXP. An essential platform for anyone interested in the experimental study of the human condition.

Yalom, I.D. (2008) *Staring at the Sun: Overcoming the Dread of Death.* London: Piatkus Books. A wonderfully written discussion of how knowledge of our own mortality affects the unconscious mind of every human being. Yalom combines his vast experience as a psychotherapist with his human qualities of compassion and insightfulness to present a degree of comfort in the face of our inevitable demise.

Selected websites

http://www.yalom.com/

Irvin Yalom's website.

http://www.youtube.com/watch?v=mx9RuB3s0dw

Radio interview with Irvin Yalom regarding *Staring at the Sun.* Several links to other interviews regarding his work as a psychotherapist.

http://www.ernestbecker.org/

The Ernest Becker Foundation, which 'seeks to illuminate how the unconscious denial of mortality profoundly influences human behaviour, giving rise to acts of hate and violence as well as noble, altruistic striving'. Includes video material.

Chapter 9: Culture: The crucial feature?

Key questions

- What do we mean by 'culture'?

- Is culture uniquely human?

- What claims have been made for non-human culture?

- What is the relationship between culture and religion?

- What is the relationship between culture and other attributes that have been claimed to be uniquely human, such as language and other symbolic abilities?

- What do cultural differences tell us about how culture developed?

- What is the relationship between culture and the perception of time?

- What is the relationship between culture and morality?

Introduction

Culture – both its nature and its relationship to other contenders for what it is that makes us human – has been a theme running through earlier chapters of this book. In Chapter 1, for example, we noted Dunbar's (2007) claim that '... [it] is in humans' capacity for culture, to live in a world constructed by ideas, that we really differ from the other apes'. This capacity for culture, in turn, is one manifestation of our status as symbolic creatures, with language being the ultimate symbolic activity (Tattersall, 2007).

Language enables us to stand back from the real world and ask if it could have been otherwise than it is. Literature and science, both fundamental features of (Western) culture, are prominent examples of the human ability to imagine different worlds; religion is another example. In Chapter 8, we discussed religion in relation to terror management theory (TMT), where it's given a major role, both as a cultural institution and as a personal belief system. As a cultural institution, religion may represent a major component of cultural worldviews, which provide beliefs about the nature of reality that function to reduce death-related anxiety (the mortality salience/MS hypothesis). The MS hypothesis is, in turn, related to worldview defence (see Chapter 8, page 228).

According to Baron-Cohen (2006), second-order (and other meta-) representations equip us with the ability to imagine and are essential for mind-reading or **theory of mind** (**ToM**) (Baron-Cohen, 1995). In turn, ToM is essential for both face-to-face social interaction and, more broadly, the development and maintenance of culture.

As we also noted in Chapter 5, the making and use of tools were once taken to be defining features of human behaviour. Goodall's pioneering observational studies of wild chimpanzees showed that 'deep chasm' argument to be mistaken (see Chapter 1). Based on de Waal's (2001) definition of culture as 'knowledge and habits [that] are acquired from others', which may explain why 'two groups of the same species may behave differently', many animal species can be regarded as having culture.

However, some 'deep chasm'/exceptionalism theorists remain; these include Malik (2006), who claims that 'All animals have an evolutionary past. Only humans make history' and Blackmore, who challenges Malik's claim by arguing that human brains are inhabited by *memes* (units of culture), which strive to get themselves copied: what makes humans unique is that they are 'meme machines' (e.g. Blackmore, 2007: see Chapter 1).

What do we mean by 'culture'?

> ### Time for reflection
> - How do you understand the term 'culture'?
> - Is it important to distinguish between narrow definitions, that would automatically exclude the possibility of non-human species possessing it, and broader, more inclusive definitions, that would allow for this possibility?

One early definition of culture as 'the human-made part of the environment' (Herskovits, 1955) is narrow and exclusive. While it was meant to contrast human beings' contribution to the environment with that of nature, it implies that non-humans have no culture. The 'human-made' part can be subdivided into:

1. *Objective* aspects (such as tools, roads and radio stations).

2. *Subjective* aspects (such as categorisations, associations, norms, roles and values). Value systems have a significant impact on various other aspects of culture, including child-rearing techniques, patterns of socialisation, identity development, kinship networks, work and leisure, religious beliefs and practices (Laungani, 2007).

As far as objective aspects are concerned, we've already seen how tool making and use are no longer considered uniquely human abilities. While there's no evidence of any non-humans building roads or radio stations, that may (simply) reflect the fact that they don't *need* them. In turn, this may suggest that there's only a quantitative difference between human and non-human culture. Regarding subjective aspects, most of the examples given above are, without question, uniquely human behaviours (many of which are based, directly or indirectly, on language or other symbolic abilities). However, kinship networks are common to all social animals, human and non-human.

What these 'exceptions to the rule' suggest is that, rather than taking the possession of culture as an absolute (a species either has it or it doesn't), we need to specify which aspect(s) of culture we're interested in. Some, like religion, are indisputably uniquely human, while others, such as imitation and other forms of social learning (arguably central to cultural transmission) are evident in chimpanzees and orang-utans as well as humans. These are all discussed in detail below.

For Triandis (1994), as for all cross-cultural and cultural psychologists (see Gross, 2010), culture is an unambiguously human characteristic:

> *Culture is to society what memory is to individuals. In other words, culture includes traditions that tell 'what has worked' in the past. It also encompasses the way people have learned to*

look at their environment and themselves, and their unstated assumptions about the way the world is and the way people should act. (Triandis, 1994).

While culture is made by humans, it also helps to 'make' them: humans have an interactive relationship with culture (Moghaddam *et al.,* 1993).

If we simply define culture as 'the non-genetic spreading of habits' (de Waal, 2001) – and insist that the rest is nothing else than 'embellishment' – or that culture is 'those group-typical behaviour patterns shared by members of a community that rely on socially learned and transmitted information' (Laland and Hoppit, 2003), then a number of species, from birds to whales to elephants and **primates** can be granted membership to the 'culture club' (Hogh-Oleson, 2010).

According to Kendal (2008), there are three key questions we need to ask about culture:

1. Does social learning equate to culture?

2. Do teaching and imitation equate to culture?

3. Do norms and ethnic markers equate to culture?

While question 3 clearly applies only to human culture, questions 1 and 2 can help us determine whether non-humans can truly be said to possess culture. Hopper (2010) observes that in recent years, there's been an explosion in the number of articles written, and conferences held, debating whether non-humans are capable of social learning (with imitation the major form) and, more relevantly here, whether those species that are capable of social learning also display signs of having their own 'cultures'. Kendal's (2008) article, entitled 'Animal "culture wars"', showed how this fascinating question has captured the imagination of both the academic community and the general public. Do non-humans exhibit behavioural traditions that can, in any way, be compared to our own rich and diverse culture? (Hopper, 2010).

Identifying social learning

Kendal (2008) notes that, based on long-term field studies of primates and *cetaceans* (dolphins, whales and porpoises), researchers have observed such diverse behaviours as chimps fishing for termites (see Chapter 5), orang-utans blowing raspberries before bedtime, capuchin monkeys playing bizarre ritualised games, dolphins wearing sponges on their noses while foraging, and humpback whales singing distinctive songs.

> *... In a pattern evocative of human cultural variation, animal populations vary in either the way they perform the behaviour or whether they perform it at all, purportedly due to differences in the spread of learned information between individuals (or social learning).* (Kendal, 2008)

Time for reflection
- Why should psychologists be interested in these examples of animal behaviour?
- What do you think the advantages are for individuals (animal or human) of social learning?
- What might be the evolutionary implications of social learning?

Social learning (SL) affords naive individuals (human or non-human) access to adaptive behaviour invented by more knowledgeable others. As a consequence, individual behaviour is governed by the trade-offs between knowledge obtained by oneself and gained from others. In the former case, time and energy are expended, as well as facing risks, such as encountering toxic foods. In the latter, time, effort, and risks are all reduced, but at the cost of less reliability (Kendal *et al.*, 2005).

There's a vigorous debate amongst psychologists as to whether social and asocial (or individual) learning involve the same underlying cognitive processes and whether evidence for certain forms of SL imply the existence of complex psychological abilities, such as theory of mind (ToM) (see Chapter 4).

As SL can influence survival (e.g. through enhancing foraging) and reproduction (e.g. preferences for exaggerated traits in mates), it also has evolutionary implications. Indeed, it may well have been key in promoting the evolution of intelligence in animals, including humans (Whiten and van Schaik, 2007). Conversely, it's also responsible for the spread of maladaptive behaviours, such as smoking (Kendal, 2008).

Identifying social learning through field work

Time for reflection

- Try to identify the advantages and disadvantages of field work compared with the laboratory experiment.

Box 9.1 Fieldwork (based on Kendal, 2008)

Fieldwork is both time-consuming and difficult, but it's essential if we want to try to understand the selection pressures that promote the evolution of 'culture'. However, evidence from the wild is often indirect and, by the standards used to judge laboratory experiments, lacking rigour.

The predominant **ethnographic method** pioneered by Andrew Whiten (Whiten *et al.*, 1999) involves comparing variation in behavioural traits at multiple sites. Such variation is judged to be cultural if there's no reason to believe that it stems from inter-site genetic or ecological differences. A second approach, involving factorial analyses, provides a quantitative means of evaluating the relative influence of ecological, genetic and social influences on behavioural similarity among individuals.

Such techniques don't (cannot) directly assess whether SL is required to produce the observed pattern of behavioural variation; as a consequence, they leave us open to both over- and underestimating its role. This means that whether behavioural variation in the wild is judged to be cultural is largely a matter of expert opinion; heated debates have taken place, which some (e.g. McGrew, 2002) have gone so far as to describe as 'war'.

The problem with field evidence to date is that it cannot quantify the likelihood that the behavioural traits in question could be learnt without SL being involved. One attempt to overcome this is the 'option bias method', which assumes that, within a group, SL will generate a greater than expected homogeneity in the behavioural options used to solve a task (e.g. the use of a short or long twig). The researchers test whether a group's bias towards one option can be taken as evidence of SL by comparing it to a probability distribution of the bias that would arise under individual learning. As collecting these data in the wild is usually impossible, these probabilities are computed through simulating what is essentially an individual learning (or control) condition. This simulation allows other factors to be considered – other than SL – that may cause a bias (e.g. there could be a bias toward short twigs because they're more readily available in the environment than long ones).

Kendal considers the much-debated example of chimp termite-fishing (or ant-dipping) (see Chapter 5), which is often cited as one of the strongest pieces of evidence for culture in the wild (Whiten *et al.*, 1999: note that one of Whiten's co-researchers is Jane Goodall). At Gombe National Park in Tanzania, chimps insert a long wand into ant nests, withdraw it as the termites swarm upwards, and then run it through their hand forming the ants into a ball that they put in their mouth. In contrast, in the Tai forest of the Ivory Coast a short stick is used which is then pulled directly through the mouth. Why should the Tai chimps use this seemingly less efficient technique when sticks of varying lengths are available at both sites? Could the difference be (purely) cultural?

At a third site, Bossou, researchers discovered that the technique used was correlated with the species of ant being captured (Humle and Matsuzawa, 2002). Using themselves as guinea pigs, they showed that black ants swarm up sticks more aggressively and give more painful bites than red ants. It's not surprising, therefore, that chimps at Bossou use long sticks for black ants and short sticks for red ants.

So, might the different techniques found at Tai and Gombe reflect differing ant species? Schoning *et al.* (2008) compared ant-dipping at 13 African sites. They suggested that variation in techniques cannot be explained by the species of ant present. For Byrne (2006), the issue of how different ant species influence the technique used is irrelevant: the hallmark of culture is intricate complexity of behaviour, and as the skill of ant-dipping is intricate and unlikely to be learnt in its entirety by a solitary chimp, there's an implied role for SL. Byrne's argument is supported by a study by Sanz *et al.* (2009), which is described in Box 9.2.

Box 9.2 A chimpanzee ant-dipping tool set (Sanz *et al.*, 2009)

Several populations of chimps have been reported to prey upon *Dorylus* army ants. The most common tool-using technique used for gathering these ants is with 'dipping' probes, which vary in length in relation to the aggressiveness and lifestyle of the prey species.

Sanz *et al.* report the use of a tool set used in preying on army ants by chimps in the Goualougo Triangle, Republic of Congo. Based on the recovery of 1,060 tools and video-tapes of chimp tool-using behaviour at ant nests, the researchers distinguished two different types of tool, based on their form and function. The chimps use a woody sapling to perforate the nest, and then a herb stem as a dipping tool to harvest the ants.

All of the ant species preyed upon in Goualougo are present and consumed by chimps at other sites, but there are no other reports of such a regular and widespread use of more than one type of tool to prey upon *Dorylus* ants. Furthermore, this tool set differs from other types of tool combinations used by chimps at this site for preying upon termites or gathering honey. Based on these findings, Sanz *et al.* conclude that these chimps have developed a specialised method for preying upon army ants which involves the use of an additional tool for opening nests. However, they say that further research is needed to determine which specific ecological and social factors may have shaped the emergence and maintenance of this technique.

Echoing Sanz *et al.*'s point regarding the need for further research, Kendal (2008) notes that the hard evidence for SL is missing, largely because there are no methods for generating such evidence in the wild. However, other researchers have gone some way to identifying SL more directly in the wild using 'proxy measures', such as patterns of affiliation and observation. For example, there's evidence in both capuchins and chimps that individuals selectively watch others from whom they can learn skills they've yet to master (Biro *et al.*, 2003; Perry *et al.*, 2003). Biro *et al.* took advantage of a natural forest clearing, through which chimps travelled daily, in order to introduce them to novel nuts and observe the spread of any nut-cracking behaviour through the group.

Studies of captive chimps have shown they can sustain foraging traditions, across pseudo-generations, through what Kendal (2008) calls 'high-fidelity' SL (ensuring the behaviour remains unaltered over time). Although these findings add credibility to the belief that SL is behind inter-site variation in behaviour, it doesn't tell us whether SL is implicated in natural behavioural variation.

Does social learning equate to culture?

For many, confidence in the role of SL in behavioural variation is sufficient for the animals in question to be said to have culture (Kendal, 2008). For example, Laland and Janik (2006) state that culture represents 'group-typical behavioural patterns, shared by community members that rely upon socially learned and transmitted information'. They believe that human culture is just a more complex elaboration of similar behavioural processes in non-humans, and understanding these can provide insights into human culture.

According to this view, it might be claimed that the best evidence for culture can be found in fish or rats. They're certainly more experimentally manipulable than primates or cetaceans, as demonstrated by Warner (1988), who showed that mating sites are socially learned in wrasse (a fish species). He did this by exchanging fish, noting that 'immigrants' adopted the traditional mating sites of residents. Similarly, pine-seed eating by rats in Israel, which aids their survival in pine forests, is arguably the strongest demonstration of SL in the wild: rats born to pine-cone stripping mothers, but then fostered by non-pine-stripping rats, failed to learn to access pine seeds, while those born to non-pine-strippers and fostered by strippers did (Terkel, 1996). Further experiments showed that pups merely needed the 'tip-off' of exposure to partially stripped cones to acquire that behaviour.

Apart from ant/termite-fishing discussed above, probably the most frequently cited demonstration of animal culture is sweet potato washing by Japanese macaques. This is discussed in Box 9.3.

Box 9.3 Japanese macaque sweet-potato washing (Kawai, 1965; Kawamura, 1959): culture or tradition?

In 1953, an 18-month-old female macaque (Imo) began to take sand-covered pieces of sweet potato (given to her and the rest of the Koshima troop by researchers) first to a stream, then to the ocean, to wash the sand off the potato pieces before eating them. Most Japanese macaques brush sand off with their hands. About three months after this first happened, Imo's mother and two of her playmates (and then their mothers) began to do the same thing. During the next two years, seven other youngsters also began to wash their potatoes, and within three years of Imo's first potato washing, 40 per cent of the troop was doing it. By 1958, 14 of 15 juveniles and two of 11 adults in the Koshima troop had started washing potatoes (Itani and Nishimura, 1973; Nishida, 1987).

This spread of potato washing behaviour is often explained in terms of naive monkeys observing Imo and others and then imitating them: sweet potato washing is cultural, so it's claimed (Galef, 1992). Consistent with this interpretation is the fact that it was Imo's close associates who learned the behaviour first and their associates directly after that. Also, one property of sweet potato washing that makes it seem a likely candidate for being passed on through imitation is its bizarreness. It's intuitively improbable that so many monkeys could learn the behaviour independently of each other (Galef, 1992).

However, sweet potato washing has been observed in four other human-provisioned troops of Japanese macaques in addition to the Koshima troop (Kawai, 1965); it simply is less unusual a form of behaviour than originally thought. This finding also implies that at least four individuals learned the behaviour independently: Imo wasn't the creative 'genius' that has been suggested by some, and potato washing isn't as improbable a behaviour for monkeys to develop independently as one might imagine. Also, in captivity, individuals of other monkey species learn quite quickly on their own to wash their food when presented with sandy foods and bowls of water (Visalberghi and Fragaszy, 1990).

Another problem with the imitation/culture explanation relates to the time it took for the behaviour to spread within the troop. According to Galef (1992), one sign of SL should be relatively rapid spread, but in fact the spread was 'painfully slow': the average time for acquisition by all the troop members that learned it was two years. Also, the rate of spread didn't increase as the number of users increased. If imitation was the mechanism of transmission, we'd expect an increased rate as more demonstrators/models become available over time. The slow rate is more consistent with individual learning, rather than imitative learning (Galef, 1992; Tomasello, 1999).

Finally, the fact that Imo's friends and relatives were first to learn the behaviour may be due to the fact that they tend to stay close to one another: they very likely went near the water more often during feeding than other troop members, increasing their chances for individual discovery (Tomasello, 1999).

According to Kendal (2008):

> *Even if the case for animal culture is accepted, it is obvious that the consequences of human culture are further reaching than that of non-humans. Human culture has enabled us to drastically alter [the] environment and even walk on the moon; niche construction on an unprecedented scale (Odling-Smee et al., 2003) ...* (Kendal, 2008)

Do teaching and imitation equate to culture?

In asking this question, Kendal (2008) turns to the issue of what might set human culture apart from that of non-humans.

Culture versus traditions

According to Galef (1992):

> *The question of whether animals exhibit culture is part of ... [the] wider debate regarding the relationship between human and animal behaviour and the appropriate way to discuss the complex behaviours of animals.*

Sahlins (1976) views culture as an **emergent property** of only the most complex brains (see Chapter 4). He suggests that 'Culture ... developed in the hominid line about three million years ago' and implies that culture is uniquely human. In contrast, Wilson (1975) has suggested that 'culture, aside from its involvement with language, which is truly unique, differs from animal tradition only in degree'. Galef (1992) classifies Sahlins as a 'splitter' and Wilson as a 'lumper' (corresponding to 'deep chasm' and 'continuity' theorists respectively as discussed in Chapter 1).

Galef describes himself as a splitter. But unlike Sahlins, he distinguishes between different types of traditions (of which culture is an instance) based not on differences in the supposed complexity of vertebrate brains, but on differences in the behavioural processes that support particular traditions. So, what is the difference between **tradition** and culture?

According to Galef (1992), 'traditional' usually describes a behaviour that has both been learned in some way from others and can be passed on to naive individuals. The English word 'tradition' comes from the Latin *traditio* meaning the act of handing something over to another or of delivering up a possession. Consequently, labelling a behaviour 'traditional' implies that social learning of some sort played a part in the acquisition of the behaviour by those who exhibit it.

While some animal behaviourists have proposed that the words 'culture' and 'tradition' are synonymous, this is based on *analogy* rather than *homology*.

Time for reflection

- In evolutionary terms, what do you understand by the terms 'analogy' and 'homology'?
- What do you understand by the term 'convergent evolution' (or **'evolutionary convergence'**)?
- How does their meaning relate to the distinction between culture and tradition?

In evolutionary theory, 'homology' refers to traits inherited by two different organisms from a common ancestor, while 'analogy' denotes a similarity that results from *convergent evolution* – not from common ancestry. (Convergent evolution refers to evolutionary change in two or more unrelated organisms that leads to the independent development of similar adaptations to similar environmental conditions.) More generally, 'homology' conveys a similarity of structure and/or function, while 'analogy' implies a comparison based on similar overt features or characteristics.

An example of a definition that confuses analogy with homology is that of Kummer (1971):

> ... [an] individual's behaviour can also be modified by its mother or by the group in which it is raised. If such social modification spreads and perpetuates a particular variant over many generations, then we have 'culture' in the broad sense in which a student of animals can use the term ... The definition states nothing about the precise mechanism of social modification (because it is unknown in most cases).

For Galef (1992), it's precisely because Kummer's definition 'states nothing about the precise mechanism of social modification' that it's inadequate and misleading: it explicitly accepts as cultural *all* – and any – traditions, i.e. all socially transmitted modifications of behaviour. For example, a scent trail that resulted in many generations of an ant population following the same path each day from nest entrance to feeding ground would be defined as an agent for the propagation of culture. Galef believes that this violates the usual meaning of 'culture'. Animal traditions are *analogs* rather than *homologs* of human culture.

An oft-cited criterion of human culture of relevance here is that it comprises a *repertoire* of behavioural traditions: human cultures are distinguished by the 'suite of traditions' that make them unique (Kendal, 2008). However, it has been claimed that chimp, orang-utan and capuchin monkey communities display unique sets of traditions, relating to activities such as foraging, grooming and retiring for the night (Whiten and van Schaik, 2007). Similarly, sperm whale clans co-existing in the same habitat have unique vocal repertoires that co-vary with distinctive movement strategies (Rendell and Whitehead, 2001).

However, a case study by Lonsdorf *et al.* (2004) may help to clarify the distinction between culture and tradition. The researchers found that chimps that spent more time observing their mothers fishing for termites acquired skills (such as knowing the depth to which their tools needed to be inserted) earlier; however, this applied only to females. While this seems to demonstrate the role of SL in the development of a behaviour, some would claim that termite fishing has little to do with 'culture'. We see that SL in the form of local enhancement (attraction to termite mounds) or emulation (a desire to obtain termites) is functional for chimps and that females learn something of the form of the behaviour (i.e. imitation) too. However, as males apparently learn how to termite fish *independently* of their mothers, 'imitation' would seem not to be necessary for transmission of this behaviour. For some, this warrants the label 'tradition' (as opposed to 'culture'), but, according to Kendal (2008), this distinction is far from clear-cut.

So, what exactly are the defining features of culture?

Teaching, imitation and the cumulative nature of culture
According to Tomasello (1999):

> ... the most distinctive characteristic of human cultural evolution as a process is the way that modifications to an artefact or a social practice made by one individual or group of individuals often spread within the group, and then stay in place until some future individual or individuals make further modifications – and these then stay in place until still further modifications are made ... This process of cumulative cultural evolution works because of a kind of 'ratchet effect': Individual and group inventions are mastered relatively faithfully by conspecifics, including youngsters, which enables them to remain in their new and improved form from within the group until something better comes along.

Similarly, Galef (1992) observes that one of the key differences between human culture and animal tradition is that '... human culture accumulates over generations and can lead to invention and transmission of increasingly complex behaviours'.

According to Hogh-Oleson (2010), other species may have different cultural features, but a distinctive feature of human culture is its *cumulative* nature:

> Behaviours and artifacts are transmitted, modified, and further developed over many generations, leading to more complex artefacts and behaviours ... complex innovations are not invented by individuals, but evolve gradually over many generations.

(There's currently little evidence, in animals, for the gradual accumulation of beneficial modifications to a behaviour (Kendal, 2008; Marshall-Pescini and Whiten, 2008; Richerson and Boyd, 2005). Boesch (2003) claims that nut-cracking in chimps has increased in complexity and efficiency from banging nuts against trees, to using a stone hammer, to additionally using a stone anvil on which the nut is placed, and finally to use of a stone to stabilise the anvil. Also, New Caledonian crows have developed more complex ways of catching caterpillars using tools made from leaves, moving from simple step-shaped tools to those with a thick handle and tapering tip (Hunt and Gray, 2003: see Chapter 5).

However, both these examples merely record diversity of behaviour, *consistent* with cumulative evolution, rather than actually monitoring the accumulation of modifications through SL. In order to claim that chimps and New Caledonian crows possess culture, we need to demonstrate that these behaviours can only arise in individuals through interaction with conspecifics, rather than independently through interaction with the physical environment.

The ontogeny of human cultural learning

According to Tomasello (1999), the major part of the 'ratchet' in the cumulative evolution of human societies takes place during childhood: each new generation of children develops in the 'ontogenetic niche' characteristic of its culture, mastering the artefacts and social practices that exist at that time. This is echoed in the theory of cognitive development proposed by the Russian psychologist, Lev Vygotsky (see Box 9.4).

Box 9.4 The child as apprentice (Vygotsky, 1962, 1981)

According to Vygotsky's *social constructivist* account, child development doesn't occur in a vacuum: knowledge is constructed as a result of the child's active interaction with the social and cultural environment. As Schaffer (2004) says:

> *Human nature cannot be described in the abstract; whatever course children's mental growth takes is to a large extent a function of the cultural tools that are handed down to them by other people.*

So, cognitive development is a thoroughly *social* process. Vygotsky's aim was to spell out and explain how the higher mental functions (reasoning, understanding, planning, remembering and so on) arise out of the child's social experiences. He did this by considering human development in terms of three levels: the *cultural, interpersonal* and *individual.*

At the cultural level, children don't need to 'reinvent the world anew'; they can benefit from the accumulated wisdom of previous generations. Indeed, they cannot avoid doing so through interactions with caregivers. So, each generation stands on the shoulders of the previous one, taking over the particular culture – including its intellectual, material, scientific and artistic achievements – in order to develop it further before handing it on, in turn, to the next generation (Schaffer, 2004). *Cultural tools* are what the child 'inherits'.

Time for reflection

- Can you think of examples of cultural tools that might be especially important for children's cognitive – and social – development (especially the last and current generations)?

Cultural tools can be (a) *technological* (computers, clocks, bicycles and other physical devices); (b) *psychological* (concepts and symbols, such as language, literacy, maths and scientific theories); and (c) *values* (such as speed, efficiency and power). It's through such tools that children learn to conduct their lives in socially effective and acceptable ways, as well as understanding how the world works. Schaffer (2004) gives the example of computers as a major – and relatively recent – cultural tool:

> *There are few instances in history where a new technical invention has assumed such a dominant role in virtually all spheres of human activity as the computer ... in the space of just a few decades computing expertise is regarded as an essential skill for even quite young children to acquire.* (Schaffer, 2004)

For Vygostksy, writing long before the invention of the computer (his works were originally published in the former Soviet Union in the 1920s and 1930s and not translated into English until the early 1960s), language represented the pre-eminent means of passing on society's accumulated knowledge. How others speak and what they speak about is the main channel of communicating culture from adult to child. Language enables children to regulate their own activities.

It's at the *interpersonal* level that culture and the individual meet, and this is where Vygotsky made his major contribution (see Gross, 2010).

According to Tomasello (1999):

> *... It is only because human children are so good at social learning (and in some cases adults are so good at teaching) that an artefact or social practice may conserve its form over many generations of stasis, until eventually a modification that group members find worthwhile is made and the cycle starts anew. For this process to work, therefore, human beings not only need to be inventive, they need to be good at preserving those inventions by imitatively learning, and sometimes explicitly teaching, the inventions of others ...*

As Goodall (1973) says, whether behaviours may be considered to have been influenced by culture 'depends on the manner in which they were acquired by the individual, i.e. the kind of learning process involved'. This is her way of making the culture/tradition distinction (see above): only behaviour acquired through specific SL processes can be described as illustrating 'culture', namely teaching and imitation (Galef, 1992; Goodall, 1973; Tomasello, 1999). By contrast, animal traditions are generally a result of such processes as 'local enhancement' ('apparent imitation resulting from directing the animal's attention to a particular object or to a particular part of the environment': Thorpe, 1963) or 'social facilitation' (the energising of responses as the result of the simple presence of conspecifics: Clayton, 1978; Zajonc, 1965: see Gross, 2010). These are quite different from behavioural mechanisms underlying human cultural evolution.

The complexity of imitation

In discussing termite 'fishing' at Gombe National Park (see page 256), Goodall (1986) has suggested that infant chimps learn the tool-using patterns of the community 'through a mixture of social facilitation, observation, imitation, and practice – with a good dose of trial and error thrown in'. However, her account is often reduced by others (Bonner, 1980; McFarland, 1985) to the claim that learning by imitation and 'culture' are responsible either for the development of termite fishing generally or for development of the variations found in different chimp communities.

Contrary to some of the evidence discussed above (see Box 9.2), Galef (1992) cites studies that point to the influence of both the behaviour of different species of insect prey and differences in the availability of materials used as probes. For example, the genus of termite that the Gombe chimps fish for is absent from the main study area at Mahale, where the termites produce a distasteful defensive secretion that protects them from chimp predation (Collins and McGrew, 1987; Nishida and Uehara, 1980). We therefore don't need 'tradition' to explain the fact that Gombe chimps fish for termites while Mahale chimps don't.

On the other hand, there is no currently available ecological explanation for the observation that Gombe chimps are more likely to use both ends of a probe before discarding it compared with chimps at Assirik in Senegal (West Africa) or that only Assirik chimps peel the bark from twigs used as probes (McGrew *et al.*, 1979). However, the lack of an ecological explanation for locale-specific behaviours does not justify the inference that they reflect learning through imitation (Tomasello, 1990). Even if, as Goodall (1986) claims, imitation is involved in the acquisition of locale-specific behaviour such as peeling bark from a termite probe, it's not sufficient on its own to explain it. Teleki (1974) spent several months carefully observing Gombe chimps' termite fishing but was unable to locate tunnel entrances or select appropriately rigid twigs or grasses as probes. This suggests that there's more to reproducing such skills than just observation/imitative learning (Galef, 1992).

Similarly, Tomasello (1999) argues that imitative learning is more complex than it might seem at first glance. In relation to human children, he says that:

> ... *Imitative learning does not just mean mimicking the surface structure of a poorly understood behaviour, the way a parrot mimicks human speech, with no understanding of its communicative significance, it also means reproducing an instrumental act understood intentionally, that is reproducing not just the behavioural means but also the intentional end for which the behavioural means was formulated. This requires some specially adapted skills of social cognition.*

Unlike the young of any other primate species, human children grow up in the midst of the accumulated wisdom of their social group (see Box 9.3. above); children are specifically adapted to make use of this wisdom. As we've seen, human children grow up in the 'ontogenetic niche' of their culture, which, in a sense, exists before they're born. But children also need to have certain social cognitive skills if they are to exploit the pre-existing cultural resources in a species-typical manner (Tomasello, 1999). These skills cannot simply be taken-for-granted, as demonstrated by autistic children's lack of a theory of mind/ToM (see Chapter 4).

Typically, however, starting at about 12 months, infants begin to imitatively learn the use of all kinds of tools, artefacts and symbols. Some examples are described in Box 9.5.

Box 9.5 The complexity and sophistication of imitative learning

In a study by Meltzoff (1988a), 14-month-old infants observed an adult bend at the waist and put its head against a panel, thereby turning on a light. The infants reproduced this rather unusual and awkward behaviour – even though it would have been easier and more natural for them simply to push the panel with their hand. One interpretation of this behaviour is that infants understood that (a) the adult had the goal of turning on the light and then chose one means of achieving this from among other possible means; and (b) if they had the same goal, they could choose the same means. According to Tomasello (1999):

> **Box 9.5** *Continued*
>
> *... Cultural learning of this type thus relies fundamentally on infants' tendency to identify with adults, and on their ability to distinguish in the actions of others the underlying goal and the different means that might be used to achieve it ...*

This interpretation is supported by a further study (Meltzoff, 1995), which found that 18-month-old infants also imitatively learned actions that adults intend to perform – even if they were unsuccessful in doing so. Similarly, Carpenter *et al.* (1998) found that 16-month-old infants imitatively learned from a complex behavioural sequence only those behaviours that appear intentional, ignoring those that appear accidental. Young children don't just mimic the limb movements of other people, they attempt to reproduce others' *intended* actions in the world.

Imitation and language

Although it is not obvious at first glance, something like this same imitative learning process must take place if children are to learn the symbolic conventions of their native language (see Chapter 6). While it's often assumed that children acquire language as adults stop what they're doing, hold up objects, and name these objects for them, such linguistic 'lessons' (a) are given only by some parents in some cultures; and (b) are only given for concrete nouns and some actions. In general, for the vast majority of words in their language, children must find a way to learn in the ongoing flow of social interaction, sometimes from speech not even addressed to them (Brown, 1999).

Tomasello (1999) cites his own research which captures some aspects of this process. Studies have shown that, as children learned words in situations in which the adult wasn't specifically intending that they learn a word, the referent wasn't perceptually available when the word was said. In addition, there were multiple potential referents in the situation that the child had to choose among based on various kinds of adult social-pragmatic cues. For example, an adult announced her intention to 'dax Mickey Mouse' and then proceeded to perform one action accidentally and another intentionally (or sometimes in reverse order). Children learned the word for the intentional, not the accidental action, regardless of which came first in the sequence (Tomasello and Barton, 1994).

Tomasello *et al.* (1993a) call this kind of imitative learning *cultural learning*: the child isn't just learning things from other people, he or she is learning things *through* them, in the sense that he or she must know something of the adult's perspective on a situation in order to be able to learn the active use of this same intentional act. The adult in studies like that of Tomasello and Barton isn't just moving and picking up objects randomly; the child must know this to make enough sense of the adult's behaviour to connect the new word to the adult's intended referent:

> *... The main theoretical point is that an organism can engage in cultural learning of this type only when it understands others as intentional agents, like the self, who have a perspective on the world that can be followed into, directed, and shared. Indeed, a strong argument can be made that children can only understand a symbolic convention in the first place if they understand their communicative partner as an intentional agent with whom one may share attention – since a linguistic symbol is nothing other than a marker for an inter-subjectively shared understanding of a situation ...* (Tomasello, 1999)

As a point of comparison, children with autism *don't* understand other people as intentional agents, or they do so only to a very limited degree. They do poorly at imitative learning of intentional actions in general (Smith and Bryson, 1994). Only half of them ever learn any language at all, and those that do perform poorly in word-learning situations such as those described above (Baron-Cohen *et al.*, 1997). Non-human primates aren't very human-like in these kinds of social-cognitive and cultural learning skills either (Tomasello, 1999).

Enculturated apes and deferred imitation

According to Galef (1992), evidence of an ability of chimps (or other primates) to learn novel behaviours by observing and then imitating their fellow primates is surprisingly limited, almost entirely anecdotal, and probably irrelevant to understanding the spread of goal-directed behaviours like fishing for insects.

Based on his studies of problem-solving by chimps in captivity (see Chapter 5), Köhler (1925) emphasised two limits on their imitation of meaningful acts: (a) the chimps have to be able to perceive the crucial relationships leading to the solution of a problem; and (b) naive chimps cannot simply copy movements made by a skilled chimp. In other words, chimps in problem-solving situations imitate only what Köhler called the *substance* of an action (the purpose of the sequence of actions), rather than its *form* (the movements themselves). According to Galef (1992), it's hard to imagine a situation in which observation is less likely to lead to 'perception of crucial relationships' or in which the 'substance' of an action would be more obscure than it is in termite fishing.

Consistent with Köhler's interpretation, Tomasello *et al.* (1987) found that naive chimps that observed a trained chimp use a rake to reach food outside its cage were more likely to learn to use the rake for the same purpose than were naive chimps that lacked the observational experience. However, the observer chimps didn't use the same motor patterns as the trained chimp had used. Acquisition of the motor patterns needed to obtain food efficiently was the result of individual trial-and-error learning. Relating this to the wild:

> ... it seems intuitively improbable that each chimpanzee discovers for itself the effectiveness of using twigs or blades of grass to fish in termite mounds for food. It is, however, easy to underestimate the complexity of the motor patterns that infant chimpanzees develop in the course of their unrewarded (playful) interactions with the environment ... (Galef, 1992)

However, there are a number of convincing reports of chimp imitation; significantly, though, these tend to involve chimps that have had extensive amounts of human contact (i.e. *enculturated apes*). Box 9.6 describes **enculturation**.

Box 9.6 What is enculturation?

'Enculturation' describes the process whereby animals, particularly apes, are reared by human caregivers in an intensive environment resembling the upbringing of a human infant (Hopper, 2010). The classic example is that of Vicki, the chimp raised by psychologists Keith and Catherine Hayes in their home during the 1950s. This took the form of intentional instruction involving human encouragement of behaviour and attention, and even direct reinforcement for imitation for many months. This raises the possibility that imitative learning skills may be influenced, or even enabled, by certain kinds of social interaction during early development (Tomasello, 1999).

According to Tomasello *et al.* (1993a), in order to be able to imitate, an individual must be able to understand the intentions of the demonstrator being observed. In order for chimps to be capable of this perspective-taking, they must be raised in a human-oriented environment. Specifically:

> ... *chimpanzees enculturated by human beings seem to show more sophisticated skills of perspective-taking ... enculturated chimpanzees have been subjected to what Vygotsky calls the 'socialisation of attention': They have been raised in an environment in which joint attention to objects is a regular and important part of their social lives with their human caregivers.*
> (Tomasello et al., 1993a)

The imitative ability described by Tomasello *et al.* (1993a) refers to chimps matching the behaviours of human demonstrators, not other chimps; for this reason, other researchers, including Hopper (2010), take issue with their view. As imitation has been shown in species as varied as rats, pigeons and Japanese quail, 'the responsible mechanism is not likely to be theory of mind or perspective taking' (Zentall, 2001: see Chapter 4).

Nonetheless, Hopper (2010) acknowledges that the few experimental studies of **deferred imitation**, most of which have involved enculturated animals, tend to support Tomasello *et al.*'s (1993a) view.

Time for reflection

- What do you understand by the term 'deferred imitation'?
- Is it likely to involve different underlying cognitive processes compared with (immediate) imitation?
- How might deferred imitation be important in relation to the transmission of traditions and/or culture?

Courage and Howe (2002) defined deferred imitation as 'the ability to reproduce a previously witnessed action or sequence of actions in the absence of current perceptual support for the actions'. Instead of copying what's currently occurring, the individual repeats the act sometime after he or she first observed it. Deferred imitation is of particular importance because it may reveal a more complex underlying cognitive process: the individual has to be able to both retain the information and recall it later, allowing her to reproduce the behaviour. Indeed, it's been proposed that deferred imitation may not only shed light on mental representations and long-term memory, but also on how such information is perceived and encoded (Hopper, 2010: see Chapter 7). In addition:

Deferred imitation is vital to the transmission of behaviours and development of traditions because it allows for actions to be reproduced by individuals at a different time and location from when and where they were first witnessed ... (Hopper, 2010)

Hopper calls this '**horizontal**' transmission.

Tomasello *et al.* (1993b) compared the imitative learning abilities of mother-reared captive chimps, enculturated chimps (raised like human children and exposed to a language-like system of communication), and two-year-old human children. Each subject/participant was shown 24 different and novel actions on objects, and each was scored as to whether their behaviour successfully reproduced (a) the end result of the demonstrated action and/or (b) the behavioural means used by the demonstrator/model. The main finding was that the mother-reared chimps hardly reproduced either (a) or (b), that is, they hardly imitatively learned them at all. In contrast, the enculturated chimps and the human children imitatively learned the novel actions much more often – and to an equal extent. This finding is supported by an earlier study, in which the same enculturated chimps acquired many human-language-like symbols through imitative learning (Savage-Rumbaugh, 1990: see Chapter 6).

What are the implications of these findings for chimp culture in the wild? Tomasello (1999) asks which group of captive chimps is more representative of chimps in their natural habitats: mother-reared or enculturated? Are enculturated chimps simply displaying more species-typical imitative learning skills because their more enriched rearing conditions more closely resemble those of wild chimps than do the impoverished rearing conditions of other captive chimps? Or might the human-like socialisation process experienced by enculturated chimps differ significantly from the natural state, such that it helps to create a set of species-*atypical* abilities more like those of humans? While there can be no definitive answer, it's possible that a human-like sociocultural environment is an essential component in the development of human-like social-cognitive and imitative learning skills – regardless of the species. A human child raised in an environment that lacks intentional interactions and other cultural characteristics would most likely not develop human-like skills of imitative learning. Tomasello concludes that captive mother-reared chimps are a better model for wild chimps than are enculturated chimps, because wild chimps receive little in the way of direct instruction from other chimps.

Is there any evidence that would challenge Tomasello's conclusion? This is discussed in Box 9.7.

Box 9.7 Can non-humans teach?

According to Barnett (1968), to identify teaching we need to establish two things: 'first, the behaviour of the putative teacher must induce a specific change in the behaviour of another ..., second, the teacher's behaviour must be persisted in, and perhaps, adapted, until the pupil achieves a certain standard of performance'.

As far as we know, no non-human animal teaches in Barnett's sense of the term (Galef, 1992). Even adult chimps rarely handle objects in such a way as to engage the attention of infants (Bard and Vauclair, 1984), although Boesch (1991) would argue otherwise. Most claims of teaching among animals are restricted to a few observations (mostly of primates) either preventing infants or juveniles from making contact with potentially dangerous objects (Goodall, 1973; Kawamura, 1959; Menzel, 1966; Nishida *et al.,* 1983) or 'encouraging' an infant to walk by moving a short distance from it and

---

> **Box 9.7** *Continued*
>
> then standing still (Altmann, 1980; Milton, 1988). In the former case, the effectiveness of the adults' behaviour has never been assessed; in the latter, there's no evidence that the adults are teaching.
>
> Galef (1992) agrees with others (e.g. Hinde, 1971; Premack, 1991) who reject such observations as evidence of teaching in non-human animals. However, Thornton and McAuliffe (2006) describe what they consider to be evidence of teaching among meerkats.
>
> It follows from Tomasello's (1999) conclusion regarding the lack of direct teaching among chimps, that the learning skills they develop in the wild (i.e. skills involving individual learning supplemented by emulation learning and ritualisation) are sufficient to create and maintain their species-typical 'cultural' activities (traditions), but they aren't sufficient for human-like cultural activities displaying the ratchet effect and cumulative cultural evolution.

In advocating a strict distinction between tradition and culture (see above), Zihlman and Bolter (2004) claim that the defining feature of culture proper is the transmission of knowledge through symbols with an abstract reference. This allows cultural learning to take place *without the physical presence of living models.* In this view, 'imitative learning' takes on a whole new significance, or, rather, it loses its significance. Perhaps some kind of 'immersion' (in the culture) might be the key learning process (through books, computers, the arts and so on).

Do norms and ethnic markers equate to culture?

Kendal (2008) cites E.B. Tyler, the founder of cultural anthropology, who proposed that culture includes the regulation of individual behaviour (law) and the development of a symbolic reinforcement apparatus for that regulation (religion and morals: see later in this chapter). She states that seemingly arbitrary, non-functional traits acquire moral significance such that a group is defined by the trait and inter-group competition is based upon differences in this 'symbolic ethnic marker'. She gives the example of the 'uniforms' adopted by football supporters and the abuse some suffer because of it:

> *So, in humans one 'culture' does not simply view another culture's behaviour as different to theirs but often, in some sense wrong. There is currently little evidence that, for example, capuchins attempting to remove fruit from a husk by pounding it, are morally outraged at the sight of others scrubbing their fruit such that they punish these deviant 'scrubbers'...* (Kendal, 2008)

In other words, human culture helps to create an 'us and them' mentality: those who are seen as different are (typically) judged as behaving 'inappropriately', even 'unnaturally'. We perceive the world through the lens of our own cultural worldview (see Chapter 8), which serves to define 'normality' (see Gross, 2009) and provides us with a sense of identity. None of these things seems to apply to non-humans. Whiten *et al.* (1999) have documented the, apparently non-functional, hand-clasp of wild chimps during grooming. However, the spontaneous spread of this behaviour in a captive group indicated that the behaviour symbolises a close relationship between the groomers rather than being a candidate for a symbol of group identity (Bonnie and de Waal, 2006). Similarly, Perry *et al.* (2003) reported many bizarre rituals amongst wild capuchins, including inserting fingers into each other's nostrils and other ritualised games. Although initially the researchers believed these rituals may signal group identity, on closer inspection this turned out not to be the case.

Imitation and mimetics: Are we just meme machines?

The American developmental psychologist, Andrew Meltzoff (1988b), has dubbed us *Homo imitans*; the British psychologist, Susan Blackmore (2007) claims that 'To be human is to imitate'. While these two writers may seem to be making very similar claims, in fact they're radically different: Meltzoff's focus is on the infant's ability to reproduce other people's behaviour (such as their facial expressions), while Blackmore (1999) regards humans as 'meme machines' (a claim she acknowledges to be both strong and contentious: Blackmore, 2007).

Universal Darwinism

According to Blackmore (2010), the idea of natural selection acting on **genes** isn't the only way of applying evolutionary theory to the mind (see Chapter 2). The process of natural selection can be thought of as a simple algorithm (i.e. a set of precise rules or instructions that can predict a precise outcome from a known starting point): if you have variation, selection, and heredity, then you must get evolution. This means that evolution can work on anything that is varied and selectively copied; that is, you can have other replicators (apart from genes) and other evolutionary systems. In *The Selfish Gene* (1976), Dawkins calls this principle 'Universal Darwinism'.

As Darwin (1859) first pointed out, if you have creatures that vary, and if most of them die, and if the survivors pass on to their offspring whatever it was that helped them survive, then most offspring must, on average, be better adapted to the environment in which that selection took place than their parents were. It's the inevitability of this process that makes it such an elegant and beautiful explanation of the origins of biological design (Blackmore, 2007).

The selfish gene and the selfish meme

However, this evolutionary process shouldn't be confined to biology. As we've seen, according to the 'evolutionary algorithm', given variation, selection and heredity, you *must* get evolution: this is a simple, mindless procedure which produces 'Design out of Chaos without the aid of Mind' (Dennett, 1995). Dawkins (1976) coined the term 'replicator' to refer to the information that is copied with variations or errors; its nature influences its own probability of replication. The most familiar replicators are genes, which build themselves machines (Dawkins, 1976) or interactors (Hull, 1988) in the form of bodies that protect the genes and transport them.

While individual bodies die, the replicators are copied reasonably intact through successive replications and are the ultimate beneficiary of the evolutionary process. It's in this sense that genes are selfish: they will be copied and proliferate if they can, without concern for the organism that carries them, or indeed for anything else, unless it affects their own chances of being copied. In explaining Universal Darwinism, Dawkins wanted to break people's habit of thinking only about genes, and so he proposed a new replicator: whenever people copy skills, habits, or behaviours through imitation of others, a new replicator is at work:

> *We need a name for the new replicator, a noun that conveys the idea of a unit of cultural transmission, or a unit of* imitation. *'Mimeme' comes from a suitable Greek root, but I want a monosyllable that sounds a bit like 'gene'. I hope my classicist friends will forgive me if I abbreviate mimeme to* meme *... Examples of memes are tunes, ideas, catch-phrases, clothes, fashions, ways of making pots or of building arches.* (Dawkins, 1976; emphasis in original.)

Other examples given by Dawkins are popular songs, stiletto heels, the idea of God and Darwinism. So, the literal meaning of 'meme' is 'that which is imitated'. A meme is a *cultural* (as distinct from a *biological*) replicator, a 'unit of cultural transmission'. **Memetics** refers to the scientific study of memes (Blackmore, 1999).

Time for reflection

● Other examples include gestures and games, urban myths and financial and political institutions, scientific theories (and whole sciences), and complex technologies (Blackmore, 2007).

● How do these examples relate to the subjective and objective aspects of Herskovits' (1955) 'human-made part of the environment'? (See above.)

Box 9.8 Memeplexes, selfplexes and viral memes (based on Blackmore, 2007, 2010)

● The examples that Blackmore gives above aren't simple memes but 'co-adapted meme-complexes' or **'memeplexes'**, that is, groups of memes that fare better together than they would individually. For this reason, they tend to stick together, and get copied and passed on together. Memeplexes range from small groups of words, such as sentences and stories, to religions and works of art.

● A sub-group of memeplexes are **selfplexes**, a memeplex formed when people use language that includes references to the self. Sentences such as 'I believe X', 'I think Y', and 'In my opinion, Z is ...' are preferable to simply stating X, Y and Z, because they create the (false) belief that there is an 'I' (or 'me') who has the beliefs and opinions. In this way, the memes are spread.

● Some memes succeed because they're true or useful or beautiful, while **viral memes** succeed by using various tricks to persuade people to copy them. Viral memes include chain letters, email viruses and ineffective diets and therapies. Dawkins (1976) refers to religions as 'viruses of the mind': they infect people by using threats and promises, as well as tricks such as rewarding faith and discouraging doubt (see Chapter 8 and later in this chapter).

Memes are copied by imitation, teaching and reading, photocopying and all the computer and other digital technology that's so much a feature of modern life. Sometimes the copies are perfect, but not always. For example, when we mis-remember something or forget it, or when old memes are combined in new ways that produce new memes:

> *... This means that the whole of human culture can be seen as a vast new evolutionary process based on memes, and human creativity can be seen as analogous to biological creativity. On this view, biological creatures and human inventions are both designed by the evolutionary algorithm. Human beings are the meme machines that store, copy and recombine memes ...* (Blackmore, 2010)

Blackmore (2007) claims that memetics provides the best explanation of what makes us human (see Chapter 1). It can help account for many aspects of human behaviour and evolution, including the origins of our large brains (see Chapter 3) and, perhaps more importantly, abilities and characteristics that the brain equips us with and which have been claimed as uniquely human – in particular – language (see Chapter 6) and consciousness (see Chapter 4).

Is culture just a collection of memes?

According to Blackmore (2007):

> *What makes us human? In the beginning it was imitation and the appearance of memes. Now it is the way we work as meme machines, living in the culture that the memes have used us to build.*

She asks if it is depressing to think of ourselves in this way – as machines created by the competition between genes and memes, and in turn creating more genes and memes. She doesn't think so:

> *... We have got used to the idea that we need no God to explain the evolution of life, and that we humans are part of the natural world. Now we have to take a step further in the same direction and change yet again the way we think about ourselves, our consciousness and free will ... But this is precisely what makes it so exciting being human – that as meme machines we can, and must, reflect on our own nature.* (Blackmore, 2007)

However, not everyone agrees. Blackmore (2007) herself acknowledges that after more than thirty years, memetics is still not a thriving science. She lists a number of reasons for this.

1. There are legitimate criticisms of memetics and many difficulties to be overcome (Aunger, 2000; Distin, 2005; Jablonka and Lamb, 2005).

2. There are repeated misunderstandings which cause people to abandon memetic explanations, such as thinking that memes must always exist as units, thinking that memetic inheritance is Lamarckian (i.e. evolution occurs through *acquired* characteristics passed from parent to offspring) and so cannot occur, or thinking of memes as some kind of entity that may or may not exist rather than as the actual songs, stories or whatever is copied (Aunger, 2000; Midgley, 2000; Richerson and Boyd, 2005).

3. Some writers seem to find memetics deeply unsettling in the way that it undermines free will and the power of human creativity and consciousness (Donald, 2001; Midgley, 2000). Blackmore maintains that fear is not a good reason for rejecting any theory and that memetics provides the best explanation of what makes us human.

If Blackmore is saying that culture is what makes us human, then there are many who would agree with her. However, many cannot accept claims such as the following:

> *Instead of thinking of our ideas as our own creations, and working for us, we have to think of them as autonomous selfish memes, working only to get themselves copied ...* (Blackmore, 1999)

Since 'we cannot find either beliefs or the self that believes' by looking into somebody's head, she argues, so we must conclude that there are no such things as beliefs or selves, 'only a person arguing, a brain processing the information, memes being copied or not'.

According to Malik (2006), the trouble with arguments like these is that, by their own criteria, they provide us with no reasons for believing in them:

> *... From an evolutionary point of view, truth is contingent. Darwinian processes are driven by the need, not to ascertain truth, but to survive and reproduce. Of course, survival often requires organisms to have correct facts about the world. A zebra that believed that lions were friendly, or a chimpanzee that enjoyed the stench of rotting food, would not survive for long.*

But although natural selection often ensures that an organism possesses the correct facts, it does not always do so. Indeed, the argument that self-consciousness and agency are illusions designed by natural selection relies on the idea that evolution can select for untruths about the world because such untruths aid survival. (Malik, 2006)

Malik is saying that the logic of Blackmore's argument undermines our confidence in its own truth: if we are simply sophisticated animals or machines, then we cannot have any confidence in the claim that we are only sophisticated animals or machines (i.e. the claim is unreliable because it is made by mere machines!). Humans are only able to do science 'because we possess the capacity to transcend our evolutionary heritage, because we exist as subjects, rather than simply as objects'. The relationship between humans as physically determined beings (humans as objects) and humans as conscious agents (humans as subjects) is clearly one of the most difficult problems for both scientists and philosophers (see Gross, 2009). We currently have no conceptual framework for considering such an ontological peculiarity, but denying one or the other aspect of our humanness isn't a way of solving the conundrum. What makes humans 'exceptional' is this 'dual character' of being simultaneously both object and subject of scientific enquiry – both the scientist and what is being investigated (Malik, 2006).

Malik puts this another way:

... human nature is not simply natural ... On the one hand, human nature means that which expresses the essence of being human, what Darwinists call 'species-typical' behaviour. On the other hand, it means that which is constituted by nature; in Darwinian terms, that which is the product of natural selection.

In non-human animals the two meanings are synonymous, but this isn't necessarily true of humans. Much of the preceding chapters have been concerned with trying to determine just what can be considered human species-specific abilities and behaviours. However, unlike non-humans,

... humans ... can also forge universal values and behaviours through social interaction and historical progress. In this sense the human essence – what we consider to be the common properties of our humanity – is as much a product of our historical and cultural development as it is of our biological heritage ... Being both social and rational means that the common social goals, opportunities and constraints are often tackled in a similar fashion in different societies. (Malik, 2006)

According to Høgh-Oleson (2010), culture is sharing by learning, and human culture differs from those of non-humans in what it is that can be shared:

... a substantial part of human culture (from religion and marriage to the latest hip thing in fashion) consists of 'social constructions', which cannot be reduced beyond the common intentional states and agreements of the individuals making up these forms (Plotkin, 2007). A sum of Euros is not just a unit of currency, it is also an agreement among a group of individuals to use it as the basis for trading relationships, and such imagined worlds and symbolic tokens, made real by collective agreements only, are not seen in other species.
(Høgh-Oleson, 2010)

Morality: Culture's support system for individuals

As Høgh-Oleson (2010) observes, morality stems from the fact that, as social creatures, we are each other's means to common goals, and hence rely on a support system for our survival. A solitary organism has no need for moral rules, nor does a creature that lives among others without mutual dependency.

The fact that many of our highest moral impulses are rooted in our mammalian and primate sociality and based on spontaneous, emotional intuitions and 'gut feelings', rather than 'pure reason' (see Chapter 3), doesn't exclude the possibility that some of our moral choices may be both exclusively human and strictly rational (Høgh-Oleson, 2010). A much-cited example is the trolley dilemma, as shown in Figure 9.1.

Time for reflection

● In Figure 9.1 below, you are asked to choose between (a) pressing a shift that will lead a runaway trolley from one track, where it would have killed five innocent people, to another track, where only one innocent person will be killed (i.e. sacrificing one to save five); and (b) pushing this person onto the track yourself (still sacrificing one to save five).

● Which would you choose – and why?

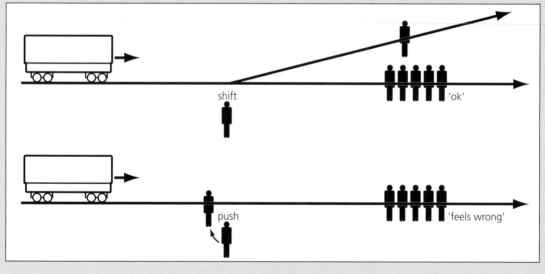

▲ Figure 9.1 The trolley dilemma

A clear majority presented with the trolley dilemma flatly refuses to push the person onto the tracks themselves: it simply 'feels wrong'. A fMRI scan of participants' brains showed that several old mammalian brain areas (more specifically the Precuneus area: see Chapter 3) were activated during this kind of problem-solving situation (Greene and Haidt, 2002). This supports the claim that substantial parts of our morality may be anchored in mammalian sociality (Høgh-Oleson, 2010). However, those who opted for (b) took longer to decide and showed more activity in prefrontal brain areas, indicating that they engaged in more cognitive processing before making their decision:

... this morally rational choice, in which higher cognitive processes apparently overrule more basic programs, could be an example of a moral choice, which no other social animal than us would be able to make! (Høgh-Oleson, 2010)

Høgh-Oleson gives examples of what he describes as an organising 'top-down' control over some of our basic impulses:

● a child choosing to inhibit the spontaneous crying reflex when hurt until others who can comfort it are visible

● a monk choosing celibacy

● a mountaineer overruling basic needs for body temperature, oxygen and food in order to climb Mount Everest.

So, some of our basic needs/impulses aren't so basic after all! We're motivated by 'ought to' and 'should' to lead lives governed by principles and values so important that they're worth dying for, and to strive to be impartial, courageous, responsible, honest, unselfish, and so on. Similarly, we can be tormented by complex, self-reflective emotions such as shame and guilt when we fail to live up to our standards. All of these things distinguish us from non-humans.

Apes may sometimes be helpful, caring, and brave, but that is not because they think they should be, and that is a crucial difference ... Our neo-cortical superstructures have given us the ability to consider and reflect on any number of different scenarios for the future, and that gives us, as probably the only creatures, the ability to see before our mind's eye the world as it could be. (Høgh-Oleson, 2010) (emphasis in original.)

According to Malik (2006), while our *capacity* for moral thought is most likely an evolved trait, this isn't the same as saying that *values* are natural. Take the question of slavery and the idea of equal human worth. For most of human history slavery has been regarded as natural as individual freedom is today. Only in the past 200 years have we begun to view the practice with revulsion. This has happened partly because of the political ideas generated by the Enlightenment, partly because of the changing economic needs of capitalism, and partly because of the social struggles of the enslaved and the oppressed.

... Certainly, today we view opposition to slavery as an essential aspect of our humanity, and see those who advocate slavery as in some way inhuman – *but that's a belief we have arrived at historically, not naturally. To understand human values such as the belief in equality we need to explore not so much human psychology as human history.* (Malik, 2006) (emphasis in original)

Why we believe: Religion as a human universal

According to Norenzayan (2010):

In a species with tremendous cultural diversity, the suite of propensities we call 'religion' tops the list of species-specific human universals. Most people in most cultures throughout history are, and have been deeply religious, yet evolutionary science is only beginning to catch up with this phenomenon that is both a product and a shaper of the human mind ...

As we saw in Chapter 8, some theorists (e.g. Becker, 1973; Solomon *et al.*, 2004) maintain that religion's adaptive value springs from its capacity to provide hope and immortality in the face of debilitating existential anxieties, in particular the terror of contemplating one's own death. However, Norenzayan argues that religion isn't an evolutionary adaptation as such; in fact, she and others claim that 'religion' isn't even a structure with unitary design and a specific function, like vertebrate vision. Rather, it denotes a set of converging, overlapping cultural by-products, rooted in innate psychological tendencies that constrain and channel, but don't wholly determine, the transmission and survival of certain beliefs and practices.

Norenzayan describes the Four Cs of religion:

- *Counterintuition:* supernatural agents
- *Commitment:* costly sacrifice
- *Compassion:* relief from existential anxieties
- *Communion:* emotion-arousing ritual.

These are themselves cultural manipulations of psychological adaptations:

> ... *In all societies there is an evolutionary canalization of these four features that tends toward what is commonly referred to as 'religion'; passionate, ritualised communal displays of costly commitments to counterintuitive worlds governed by supernatural agents. These features of religion emerge in all known cultures and animate the majority of individual human beings in the world (Atran, 2002). In this respect, the four Cs of religion are existential universals (Norenzayan and Heine, 2005); they recruit psychological tendencies that are in principle available in the psychological repertoire of human beings everywhere, although the degree to which these tendencies are invoked can vary from culture to culture and across individuals, and the situations under which these tendencies are triggered can also vary.* (Norenzayan, 2010)

Culture and the perception of time

Just as morality and religion are human universals, so are language and other symbols. As we've seen throughout the preceding chapters, language is at the heart of many of the abilities and characteristics that have been claimed as uniquely human, including mental time travel (see Chapter 7). Also, just as morality, religion and language are extremely culturally diverse (at the same time as being universals), so is the perception of time.

According to Ezzell (2006),

> *Time is elastic in many cultures, but snaps taut in others. Indeed, the way members of a culture perceive and use time reflects their society's priorities and even their own worldview.*

Time for reflection

- How would you describe the 'traditional', commonsense view of time as described in Chapter 7?
- How would you describe your attitude to time?
- What do you understand by 'individualist' and 'collectivist' cultures'?

Roughly speaking, capitalist politico-economic systems are associated with **individualism**, while socialist societies are associated with **collectivism**. Individualist cultures also tend to be Western, while collectivist cultures tend to be non-Western, traditional and often non-industrialised. Individualism–collectivism represents a major 'cultural syndrome', which Triandis (1990) defines as 'a pattern of values, attitudes, beliefs, norms and behaviours that can be used to contrast a group of cultures to another group of cultures'.

The predominant Western (Eurocentric) concept of time is *linear*: it travels in a straight line from past, through present, to future, and it's measured objectively in discrete units (see Chapter 7). Non-Western (especially Eastern) cultures are more likely to see time as a wheel in which past, present and future revolve endlessly. Individualist cultures also see time as a commodity, a precious resource which can be 'used', 'saved', 'bought', 'wasted', and which should be rationed and controlled through the use of schedules and appointments. In collectivist cultures, time is regarded as a limitless, 'elastic' resource, which enables individuals to meet their obligations to various members of the community to whom they are bound (Owusu-Bempah and Howitt, 2000).

Box 9.9 The importance of a balanced time perspective

According to Boniwell and Zimbardo (2003), one key to learning how to live a fulfilling life is discovering how to achieve a balanced **time perspective (TP)**. One's TP refers to the subjective conception of focusing on various temporal (time-related) categories or time frames when making decisions and taking action. It represents one of the most powerful influences on almost all aspects of human behaviour.

Western ways of life have become predominantly goal- and future-oriented. Time-saving technological devices help to increase productivity and efficiency, but they fail to free up actual time to enjoy oneself (Zimbardo, 2002, in Boniwell and Zimbardo, 2003). The concept of 'time famine' refers to the lack of time and people's difficulty in finding an optimal balance in their use of time. For example, do emails save us time or do we spend time sending more of them, both necessary and unnecessary?

Some cultures confound time and space, as in the Australian Aborigines' concept of 'Dreamtime', which encompasses not only a creation myth but a method of finding their way around the countryside. These same people also don't draw neat distinctions between past, present and future; they believe that their ancestors crawled out of the ground during the Dreamtime, 'sang' the world into existence as they moved about naming each feature and living thing, which brought them into being. Even today, an entity doesn't exist unless an Aborigine 'sings' it (Ezzell, 2006).

Sardar (in Ezzell, 2006), a British Muslim author and critic, has written about time and Islamic cultures, particularly the fundamentalist Wahhabism sect. Muslims always 'carry the past with them'. In Islam, time is a tapestry incorporating the past, present and future; the past is ever present. Sardar claims that the West has 'colonised' time by spreading the expectation that life should become better as time passes: 'If you colonise time, you also colonise the future. If you think of time as an arrow, of course, you think of the future as progress, going in one direction. But different people may desire different futures' (Sardar, in Ezzell, 2006).

Space, time and language

As we noted above, the Australian Aborigines' 'Dreamtime' concept confuses time and space. Consistent with examples discussed in Chapter 6, Boroditsky (2011) reports that speakers of Kuuk Thaayorre (in Pormpuraaw, a small Aboriginal community in northern Australia) don't use relative spatial terms such as left and right. Rather, they talk in terms of absolute cardinal directions (north, south, east, west, and so on), and these are used at all scales/distances (for example, 'the cup is southeast of the plate'; or 'the boy standing to the south of Mary is my brother'). In Pormpuraaw, one must always stay oriented, just to be able to speak properly!

People who think differently about space are also likely to think differently about time. For example, Boroditsky and Gaby (2010) gave Kuuk Thaayorre speakers sets of pictures that showed temporal progression: a man ageing, a crocodile growing, a banana being eaten. They were then asked to arrange the shuffled pictures on the ground to indicate the correct temporal order. Each participant was tested twice, each time facing in a different cardinal direction. English speakers given this task will arrange the pictures so that time proceeds from left to right; Hebrew speakers (used to reading and writing from right to left) will tend to lay the pictures from right to left. This shows that reading/writing direction influences how we organise time. However, the Kuuk Thaayorre speakers didn't routinely arrange the pictures in a left/right or right/left way: they arranged from *east to west*. When they were seated facing south, the cards went from left to right; when they faced north, the pictures went from right to left. When they faced east, the pictures came towards the body, and so on. The researchers never told anyone which direction they were facing: the Kuuk Thaayorre knew that already and spontaneously used this spatial orientation to construct their representation of time.

Miles *et al.* (2010) found that English speakers unconsciously sway their bodies *forwards* when thinking about the future and *backwards* when thinking about the past. But in Aymara, a language spoken in the Andes of South America, the past is said to be in front and the future behind; the Aymara speakers' body language matches their way of talking (Boroditsky, 2011).

Conclusions: The evolution of culture

According to Bodmer (2007):

> ... *cultural evolution, which depends both on transmission and innovation just as biological evolution depends on Mendelian inheritance and genetic variability, is hugely more developed in humans than in any other animals. It seems doubtful that the brain has evolved significantly, in biological or genetic terms, since the development of the potential for sophisticated language, which must have been a major factor in enabling the possibility of comparatively rapid cultural evolution.*

In other words, cultural evolution is as real a phenomenon as biological evolution, and is distinct from it. Since human beings began to use language, changes in their behaviour have been due to cultural as opposed to biological evolution (such as changes in the structure/function of the brain). For example, the evolution of the use of clothing, after nakedness had evolved to help avoid parasite infections (Pagel and Bodmer, 2003: see Chapter 2), must have been essential for survival in the colder, mainly northern, climates to which *Homo sapiens* migrated after the end of the last Ice Age.

The key feature of cultural evolution is *horizontal* transmission within generations (rather than vertical transmission across generations). This horizontal process in humans, which depends largely on our superior cognitive abilities, is enormously more rapid than conventional biological evolution:

> ... *This undoubtedly is the major determinant of the extraordinarily rapid development of human society over the last few thousand years, which are hardly a tick in the usual time frame of the clock of biological evolution ...* (Bodmer, 2007)

Much of the extreme development of human culture, such as music, science, mathematics and literature, may simply be a by-product of our superior cognitive abilities, which were selected for our better survival and adaptation to rapidly changing environmental conditions. Culture is nowadays largely passed on from generation to generation (i.e. vertically) through education, and language, in one form or another, remains the main vehicle for cultural transmission (Bodmer, 2007: see Chapter 6).

To illustrate cultural diversity, Bodmer asks us to consider so-called primitive or hunter-gatherer peoples, such as are still found in the Amazon basin of South America. Assuming that they have the same cognitive potential as a modern educated European or American (and there's no reason to believe otherwise), if a newborn 'hunter-gatherer' baby were raised by, say, a typical British family, then it would develop ways of thinking that were just like native-born British children.

> ... *That surely emphasises the overriding importance of culture in determining our ways of thinking. Widely different human cultures have been superimposed upon the presumed unique cognitive features of humans.* (Bodmer, 2007)

However, there are many who take a very different view of culture; while acknowledging that it can seem to have a limited independence, in the long run it must be subordinated to nature. For example, E.O. Wilson, the founder of socio-biology, in *Consilience: The Unity of Knowledge* (1998) promises to synthesise science and the humanities. He concludes that features of culture *may* emerge that *reduce* Darwinian fitness (thereby contradicting a fundamental evolutionary principle) – but only 'for a time. Culture can indeed run wild for a time'. The clear implication is that this wildness will not last: human beings will be duly reined in to ensure that society continues to function on behalf of biology (Belsey, 2006).

Wilson's own theory of '**gene-culture co-evolution**' initially sounds as if it might attribute a degree of autonomy to culture. However, 'Gene-culture co-evolution is a special extension of the process of evolution by natural selection' (Wilson, 1998). In other words, culture is no more than the instrument of biology. The 'co' in co-evolution turns out to work as follows: genes prescribe rules, but culture helps to determine which genes survive; newly successful genes change the rules, which change the culture. At this point, there's a degree of 'play' in the system, but this will be contained in due course (Belsey, 2006). However,

> ... *This falls a long way short of any account that allows culture, once it has evolved, a significant contribution to the process of shaping human destiny in all its waywardness.* (Belsey, 2006)

Returning to the theme of Chapter 1, Malik (2007) states that for many natural scientists, any claim for **human exceptionalism** smacks of mysticism. For instance, the primatologist Frans de Waal (2001) suggests that the traditional distinction between nature and culture is yet one more expression of 'outdated Western dualism' (see Chapter 1). He argues that natural selection 'has produced our species, including our cultural abilities. Culture is part of human nature'. Since human nature can be understood through 'a combination of neurophysiology and deep genetic history' (Wilson, 1998), all that appears distinctive about human beings – language, morality, reason, culture itself – isn't after all that exceptional and can be understood in the same way as can any natural phenomenon.

Similarly, Pinker (2002) in *The Blank Slate*, claims that individual and cultural differences are merely the local manifestation of organically rooted drives that we share with all other human beings. Evolutionary psychology 'exposes the psychological unity of our species beneath the superficial differences of physical appearance and parochial culture'. This unity is understood in terms of innate, genetically based, responses to the environment. Surface diversity masks the underlying sameness of a biologically determined, foundational human nature (Belsey, 2006).

Against this view, Belsey (2006), and many others (e.g. Wolpert, 2007) contends that a more accurate view of culture would be to allow that:

> ... once it has evolved, as it did some 40,000 years ago, culture has its own history and its own imperatives, which interact with biology in ways that are not always harmonious, driven by a survival mechanism, or instrumental in conferring reproductive advantage. The Darwinian story of natural selection, invoked to explain changes in species over millions of years, does not do justice ... (Besley, 2006)

Chapter summary

- Herskovits' definition of culture excludes the possibility that non-humans might be considered to have culture.

- Objective aspects of the human-made part of the environment include tool making and use, which are no longer considered uniquely human abilities; most subjective aspects are uniquely human, many based on language or other symbolic abilities.

- According to Kendal (2008), there are three key questions that we need to ask about culture: (1) Does social learning equate to culture? (2) Do teaching and imitation equate to culture? (3) Do norms and ethnic markers equate to culture? While (3) clearly applies only to human culture, (1) and (2) can help us determine whether non-humans can truly be said to possess culture.

- Long-term field studies of primates and cetaceans show that animal populations vary in both how they perform certain behaviour or whether they perform it at all, reflecting differences in social learning (SL).

- There's a vigorous debate amongst psychologists as to whether social and asocial (or individual) learning involve the same underlying cognitive processes and whether evidence for certain forms of SL imply the existence of complex psychological abilities, such as theory of mind (ToM).

- As SL can influence survival and reproduction, it also has evolutionary implications. Indeed, it may well have been key in promoting the evolution of intelligence in animals, including humans.

- The predominant ethnographic method pioneered by Whiten involves comparing variation in behavioural traits at multiple sites. Such variation is judged to be cultural if there's no reason to believe that it stems from inter-site genetic or ecological differences. A second approach provides quantitatively evaluating the relative influence of ecological, genetic and social influences on behavioural similarity amongst individuals.

- Researchers using the 'option bias method' test whether a group's bias towards one behavioural option used to perform a task can be taken as evidence of SL by comparing it to a probability distribution of the bias that would arise through individual learning.

- A much-debated example that's often cited as the strongest evidence for culture in the wild is chimpanzees' termite-fishing (or ant-dipping). Whiten *et al.* have observed differences in how this is done between chimpanzees at Gombe National Park (Tanzania) and those in the Tai forest (Ivory Coast).

- The discovery at Bossou that the technique used was correlated with the ant species being captured, suggests that the Gombe-Tai difference may reflect the ant species present rather than SL.

- Byrne argues that the issue of different ant species is irrelevant and is supported by Sanz *et al.*'s discovery of chimpanzees' use of a tool set in the Goualougo Triangle (Republic of Congo).

- While there may be no means of generating hard evidence for SL in the wild, the use of 'proxy measures', such as patterns of affiliation and observation, can help identify SL more directly.

- For many, evidence of SL in behavioural variation is sufficient for the animals in question (such as pine-cone stripping Israeli rats) to be said to have culture. Human culture is just a more complex elaboration of similar behavioural processes.

- Another frequently cited example of animal culture is sweet potato washing by Japanese macaques, but there are several difficulties involved in interpreting such behaviour in this way.

- Galef and others distinguish between 'culture' and 'tradition', culture being one instance of tradition. 'True' culture is usually reserved to describe uniquely human tradition. While some animal behaviourists have equated the two terms, this is based on a confusion between analogy and homology.

- A key distinguishing feature of human culture is its cumulative nature: complex innovations aren't invented by individuals, but evolve gradually over many generations. There is currently little evidence in animals for the gradual accumulation of beneficial behavioural modifications.

- According to Tomasello, each new generation of children develops in the 'ontogenetic niche' characteristic of its culture, mastering the current artefacts and social practices.

- This is similar to Vygotsky's social constructionist account of the child as apprentice: cognitive development is a thoroughly social process. At the cultural level, children benefit unavoidably from the accumulated wisdom of previous generations, 'inheriting' technological and psychological tools and values.

- Goodall, Galef, Tomasello and others argue that what defines behaviour as culturally influenced is the kind of learning process involved: only behaviour acquired through specific SL processes can be described as 'cultural', namely teaching and imitation.

- By contrast, animal traditions are generally a result of processes such as 'local enhancement' or 'social facilitation'.

- Even if imitation is involved in the acquisition of locale-specific behaviour, it's not sufficient to explain it. Imitation is more complex that it might seem. In relation to human children, they don't just mimic other people's limb movements, but attempt to reproduce others' intended actions in the world.

- According to Tomasello, much of children's imitation is better described as cultural learning. The child is learning things from and through other people: he or she must know something of the adult's perspective on a situation in order to be able to learn the active use of this same intentional act.

- Neither children with autism, nor non-human primates, understand conspecifics as intentional agents – or only to a very limited degree. The most convincing reports of chimpanzee imitation (including the few experimental studies of deferred imitation) tend to involve enculturated apes.

- Tomasello concludes that captive mother-reared chimps are a better model for wild chimps than are enculturated chimps, because wild chimps receive little in the way of direct instruction from other chimps.

- Unlike animals, human culture helps to create an 'us and them' mentality: those who are seen as different are (typically) judged as behaving 'inappropriately', even 'unnaturally'. We perceive the world through the lens of our own cultural worldview, which defines 'normality' and provides us with a sense of identity.

- According to Dawkins, 'Universal Darwinism' is the principle according to which evolution can apply to replicators other than genes, including non-biological memes. Blackmore identifies three major types of cultural replicator, namely memeplexes, selfplexes and viral memes.

- Blackmore argues that the whole of human culture can be seen as a vast new evolutionary process based on memes; memetics provides the best explanation of what makes us human.

- According to Malik, if, as Blackmore claims, humans are just meme machines, then we cannot have any confidence in the claim that we're simply sophisticated animals or machines: the claim is unreliable because it's made by mere machines.

- What we consider to be the common properties of our humanity is as much a product of our historical and cultural development as it is of our biological heritage. A substantial part of human culture comprises social constructions based on the common intentional states and agreements between people.

- While several old mammalian brain areas (specifically, the Precuneus area) are activated during problem-solving situations such as the trolley dilemma, prefrontal areas may also be involved that overrule these more basic programs. Only humans are motivated by 'ought to' and 'should' and are capable of morally rational choices.

- According to Malik, while our capacity for moral thought is most likely an evolved trait, this isn't the same as saying that values are natural. To understand human values, we need to explore human history rather than human psychology.

- Religion is, arguably, the most distinctive species-specific human universal. But rather than being an evolutionary adaptation as such, 'religion' denotes a set of converging cultural by-products.
- According to Norenzayan, the Four Cs of religion (counterintuition, commitment, compassion and communion) are cultural manipulations of psychological adaptations.
- Just as morality, religion and language are extremely culturally diverse, as well as being human universals, so is the perception of time. Individualist and collectivist cultures see time as a precious commodity and an 'elastic' obligation-to-others-related resource respectively.
- Some cultures confound time and space, as in the Australian Aborigines' concept of 'Dreamtime'; evidence shows that people who think differently about space are also likely to think differently about time.
- The key feature of cultural evolution is horizontal transmission within generations (rather than vertical transmission across generations). This depends largely on our superior cognitive abilities and is enormously more rapid than biological evolution.
- According to Wilson's 'gene-culture co-evolution' theory, culture is no more than the instrument of biology; culture is part of human nature. But Bodmer and others argue that cultural evolution is as real as biological evolution and is distinct from it.

Suggested further reading

Blackmore, S. (1999) *The Meme Machine.* Oxford: Oxford University Press. The definitive account of memetics, with an introduction by Richard Dawkins.

Gould, S.J. (1987) 'Genes on the brain'. In S.J. Gould (ed.) *An Urchin in the Storm.* London: Penguin Books. This is one of a collection of superb essays by the late distinguished palaeontologist, evolutionary biologist and historian of science. In a review of C.L. Lumsden & E.O. Wilson's (1983) *Promethean Fire: Reflections on the Origin of Mind,* Gould argues against the theory of gene-culture co-evolution.

Høgh-Oleson, H. (ed.) (2010) *Human Morality and Sociality: Evolutionary and Comparative Perspectives.* Basingstoke: Palgrave Macmillan. A collection of nine original chapters by leading researchers from a number of different disciplines (including Christophe Boesch, Leda Cosmides & John Tooby, Dennis Krebs and Frans B.M. de Waal). This interdisciplinary reader explores the unique characteristics that define humanity and society, including morality and religion.

Tomasello, M. (1999) 'The Human Adaptation for Culture'. *Annual Review of Anthropology,* 28, 509–29. An excellent discussion of the nature of human culture and how this distinguishes us from chimpanzees.

Selected websites

http://www.youtube.com/watch?v=KIXFeTx9r-g&feature=related

Interview with Steven Pinker: How Far Can Darwin Take Us? Links to many other Pinker clips.

www.dur.ac.uk/anthropology

University of Durham's Department of Anthropology website (including the Evolutionary Anthropology Research Group). The staff includes Rachel Kendal (author of 'Animal "Culture Wars"', 2009).

http://darwin.st.andrews.ac.uk/documents/whiten.pdf

Power-point presentations (no text) on 'The Evolution of Culture' by Andrew Whiten: Centre for Social Learning and Cognitive Evolution, University of St Andrews.

http://www.onelife.com/evolve/index.html

Site devoted to 'The Evolution of the Human', including the History of Man, the Neanderthal, How Evolution Works, Instinct and Intelligence and the Evolution of the Brain, plus other useful links.

Glossary

Access consciousness: The sense in which mental representations may be poised for use in rational control of action or speech. According to Block (1995), speech isn't a prerequisite for access consciousness.

Affective priming paradigm: An experimental technique used to investigate the emotional (affective) influence of one kind of stimulus on another, by measuring the time it takes to respond to the second stimulus (such as the effect of the word 'love' or a consonant chord on the time it takes to process 'hate' or a dissonant chord).

Agonistic screams: Those produced by chimpanzees in aggressive encounters with other chimpanzees.

Altricial: Species (including humans) in which the young are highly dependent on adults for their survival, mature slowly, and rely much more on learning compared with *precocial* species.

AMY1: A gene which encodes salivary amylase, an enzyme involved in digesting starch. This gene had to change in order to allow early *Homo* species to digest high-starch foods, which became more accessible with the agricultural revolution (about 10,000 years ago). While found in all mammals, humans have an especially large number of copies of *AMY1* compared with other primates.

Anterior cingulate cortex (ACC): Part of the cingulate cortex which surrounds the amygdala and hypothalamus. The ACC is linked to the *dorsolateral prefrontal cortex* (DPFC) and both are involved in speech production and verbal fluency. The cingulated cortex is part of the limbic system.

Anterograde amnesia: The inability to form new memories.

Anthropomorphism: The attribution of human characteristics and abilities to non-human animals and physical objects/aspects of the physical environment. Related to *artificialism* in the child.

Aphasia: A disorder of speech, such as motor (or expressive), aphasia, the ability to produce speech (associated with Broca's area), or receptive aphasia, the ability to understand speech (one's own or someone else's) (associated with Wernicke's area).

Archaeological record: The appearance of the first – very simple – stone tools, about 2.5 million years ago.

Arcuate fasciculus: In the classical model of language processing, a fibre bundle to which Wernicke's area conveys what we intend to say, before sending it on to Broca's area.

Articulatory phonology: The view that speech isn't so much a system for producing sound as a system for producing articulatory gestures, through the independent action of the articulatory organs – the lips, velum (the soft palate behind the hard palate), larynx and tongue.

Articulatory suppression: An experimental technique in which participants are asked to repeat aloud the same word over and over again in order to interfere with/prevent speech production processes (such as sub-vocal articulation, which is thought to be important for understanding text).

Artificialism: Young children's perception of the natural world as existing solely to solve human problems (Piaget, 1965).

Association areas: Situated between the sensory and motor areas of the (neo)cortex, these have no direct connections outside the cortex. Instead, they communicate only to each other and to other cortical neurons. In humans, the association areas include the massive *prefrontal cortex* and regions of the occipital, temporal and parietal lobes. The 'association cortex' is where the 'higher mental functions' (thinking, reasoning, planning, deciding and so on) probably 'occur'.

Australopithecines: Literally, 'southern apes', the generic name for the early walking (bipedal) apes (referred to as '*Australopithecus*'). They were replaced soon after the start of the *Pleistocene period* (just under two million years ago) in the African savannah by two diverging lines of walking apes: (a) the first line of the meat-eating *Homo* genus, including the tool-making *Homo habilis*; and (b) the vegetarian *Paranthropus*.

Australopithecus afarensis: One of the early walking (bipedal) apes, including 'Lucy'; shorter than modern humans and still closer to chimpanzees above the neck with smaller brains.

Australopithecus africanus: A walking ape, living 2–3 million years ago, the same size as chimpanzees but with a slightly larger average brain size.

Australopithecus anamensis: A walking ape dating from four million years ago, providing the first clear evidence of bipedalism. Such claims have also been made for *Ardipithecus ramidus* (4–5 million years ago) and *Ororrin tugenensis* (6 million years ago).

Biological time: The various biological 'clocks' which control the fluctuation of basic physiological processes (including blood pressure, body temperature, heart rate, hormone secretion and alertness). This fluctuation (or periodicity) can occur as a *circadian, circannual, infradian* or *ultradian rhythm*.

Bipedalism: Upright evolution (walking on two legs). Considered by some to be an essential evolutionary development in the emergence of ancient hominids from other apes. It marks a split between human ancestors and those of chimpanzees, but predates *Homo sapiens* by several million years.

Blindsight: The ability to perform various visual tasks (such as describing an object's shape) despite the absence of any conscious awareness ('unconscious vision') (Weiskrantz, 1986).

Bodily rhythm: A cyclical variation over some period of time (from less than 24 hours to one year) in physiological or psychological processes.

Broca's area: A certain part of the left hemisphere (located just above the left ear, abutting the cortical areas that control movement of the face, tongue, jaw and throat), damage to which causes the patient's speech to become slow and laboured (motor/expressive aphasia), but without affecting the ability to understand speech. More recently, it is seen as controlling the semantic aspects of language.

Circadian rhythm: Fluctuations in physiological or psychological processes that occur within a 24-hour cycle ('circa' = 'about', 'diem' = 'a day').

Circannual rhythm: Yearly rhythms, a subset of *infradian rhythms*.

Cognitive unconscious: Unconscious, automatic, psychological processes involved in perception, memory and action. *Blindsight* is a major example.

Collectivism: Part of one of the major cultural syndromes (individualism–collectivism), in which one's identity is defined by characteristics of the collective group one is permanently attached to (family, tribal or religious group, or country). This is the emphasis in Eastern and socialist societies.

Comatose: A state that involves the absence of both wakefulness (the person is described as 'unconscious') and consciousness content (the person lacks awareness of anything around them).

Combinatorial generative computation: The putting together of discrete elements to produce new ideas, which can be expressed, for example, as novel words or musical forms. Other important examples include the use and manufacture of tools.

Continuity argument: The view, according to which all species, including humans, have evolved through the same process of natural selection, making them all unique. We would, therefore, expect to find that close evolutionary relatives, such as humans (*Homo sapiens*) and chimpanzees (*Pan troglodytes*) share certain abilities and behaviours. Attempts to define 'human nature' are made by comparison with chimpanzees, rather than with species lower down the evolutionary (phylogenetic) scale.

Conventionalisation: The shift from iconic gestures (which 'mimic' the object or action) to arbitrary symbols; it represents a more economical communications system.

Convolution: The characteristic folded/wrinkled appearance of the cortex: this is necessary if its 2,500 cm^2 surface area is to fit inside the relatively small skull.

Corvids: Technical name for the crow family, a group of intelligent birds that include crows, magpies, ravens, rooks, jackdaws and jays.

Creationism: The belief that the universe and everything in it was created by God (or some supernatural being), as opposed to the claims made by evolutionary theory.

Creativity: In relation to the use of language, the ability to produce/understand an infinite number of novel utterances; also known as productivity.

Declarative memory: The acquisition of factual knowledge (knowing *that*), which may be of a 'public' or very personal kind (as in *episodic/autobiographical memory*).

Deep social mind: A human exceptionalism account (Whiten, 1999, 2007), according to which there exists a special degree of cognitive penetration between individuals. This makes us the most deeply social species on earth. It comprises mind-reading, culture, language and communication and cooperation. It's the combination of these characteristics which is distinctively human.

Deep structure: The *meaning* of a sentence; when we hear a spoken sentence, we transform the *surface structure* into its deep structure.

Deferred imitation: The ability to reproduce a previously witnessed action or sequence of actions when the model is no longer present, i.e. instead of copying what's currently occurring, the individual repeats that act some time after it was first observed.

Déjà vu: French for 'already seen'. The sense of having encountered a situation before, identical in every detail, even though we know that we haven't been there or done that before.

Depersonalisation: The sudden, generally brief experience in which everything that's normally familiar to us strikes us as strange, new and unreal.

Descent with modification: In the context of evolution, the modification or co-opting of abilities or capacities relevant to ancient traits in the service of other developing traits. For example, the right hemisphere, which is largely responsible for emotional arousal, was originally specialised for detecting and responding to unexpected environmental stimuli.

Developmental cognitive neuroscience (DCN): A subfield that's concerned with trying to relate developmental changes in perception, cognition and behaviour to underlying growth of the brain.

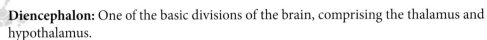

Diencephalon: One of the basic divisions of the brain, comprising the thalamus and hypothalamus.

Displacement: In relation to the use of language, reference to things that aren't present in time or space.

Dopamine loop: A neural circuit fuelled by the neurotransmitter dopamine which encodes the notion of flowing time. Each circuit or 'loop' of activity takes, on average, 100 milliseconds to complete and events registered by the brain within the duration of a single loop are experienced as a single occurrence. Part of the concept of an interval timer (IT).

Dorsolateral prefrontal cortex (DPFC): The part of the *prefrontal cortex* (PFC) where we play around with our thoughts and feelings, where we think about them; the main site of *working memory* (WM).

Dysfunctional metacognitive beliefs: Hallucinating patients' beliefs about their own mental processes that lead them to make self-defeating efforts to control their thoughts (they perceive them as unintended and, therefore, alien).

Echo phonology: The parallel movements of the mouth and the hand(s). For example, the mouth may open and close in synchrony with the opening and closing of the hand.

Electroencephalogram (EEG): A way of recording the brain's electrical activity by fitting electrodes (passive sensors) to the scalp. The EEG records output from large groups of neurons, which are traced on paper; this output takes the form of brainwave patterns.

Electromyogram (EMG): A way of recording the electrical activity of muscles by, for example, placing electrodes on the wrist.

Emergent property: A characteristic of a system (such as the brain) that is a product of the interactions between all the individual units composing the system (neurons). Examples include consciousness, intelligence and memory, none of which could possibly be characteristics of individual neurons.

Enculturation: The process whereby animals, particularly apes (and especially chimpanzees) are reared by human caregivers in an intensive environment that resembles the upbringing of a human infant.

Endogenous pacemakers: In the absence of *exogenous zeitgebers*, internal timing devices (internal biological clocks) control behaviours that show rhythmical fluctuation/periodicity.

Episodic memory (EM): A form of autobiographical memory that stores a record of our past personal experiences.

Ethnographic method: Methodological approach derived from social anthropology, involving 'immersion' in a setting and an attempt to reflect that context from the perspective of group/culture members (Coolican, 2009).

Evolutionary convergence: The appearance of the same functionally advantageous trait in two or more species quite independently of each other. Also referred to as convergent evolution.

Exaptation: The take-over of structures or processes originally evolved as an adaptation to one function for use in a totally different way.

Existentialism: An approach to philosophy, associated with Kierkegaard, Heidegger and Sartre among others, concerned with the meaning of human existence, including the themes of freedom, decision, responsibility, finitude, guilt, alienation, despair and death.

Exogenous zeitgebers: Environmental factors such as light–dark cycles, and clocks, that provide clues to bodily rhythms. ('Zeitgeber' = German for 'time-givers').

Experimental Existential Psychology (XXP): The use of traditional methodologies from mainstream psychology to investigate Yalom's *givens of existence* and other existential concerns. Central to XXP is *terror management theory* (*TMT*).

Extrinsic religiosity: An approach to religion that treats it more as a means to an end (such as social acceptance or increased status), rather than a deep faith characterised by striving for meaning and value (*intrinsic religiosity*).

Flashbulb memories: A special kind of episodic memory (EM), in which we can recall vivid and detailed recollections of where we were and what we were doing when we first heard about some major public national/international event.

FOXP2: A gene located on chromosome 7, believed to be necessary for the acquisition of normal speech, including *morphosyntax*. A point mutation on the gene is implicated in the specific language disorder found in the KE family. Dubbed the 'grammar gene' by Pinker (1994).

Functional lateralisation: A feature of the human brain, in which areas specialised for particular psychological functions (such as language) are found only in one or other hemisphere. For example, Broca's area and Wernicke's area are found only in the *left* hemisphere. Also known as *hemispheric asymmetry.*

Functional magnetic resonance imaging (fMRI): This monitors blood flow in the brain over time as people perform different kinds of tasks. While MRI can identify, for example, the smallest tumour, it's limited to producing still images of brain slices. The ability of fMRI to monitor blood flow over time can tell us much about brain function.

Functionally referential communication: The use of vocalisations to 'pick out' a specific aspect of the external world and direct others' attention to it.

Functors: Terms that convey purely 'grammatical' meaning, such as the verb 'to be', plurals and possessives.

Generative computation: The ability to create a virtually infinite variety of words and things, such as arrangements of words, sequences of musical notes, combinations of actions or strings of mathematical symbols. Involves two types of operation: recursive and combinatorial. One aspect of Hauser's (2009) theory of *humaniqueness.*

Genome: The total set of biological information needed to build and maintain a living individual of any particular species. It can be used to describe/define an individual member of that species or the species as a whole. The biological information is encoded in the form of *genes.*

Gene: A strand of deoxyribonucleic acid (DNA), the basic unit of heredity/heriditary transmission. A DNA chain is composed of four chemical bases: adenine (A), cytosine (C), guanine (G), and thymine (T); these are arranged in the form of a double helix. The estimated 23, 500 human genes are found strung along the 23 pairs of chromosomes, one member of each pair being inherited from each parent.

Gene-culture Co-evolution: According to Wilson (1998), a special extension of evolution by natural selection, in which culture is no more than the instrument of biology.

Givens of existence: Yalom's (1980) term for fundamental human concerns that affect us all, namely, fear of death, freedom, existential isolation and meaninglessness.

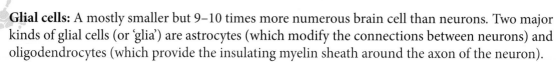

Glial cells: A mostly smaller but 9–10 times more numerous brain cell than neurons. Two major kinds of glial cells (or 'glia') are astrocytes (which modify the connections between neurons) and oligodendrocytes (which provide the insulating myelin sheath around the axon of the neuron).

Grammar: The complex and yet intuitive understanding needed to make sense of any sentence we might hear and the complementary ability to produce such sentences. Often referred to as mental grammar. More formally, the general term for *phonology*, morphology, and *syntax*, a finite set of rules that generate the sentences in a language.

Handedness: A form of asymmetry in which one side (hand or paw) is proficient and the other less so. While the pawedness of cats, mice and rats is equally split between right and left, about 90 per cent of all humans are right-handed.

Haplorhine species: Includes New and Old World monkeys, apes and humans.

(*HAR1*) Human accelerated region 1: A part of the human genome that has undergone greatest modification since *Homo* split from chimpanzees. Found in the genomes of rats, mice, chickens and 12 other vertebrate species, as well as chimpanzees and humans, *HAR1* evolved extremely slowly until humans came along.

Higher-order consciousness: The recognition by a thinking subject of his or her own acts or affections: conscious of being conscious. It involves direct awareness and is what humans have in addition to *primary consciousness*. Related to *self-consciousness* and *second-order representations*.

Hippocampus: A part of the limbic system that plays a central role in human memory (especially spatial memory); has been called a 'cognitive map'.

Hominid: The human family of species; *Homo* (human) is reserved for people that display our own level of intelligence, moral sense and depth of introspective consciousness. At its most basic, 'human' simply denotes *bipedal* apes, and includes *Homo habilis, Homo rhodesiense, Homo erectus* (Asia) and *Homo neanderthalensis* (Europe) or 'Neanderthal', *Homo ergaster,* and *Homo floreseinsis.*

Homo ergaster: The first hominid to leave Africa (1.95 million years ago), becoming the Asian *Homo erectus*; they spread rapidly to the Middle East, Russia, India, the Far East and Southeast Asia.

Homo habilis: A possible precursor to *Homo floreseinsis* (the 'Hobbits'), the latest-surviving extinct hominid (as recently as 18,000 years ago).

Homology: In evolutionary biology, any similarity in the characteristics of different species (is believed to be) due to their having a common ancestor. For example, given that both chimpanzees and humans are capable of mirror self-recognition, we can infer that the ancestor common to both species also had this ability. Such traits are called homologies.

Homo neanderthalensis: Commonly referred to as simply 'Neanderthals', they survived until less than 30,000 years ago.

Homo psychologicus: Humphrey's (1896) term for human beings as 'natural psychologists': the distinguishing feature of a human-like ape would have been social intelligence and mind-reading.

Horizontal transmission: The key feature of cultural evolution, involving transmission *within* generations (rather than vertical transmission *across* generations); this is hugely more rapid than conventional biological evolution).

Human exceptionalism: The view according to which human beings are a unique species; this implies a *qualitative difference* between humans and all other species. (This is sometimes referred to as a 'deep chasm' approach.) The main alternative is the continuity argument/ approach.

Humaniqueness: Hauser's (2009) term for the key ingredients of the human mind, which, together, distinguish us from all other species. The four major ingredients are: generative computation, promiscuous combination of ideas, mental symbols and abstract thought.

Hylobatid species: Include gibbons.

Implicit memory (IM): The influence of our past experience on our current behaviour despite the fact that those experiences are unavailable to conscious awareness.

Inattentional blindness: The occasional tendency to ignore something staring us in the face, because our attention is focused on something else.

Individualism: Part of one major cultural syndrome (individualism–collectivism), in which one's identity is defined by personal choices and achievements – the autonomous individual. This is the predominant emphasis in the West and capitalist politico-economic systems.

Infant-directed speech (IDS): The way that adults quite automatically adjust their speech when interacting with babies and young children, by using high pitch, an exaggerated use of pitch and contour and slower pace. Sometimes called 'motherese' or 'baby-talk register'.

Infradian rhythm: A rhythm that has a cycle of more than 24 hours (such as the human menstrual cycle).

Insightful deception: Behaviour that requires the calculation of the consequences of one's behaviour, especially how it would be interpreted by another individual. This implies possession of a *theory of mind* (ToM) or *mind-reading ability*. It is performed in the absence of specialised genetic programming and without specific learning.

Intentionality: The philosophical term that denotes that most conscious states (thoughts, feelings and so on) are *about,* or refer to, something (as opposed to being undirected, generalised states).

Internal time-consciousness: Husserl's (1938/1991) account of how one moment of consciousness is interconnected with the previous and subsequent ones.

Interval timer (IT): The brain's 'stopwatch', marking time spans of seconds to hours. It enlists the higher cognitive powers of the cerebral cortex, which controls perception, memory and conscious thought.

Intrinsic reinforcement: A technique used by Pepperberg (1998) to teach language to a parrot, in which the reward given for a particular vocalisation is the object the vocalisation refers to.

Intrinsic religiosity: A deep, heartfelt faith characterised by striving for meaning and value.

Junk DNA: A jumble of repetitive or random sequences of DNA that's rarely or never translated/ transcribed; this describes most DNA, with only a small proportion spelling out genes.

Kinaesthetic self-concept: Explicit mental representations of the positions and movements of our own body, also found in chimpanzees.

Language acquisition device (LAD): The child's innate (inborn) knowledge of *transformational grammar* (TG), the ability to identify the features shared by all human languages (*linguistic universals*). This enables any child to acquire any language to which it might be exposed

291

(regardless of country of birth) and represents a distinct mental module or 'organ' (Chomsky, 1957, 1979).

LCT: A gene commonly found in mammals that permits the digestion of the carbohydrate lactose (milk sugar). Like *AMY1*, *LCT* has changed during the course of human evolution (around 9,000 years ago), allowing adults – and not just nursing infants – to process lactose.

Learned deception: Behaviour that only *appears* to reflect a deliberate attempt to deceive another animal but which turns out not to involve *theory of mind* (ToM) or *mind-reading*.

Limbic system: A group of interconnected telencephalic and diencephalic structures involved in feeling, feeding, fighting and sexual behaviour. The major structures are the hypothalamus, mammillary bodies, anterior nuclei of the thalamus, hippocampus, amygdala, septum, fornix and cingulate cortex (which is in a gyrus – the cingulate gyrus).

Linguistic universals: Linguistic features common to all languages, such as the use of consonants and vowels, syllables, modifiers, nouns and verbs and recursion. Collectively, they provide the *deep structure*. Sometimes referred to as universal grammar.

Lissencephaly: A severe, often fatal, congenital disorder, in which the cortex lacks its characteristic folds (convolution) and has a much reduced surface area. ('Smooth brain'.)

Machiavellian intelligence: A form of social intelligence that involves deceptions and the formation of coalitions and alliances. Found in baboons, rhesus monkeys and other primates (including apes and humans).

MC1R: A human gene believed to be responsible (along with other genes) for producing skin pigmentation (i.e. skin colour). A specific variant of *MC1R* is always found in Africans with dark pigmentation and originated 1.2 million years ago.

Meme: Literally, 'that which is imitated'. A cultural (as opposed to biological) replicator, a unit of cultural transmission (Dawkins, 1976).

Memeplexes: Groups of memes that fare better together than they would individually.

Memetics: The scientific study of memes.

Mesencephalon: One of the basic divisions of the brain, comprising the tectum and tegmentum. Sometimes referred to as the midbrain.

Metencephalon: One of the basic divisions of the brain, comprising the pons and cerebellum.

Microcephaly: A genetically determined failure of the brain to develop to its normal size; this can be reduced by up to 70 per cent.

Mind–brain (mind–body) problem: Originally a philosophical debate regarding the difficulty in explaining the relationship between something that has size, weight, shape and density, and exists in space and time (the brain) and something else that has none of those attributes (the mind). Perhaps the oldest and most commonly debated example of *reductionism*.

Mind-reading: The ability to put yourself in someone else's shoes, psychologically, to imagine the other person's thoughts and feelings (Baron-Cohen, 1995). Also referred to as *theory of mind* (ToM).

Mind time: Also referred to as 'brain time', the subjective experience of time flowing, and the related sense of time as an arrow (i.e. time travelling in a straight line from past, through present, to future).

Minimally conscious state (MCS): The state to which some *vegetative state* (VS) patients progress, in which they regain some (transient) level of awareness.

Mirror neurons: Found in both human and monkey brains, in various areas including V5 and the ventral premotor cortex, they fire in the same way when observing another individual performing an action as when the person/monkey performs the action itself. They also help us to read another person's intentions and emotions. These effects are largely automatic and unconscious.

Mitochondria: Locations within body cells where human genes can be found (most are found on the chromosomes).

Model/rival (M/R) protocol: A technique used by Pepperberg (1998) for teaching language to a parrot: two humans teach each other about particular objects while the parrot watches.

Morphosyntax: Understanding of the internal structure of words (morphology) and how words are put together to form phrases and sentences (*syntax*, a part of grammar).

Mortality salience hypothesis: The prediction that, if cultural worldviews and self-esteem function to reduce anxiety associated with death awareness, then asking people to think about their own mortality should increase their need for the beliefs provided by those worldviews and self-esteem.

Mortality salience (MS) paradigm: Reminding participants of their own mortality, typically by asking them to describe the emotions that the thought of their own death elicits or what they think will happen when they physically die.

Mutations: Errors that are sometimes produced during the replication of genes. While many mutations are neither harmful nor beneficial, in the wrong place in the genome even a single one can be fatal.

Myelencephalon: One of the basic divisions of the brain, comprising the medulla oblongata.

Myelination: The formation of myelin sheaths around the axons of neurons, which aids the transmission of nerve impulses to neighbouring neurons.

Near-threshold luminance detection: The likelihood of being able to consciously perceive a flash of light barely bright enough to see, dependent on the phase of another wave in the front of the brain (which rises and falls about seven times per second).

Neuron: The basic structural unit, or building block, of the nervous system (sometimes spelt 'neurone'); about 80 per cent of all neurons are found in the brain, particularly in the cerebral cortex.

Non-declarative memory: The acquisition of skills demonstrated through behavioural change (knowing *how*); a form of memory shared by human and non-human animals.

Objective body: How our body is experienced by others ('the body as object'), as opposed to the *phenomenal body*.

Objective time: Otherwise known as 'clock time', which is used as the objective measure against which brain or subjective time is gauged in experimental research.

Oneiric: Dream-related.

One-word stage: The second stage of language development (age 12–18 months), in which babies produce their first words ('articulate sounds').

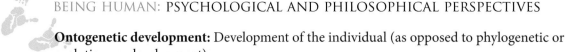

Ontogenetic development: Development of the individual (as opposed to phylogenetic or evolutionary development).

Orbitofrontal cortex (OFC): A key region within the *prefrontal cortex* (PFC) and the first to mature in the child. It lies behind the eyes, next to the amygdala and anterior cingulate gyrus. It is larger in the right hemisphere.

Paraventricular nucleus: This is prevented by the *suprachiasmatic nucleus* (SCN), in response to daylight, from producing a message that would ultimately result in the release of melatonin.

Perceptual reorganisation: Kohler's (1925) explanation, based on Gestalt principles, of his chimpanzees' ability to solve problems such as stacking boxes to acquire an out-of-reach banana. In contrast with *trial-and-error* learning, the solution came to the chimpanzees in a 'flash of insight'.

Periaqueductal grey: A region of the midbrain that plays a major role in speech. Located close to the ventricles, it's rich in hormone receptors and communicates with the amygdala and hippocampus.

Perisylvian cortex: A broad wedge of the left hemisphere, so-called because of the way it surrounds the Sylvian fissure, the deep, horizontal 'canyon' that separates the temporal from the frontal and parietal lobes; it plays an important role in language ability.

Permanent Vegetative State (VS): In the UK, a diagnosis made of a *vegetative state* (VS) patient after at least six months for non-traumatic brain injury and 12 months for traumatic ones.

Phenomenal body: How the individual experiences his/her own body (in contrast with the *objective body*).

Phenomenal consciousness: The qualitative, subjective, experiential, or phenomenological aspects of conscious experience, sometimes identified with qualia.

Phenomenology: A philosophical movement, associated with Husserl, based on the belief that there's nothing 'behind' or more fundamental than experience: the study of behaviour should begin with people's *experience*, the thing itself as it appears (i.e. the 'phenomenon'). Closely associated with *Existentialism*.

Phonology: Rules for combining basic sounds (phones or phonetic segments) into phonemes (the sounds that affect the *meaning* of what's said).

Phylogenetic development: Development/evolution of species (as opposed to *ontogenetic development*).

Phylogenetic scale: The evolutionary scale.

Pineal gland: Situated near the corpus callosum, this releases melatonin (the 'sleep hormone') on instruction from the *suprachiasmatic nucleus* (SCN). The pineal gland was believed by Descartes to be the 'seat of the mind'.

Plasticity: A key characteristic of the human brain, without which the developing nervous system would be unable to repair itself following damage or to tailor its responses to changing aspects of the outside world. Demonstrated by the ability of undamaged areas to take over the functions usually performed by damaged areas. It also refers to the in-built 'redundancy' characteristic of all developing systems. Complementary to plasticity is *specificity*.

Pongid species: Chimpanzees, bonobos, orang-utans and gorillas.

Positron emission tomography (PET): A form of brain scanning/imaging, in which radiation is used in order to compute 'brain slices' (apparent cross-sections of the brain). A radioactive tracer is added to a substance used by the body (such as oxygen or glucose); as the marked substance is metabolised, PET shows the pattern of how it's being used.

Precocial: Species (such as chickens and geese) that rely on highly specific innate capacities, adapted to one particular environmental niche. They're mobile at birth and mature quickly, in contrast with *altricial species*.

Prefrontal cortex (PFC): The front-most part of the brain (right behind the forehead), which links the sensory cortex with the emotional and survival-oriented sub-cortical structures; it is found only in humans.

Pre-linguistic stage: The first stage of language development, lasting 0–12 months, consisting largely of babbling (the production of phonemes, which, in themselves, have no meaning).

Primary consciousness: The state of being mentally aware of things in the environment, of having mental images in the present. Related to sentience, the ability to have bodily sensations (including hunger, thirst, pain, fear and anger). Most mammals and some birds probably have primary consciousness, but animals without a cortex do not. Related to *phenomenal consciousness*.

Primates: The group of animal species (mammals) to which humans belong. Two main sub-divisions are (a) *prosimians* (including lemurs and lorises) and (b) *simians* (monkeys and apes). Apes are sub-divided into *lesser apes* (including gibbons) and *great apes* (gorillas, orang-utans, common chimpanzees/*Pan troglodytes,* pygmy chimps/bonobos/*Pan paniscus,* and human beings/*Homo sapiens*). Humans have been dubbed 'the naked ape'.

Procedural memory (PM): Information from long-term memory (LTM) which cannot be inspected consciously (such as the difficulty of describing how to ride a bicycle), in contrast with *declarative memory* (DM). (Knowing *how*.)

Production-based studies: The nature of early attempts to teach language to chimpanzees and other great apes. Operant conditioning is used to reward the correct use of signs (based on American Sign Language/ASL), small plastic symbols or a special computer-controlled keyboard. In all cases, the aim is to build up a vocabulary from scratch. More recently, a comprehension-based approach has attempted to create more naturalistic environments in which the chimpanzee/bonobo acquires language more like children do.

Promiscuous combination of ideas: Connecting thoughts from different domains of knowledge, allowing us to combine our understanding of, for example, art, sex, space, causality and friendship. This can help generate new laws, social relationships and technologies. One aspects of Hauser's (2009) theory of *humaniqueness*.

Prosencephalon: The forebrain.

Prosody: The inflection and overall musical quality that lend important emphasis to verbal communication

Qualia: The collection of personal, subjective experiences, feelings and sensations that accompany awareness. They are phenomenal states (how things seem to us as human beings) and are the way that consciousness manifests itself.

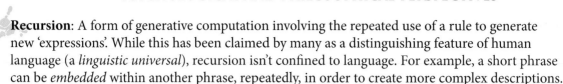

Recursion: A form of generative computation involving the repeated use of a rule to generate new 'expressions'. While this has been claimed by many as a distinguishing feature of human language (a *linguistic universal*), recursion isn't confined to language. For example, a short phrase can be *embedded* within another phrase, repeatedly, in order to create more complex descriptions.

Reductionism: Any attempt to explain some complex whole in terms of its component or constituent parts, such as the claim that psychological explanations can be replaced by explanations in terms of brain functioning or even in terms of physics and chemistry. Anti-reductionists would argue that, for example, conscious states are real and cannot be reduced to something else (they are irreducible).

Referential mapping: A technique used by Pepperberg (1998) to teach language to a parrot, in which she assigns meaning to vocalisations that the parrot produces spontaneously.

Referential opacity: A unique logical property of second-order representations, in which statements such as 'Mary believes that John is having an affair with his colleague' is true by virtue of the fact that Mary believes it's true – regardless of whether John is actually having an affair with his colleague.

REM sleep: Rapid eye movement sleep, in which pulse and respiration rates, and blood pressure, increase and become less regular. EEGs begin to resemble those of the waking state, showing that the brain is active. But it also involves muscular paralysis and resistance to being woken (hence 'paradoxical sleep'). Also referred to as 'dream sleep'.

Reminiscence bump: The finding that if older participants (over 60) are given cue words to help them recall personal events, there's a concentration of memories from a period covering about 10 years, with a 'peak' at age 20. The reminiscence bump is central to the reminiscence effect (RE).

Replication: In the context of genetics, this is the process by which a gene makes a copy of itself. DNA can replicate indefinitely, while still containing the same information.

Retrograde amnesia: Failure to recover long-term memories, that is, what happened *before* the surgery or accident that caused the amnesia.

Rhombencephalon: The hindbrain.

Second-order intentionality: The capacity to reflect on the contents of another individual's mind. This is related to *mind-reading*. Second-order intentionality also has a unique logical property, called *referential opacity*.

Self-actualisation: Realising one's full potential, 'becoming everything one is capable of becoming'; according to Maslow (1954), what makes us unique as a species.

Self-consciousness: An organism's capacity for second-order representations of its own mental states ('thoughts about thoughts'). Closely related to *theory of mind* (ToM).

Selfplexes: A sub-group of *memeplexes* formed when people use language that includes references to the self.

Self-transcendence: To place value outside oneself, to pursue some higher purpose or cause; an important function of religion.

Semanticity: The use of symbols to mean or refer to objects, actions, and so on. Also referred to as *functional referential communication*.

Semantic memory (SM): Our store of general, factual knowledge about the world, including concepts, rules, and language (a 'mental thesaurus').

Semantics: Rules for combining phonemes into morphemes, a language's basic units of meaning (consisting mainly of words).

Social cognitive neuroscience: Scientific study of how the human brain carries out social information processing. Practically, this involves the use of fMRI and neuropsychology to test hypotheses regarding social cognition, such as the relationship between how our actions are automatically affected by the other people we are with and *theory of mind* (ToM).

Source monitoring: In the context of explaining hallucinations, the capacity to distinguish between self-generated thoughts and externally presented stimuli.

Specificity: A key characteristic of the human brain, without which the brain couldn't become accurately wired; for example, nerves wouldn't be able to make the right connections between the motor cortex and muscles (via the spinal cord). Complementary to specificity *is plasticity.*

Stage 1 grammar: The third stage of language development (age18–30 months), in which children begin to construct two-word sentences; speech is largely *telegraphic.*

Stage 2 grammar: The fourth stage of language development (from 30 months to about 4–5 years), in which children begin to add functors to their sentences.

Structure dependence: The patterned nature of language; the use of 'structured chunks', such as word order.

Suprachiasmatic nucleus (SCN): A tiny cluster of about 3,000 neurons, located in the medial hypothalamus, thought to be the location of the internal (biological) clock.

Surface structure: The actual words or phrases used in a sentence (its syntactical structure). When we hear a spoken sentence, we transform it into its *deep structure.*

Syntax: Rules for combining morphemes to form phrases and sentences that are both meaningful and grammatically correct.

Telegraphic speech: Speech that uses only those words that convey the most information, called contentives; there's an absence of functors. Characteristics of children during *Stage 1 grammar.*

Telencephalon: One of the basic divisions of the brain, comprising the cerebral hemispheres/cerebrum, basal ganglia, and limbic system (which includes the hippocampus, hypothalamus and thalamus).

Teleo-functional reasoning: The tendency to believe that something exists for a purposeful reason, rather than because 'it's just there'.

Telescopy phenomenon: The tendency to date events more recently than they actually occurred; also known as 'forward telescoping'.

Terror management theory (TMT): A broad theoretical account of how we cope with the fear of death, which is the existential concern that has received the greatest attention by *experimental existential psychology* (XXP).

Theory of mind (ToM): The ability to infer the existence of mental states in others (mental state attribution) or *mind-reading.*

Third-person account: A way of referring to the scientific account of the world, implying objectivity or causal explanation.

Three-second window: As demonstrated by a number of different experiments, the duration of the 'subjective (or phenomenal) present' or the 'state of being conscious' (STOBCON). Also known as the three-second rule.

Time perspective (TP): Our subjective conception of focusing on various temporal (time-related) categories or time frames when making decisions and taking actions.

Tradition: From the Latin *traditio*, meaning the act of handing something over to another or of delivering up a possession; sometimes contrasted with 'culture', but culture can be regarded as one form that tradition may take.

Transcranial magnetic stimulation (TMS): The use of a powerful magnet, flicking on and off several times a second, held against the outside of the head inducing an electrical current that penetrates two centimetres into brain tissue, this can either enhance or suppress activity in particular brain areas. A technique used widely to test for side-effects of brain surgery and to establish the function of different brain areas.

Transformational grammar (TG): Chomsky's (1957, 1965) theory of language, in which phrase-structure rules play a central role: these specify what are acceptable/unacceptable utterances in a speaker's native language. TG also enables children to learn the rules for transforming *deep structure* into various *surface structure* items (and vice versa).

Translation: In the context of genetics, the process by which a gene 'reads' itself. It begins with the text of a gene being transcribed into a copy by *replication*, but the copy is made of ribonucleic acid (RNA), very similar to DNA. RNA uses the same base letters as DNA, except that it uses uracil (U) instead of T (thymine).

Trial and error: The kind of learning involved in operant conditioning, whereby behaviour is initially quite random and only 'correct' behaviour is reinforced/rewarded, therefore becoming more likely to be repeated. Often contrasted with insight learning, which implies perceptual restructuring of the situation leading to problem-solving.

Triune brain model (TBM): MacLean's (1973) view of the brain as comprising three brains in one, each with a different *phylogenetic* history. A 'neural chassis' corresponds to the brains of fish and amphibians; a reptilian complex comprises the basal ganglia (dominant in the brains of reptiles and birds); a paleomammalian component consists of the limbic system, which sub-divides into the amygdala and septal divisions (the thalamocingulate division) and includes the paleocortex; a neomammalian component comprises the neocortex.

Ultradian rhythm: A rhythm with a cycle of less than 24 hours, such as the 90–120 minute cycle of human sleep stages.

Upper Paleolithic Revolution: The period in Europe (the Late Stone Age in Africa) between 10,000 and 40,000 years ago during which humans began making tools from new materials (such as bone and antler), using tool kits comprising more than 100 items. Tools themselves became works of art for the first time, and beads and pendants appear in the fossil record.

Vegetative state (VS): A state in which the patient appears to be awake ('conscious') but where there's a lack of consciousness content (the person lacks awareness of anything around them).

Viral memes: Memes that succeed by using various tricks to persuade people to copy them.

Wagon wheel illusion: Visual illusion in which the wheels of a forward-moving vehicle appear to slow down or even roll backwards.

Wernicke's area: A part of the left hemisphere (located behind Broca's area), damage to which causes receptive aphasia. More recently, it's seen as controlling the syntactical aspects of language.

Working memory (WM) model: An alternative view of short-term memory (STM) as simple and unitary, in which a central executive is in overall charge of a small number of sub- or slave-systems (Baddeley & Hitch, 1974).

Worldview defence: Related to the *mortality salience (MS) hypothesis*, if the function of adopting a particular cultural worldview is to protect us against death terror, then MS should increase the need for such protection. In turn, this should increase our liking for /agreement with those who share our worldview, and increase hostility towards those who hold dissimilar worldviews.

References

Aiello, L. & Dunbar, R. (1993) 'Neocortex size, group size and the evolution of language.' *Current Anthropology*, 34, 184–193.

Aitchison, J. (1983) *The Articulate Mammal* (2nd edn). London: Hutchinson.

Allen, C. & Bekoff, M. (2007) 'Animal consciousness.' In M. Velmans & S. Schneider (eds) *The Blackwell Companion to Consciousness*. Oxford: Blackwell Publishing.

Allport, G. (1950) *The Individual and his Religion*. New York: Macmillan.

Allport, G. (1966) 'Religious context of prejudice.' *Journal for the Scientific Study of Religion*, 5, 447–57.

Allport, G. (2004) Preface. In Frankl, V.E. (1946/2004) *Man's Search for Meaning*. London: Rider.

Altmann, J. (1980) *Baboon Mothers and Infants*. Cambridge, MT: Harvard University Press.

Andreasen, N.C. & Pierson, R. (2008) 'The role of the cerebellum in schizophrenia.' *Biological Psychiatry*, 64(2), 81–8.

Arndt, J. & Greenberg, J. (1999) 'The effects of a self-esteem boost and mortality salience on responses to boost relevant and irrelevant worldview threats.' *Personality & Social Psychology Bulletin*, 25, 1331–41.

Arndt, J., Greenberg, J., & Cook, A. (2002) 'Mortality salience and the spreading activation of worldview-relevant constructs: Exploring the cognitive architecture of terror.' *Journal of Experimental Psychology: General*, 131, 307–24.

Aron, A., Aron, E.N., & Norman, C. (2001) 'Self-expansion model of motivation and cognition in close relationships and beyond.' In G.J.O. Fletcher & M.S. Clark (eds) *Blackwell Handbook of Social Psychology: Interpersonal Processes*. Malden, MA: Blackwell.

Ashworth, P. (2003) 'The origins of qualitative psychology.' In J.A. Smith (ed.) *Qualitative Psychology: A Practical Guide to Research Methods*. London: Sage Publications.

Atran, S. (2002) *In Gods We Trust: The Evolutionary Landscape of Religion*. Oxford: Oxford University Press.

Aunger, R.A. (ed.) (2000) *Darwinising Culture: The Status of Memetics as a Science*. Oxford: Oxford University Press.

Azevedo, F.A., Carvalho, L.R.B, Grinberg, L.T., *et al.*, (2009) 'Equal numbers of neuronal and non-neuronal cells make the human brain an isometrically scaled-up primate brain.' *The Journal of Comparative Neurology*, 513(5), 532–41.

Baddeley, A.D. (1990) *Human Memory*. Hove: Lawrence Erlbaum Associates.

Baddeley, A.D. & Hitch, G. (1974) 'Working memory.' In G.H. Bower (ed.) *Recent Advances in Learning and Motivation, Volume 8*. New York: Academic Press.

Bailey, P. (1987) 'Introduction: Saving the scaffolding.' In Levi, P. (1958/1987) *If This is a Man*. London: Sphere Books.

Banks, W.P. & Pockett, S. (2007) 'Benjamin Libet's work on the neuroscience of free will.' In M. Velmans & S. Schneider (eds) *The Blackwell Companion to Consciousness*. Oxford: Blackwell Publishing.

Bard, K.A. & Vauclair, J. (1984) 'The communicative context of object manipulation in ape and human adult-infant pairs.' *Journal of Human Evolution*, 13, 181–90.

Barnett, S.A. (1968) 'The instinct to teach.' *Nature*, 220, 747.

Baron, R.M. (1997) 'On making terror management theory less motivational and more social.' *Psychological Inquiry*, 8, 21–2.

Baron-Cohen, S. (1995) *Mindblindness: An Essay on Autism and Theory of Mind.* Cambridge, MA: MIT Press.

Baron-Cohen, S. (2003) *The Essential Difference.* London: Penguin.

Baron-Cohen, S. (2006) 'The biology of the imagination: How the brain can both play with truth and survive a predator.' In R. Headlam Wells & J. McFadden (eds) *Human Nature: Fact and Fiction.* London: Continuum.

Baron-Cohen, S., Baldwin, D., & Crowson, M. (1997) 'Do children with autism use the speaker's direction of gaze to crack the code of language?' *Child Development,* 68, 48–57.

Baron-Cohen, S., Leslie, A.M., & Frith, U. (1985) 'Does the autistic child have a "theory of mind"?' *Cognition,* 21, 37–46.

Barrett, W. (1958) *Irrational Man,* New York: Doubleday.

Bates, E., Benigni, L., Bretherton, I., Camioni, L., & Volterra, V. (1979) *The Emergence of Symbols: Cognition and Communication in Infancy.* New York: Academic Press.

Batson, C.D. (1976) 'Religion as prosocial: Agent or double agent?' *Journal for the Scientific Study of Religion,* 15, 29–45.

Batson, C.D. & Stocks, E.L. (2004) 'Religion: Its core psychological functions.' In J. Greenberg, S.L. Koole & T. Pyszczynski (eds) *Handbook of Experimental Existential Psychology.* New York: The Guilford Press.

Batson, C.D., Schoenrade, P.A., & Ventis, W.L. (1993) *Religion and the Individual: A Social-psychological Perspective.* New York: Oxford University Press.

Baumeister, R.F. & Leary, M.R. (1995) 'The need to belong: Desire for interpersonal attachments as a fundamental human motivation.' *Psychological Bulletin,* 117, 497–529.

Becker, E. (1962) *The Birth and Death of Meaning.* New York: Free Press.

Becker, E. (1967) *Beyond Alienation: A Philosophy of Education for the Crisis of Democracy.* New York: George Braziller.

Becker, E. (1973) *The Denial of Death.* New York: Free Press.

Bellow, S. (1965) *Herzog.* Harmondsworth: Penguin.

Belsey, C. (2006) 'Biology and imagination: The role of culture.' In R. Headlam Wells & J. McFadden (eds) *Human Nature: Fact and Fiction.* London: Continuum.

Bem, S. & Looren de Jong, H. (1997) *Theoretical Issues in Psychology: An Introduction.* London: Sage Publications.

Bentall, R.P. (2007) 'Researching psychotic complaints.' *The Psychologist,* 20(5), 293–5.

Bering, J. (2006) 'The folk psychology of souls.' *Behavioural and Brain Sciences,* 29, 453–98.

Bering, J. (2010) 'The nonexistent purpose of people.' *The Psychologist,* 23(4), 290–3.

Bickerton, D. (1990) *Language and Species.* Chicago: University of Chicago Press.

Bickerton, D. (1995) *Language and Human Behaviour.* Seattle, WA: University of Washington Press.

Binford, L. (1981) *Bones, Ancient Men and Modern Myth.* San Diego, CA: Academic Press.

Binford, L. (1985) 'Human Ancestors: Changing views of their behaviour.' *Journal of Anthropological Archaeology*, 4, 292–327.

Binofski, F. & Block, R. (1996) 'Accelerated time experience after left frontal cortex lesion.' *Neurocase,* 2, 485–93.

Binswanger, L. (1956) 'Existential analysis and psychotherapy.' In F. Fromm-Reichman & J. Moreno (eds) *Progress in Psychotherapy.* New York: Grune & Stratton.

Biro, D., Inoue-Nakamura, N., Tonooka, R. *et al.* (2003) 'Cultural innovation and transmission of tool use in wild chimpanzees.' *Animal Cognition,* 6, 213–23.

Blackham, H.J. (1961) *Six Existentialist Thinkers.* London: Routedge & Kegan Paul Ltd.

Blackmore, S. (1999) *The Meme Machine.* Oxford: Oxford University Press.

Blackmore, S. (2007) 'Imitation makes us human.' In C. Pasternak (ed.) *What Makes Us Human?* Oxford: Oneworld.

Blackmore, S. (2010) *Consciousness: An Introduction* (2nd edn). London: Hodder Education.

Blakemore, C. (1988) *The Mind Machine.* London: BBC Books.

Blakemore, S-J., Bristow, D., Bird, G., Frith, C., & Ward, J. (2005) 'Somatosensory activations during the observation of touch and a case of vision-touch synaesthesia.' *Brain,* 128, 1571–83.

Block, N. (1995) 'On a confusion about a function of consciousness.' *Behavioural and Brain Sciences,* 18, 227–47.

Bodmer, W. (2007) Foreword. In C. Pasternak (ed.) *What Makes Us Human?* Oxford: Oneworld.

Boesch, C. (1991) 'Teaching among wild chimpanzees.' *Animal Behaviour,* 41, 530–2.

Boesch, C. (2003) 'Is culture a golden barrier between human and chimp?' *Evolutionary Anthropology,* 12, 89–91.

Boniwell, L. & Zimbardo, P. (2003) 'Time to find the right balance.' *The Psychologist,* 16(3), 129–31.

Bonner, J.T. (1980) *The Evolution of Culture in Animals.* Princeton, NJ: Princeton University Press.

Bonnie, K.E. & de Waal, T.B.M. (2006) 'Affiliation promotes the transmission of a social custom.' *Primates,* 47, 27–34.

Boroditsky, L. (2011) 'How language shapes thought.' *Scientific American,* 304(2), 42–5.

Boroditsky, L. & Gaby, A. (2010) 'Remembrances of times east: Absolute spatial representations of time in an Australian aboriginal community.' *Psychological Science,* 21(11), 1635–9.

Bowlby, J. (1969) *Attachment and Loss: Attachment.* Harmondsworth: Penguin.

Boyer, P. (2001) *Religion Explained: The Evolutionary Origins of Religious Thought.* New York: Basic Books.

Boysen, S.T. (1993) 'Counting in chimpanzees: Non-human principles and emergent properties of number.' In S.T. Boysen & E.J. Capaldi (eds) *The Development of Numerical Competence: Animal and human models.* Hove: Lawrence Erlbaum Associates.

Browman, C.P. & Goldstein, L.F. (1995) 'Dynamics and articulatory phonology.' In T. van Gelder & R.F. Port (eds) *Mind as Motion.* Cambridge, MA: MIT Press.

Brown, A.S. (2004) 'Getting to grips with déjà vu.' *The Psychologist,* 17(12), 694–6.

Brown, P. (1999) 'The conversational context for language acquisition: A Tzeltal (Mayan) case study.' In M. Bowerman & S. Levinson (eds) *Language Acquisition and Conceptual Development.* Cambridge: Cambridge University Press.

Brown, R. & Kulik, J. (1977) 'Flashbulb memories.' *Cognition* 5, 73–99.

Brown, R. (1973) *A First Language: The Early Stages.* Cambridge, MA: Harvard University Press.

Burling, R. (2005) *The Talking Ape.* New York: Oxford University Press.

Busch, N.A., Dubois, J. & Van Rullen, R. (2009) 'The phase of ongoing EEG oscillations predicts visual perception.' *The Journal of Neuroscience,* 29, 7869.

Buss, D.M. (1997) 'Human social motivation in evolutionary perspective: Grounding terror management theory.' *Psychological Inquiry,* 8, 22–26.

Buss, D.M. & Schmitt, D.P. (1993) 'Sexual strategies theory – An evolutionary perspective on human mating.' *Psychological Review,* 100, 204–32.

Butler, A.B. & Hodos, W. (1996) *Comparative Vertebrate Neuroanatomy.* New York: Wiley-Liss.

Byrne, R. (1995) *The Thinking Ape: Evolutionary Origins of Intelligence.* Oxford: Oxford University Press.

Byrne, R.W. (2006) 'Culture in great apes.' *Philosophical Transactions of the Royal Society of London,* Series B, 362, 577–85.

Byrne, R. & Corp, N. (2004) 'Neocortex size predicts deception in primates.' *Proceedings of the Royal Society of London,* Series B, 271, 1693–9.

Byrne, R. & Whiten, A. (eds) (1988) *Machiavellian Intelligence: Social Expertise and the Evolution of Intellect in Monkeys, Apes, and Humans.* Oxford: Clarendon Press.

Callaway, E. (2010) 'Modern humans' Neanderthal origins.' *New Scientist,* 206(2760), 8.

Callender, C. (2010) 'Is time an illusion?' *Scientific American,* 302(6), 40–7.

Camus, A. (1942/2005) *The Myth of Sisyphus.* London: Penguin. (Originally published in French 1942, first English translation 1955).

Capirci, O., Iversson, J.M., Pizzuto, E., & Volterra, V. (1996) 'Gestures and words during the transition to two-word speech.' *Journal of Child Language,* 23, 645–73.

Carpenter, M., Akhtar, N., & Tomasello, M. (1988) 'Sixteen-month-old infants differentially imitate intentional and accidental actions.' *Infant Behavioural Development,* 21, 315–30.

Carroll, D.W. (1986) *Psychology of Language.* Monterey, CA: Brooks/Cole Publishing Co.

Carroll, J. (2006) 'Literature and evolution.' In R. Headlam Wells & J. McFadden (eds) *Human Nature: Fact and Fiction.* London: Continuum.

Carter, R. (2006) 'The limits of imagination.' In R. Headlam Wells & J. McFadden (eds) *Human Nature: Fact and Fiction.* London: Continuum.

Casler, K. & Keleman, D. (2008) 'Developmental continuity in the teleo-functional explanation: Reasoning about nature among Romanian Romani adults.' *Journal of Cognition and Development,* 9, 340–62.

Cassirer, E. (1944) *An Essay on Man.* New Haven, CT: Yale University Press.

Cavanagh, K. (2000) 'Internal clocks and human timing.' *The Psychologist,* 13(2), 82–3.

Chalmers, D. (2007) 'The hard problem of consciousness.' In M. Velmans & S. Schneider (eds) *The Blackwell Companion to Consciousness.* Oxford: Blackwell Publishing.

Chappell, J. & Kacelnik, A. (2002) 'Tool selectivity in a non-primate, the New Caledonian crow (*Corvus moneduloides*).' *Animal Cognition,* 5, 71–8.

Cheney, D.L. & Seyfarth, R.M. (1990) *How Monkeys See the World.* Chicago, ILL: University of Chicago Press.

Chomsky, N. (1957) *Syntactic Structures.* The Hague: Mouton.

Chomsky, N. (1965) *Aspects of the Theory of Syntax.* Cambridge, MA: MIT Press.

Chomsky, N. (1975) *Reflections on Language.* New York: Pantheon.

Chomsky, N. (1979) *Language and Responsibility.* Sussex: Harvester Press.

Chomsky, N. (1988) *Language and Problems of Knowledge.* Cambridge, MA: MIT Press.

Clayton, D.A. (1978) 'Socially facilitated behaviour.' *Quarterly Review of Biology,* 53, 373–91.

Coghlan, A. (2011) 'Key to humanity is in missing DNA.' *New Scientist,* 209(2803), 6–7.

Cohen, J. (2000) 'Primate education.' *Sunday Times Magazine,* 13 August, 16–23.

Cohen, N.J. & Squire, L.R. (1980) 'Preserved learning and retention of pattern-analysing skills in amnesia: Dissociation of knowing how form knowing that.' *Science,* 210, 207–10.

Collins, D.A. & McGrew, W.C. (1987) 'Termite fauna related to differences in tool use between groups of chimpanzees (*Pan troglodytes*).' *Primates,* 28, 457–71.

Coniam, M. (2001) 'Rodents to Freedom.' *Philosophy Now,* 32, 10–1.

Conillac, E.B. de (1971) *An Essay on the Origin of Human Knowledge: Being a Supplement to Mr. Locke's Essay on the Human Understanding.* Gainesville, FL: Scholars' Facsimiles and Reprints. (Originally published 1756; trans. T. Nugent.)

Connor, S. (2010) 'Say hello to X woman, your long-lost cousin.' *The Independent,* 25 March, 2011.

Conway, M.A. (1990) *Autobiographical Memory.* Milton Keynes: Open University Press.

Corballis, M. (2002) *From Hand to Mouth: The Origins of Language.* Princeton, NJ: Princeton University Press.

Corballis, M. & Suddendorf, T. (2007) 'Memory, Time, and Language.' In C. Pasternak (ed.) *What Makes Us Human?* Oxford: Oneworld.

Coren, S. (1992) *Left Hander.* London: John Murray.

Courage, M.L. & Howe, M.L. (2002) 'From infant to child: The dynamics of cognitive change in the second year of life.' *Psychological Bulletin,* 128, 250–77.

Crawley, S.E. & Pring, L. (2000) 'When did Mrs Thatcher resign? The effects of ageing on the dating of public events.' *Memory,* 8, 111–21.

Cross, I. (1999) 'Is music the most important thing we ever did?' In S.W. Yi (ed.) *Music, mind and science.* Seoul: National University Press.

Curtiss, S. (1977) *Genie: A Psycholinguistic Study of a Modern-day 'Wild Child'*. London: Academic Press.

Damasio, A.R. (2006) 'Remembering when.' *Scientific American Special Edition: A Matter of Time,* 16(1), 34–41.

Darwin, C. (1859) *On the Origin of Species by Means of Natural Selection*. London: Murray.

Darwin, C. (1871) *The Descent of Man*. London: John Murray.

Davidson, D. (1984) *Inquiries into Truth and Interpretation*. Oxford: Oxford University Press.

Davidson, D. (1985) *Actions and Events*. Oxford: Oxford University Press.

Davidson, I. & Noble, W. (1989) 'The archaeology of depiction and language.' *Current Anthropology*, 30, 125–56.

Dawkins, R. (1976) *The Selfish Gene*. Oxford: Oxford University Press (new edition with additional material, 1989).

Dawkins, R. (2006) *The God Delusion*. Bosten: Houghton Mifflin Co.

de Waal, F. (2001) *The Ape and the Sushi Master: Cultural Reflections of a Primatologist*. London: Allen Lane.

Deacon, T. (1989) 'The neural circuitry underlying primate calls and human language.' *Human Evolution,* 4, 367–401.

Deacon, T. (1997) *The Symbolic Species: The Co-evolution of Language and the Human Brain*. London: Penguin.

Dechesne, M., Greenberg, J., Arndt, J., & Schimel, J. (2000) 'Terror management and the vicissitudes of sports fan affiliation: The effects of mortality salience on optimism and fan identification.' *European Journal of Social Psychology,* 30, 813–35.

Dechesne, M., Janssen, J., & van Knippenberg, A. (2000) 'Derogation and distancing as terror management strategies: The moderating role of need for closure and permeability of group boundaries.' *Journal of Personality & Social Psychology,* 79, 923–32.

Dechesne, M., Pyszczynski, T., Arndt, J., Ransom, S., Sheldon, K., van Knippenberg, A., & Janssen, J. (2003) 'Literal and symbolic immortality: The effect of evidence of literal immortality on self-esteem striving in response to mortality salience.' *Journal of Personality & Social Psychology,* 84, 722–37.

Dennett, D. (1969) *Content and Consciousness*. London: RKP.

Dennett, D. (1995) *Darwin's Dangerous Idea*. London: Penguin.

Dennett, D. (1997) *Kinds of Minds: Towards an Understanding of Consciousness*. New York: Basic Books.

Descartes, R. (1647/1985) 'Discourse on method.' In J. Cottingham, R. Stootoff & D. Murdock (eds and trans) *The Philosophical Writings of Descartes*. Cambridge: Cambridge University Press.

Deutscher, G. (2010) *Through the Language Glass*. London: Heinemann.

Distin, K. (2005) *The Selfish Meme: A Critical Reassessment*. Cambridge: Cambridge University Press.

Dobbs, D. (2006) 'A revealing reflection.' *Scientific American Mind,* 17(2), 22–7.

Doherty-Sneddon, G., (2008) 'The great baby signing debate.' *The Psychologist,* 21(4), 300–3.

Donald, M. (1991) *Origins of the Modern Mind*. Cambridge, MA: Harvard University Press.

Donald, M. (2001) *A Mind So Rare: The Evolution of Human Consciousness*. New York: Norton.

Donaldson, I.J. & Gottgens, B. (2006) 'Evolution of candidate transcriptional regulatory motifs since the human–chimpanzee divergence.' *Genome Biology*, 7, R52.

Draaisma, D. (2004) *Why Life Speeds Up as You Get Older: How Memory Shapes our Past*. Cambridge: Cambridge University Press.

Dunbar, R. (1993) 'Coevolution of neocortical size, group size and language in humans.' *Behavioural and Brain Sciences*, 16, 681–735.

Dunbar, R. (1996) *Grooming, Gossip and the Evolution of Language*. London: Faber & Faber.

Dunbar, R. (2004) 'Can you guess what I'm thinking?' *New Scientist*, 182(2451), 44–5.

Dunbar, R. (2007) 'Why are Humans not just Great Apes?' In C. Pasternak (ed.) *What Makes Us Human?* Oxford: Oneworld.

Eagleman, D.M. & Pariyadat, V. (2009) 'Is subjective duration a signature of coding efficiency?' *Philosophical Transactions of the Royal Society B*, 364, 1841–51.

Eagleman, D.M. & Pariyadat, V. (2010) 'Duration illusions and what they tell us about the brain.' In N. Srinivasan, B.R. Kar, & J. Pandey (eds) *Advances in Cognitive Science, Vol.2*. Delhi: Sage Publications.

Edelman, G. (1989) *The Remembered Present: A Biological Theory of Consciousness*. New York: Basic Books.

Edelman, G. (1992) *Bright Air, Brilliant Fire: On the Matter of the Mind*. Harmondsworth: Penguin.

Edelman, G. & Tononi, G. (2000) *A Universe of Consciousness: How Matter Becomes Imagination*. New York: Basic Books.

Eiser, J.R. (1994) *Attitudes, Chaos and the Connectionist Mind*. Oxford: Blackwell.

Eliot, L. (1999) *Early Intelligence*. London: Penguin Books.

Empson, J. (1993) *Sleep and Dreaming* (2nd revised edn). Hemel Hempstead: Harvester Wheatsheaf.

Enard, W., Przeworski, M., Fisher, S.E., Lai, C.S.L., Wiebe, V., Kitano, T., Monaco, A.P., & Paabo, S. (2002) 'Molecular evolution of FOXP2, a gene involved in speech and language.' *Nature*, 418, 869–71.

Evans, E.M. (2000) 'The emergence of beliefs about the origins of species in school-age children.' *Merrill-Palmer Quarterly: AQ Journal of Developmental Psychology*, 46, 221–54.

Evans, N. & Levinson, S.C. (2009) 'The myth of language universals: Language diversity and its importance for cognitive science.' *Behavioural and Brain Sciences*, 32(5), 429–48.

Evans-Pritchard, E.E. (1937) *Witchcraft, Oracles and Magic among the Azande*. Oxford: Oxford University Press.

Everett, D.L. (2009a) *Don't Sleep, There are Snakes: Life and Language in the Amazonian jungle*. London: Profile Books.

Everett, D.L. (2009b) 'Piraha culture and grammar: A response to some criticisms.' *Language*, 85(2), 405–42.

Eysenck, H.J. (1987) *Decline and Fall of the Freudian Empire*. Harmondsworth: Penguin.

Ezzell, C. (2006) 'Clocking cultures.' *Scientific American Special Edition: A Matter of Time,* 16(1), 42–5.

Fadiga, L., Forgassi, L., Pavesi, G., & Rizzolatti. G. (1995) 'Motor facilitation during action observation – a magnetic stimulation study.' *Journal of Neurophysiology,* 73, 2608–11.

Feifel, H. (1969) 'Perception of death.' *Annals of the New York Academy of Sciences,* 164, 669–74.

Ferrari, P.F., Gallese, V., Rizzolatti, G. & Fogassi, L. (2003) 'Mirror neurons responding to the observation of ingestive and communicative mouth actions in the monkey ventral premotor cortex.' *European Journal of Neuroscience,* 17, 1703–14.

Festinger, L. (1954) 'A theory of social comparison processes.' *Human Relationships,* 1, 117–40.

Fields, R.D. (2004) 'The other half of the brain.' *Scientific American,* 290(4), 26–33.

Fisher, S.E., Vargha-Khadem, F., Watkins, K.E., Monaco, A.P., & Pembrey, M.E. (1998) 'Localisation of a gene implicated in a severe speech and language disorder.' *Nature,* 18, 168–70.

Fitch, W. T. (2010) 'The evolution of language.' *New Scientist,* 208(2789), i-viii.

Fitzgerald, J.M. (1992) 'Autobiographical memory and conceptualisations of the self.' In M.A. Conway, D.C. Rubin, H. Spinnler & W.A. Wagenaar (eds) *Theoretical Perspectives in Autobiographical Memory.* Dordrecht: Kluwer Academic Publishers.

Florian, V., & Kravetz, S. (1983) 'Fear of personal death: Attribution, structure, and relation to religious belief.' *Journal of Personality & Social Psychology,* 44, 600–7.

Florian, V., Mikulincer, M. & Hirschberger, G. (2001) 'An existentialist view on mortality salience effects: Personal hardiness, death-thought accessibility, and cultural worldview defence.' *British Journal of Social Psychology,* 40, 437–53.

Fodor, J.A. (1983) *The Modularity of Mind.* Cambridge, MA: MIT Press.

Forsey, J. (1999/2000) 'Humans and dumb animals.' *Philosophy Now,* 25, 29–31.

Fox, D. (2009) 'The time machine in your head.' *New Scientist,* 204(2731), 32–7.

Fraisse, P. (1964) *The Psychology of Time.* London: Eyre and Spottiswoode.

Frankenheuser, M. (1959) *Estimation of Time: An Experimental Study.* Stockholm: Almqvist and Wiksell.

Frankl, V.E. (1946/2004) *Man's Search for Meaning.* London: Rider.

Freud, S. (1900/1977) *The Interpretation of Dreams.* Pelican Freud Library (4). Harmondsworth: Penguin.

Freud, S. (1927/1964) *The Future of an Illusion.* New York: Doubleday.

Freud, S. (1930/1961) *Civilisation and its Discontents.* New York: Norton.

Frith, C. (2010) 'Social neuroscience.' In R. Gross *Psychology: The Science of Mind and Behaviour* (6th edn). London: Hodder Education.

Frith, C. & Rees, G. (2007) 'A brief history of the scientific approach to the study of consciousness.' In M. Velmans & S. Schneider (eds) *The Blackwell Companion to Consciousness.* Oxford: Blackwell Publishing.

Fritsche, I., Jonas, E., Fischer, P., Koranyl, N., Berger, N. & Fleischmann, B. (2007) 'Mortality salience and the desire for offspring.' *Journal of Experimental Social Psychology,* 43(5), 753–62.

Fromholt, P. & Larsen, S.F. (1992) 'Autobiographical memory and life-history narratives in ageing and dementia (Alzheimer type).' In M.A. Conway, D.C. Rubin, H. Spinnler & W.A. Wagenaar (eds) *Theoretical Perspectives in Autobiographical Memory.* Dordrecht: Kluwer Academic Publishers.

Fromm, E. (1950) *Psychoanalysis and religion.* New Haven, CT: Yale University Press.

Fromm, E. (1960) 'Psychoanalysis and Zen Buddhism.' In D.T. Suzuki, E. Fromm & R. De Martino (eds) *Zen Buddhism and Psychoanalysis.* London: George Allen & Unwin.

Galef, B.G. (1992) 'The question of animal culture.' *Human Nature, 3*(2), 157–78.

Gallagher, H.L. & Frith, C.D. (2004) 'Dissociable neural pathways for the perception and recognition of expressive and instrumental gestures.' *Neuropsychologia, 42,* 1725–36.

Gallagher, S. (2007) 'Phenomenological approaches to consciousness.' In M. Velmans & S. Schneider (eds) *The Blackwell Companion to Consciousness.* Oxford: Blackwell Publishing.

Gallese, V., Fadiga, L., Forgassi, L., & Rizzolatti, G. (1996) 'Action recognition on the premotor cortex.' *Brain, 119,* 593–609.

Gallup, C.G. (1998) 'Can animals empathise? Yes.' *Scientific American Presents, 9*(4), 66, 68–71.

Gallup, C.G., Anderson, J.R., & Shillito, D.J. (2002) 'The mirror test.' In M. Bekoff, C. Allen & G.M. Burghardt (eds) *The Cognitive Animal.* Cambridge, MA: MIT Press.

Gallup, G.G. (1970) 'Chimpanzees: Self-recognition.' *Science, 167,* 86–7.

Gallup, G.G. (1977) 'Self-recognition in primates.' *American Psychologist, 32,* 329–38.

Gardner, R.A. & Gardner, B.T. (1969) 'Teaching sign language to a chimpanzee.' *Science, 165,* 664–72.

Gauker, C. (1990) 'How to learn language like a chimpanzee.' *Philosophical Psychology, 3,* 31–53.

Gentilucci, M., Benuzzi, F., Gangitano, M., & Grimaldi, S. (2001) 'Grasp with hand and mouth: A kinematic study on healthy subjects.' *Journal of Neurophysiology, 86,* 1685–99.

Gentilucci, M. & Corballis, M.C. (2006) 'From manual gesture to speech: A gradual transition.' *Neuroscience & Behavioural Reviews, 30,* 949–60.

Gentilucci, M. & Corballis, M. (2007) 'The hominid that talked.' In C. Pasternak (ed.) *What Makes Us Human?* Oxford: Oneworld.

Gerhardt, S. (2004) *Why Love Matters: How affection shapes a baby's brain.* London: Routledge.

Gerstner, G.E., & Fazio, V.A. (1995) 'Evidence for a universal perceptual unit in mammals.' *Ethology, 101,* 89–100.

Giorgi, A. & Giorgi, B. (2003) 'Phenomenology.' In J.A. Smith (ed.) *Qualitative Psychology: A Practical Guide to Research Methods.* London: Sage Publications.

Goffman, E. (1972) *Strategic Interaction.* New York: Ballantine.

Golden, F. (1991) 'Clever Kanzi.' *Discover,* March 20th.

Goldenberg, J., McCoy, S., Pyszczynski, T., Greenberg, J. & Solomon, S. (2000) 'The body as a source of self-esteem: The effect of mortality salience on identification with one's body, interest in sex, and appearance monitoring.' *Journal of Personality & Social Psychology, 79,* 118–30.

Goldenberg, J.L., Pyszczynski, T., McCoy, S.K., Greenberg, J. & Solomon, S. (1999) 'Death, sex, and neuroticism: Why is sex such a problem?' *Journal of Personality & Social Psychology,* 77, 1173–87.

Goldin-Meadow, S. (1999) 'The role of gesture in communication and thinking.' *Trends in Cognitive Science,* 3, 419–29.

Goleman, D. (1996) *Emotional Intelligence.* London: Bloomsbury.

Goodall, J. (1973) 'Cultural elements in a chimpanzee community.' In W. Montagna (ed.) *Precultural Primate Behaviour.* Symposia of the Fourth International Congress of Primatology, Vol.1. Basel: Karger.

Goodall, J. (1986) *The Chimpanzees of Gombe: Patterns of Behaviour.* Cambridge, MA: Belknap Press.

Goodall, J. (1988) *In the Shadow of Man.* London: Orion Books Ltd.

Goodall, J. (2010) 'Jane of the Jungle' (interview by Kate Wong). *Scientific American,* 303(6), 62–3.

Gopnik, A. (2010) 'How babies think.' *Scientific American,* 303(1), 56–61.

Gopnik, M. (1990) 'Feature-blind grammar and dysphasia.' *Nature,* 344, 715.

Gould, S.J. (2002) *The Structure of Evolutionary Theory.* Cambridge, MA: Harvard University Press.

Green, R.E., Krause, J., Briggs, A.W., *et al.* (2010) 'A draft sequence of the Neanderthal genome.' *Science,* 328(5979), 710–22.

Greenberg, J., Martens, S., Jonas, E., Eisenstadt, D., Pyszczynski, T. & Solomon, S. (2003) 'Psychological defence in anticipation of anxiety: Eliminating the potential for anxiety eliminates the effect of mortality salience on worldview defence.' *Psychological Science,* 14, 516–19.

Greenberg, J., Pyszczynski, T., Solomon, S., Rosenblatt, A., Veeder, M., Kirkland, S. & Lyon, D. (1990) 'Evidence for terror management theory II: The effects of mortality salience on reactions to those who threaten or bolster the cultural worldview.' *Journal of Personality & Social Psychology,* 58, 308–18.

Greenberg, J., Simon, L., Pyszczynski, T., Solomon, S. & Chatel, D. (1992b) 'Terror management and tolerance: Does mortality salience always intensify negative reactions to others who threaten one's worldview?' *Journal of Personality & Social Psychology,* 63, 212–20.

Greenberg, J., Solomon, S., Pyszczynski, T., Rosenblatt, A., Burling, J., Lyon, D. & Simon, L. (1992a) 'Assessing the terror management analysis of self-esteem: Converging evidence of an anxiety-buffering function.' *Journal of Personality & Social Psychology,* 63, 913–22.

Greene, J. & Haidt, J. (2002) 'How (and when) does moral judgement work?' *Trends in Cognitive Science,* 16, 517–23.

Gregory, R.L. (1981) *Mind in Science.* Hove: Lawrence Erlbaum.

Gross, R. (2003) *Key Studies in Psychology* (4th edn). London: Hodder & Stoughton.

Gross, R. (2008) *Key Studies in Psychology* (5th edn). London: Hodder Education.

Gross, R. (2009) *Themes, Issues and Debates in Psychology* (3rd edn). London: Hodder Education.

Gross, R. (2010) *Psychology: The Science and Mind of Behaviour* (6th edn). London: Hodder Education.

Gross, R., McIlveen, R., Coolican, H., Clamp, A. & Russell, J. (2000) *Psychology: A New Introduction* (2nd edn). London: Hodder & Stoughton.

Harmon-Jones, E., Simon, L., Greenberg, J., Pyszczynski, T., Solomon, S. & McGregor, H. (1997) 'Terror management theory and self-esteem: Evidence that increased self-esteem reduces mortality salience effects.' *Journal of Personality & Social Psychology*, 72, 24–36.

Hauser, M.D. (2000) *Wild Minds: What Animals Really Think.* London: Penguin.

Hauser, M.D. (2009) 'Origin of the mind.' *Scientific American*, 301(3), 30–7.

Hauser, M.D., Chomsky, N. & Fitch, W.T. (2002) 'The faculty of language: Why is it, who has it, and how did it evolve?' *Science*, 298, 1569–79.

Hauser. M.D & Fitch, W.T. (2003) 'What are the uniquely human components of the language faculty?' In M. Christiansen & S. Kirby (eds) *Language Evolution.* Oxford: Oxford University Press.

Hayes, K.J. & Hayes, C. (1951) 'Intellectual development of a house-raised chimpanzee.' *Proceedings of the American Philosophical Society*, 95, 105–9.

Heidegger, M. (1927/1962) *Being and Time.* London: SCM Press.

Herculano-Houzel, S., Mota, B. & Lent, R. (2006) 'Cellular scaling rules for rodent brains.' *Proceedings of the National Academy of Sciences*, 103(32), 12138–43.

Herskovits, M.J. (1955) *Cultural Anthropology.* New York: Knopf.

Hinde, R.A. (1971) 'Development of social behaviour.' In A.M. Schreier & F. Stollnitz (eds) *Behaviour of Nonhuman Primates*, Vol. 3. New York: Academic Press.

Hockett, C.F. (1960) 'The origin of speech.' *Scientific American*, 203, 88–96.

Høgh-Oleson, H. (2010) 'Homo Sapiens – Homo Socious: A Comparative Analysis of Human Mind and Kind.' In H. Hogh-Oleson (ed.) *Human Morality & Sociality: Evolutionary & Comparative Perspectives.* Basingstoke: Palgrave Macmillan.

Holloway, R. (1983) 'Human paleontological evidence relevant to language behaviour.' *Human Neurobiology*, 2, 105–14.

Hopper, L.M. (2010) 'Deferred imitation in children and apes.' *The Psychologist*, 23(4), 294–7.

Horney, K. (1943) *Our Inner Conflicts: A Constructive Theory of Neurosis.* New York: Norton.

Hull, D.L. (1988) 'Interactors versus vehicles.' In H.C. Plotkin (ed.) *The Role of Behaviour in Evolution.* Cambridge, MA: MIT Press.

Humle, T. & Matsuwzawa, T. (2002) 'Ant-dipping among the chimpanzees of Bossou, Guinea, and comparisons with other sites.' *American Journal of Primatology*, 25, 551–81.

Humphrey, N. (1986) *The Inner Eye.* London: Faber & Faber.

Humphrey, N. (1992) *A History of the Mind.* London: Vintage.

Humphrey, N. (1993) *The Inner Eye* (new edn). London: Vintage.

Hunt, G.R. & Gray, R.D. (2003) 'Diversification and cumulative evolution in New Caledonian crow tool manufacture.' *Proceedings of the Royal Society B*, 270, 867–74.

Husserl, E. (1925; trans. 1977) *Phenomenological Psychology.* The Hague: Martinus Nijhoff.

Husserl, E. (1928; trans. 1991) *On the Phenomenology of the Consciousness of Internal Time (1893–1917).* The Hague: Kluwer.

Husserl, E. (1931; trans. 1960) *Cartesian Meditations: An Introduction to Phenomenology.* The Hague: Martinus Nijhoff.

Husserl, E. (1936; trans. 1970) *The Crisis of European Sciences and Transcendental Phenomenology.* Evanston, IL: Northwestern University Press.

Iacoboni, M., Woods, R.P., Brass, M., Bekkering, H., Mazziotta, J.C. & Rizzolatti, G. (1999) 'Cortical mechanisms of human imitation.' *Science, 286,* 2526–8.

International Dictionary of Psychology. N.S. Sutherland (ed.) (1989). New York: Continuum.

Isaac, G. (1976) 'Stages of cultural elaboration in the Pleistocene.' In S.R. Harnad, H.D. Steklis & J. Lancaster (eds) *Origins and Evolution of Language and Speech.* New York: New York Academy of Sciences.

Itani. J. & Nishimura, A. (1973) 'The study of infrahuman culture in Japan.' In E.W. Menzel (ed.) *Vol.1 of Symposia of 4th International Congress of Primatology.* Chicago, IL: University of Chicago Press.

Jablonka, E. & Lamb, M.J. (2005) *Evolution in Four Dimensions: Genetic, Epigenetic, Behavioural and Symbolic Variations in the History of life.* Cambridge, MA and London: Bradford Books.

Jablonski, N.G. (2010) 'The naked truth.' *Scientific American,* 302(2), 28–35.

Jackendoff, R. (1993) *Patterns in the Mind: Language and Human Nature.* Hemel Hempstead: Harvester Wheatsheaf.

Jackson, J.H. (1888) 'On a particular variety of epilepsy "intellectural aura", one case with symptoms of organic brain disease.' *Brain,* 11, 179–207.

James, W. (1890) *The Principles of Psychology.* London: MacMillan.

James, W. (1902) *The Varieties of Religious Experience.* New York: Longmans.

Jansari, A. & Parkin, A.J. (1996) 'Things that go bump in your life: Explaining the reminiscence bump in autobiographical memory.' *Psychology and Ageing,* 11, 85–91.

Jerison, H. (1991) 'Brain size and the evolution of mind.' *The Fifty-Ninth James Arthur Lecture on the Human Brain.* New York: American Museum of Natural History.

Jerison, H.J. (1955) 'Brain to body ratios and the evolution of intelligence.' *Science,* 121(3144), 447–8.

Johnson, M.H. (2005) *Developmental Cognitive Neuroscience: An Introduction* (2nd edn). Oxford: Blackwell.

Johnson, M.H. (2009) 'Developing human brain functions.' *The Psychologist,* 22(11), 924–6.

Jonas, E. & Fischer, P. (2006) 'Terror management and religion: Evidence that intrinsic religiousness mitigates worldview defence following mortality salience.' *Journal of Personality & Social Psychology,* 19(3), 553–67.

Jonas, E., Schimel, J., Greenberg, J. & Pyszczynski, T. (2002) 'The Scrooge effect: Evidence that mortality salience increases prosocial attitudes and behaviour.' *Personality and Social Psychology Bulletin,* 28, 1342–53.

Jones, D. (2008) 'Running to catch the sun.' *The Psychologist,* 21(7), 580–583.

Jones, S. (1994) *The Language of the Genes.* London: Flamingo.

Joos, M. (1948) *Acoustic Phonetics. Language Monograph No. 23.* Baltimore, MD: Linguistic Society of America.

Jung, C.G. (1935) *The Relations between the Ego and the Unconscious* (Collected Works 7.) Princeton, NJ: Princeton University Press.

Jung, C.G. (1938) *Psychology and Religion* (Collected Works 11.) Princeton, NJ: Princeton

Jung, C.G. (1977) *The Structure and Dynamics of the Psyche* (Collected Works 8). London: Routledge.

Jung, C.G. (ed.) (1964) *Man and his symbols.* London: Aldus Books.

Karmiloff-Smith, A. (2000) 'Why babies' brains are not Swiss army knives.' In H. Rose & S. Rose (eds) *Alas, Poor Darwin: Arguments Against Evolutionary Psychology.* London: Jonathan Cape.

Kasser, T. & Sheldon, K.M. (2000) 'Of wealth and death: Materialism, mortality salience, and consumption behaviour.' *Psychological Science,* 11, 348–51.

Kawai, M. (1965) 'Newly acquired pre-cultural behaviour of the natural troop of Japanese monkeys on Koshima Islet.' *Primates,* 6, 1–30.

Kawamura, S. (1959) 'The process of sub-culture propagation among Japanese macaques.' *Primates, 2,* 43–54.

Keller, H. (1902, 1908) *The Story of My Life.* New York: Doubleday, Page & Co.

Kellogg, W.N. & Kellogg, L.A. (1933) *The Ape and the Child.* New York: McGraw-Hill.

Kelly, K. (2010) *What Technology Wants.* New York: Viking Adult.

Kendal, R.L. (2008) 'Animal "culture wars".' *The Psychologist,* 21(4), 312–5.

Kendal, R.L., Coolen, I., van Bergen, Y. & Laland, K.N. (2005) 'Tradeoffs in the adaptive use of social and asocial learning.' *Advances in the Study of Behaviour, 35,* 333–79.

Kenneally, C. (2010) 'Talking heads.' *New Scientist,* 206(2762), 33–5.

Kierkegaard, S. (1844) *The Concept of Dread.* (Trans. W. Lowrie 1944). Princeton, NJ: Princeton University Press.

Kihlstrom, J.F. (1987) 'The cognitive unconscious.' *Science,* 237(4821), 1445–52.

Kirkpatrick, L.A. (1994) 'The role of attachment in religious belief and behaviour.' In K. Bartholomew & D. Perlman (eds) *Attachment Processes in Adulthood* (Vol. 5). Bristol, PA: Kingsley.

Kirkpatrick, L.A. (1997) 'A longitudinal study of changes in religious belief and behaviour as a function of individual differences in adult attachment style.' *Journal for the Scientific Study of Religion,* 36, 207–17.

Kirkpatrick, L.A. (1998) 'God as a substitute attachment figure: A longitudinal study of adult attachment style and religious change in college students.' *Personality and Social Psychology Bulletin,* 24, 961–73.

Kirkpatrick, L.A. (1999) 'Attachment and religious representations and behaviour.' In J. Cassidy & P.R. Shaver (eds) *Handbook of Attachment : Theory, Research, and Clinical Applications.* New York: Guilford Press.

Kirkpatrick, L.A. (2005) *Attachment, Evolution, and the Psychology of Religion.* New York: Guilford Press.

Kirkpatrick, L.A. & Navarette, C.D. (2006) 'Reports of my death anxiety have been greatly exaggerated: A critique of terror management theory from an evolutionary perspective.' *Psychological Inquiry,* 17(4), 288–98.

Køelsch, S., Schultz, K., Sammler, D. *et al.*, (2008) 'Functional architecture of verbal and tonal working memory.' *Human Brain Mapping,* 30(3), 859–73.

Köhler, E., Keysers, C., Umital, M.A., Forgassi, L., Gallese, V. & Rizzolatti, G. (2002) 'Hearing sounds, understanding actions: Action representation in mirror neurons.' *Science,* 297, 846–8.

Köhler, W. (1925) *The Mentality of Apes.* New York: Harcourt Brace.

Kummer, H. (1971) *Primate Societies.* Chicago: Aldine.

Lai, C.S., Fisher, S.E., Hurst, J.A., Vargha-Khadem, F. & Monaco, A.P. (2001) 'A novel forkhead-domain gene is mutated in a severe speech and language disorder.' *Nature,* 413, 519–23.

Laitman, J.T. (1984) 'The anatomy of human speech.' *Natural History,* August, 20–27.

Laland, K.N. & Hoppit, W. (2003) 'Do animals have culture?' *Evolutionary Anthropology,* 12, 150–9.

Laland, K.N. & Janik, V. (2006) 'The animal cultures debate.' *Trends in Ecology and Evolution,* 21, 542–7.

Lamson, M.S. (1881) *Life and Education of Laura Dewey Bridgman, the Deaf, Dumb, and Blind Girl.* Boston: Houghton, Mifflin Co.

Langer, S.K. (1951) *Philosophy in a New Key.* New York: Mentor.

Larkin, P. (1977) Aubade. *Times Literary Supplement,* 23 December.

Laungani, P.D. (2007) *Understanding Cross-Cultural Psychology.* London: Sage.

Le Page, M. (2010) 'RNA rules, OK.' *New Scientist,* 206(2765), 34–5.

Leakey, R. (1994) *The Origin of Humankind.* London: Weidenfeld & Nicolson.

Leary, M.R. (1999) 'Making sense of self-esteem.' *Current Directions in Psychological Science,* 8, 32–5.

Leary, M.R. & Downs, D.L. (1995) 'Interpersonal functions of the self-esteem motive: The self-esteem system as a sociometer.' In M.H. Kernis (ed.) *Efficacy, Agency and Self-esteem.* New York: Plenum Press.

Leary, M.R., Tambour, E.S., Terdal, S.K. & Downs, D.L. (1995) 'Self-esteem as an interpersonal monitor: The sociometer hypothesis.' *Journal of Personality & Social Psychology,* 68, 518–30.

Lenneberg, E.H. (1967) *Biological Foundations of Language.* New York: Wiley.

Leslie, A.M. (1987) 'Pretense and Representation: The origins of "Theory of Mind".' *Psychological Review,* 94, 412–26.

Levi, P. (1958/1987) *If This Is A Man.* London: Sphere Books.

Lewin, R. (1991) 'Look who's talking now.' *New Scientist,* 27 April, 48–52.

Lewis, M. & Brooks-Gunn, J. (1979) *Social Cognition and the Acquisition of Self.* New York: Plenum.

Liberman, A.M., Cooper, F.S., Shankweiler, D.S. & Studdert-Kennedy, M. (1967) 'Perception of the speech code.' *Psychological Review,* 74, 431–461.

Libet, B. (1985) 'Unconscious cerebral initiative and the role of conscious will in voluntary action.' *Behavioural and Brain Sciences,* 8, 529–66.

Libet, B. (1994) 'A testable field theory of mind–brain interaction.' *Journal of Consciousness Studies,* 1,119–26.

Libet, B. (2004) *Mind Time: The Temporal Factor in Consciousness.* Cambridge, MA: Harvard University Press.

Libet, B., Gleason, C.A., Wright, E.W. & Pearl, D.K. (1983) 'Time of conscious intention to act in relation to onset of cerebral activity (readiness potential): The unconscious initiation of a freely voluntary act.' *Brain,* 106, 623–42.

Lieberman, P. (2000) *Human Language and our Reptilian Brain: The Subcortical Bases of Speech, Syntax and Thought.* Cambridge, MA: Harvard University Press.

Liegeois, F., Baldeweg, T., Connelly, A., Gadian, D.G., Mishkin, M. & Vargha-Khadem, F. (2003) 'Language fMRI abnormalities associated with FOXP2 gene mutation.' *Nature Neuroscience,* 6, 1230–7.

Liepelt, R., Ullsperger, M., Obst, K., Spengler, S., Von Cramon, D.Y. & Brass, M. (2009) 'Contextual movement constraints of others modulate motor preparation in the observer.' *Neuropsychologia,* 47, 268–75.

Lifton, R.J. (1979) *The Broken Connection.* New York: Simon & Schuster.

Lifton, R.J. & Olson, E. (1974) *Living and Dying.* New York: Praeger.

Lodge, D. (2002) 'Sense and sensibility.' *Guardian Review,* 2 November, 4–6.

Loehlin, J.C. (1959) 'The influence of different activities on the apparent length of time.' *Psychological Monograph,* 73, 4.

Loftus, E.F. & Pickrell (1995) 'The formation of false memories.' *Psychiatric Annals,* 25, 720–5.

Lombrozo, T., Keleman, D. & Zaitchik, D. (2007) 'Inferring design: Evidence of a preference for teleological explanations in patients with Alzheimer's disease.' *Psychological Science,* 18, 999–1006.

Lonsdorf, E.V., Pusey, E.A. & Eberly, L. (2004) 'Sex differences in learning in chimpanzees.' *Nature,* 428, 715–6.

Mack, A. & Rock, I. (1998) *Inattentional Blindness.* Cambridge, MA: MIT Press.

MacLean, P.D. (1973) *A Triune Concept of the Brain and Behaviour.* Toronto: University of Toronto Press.

MacLean, P.D. (1985) 'Evolutionary psychiatry and the triune brain.' *Psychological Medicine,* 15, 219–21.

MacNamara, J. (1982) *Names for Things.* Cambridge, MA: MIT Press.

MacNeilage, P.F. (1998) 'The frame/content theory of evolution of speech.' *Behavioural Brain Science,* 21, 499-546.

MacNeilage, P.F., Rogers, L.J. & Vallortigara, G. (2009) 'Origins of the left and right brain.' *Scientific American,* 301(1), 48–55.

Macquarrie, J. (1972) *Existentialism.* Harmondsworth: Pelican.

Malik, K. (2006) 'What science can and cannot tell us about human nature.' In R. Headlam Wells & J. McFadden (eds) *Human Nature: Fact and Fiction.* London: Continuum.

Malinowski, B. (1954) *Magic, Science and Religion and Other Essays.* New York: Doubleday.

Mangan, B. (2007) 'Cognition, fringe consciousness, and the legacy of William James.' In M. Velmans & S. Schneider (eds) *The Blackwell Companion to Consciousness.* Oxford: Blackwell Publishing.

Mangan, P.A. (1996) *Report for the Annual Meeting of the Society for Neuroscience.* Washington, DC: Society for Neuroscience.

Manhart, K. (2004) 'The limits of multitasking.' *Scientific American Mind,* 14(5), 62–7.

Mareschal, D., Johnson, M.H., Sirois, S., *et al.* (2007) *Neuroconstructivism: Vol.1. How the brain constructs cognition.* Oxford: Oxford University Press.

Marshall-Pescini, S. & Whiten, A. (2008) 'Chimpanzees (*Pan troglodytes*) and the question of cumulative culture: An experimental approach.' *Animal Cognition,* 11, 449–56.

Maslow, A.H. (1954) *Motivation and Personality.* New York: Harper.

Maslow, A.H. (1964) *Religions, Values, and Peak-experiences.* Columbus, OH: Ohio State University Press.

Maslow, A.H. (1970) *Motivation and Personality* (2nd edn). New York: Harper & Row.

Matell, M.S. & Meck, W.H. (2000) 'Neuropsychological mechanisms of Interval Timing.' *BioEssays,* 22(1), 94–103.

May, R. (1953) *Man's Search for Himself.* New York: Norton.

May, R. (1969) *Love and Will.* New York: Norton.

McBrearty, S. & Brooks, A.S. (2000) 'The revolution that wasn't: A new interpretation of the origin of modern human behaviour.' *Journal of Human Evolution,* 39, 453–563.

McCormack, P.D. (1979) 'Autobiographical memory in the aged.' *Canadian Journal of Psychology,* 33, 118–24.

McEwan, I. (2006) 'Literature, science and human nature.' In R. Headlam Wells & J. McFadden (eds) *Human Nature: Fact and Fiction.* London: Continuum.

McFarland, D. (1985) *Animal Behaviour.* Bath: Pitman Press.

McGregor, I. (2006) 'Offensive defensiveness.' *Psychological Inquiry,* 17, 299–308.

McGrew, W.C. (1991) 'Chimpanzee material culture: What are the limits and why?' In R. Foley (ed.) *The Origins of Human Behaviour.* London: Unwin Hyman.

McGrew, W.C. (2002) 'Ten dispatches from the chimpanzee culture wars.' In F.B.M. de Waal & P.L. Tyack (eds) *Animal Social Complexity.* Cambridge, MA: Harvard University Press.

McGrew, W.C., Tutin, C.E.G. & Baldwin, P.J. (1979) 'Chimpanzees, tools, and termites: Cross-cultural comparisons of Senegal, Tanzania, and Rio Muni.' *Man,* 14, 185–214.

McKellar, P. (1957) *Imagination and Thinking.* London: Cohen and West.

McKellar, P. (1968) *Experience and Behaviour.* Harmondsworth: Penguin.

McLean, C.Y., Reno, P.L., Pollen, A.A. *et al.* (2011) 'Human-specific loss of regulatory DNA and the evolution of human-specific traits.' *Nature,* 471, 216–19.

McMullen. E.& Saffran, J.R. (2004) 'Music and language: A developmental comparison.' *Music Perception,* 21(3), 289–311.

Mellars, P.A. & Stringer, C.B. (1989) (eds) *The Human Revolution: Behavioural and Biological Perspectives on the Origins of Modern Humans.* Edinburgh: Edinburgh University Press.

Meltzoff, A.N. (1988a) 'Infant imitation after a one-week delay: Long term memory for novel acts and multiple stimuli.' *Developmental Psychology,* 24, 470–6.

Meltzoff, A.N. (1988b) 'The human infant as *Homo imitans*.' In T.R. Zentall & B.G.J. Galef (eds) *Social Learning.* Hillsdale, NJ: Lawrence Erlbaum Associates.

Meltzoff, A.N. (1995) 'Understanding the intentions of others: Re-enactment of intended acts by 18-month-old children.' *Developmental Psychology,* 31, 838–50.

Menzel, E.W. (1966) 'Responsiveness to objects in free-ranging Japanese monkeys.' *Behaviour,* 26, 130–49.

Merleau-Ponty, M. (1962) *The Phenomenology of Perception.* London: RKP.

Merleau-Ponty, M. (1968) *The Visible and the Invisible.* Evanston, ILL: Northwestern University Press.

Midgley, M. (2000) 'Why memes?' In H. Rose & S. Rose (eds) *Alas, Poor Darwin.* London: Cape.

Mikulincer, M. & Florian, V. (2002) 'The effects of mortality salience on self-serving attributions: Evidence for the function of self-esteem as a terror management mechanism.' *Basic and Applied Social Psychology,* 24, 261–71.

Mikulincer, M. & Shaver, P.R. (2003) 'The attachment behavioural system in adulthood: Activation, psychodynamics, and interpersonal processes.' In M.P. Zanna (ed.) *Advances in Experimental Social Psychology* (Vol. 35). New York: Academic Press.

Mikulincer, M., Florian, V. & Hirschberger, G. (2003) 'The existential function of close relationships: Introducing death into the science of love.' *Personality and Social Psychology Review,* 7, 20–40.

Mikulincer, M., Florian, V., & Hirschberger, G. (2004) 'The terror of death and the quest for love: an existential perspective on close relationships.' In J. Greenberg, S.L. Koole & T. Pyszczynski (eds) *Handbook of Experimental Existential Psychology.* New York: The Guilford Press.

Miles, L., Nind, L. & Macrae, N. (2010) 'Moving through time.' *Psychological Science,* published on line, 8 January.

Milner, A.D. & Goodale, M.A. (1995) *The Visual Brain in Action.* Oxford: Oxford University Press.

Milton, K. (1988) 'Foraging behaviour and the evolution of primate intelligence.' In R.W. Byrne & A. Whiten (eds) *Machiavellian Intelligence.* Oxford: Oxford University Press.

Mitchell, P. (1997) *Introduction to Theory of Mind: Children, Autism and Apes.* London: Arnold.

Mithen, S. (1996) *The Prehistory of the Mind.* London: Thames & Hudson.

Mithen, S. (2001) 'The evolution of imagination: an archaelogical perspective.' *SubStance,* 30, 41.

Mithen, S. (2005) *The Singing Neanderthals: The Origins of Music, Language, Mind and Body.* London: Weidenfeld & Nicolson.

Moghaddam, F.M., Taylor, D.M. & Wright, S.C. (1993) *Social Psychology in Cross-Cultural Perspective.* New York: W.H. Freeman.

Montgomery, S.H., Capellini, I., Barton, R.A. & Mundy, N.I. (2010) 'Reconstructing the ups and downs of primate brain evolution: Implications for adaptive hypotheses and *Homo floresiensis*.' *BMC Biology,* 8, 9. http://www.biomedcentral.com/1741-7007/8/9/

Motluk, A. (2010) 'It's not what you've got ...' *New Scientist,* 207(2771), 38–41.

Muthukumaraswamy, S.D., Johnson, B.W. & McNair, N.A. (2004) 'Mu rhythm modulation during observation of an object-directed grasp.' *Cognitive Brain Research, 19,* 195–201.

Nagel, T. (1974) 'What is it like to be a bat?' *Philosophical Review, 83,* 435–50.

Nagel, T. (1979) *Mortal Questions.* Cambridge: Cambridge University Press.

Nagel, T. (1987) *What Does it All Mean?* Oxford: Oxford University Press.

Navarette, C.D. (2005) 'Mortality concerns and other adaptive challenges: The effects of coalition-relevant challenges on worldview defence in the US and Costa Rica.' *Group Processes and Intergroup Relations,* 8(3), 411–27.

Navarette, C.D., Kurzban, R., Fessler, D.M.T. & Kirkpatrick, L.A. (2004) 'Anxiety and intergroup bias: Terror management or coalition psychology?' *Group Processes and Intergroup Relations,* 7(4), 370–97.

Neppe, V.M. (1983) *The Psychology of Déjà Vu: Have I Been Here Before?* Johannesburg: Witwatersrand University Press.

Newton, Isaac (1687) *Principia (Mathematical Principles of Natural Philosophy).* Cambridge: Cambridge University Library Newton Manuscripts, Series 2.

Nisbett, R.E. & Wilson, T.D. (1977) 'Telling more than we can know: Verbal reports on mental processes.' *Psychological Review, 84,* 231–59.

Nishida, T. (1987) 'Local traditions and cultural tradition.' In B.B. Smuts, D.L. Cheney, R.M. Seyfarth, R.W. Wrangham & T.T. Struhsaker (eds) *Primate Societies.* Chicago: University of Chicago Press.

Nishida, T. & Uehara, S. (1980) 'Chimpanzees, tools, and termites: Another example from Tanzania.' *Current Anthropology, 21,* 671–2.

Nishida, T., Wrangham, R., Goodall, J. & Urhara, S. (1983) 'Local differences in plant feeding habits of chimpanzees between the Mahale Mountains and the Gombe National Park, Tanzania.' *Journal of Human Evolution, 12,* 467–80.

Norenzayan, A. (2010) 'Why we believe – Religion as a human universal.' In H. Høgh-Oleson (ed.) *Human Morality & Sociality: Evolutionary & Comparative Perspectives.* Basingstoke: Palgrave Macmillan.

Norenzayan, A., & Heine, S. (2005) 'Psychological universals: What are they and how can we know?' *Psychological Bulletin, 135,* 763–84.

Odling-Smee, F.J., Laland, K.N. & Feldman, M.W. (2003) *Niche construction.* Princeton, NJ: Princeton University Press.

Ogden, R.S. & Jones, L.A. (2009) 'More is still better: Testing the perturbation model of temporal reference memory across different modalities and tasks.' *Quarterly Journal of Experimental Psychology,* 62(5), 909–24.

O'Keefe, J. & Nadel, L. (1978) *The Hippocampus as a Cognitive Map.* Oxford: Oxford University Press.

Oppenheimer, S. (2003) *Out of Eden: The Peopling of the World.* London: Constable.

Oppenheimer, S. (2007) 'What makes us human? – Our ancestors and the weather.' In C. Pasternak (ed.) *What Makes Us Human?* Oxford: Oneworld.

Orbach, A. (1999) *Life, Psychotherapy and Death: The End of our Exploring*. London: Jessica Kingsley Publishers.

Owusu-Bempah, K. & Howitt, D. (2000) *Psychology Beyond Western Perspectives*. Leicester: British Psychological Society.

Pagel, M. & Bodmer, W. (2003) 'A naked ape would have fewer parasites.' *Proceedings of the Royal Society of London B* (Suppl.), 270, S117–S119.

Panati, C. (1996) *Sacred Origins of Profound Things: The Stories behind the Rites and Rituals of the World's Religions*. New York: Penguin Books.

Pasternak, C. (2007) 'Curiosity and quest.' In C. Pasternak (ed.) *What Makes Us Human?* Oxford: Oneworld.

Patel. A.D. (2003) 'Language, music, syntax, and the brain.' *Nature Neuroscience*, 6(7), 674–81.

Patel, A.D. (2008) *Music, Language, and the Brain*. New York: Oxford University Press.

Patterson, F.G. (1978) 'The gestures of a gorilla: Language acquisition in another pongid.' *Brain and Language*, 5, 72–97.

Patterson, F.G. (1980) 'Innovative use of language by a gorilla: A case study.' In K. Nelson (ed.) *Children's Language*, Vol. 2. New York: Gardner Press.

Patton, P. (2008/2009) 'One world, many minds.' *Scientific American Mind*, 19(6), 72–9.

Pavlov, I.P. (1927) *Conditioned Reflexes*. Oxford: Oxford University Press.

Peplau, L.A. & Perlman, D. (eds) (1982) *Loneliness: A Sourcebook of Current Theory, Research, and Therapy*. New York: Wiley.

Pepperberg, I.M. (1998) 'Talking with Alex: Logic and speech in parrots.' *Scientific American Exploring Intelligence*, 9(4), 60–5.

Peretz, I. & Zatorre, R. (2005) 'Brain organisation for music processing.' *Annual Review of Psychology*, 56, 89–114.

Perry, S., Baker, M., Fadigan, L. *et al.*, (2003) 'Social conventions in wild white-faced capuchin monkeys.' *Current Anthropology*, 44, 241–68.

Phillips, P. (1997) 'Talking to the Animals.' *Philosophy Now*, 18, Summer, 5–9.

Piaget, J. (1965) *The Moral Judgement of the Child*. New York: Free Press.

Pinker, S. (1994) *The Language Instinct*. New York: Morrow.

Pinker, S. (2002) *The Blank Slate: The Modern Denial of Human Nature*. London: Allen Lane.

Pinker, S. (2004) *The Language Instinct*. New York: Morrow.

Pinker, S. (2006) 'The biology of fiction.' In R. Headlam Wells & J. McFadden (eds) *Human Nature: Fact and Fiction*. London: Continuum.

Pinker, S. & Bloom, P. (1990) 'Natural language and natural selection.' *Behavioural and Brain Sciences*, 13, 707–784.

Ploog, D. (2002) 'Is the neural basis of vocalisation different in non-human primates and *Homo sapiens*?' In T.J.Crow (ed.) *The Speciation of Modern* Homo Sapiens. Oxford: Oxford University Press.

Plotkin, H. (2007) 'The power of culture.' In R. Dunbar & L. Barrett (eds) *The Oxford Handbook of Evolutionary Psychology*. Oxford: Oxford University Press.

Plotnik, J.M., de Waal, F.B.M., & Reiss, D. (2006) 'Self-recognition in an Asian elephant.' *Proceedings of the National Academy of Sciences of the USA,* 103, 17053–7.

Pollard, K.S. (2009) 'What makes us human?' *Scientific American,* 300(5), 32–7.

Pollard, K.S., Salama, S.R., Lambert, N., *et al.* (2006) 'An RNA gene expressed during cortical development evolved rapidly in humans.' *Nature,* 443, 167–72.

Poppel, E. (1997) 'A hierarchical model of temporal perception.' *Trends in Cognitive Sciences,* 1, 56–61.

Poppel, E. (2004) 'Lost in time: A horizontal frame, elementary processing units and the 3-second window.' *Acta Neurobiologiae Experimentalis,* 64, 295–301.

Poppel, E. (2009) 'Pre-semantically defined temporal windows for cognitive processing.' *Philosophical Transactions of the Royal Society B,* 364(1525), 1887–96.

Poppel, E. & Logothetis, N. (1986) 'Neural oscillations in the human brain: Discontinuous initiations of pursuit eye movements indicate a 30-Hz temporal framework for visual information processing.' *Naturwissenschaften,* 73, 267–8.

Popper, K. (1959) *The Logic of Scientific Discovery.* London: Hutchinson.

Popper, K.R. (1972) *Objective Knowledge: An Evolutionary Approach.* Oxford: Oxford University Press.

Povinelli, D.J. (1993) 'Reconstructing the evolution of mind.' *American Psychologist,* 48, 493–509.

Povinelli, D.J. (1998) '... Maybe not.' *Scientific American Presents,* 9(4), 67, 72–5.

Povinelli, D.J. (2000) *Folk Physics for Apes.* Oxford: Oxford University Press.

Povinelli, D.J. & DeBlois, S. (1992) 'Young children's (*Homo sapiens*) understanding of knowledge formation in themselves and others.' *Journal of Comparative Psychology,* 106, 228–38.

Povinelli, D.J. & Eddy, T.J. (1996a) 'Chimpanzees: Joint visual attention.' *Psychological Science,* 7, 129–35.

Povinelli, D.J. & Eddy, T.J. (1996b) 'What young chimpanzees know about seeing.' *Monographs of the Society for Research in Child Development,* 61(3), 1–191.

Povinelli, D.J., Nelson, K.E. & Boysen, S.T. (1990) 'Inferences about guessing and knowing in chimpanzees (*Pan troglodytes*).' *Journal of Comparative Psychology,* 104, 203–10.

Povinelli, D.J., Nelson, K.E. & Boysen, S.T. (1992) 'Comprehension of role reversal by chimpanzees: Evidence of empathy?' *Animal Behaviour,* 43, 633–40.

Povinelli, D.J., Rulf, A.B., Landau, K.R. & Bierschwale, D.T. (1993) 'Self-recognition in chimpanzees (*Pan troglodytes*): Distribution, ontogeny and patterns of emergence.' *Journal of Comparative Behavioural Biology,* 107, 347–72.

Povinelli, D.J., Rulf, A.B. & Bierschwale, D. (1994) 'Absence of knowledge attribution and self-recognition in young chimpanzees (*Pan troglodytes*).' *Journal of Comparative Psychology,* 108, 74–80.

Premack, D. (1971) 'Language in chimpanzee?' *Science,* 172, 808–22.

Premack, D. (1991) 'The aesthetic basis of pedagogy.' In R.R. Hoffman & D.S. Palermo (eds) *Cognition and the Symbolic Processes.* Hillsdale, NJ: Lawrence Erlbaum Associates.

Premack, D. & Woodruff, G. (1978) 'Does the chimpanzee have a theory of mind?' *Behavioural and Brain Sciences,* 4, 515–26.

Prior, H., Schwarz, A. & Gunturkun, O. (2008) 'Mirror-induced behaviour in the Magpie (*Pica pica*): Evidence of self-recognition.' *PloS Biology*, 6(8).

Pyszczynski, T., Greenberg, J., & Kolole, S.L. (2004) 'Experimental existential psychology: Exploring the human confrontation with reality.' In J. Greenberg, S.L. Koole & T. Pyszczynski (eds) *Handbook of Experimental Existential Psychology*. New York: The Guilford Press.

Rank, O. (1934) *Psychology and the Soul*. New York: Dover.

Rank, O. (1944) 'Beyond Psychology.' *Psychoanalytic Quarterly*, *13*, 371-376.

Rank, O. (1958) *Beyond Psychology* (Original work published 1941). New York: Dover Books.

Rao, S.M., Mayer, A.R. & Harrington, D.L. (2001) 'The evolution of brain activation during temporal processing.' *Nature Neuroscience*, 4(3), 317–23.

Reiss, D. & Marino, L. (2001) 'Mirror self-recognition in the bottlenose dolphin: A case of cognitive convergence.' *Proceedings of the National Academy of Sciences of the USA*, 98, 5937–42.

Rendell, L. & Whitehead, H. (2001) 'Culture in whales and dolphins.' *Behaviour and Brain Sciences*, 24, 309–24.

Richerson, P.J. & Boyd, R. (2005) *Not by Genes Alone: How Culture Transformed Human Evolution*. Chicago: University of Chicago Press.

Ridley, M. (1999) *Genome: The Autobiography of a Species in 23 Chapters*. London: Fourth Estate.

Ridley, M. (2003) *Nature Via Nurture: Genes, Experience and What Makes Us Human*. London: Fourth Estate.

Rilling, J.K. & Insel, T.R. (1998) 'Evolution of the cerebellum in primates: Differences in relative volume among monkeys, apes and humans.' *Brain, Behaviour and Evolution*, 52, 308–14.

Rilling, J.K. & Insel, T.R. (1999) 'The primate neocortex in comparative perspective using magnetic resonance imaging.' *Journal of Human Evolution*, 37(2), 191–223.

Ritchie, A.D. (1936) 'The Natural History of the Mind.' *International Journal of Psychoanalysis*, 17, 384–385.

Rizzolatti, G. & Arbib, M.A. (1998) 'Language within our grasp.' *Trends in Neuroscience*, 21, 188–94.

Rizzolatti, G., Camarda, M., Forgassi, L., Gentilucci, M., Luppino, G. & Matelli, M. (1988) 'Functional organisation of interior area 6 in the macaque monkey. II Area 5 and the control of distal movements.' *Experimental Brain Research*, 71, 491–507.

Rizzolatti, G., Fadiga, L., Gallese, V. & Forgassi, L. (1996) 'Premotor cortex and the recognition of motor actions.' *Cognitive Brain Research*, 3, 131–41.

Rizzolatti, G., Forgassi, L. & Gallese, V. (2001) 'Neurophysiological mechanisms underlying the understanding and imitation of action.' *Nature Review Neuroscience*, 2, 661–70.

Rizzolatti, G., Forgassi, L. & Gallese, V. (2006) 'Mirrors in the mind.' *Scientific American*, 295(5), 30–37.

Rogers, A.R., Iltis, D. & Wooding, S. (2004) 'Genetic variation at the MC1R Locus and the time since loss of human body hair.' *Current Anthropology*, 45(1), 105–8.

Rolls, G. (2010) *Classic Case Studies in Psychology* (2nd edn). London: Hodder Education.

Rose, D. (2006) *Consciousness: Philosophical, Psychological and Neural Theories.* Oxford: Oxford University Press.

Rose, S. (2003) *The Making of Memory: From Molecules to Mind* (revised edition). London: Vintage.

Rose, S. (2005) *The 21ˢᵗ-Century Brain: Explaining, Mending and Manipulating the Mind.* London: Vintage Books.

Ross, P.E. (2004) 'Draining the language out of colour.' *Scientific American,* 290 (4), 24–25.

Ruben, R.J. (2005) 'Sign language: Its history and contribution to the understanding of the biological nature of language.' *Acta Oto-Laryngologica,* 125, 464–7.

Rubin, D.C. & Schulkind, M.D. (1997) 'The distribution of autobiographical memories across the lifespan.' *Memory and Cognition,* 25, 859–66.

Rumbaugh, D.M., Warner, H. & Von Glaserfeld, E. (1977) 'The Lana project: Origin and tactics.' In D.M. Rumbaugh (ed.) *Language Learning by a Chimpanzee: The LANA Project.* New York: Academic Press.

Sahlins, M. (1976) *The Use and Abuse of Biology.* London: Tavistock.

Sanz, C.M., Schoning, C. & Morgan, D.B. (2009) 'Chimpanzees Prey on Army Ants with Specialised Tool Set.' *American Journal of Primatology,* 71, 1–8.

Sartre, J.P. (1956) *Being and Nothingness: An Essay on Phenomenological Ontology.* (Trans. Hazel Barnes; French original, 1943). New York: Philosophical Library.

Savage-Rumbaugh, S. (1990) 'Language as a cause–effect communication system.' *Philosophical Psychology,* 3, 55–76.

Savage-Rumbaugh, S. & Lewin, R. (1994) *Kanzi: The Ape at the Brink of the Human Mind.* New York: John Wiley.

Savage-Rumbaugh, S., Rumbaugh, D.M. & Boysen, S.L. (1980) 'Do apes use language?' *American Scientist,* 68, 49–61.

Savage-Rumbaugh, S., Shanker, S.G. & Taylor, T.J. (1998) *Apes, Language, and the Human Mind.* New York: Oxford University Press.

Schachter, S. (1959) *The Psychology of Affiliation.* Stanford, CA: Stanford University Press.

Schacter, D.L. (1987) 'Implicit memory: History and current status.' *Journal of Experimental Psychology: Learning, Memory and Cognition,* 13, 501–18.

Schaffer, H.R. (2004) *Introducing Child Psychology.* Oxford: Blackwell Publishing.

Schick, K.D. & Toth, M. (1993) *Making Silent Stones Speak.* London: Weidenfeld & Nicolson.

Schoning, C., Hulme, T., Mobius, Y. & McGrew, W.C. (2008) 'The nature of culture: Technical variation on chimpanzee predation on army ants revisited.' *Journal of Human Evolution,* 55, 48–59.

Schore, A. (2003) *Affect Dysregulation and Disorders of the Self.* New York: Norton.

Schrock, K. (2009) 'Why music moves us.' *Scientific American Mind,* 20(4), 32–7.

Schultz, N. (2010) 'Southpaws.' *New Scientist,* 206(2758), 36–9.

Scollon, R. (1976) *Conversations with a One-Year-Old.* Honolulu: University of Hawaii Press.

Searle, J.R. (2007) 'Biological naturalism.' In M. Velmans & S. Schneider (eds) *The Blackwell Companion to Consciousness.* Oxford: Blackwell Publishing.

Segall, M.H., Dasen, P.R., Berry, J.W. & Poortinga, Y.H. (1999) *Human Behaviour in Global Perspective: An Introduction to Cross-Cultural Psychology* (2nd edn). Needham Heights, MA: Allyn & Bacon.

Seidenberg, M.S. & Petitto, L.A. (1987) 'Communication, symbolic communications and language: Comment on Savage-Rumbaugh, McDonald, Sevcik, Hopkins, and Rupert.' *Journal of Experimental Psychology: General,* 116, 279–87.

Seyfarth, R.M., Cheney, D.L. & Marler, P. (1980) 'Vervet monkey alarm calls: Semantic communication in a free-ranging primate.' *Animal Behaviour,* 28, 1070–94.

Shaw, P., Greenstein, D., Lerch, J., Clasen, L., Lenroot, R., Gogtay, N., Evans, A., Rapoport, J. & Giedd, J. (2006) 'Intellectual ability and cortical development in children and adolescents.' *Nature,* 440, 676–79.

Shum, M.S. (1998) 'The role of temporal landmarks in autobiographical memory processes.' *Psychological Bulletin,* 124, 423–42.

Siffre, M. (1975) 'Six months alone in a cave.' *National Geographic,* March, 426–35.

Simon, L. Greenberg, J., Harmon-Jones, E. & Solomon, S. (1996) 'Mild depression, mortality salience, and defence of the worldview: Evidence of intensified terror management in the mildly depressed.' *Personality and Social Psychology Bulletin,* 22, 81–90.

Skowranski, J.J. & Thompson, C.P. (1990) 'Reconstructing the dates of personal events: Gender differences in accuracy.' *Applied Cognitive Psychology,* 4, 371–81.

Sloboda, J. (1985) *The Musical Mind: The Cognitive Psychology of Music.* Oxford: Oxford University Press.

Sloboda, J. (1999) 'Music – where cognition and emotion meet.' *The Psychologist,* 12(9), 450–5.

Slocombe, K. E. (2008) 'The calls of the wild.' *The Psychologist,* 21(10), 854–7.

Slocombe, K.E., Kaller, T., Call, J. & Zuberbühler, K. (2010) 'Chimpanzees extract social information from agonistic screams.' www.plosone.org/article/info%3Adoi%2F10.1371%2Fjournal.pone.0011473

Slocombe, K.E. & Zuberbühler, K. (2005a) 'Agonistic screams in wild chimpanzees (*Pan troglodytes schwinfurthii*) vary as a function of social role.' *Journal of Comparative Psychology,* 119(1), 67–77.

Slocombe, K.E. & Zuberbühler, K. (2005b) 'Functionally referential communication in a chimpanzee.' *Current Biology,* 15(19), 1779–84.

Slocombe, K.E. & Zuberbühler, K. (2006) 'Food-associated calls in chimpanzees: Responses to food types or food preferences?' *Animal Behaviour,* 72, 989–99.

Slocombe, K.E. & Zuberbühler, K. (2007) 'Chimpanzees modify recruitment screams as a function of audience composition.' *Proceedings of the National Academy of Science,* 104, 17228–33.

Smith, I.M., & Bryson, S.E. (1994) 'Imitation and action in autism: A critical review.' *Psychological Bulletin,* 116, 259–73.

Sober, E. (1998) 'Morgan's Canon.' In D.D. Cummins & C. Allen (eds) *The Evolution of Mind.* Oxford: Oxford University Press.

Solomon, S., Greenberg, J., & Pyszczynski, T. (1991a) 'A terror management theory of social behaviour: The psychological functions of self-esteem and cultural worldviews.' In M. Zanna (ed.) *Advances In Experimental Social Psychology,* Vol. 24. Orlando, FL: Academic Press.

Solomon, S., Greenberg, J., & Pyszczynski, T. (1991b) 'A terror management theory of self-esteem.' In C.R. Snyder & D. Forsyth (eds) *Handbook of Social and Clinical Psychology: The Health Perspective.* New York: Pergamon Press.

Solomon, S., Greenberg, J. & Pyszczynski, T. (2004) 'The cultural animal: Twenty years of terror management theory and research.' In J. Greenberg, S.L. Koole & T. Pyszczynski (eds) *Handbook of Experimental Existential Psychology.* New York: The Guilford Press.

Solso, R.L. (1995) *Cognitive Psychology* (4th edn). Boston: Allyn & Bacon.

Soper, K. (1995) *What is Nature? Culture, Politics and the Non-human.* Oxford: Blackwell.

Spatt, J. (2002) 'Déjà vu': Possible parahippocampal mechanisms.' *Journal of Neuropsychiatry and Clinical Neuroscience, 14,* 6–10.

Steinbeis, N. & Koelsch, S. (2008) 'Comparing the processing of music and language meaning using EEG and fMRI provides evidence for similar and distinct neural representations.' *PLoS ONE, 3*(5), (e2226:doi: 10.1371/journal.pone.0002226).

Stetson, C., Fiesta, M.P. & Eagleman, D.M. (2007) 'Does time really slow down during a frightening event?' *PLoS ONE, 2*(12), p e:1295 (doi: 10.1371/journal.pone.0001295).

Stevens, A. & Price, J. (2000) *Evolutionary Psychiatry: A New Beginning* (2nd edn). London: Routledge.

Sullivan, H.S. (1953) *The Interpersonal Theory of Psychiatry.* New York: Norton.

Sully, J. (1881) *Illusion: A Psychological Study.* London: Kegan Paul.

Swartz, K.B. & Evans, S. (1991) 'Not all chimpanzees (*Pan troglodytes*) show self-recognition.' *Primates, 32,* 483–96.

Tattersall, I. (2007) 'Human evolution and the human condition.' In C. Pasternak (ed.) *What Makes Us Human?* Oxford: Oneworld.

Taylor, C. (1985) *Human Agency and Language.* Cambridge: Cambridge University Press.

Taylor, T. (2010) *The Artificial Ape: How Technology Changed the Course of Human Evolution.* Basingstoke: Palgrave Macmillan.

Teichman, J. (1988) *Philosophy and the Mind.* Oxford: Blackwell.

Teleki, G. (1974) 'Chimpanzee subsistence technology: Materials and skills.' *Journal of Human Evolution, 3,* 575.

Terkel, J. (1996) 'Cultural transmission of feeding behaviour in the black rat (*Rattus rattus*).' In C.M. Heyes & B.G. Galef (eds) *Social Learning in Animals.* San Diego, CA: Academic Press.

Terrace, H.S. (1979) *Nim.* New York: Knopf.

Terrace, H.S. (1987) 'Thought without words.' In C. Blakemore & S. Greenfield (eds) *Mindwaves.* Oxford: Blackwell Publishing.

Thornton, A. & McAuliffe, K. (2006) 'Teaching in wild meerkats.' *Science, 313,* 227–9.

Thorpe, W.H. (1963) *Learning and Instinct in Animals* (2nd edn). London: Methuen.

Tillich, P. (1974) *The Courage to Be.* London: Collins.

Tolstoy, L. (1904) *My Confessions.* Boston: Dana Estes.

Tomasello, M. (1990) 'Cultural transmission in the tool use and communicatory signalling of chimpanzees.' In S. Parker & K. Gibson (eds) *'Language' and Intelligence in Monkeys and Apes: Comparative Developmental Perspectives.* Cambridge: Cambridge University Press.

Tomasello, M. (1999) 'The human adaptation for culture.' *Annual Review of Anthropology,* 28, 509–29.

Tomasello, M. & Barton, M. (1994) 'Learning words in non-ostensive contexts.' *Developmental Psychology,* 30, 639–50.

Tomasello, M., Davis-Dasilva, M., Camak, L. & Bard, K. (1987) 'Observational learning of tool-use by young chimpanzees.' *Human Evolution,* 2, 175–83.

Tomasello, M., Kruger, A. & Ratner, H. (1993a) 'Cultural learning.' *Behavioural and Brain Sciences,* 16, 495–52.

Tomasello, M., Savage-Rumbaugh, S. & Kruger, A. (1993b) 'Imitative learning of actions on objects by children, chimpanzees and enculturated chimpanzees.' *Child Development,* 64, 1688–1705.

Tononi, G. (2007) 'The Information Integration Theory of Consciousness.' In M. Velmans & S. Schneider (eds) *The Blackwell Companion to Consciousness.* Oxford: Blackwell Publishing.

Tooby, J. & Cosmides, L. (1990) 'The past explains the present: Emotional adaptations and the structure of ancestral environments.' *Ethology and Sociobiology,* 11, 375–424.

Trainor, L.J., Auatin, C.M. & Desjardins, R.N. (2000) 'Is infant-directed speech prosody a result of the vocal expression of emotion?' *Psychological Science,* 11(3), 188–95.

Trainor, L.J. & Desjardins, R.N. (2002) 'Pitch characteristics of infant-directed speech affect infants' ability to discriminate vowels.' *Psychological Bulletin and Review,* 9(2), 335–40.

Trehub, S.E., Schellenberg, E.G. & Kamenetsky, S.B. (1999) 'Infants' and adults' perception of scale structure.' *Journal of Experimental Psychology: Human Perception and Performance,* 25, 965–75.

Triandis, H.C. (1990) 'Theoretical concepts that are applicable to the analysis of ethnocentrism.' In R.W. Brislin (ed.) *Applied Cross-Cultural Psychology.* Newbury Park, CA: Sage.

Triandis, H. (1994) *Culture and Social Behaviour.* New York: McGraw-Hill.

Tulving, E. (1972) 'Episodic and semantic memory.' In E. Tulving & W. Donaldson (eds) *Organisation of Memory.* New York: Academic Press.

Tulving, E. (1985) 'Memory and consciousness.' *Canadian Psychology,* 26, 1–12.

Turner, J. (2000) *On the Origin of Human Evolutions.* Palo Alto, CA: Stanford University Press.

Van Hoof, J.A.R.A.M. (1962) 'Facial expressions in higher primates.' *Symposium of Zoological Society of London,* 28, 635–73.

Van Hoof, J.A.R.A.M. (1967) 'The facial displays of the catarrhine monkeys and apes.' In D. Morris (ed.) *Primate Ethology.* London: Weidenfeld & Nicolson.

Van Rullen, R., Pascual-Leone, A. & Battelli, L. (2008) 'The Continuous Wagon Wheel Illusion and the "When" Pathway of the right parietal lobe: A repetitive transcranial magnetic stimulation study.' *PLoS ONE,* 3(8) p e2911 (doi:10.1371/journal.pone.0002911).

Vargha-Khadem, F., Watkins, K.E., Alcock, K.J., Fletcher, P. & Passingham, R. (1995) 'Praxic and nonverbal cognitive deficits in a large family with a genetically transmitted speech and language disorder.' *Proceedings of the National Academy of Science, USA, 92, 930–3.*

Velmans, M. (2003) 'Preconscious free will.' *Journal of Consciousness Studies,* 10(12), 42–61.

Visalberghi, E. & Fragaszy , D.M. (1990) 'Food washing behaviour in tufted capuchin monkeys (*Cebus paella*) and crabeating macaques (*Macaca fascularis*).' *Animal Behaviour* 40, 829–36.

Vygotsky, L.S. (1962) *Thought and Language.* Cambridge, MA: MIT Press. (Originally published 1934.)

Vygotsky, L.S. (1981) 'The genesis of higher mental functions.' In J.V. Wertsch (ed.) *The Concept of Activity in Soviet Psychology.* Armonk. NY: Sharpe.

Wallisch, P. (2008) 'An odd sense of timing.' *Scientific American Mind,* 19(1), 37–43.

Wallman, J. (1992) *Apeing Language.* Cambridge: Cambridge University Press.

Warner, R.R. (1988) 'Traditionality of mating-site preferences in a coral reef fish.' *Nature,* 335, 719–21.

Watkins, K.E., Dronkers, N.F. & Vargha-Khadem, F., (2002) 'Behavioural analysis of an inherited speech and language disorder: Comparison with acquired aphasia.' *Brain,* 125, 452–64.

Weiskrantz, L. (1986) *Blindsight: A Case Study and Implications.* Oxford: Oxford University Press.

Weiskrantz, L. (2007) 'The case of blindsight.' In M. Velmans & S. Schneider (eds) *The Blackwell Companion to Consciousness.* Oxford: Blackwell Publishing.

Weiskrantz, L., Warrington, E.K., Sanders, M.D. & Marshall, J. (1974) 'Visual capacity in the hemianopic field following a restricted occipital ablation.' *Brain,* 97, 709–28.

White, R. (1985) 'Thoughts on social relationships and language in hominid evolution.' *Journal of Social and Personal Relationships,* 2, 95–115.

Whiten, A. (2007) 'The place of "deep social mind" in the evolution of human nature.' In C. Pasternak (ed.) *What Makes Us Human?* Oxford: Oneworld.

Whiten, A., Goodall, J., McGrew, W.C., Nishida, T., Reynolds, V., Sugiyama, Y., Tutin, C.E.G., Wrangham, R. & Boesch, C. (1999) 'Cultures in chimpanzees.' *Nature,* 399, 682–5.

Whiten, A. & van Schaik, C.P. (2007) 'The evolution of animal "cultures" and social intelligence.' *Philosophical Transactions of the Royal Society B,* 362, 603–20.

Williamson, V. (2009) 'In search of the language of music.' *The Psychologist,* 22(12), 1022–25.

Wilson, E.O. (1975) *Sociobiology: The Abridged Version.* Cambridge, MA: Belknapp Press.

Wilson, E.O. (1998) *Consilience: The Unity of Knowledge.* London: Little Brown.

Wise, S.M. (1999) *Rattling the Cage: Towards Legal Rights for Animals.* London: Profile Books.

Wisman, A. & Goldenberg, J.L. (2005) 'From the grave to the cradle: Evidence that mortality salience engenders a desire for offspring.' *Journal of Personality & Social Psychology,* 89(1), 46–61.

Wittgenstein, L. (1953) *Philosophical Investigations.* Oxford: Basil Blackwell.

Wolfradt, U. (2005) 'Strangely familiar.' *Scientific American Mind,* 16(1), 32–37.

Woll, B. (2002) 'The sign that dares to speak its name: Echo phonology in British Sign Language (BSL).' In P. Boyes-Braem & R. Sutton-Spence (eds) *The Hands are the Head of the Mouth: The Mouth as Articulator in Sign Language.* Hamburg: Signum-Verlag.

Woll, B. & Sieratzki, J.S. (1998) 'Echo phonology: Signs of a link between gesture and speech.' *Behavioural and Brain Sciences,* 21, 531–2.

Wolpert, L. (2007) 'Causal belief makes us human.' In C. Pasternak (ed.) *What Makes Us Human?* Oxford: Oneworld.

Wong, K. (2009) 'The Human Pedigree.' *Scientific American,* (Special Issue), 300(1), 46–9.

Woodruff, G. & Premack, D. (1979) 'Intentional communication in the chimpanzee: The development of deception.' *Cognition,* 7, 333–62.

Workman, L. & Reader, W. (2008) *Evolutionary Psychology: An Introduction* (2nd edn). Cambridge: Cambridge University Press.

Wright, K. (2006) 'Times of our Lives.' *Scientific American Special Edition: A Matter of Time,* 16(1), 26–33.

Wynn, T. & McGrew, W.C. (1989) 'An ape's view of the Oldowan.' *Man ,* 24, 383–98.

Yalom, I.D. (1980) *Existential Psychotherapy.* New York: Basic Books.

Yalom, I.D. (2008) *Staring at the Sun: Overcoming the Dread of Death.* London: Piatkus Books.

Yarrow, K., Haggard, P., Heal, R., Brown, P., & Rothwell, J.C. (2001) 'Illusory perceptions of space and time preserve cross-saccadic perceptual continuity.' *Nature,* 414, 302–5.

Zajonc, R.B. (1965) 'Social facilitation.' *Science,* 149, 269–74.

Zentall, T.R. (2001) 'Imitation in animals: Evidence, function, and mechanisms.' *Cybernetics and Systems,* 32, 53–96.

Zihlman, A.L. & Bolter, D.R. (2004) 'Mammalian and primate roots of human sociality.' In R.W. Sussman & A.R. Chapman (eds) *The Origins and Nature of Sociality.* New York: Aldine de Gruyter.

Zilboorg, G. (1943) 'Fear of Death.' *Psychoanalytic Quarterly,* 12, 465–75.

Index